Women Adventurers, 1750–1900

ALSO BY MARY F. MCVICKER

Women Composers of Classical Music:
369 Biographies from 1550 into the 20th Century
(McFarland, 2011)

Women Adventurers, 1750–1900

A Biographical Dictionary,
with Excerpts from
Selected Travel Writings

Mary F. McVicker

McFarland & Company, Inc., Publishers
Jefferson, North Carolina, and London

The present work is a reprint of the illustrated case bound edition of Women Adventurers, 1750–1900: A Biographical Dictionary, with Excerpts from Selected Travel Writings, *first published in 2008 by McFarland.*

LIBRARY OF CONGRESS CATALOGUING-IN-PUBLICATION DATA

McVicker, Mary Frech.
Women adventurers, 1750–1900 : a biographical dictionary, with
excerpts from selected travel writings / Mary F. McVicker.
p.   cm.
Includes bibliographical references and index.

ISBN 978-0-7864-7509-4
softcover : acid free paper ∞

1. Women adventurers — Great Britain — Biography — Dictionaries.
2. Women travelers — Great Britain — Biography — Dictionaries.
3. Women adventurers — Biography — Dictionaries.   4. Women
travelers — Biography — Dictionaries.   I. Title.
G245.M38   2013   910.4092'241 — dc22   2007045995

BRITISH LIBRARY CATALOGUING DATA ARE AVAILABLE

On the cover: lithograph of Lady Hester Stanhope,
1846 (Carl H. Pforzheimer Collection of Shelley and His Circle,
New York Public Library); title frame (Hemera/Thinkstock)

Manufactured in the United States of America

*McFarland & Company, Inc., Publishers
Box 611, Jefferson, North Carolina 28640
www.mcfarlandpub.com*

Acknowledgments

This book owes its existence largely to libraries, the resource of inter-library loans, and the skills and helpfulness of librarians. In particular, I drew heavily on the resources of the Newberry Library in Chicago, the Regenstein Library at the University of Chicago, and the Osterle Library at North Central College in Naperville, Illinois.

June Johnson, librarian extraordinaire at Osterle, never flagged in her support, enthusiasm, and enterprise in locating many obscure books, which she regarded as a challenge. She greeted the arrival of the many dozens of books with interest; yet the paperwork and processing must have been daunting and tedious at times.

Thank you, June.

And thank you, Don, not only for your encouragement and support in my undertaking this project, but for the practical matter of toting loads of books to and from libraries.

Contents

Introduction

I can never forget my feelings of joy and exultation when I realized that I was at last in Persia, on the threshold of a new life, which I ardently trusted might have its quantum of adventure. I had been civilized all my days, and now I felt a sense of freedom and expansion which quickened the blood and made the pulse beat high. The glamour of the East penetrated me from the first moment of landing on its enchanted shores, and although many a time I encountered hard facts, quite sufficient to destroy the romantic illusions of most folk, yet they struck against mine powerlessly. —Ella Sykes, *Through Persia on a Side-Saddle* (London: Innes, 1898), pages 2–3.

Ella Sykes wasn't the only traveler who expressed such sentiments.

Adela Breton wrote a close friend, "In the gilded cage of English civilization, I think longingly of American wilds and anything that reminds me of them is a pleasure" (Mary McVicker, *Adela Breton: A Victorian Artist Amid Mexico's Ruins* [Albuquerque: University of New Mexico Press, 2005], page 112).

And Gertrude Bell began *The Desert and the Sown* (London: Heinemann, 1907; page 1) with, "To those bred under an elaborate social order few such moments of exhilaration can come as that which stands at the threshold of wild travel."

Travel has given many women a sense of independence and often a sense of purpose. And for many, travel often provided not only new sights and experiences, but sometimes a sharp edge of adventure.

Most of these women are known to us because they wrote books about their travel. We can only wonder how many other women took journeys equally adventurous as those in this book, but of whom we find only minimal or no trace.

To compile this directory I considered about 250 women, examining the books, when available, of most of them. I was looking for women whose travel had been adventurous; about half of the women I originally considered aren't included in this book. The judgment of "adventurous" is admittedly subjective; nonetheless it was the strongest criterion for selecting women to be included in the directory.

Time is relative and thus relevant. Traveling "off the beaten path" in Europe in 1740 was considerably more adventurous and exploratory than it would be even fifty years later. Hester Piozzi, for example, wouldn't be included if her travels had been much later. Similarly, traveling up the Nile in the 1850s was a different matter than the same journey in the 1880s, when at certain seasons the river was a veritable thoroughfare for dahabeeyahs, or houseboats.

Many women traveled throughout the British Empire. Certainly to us the multi-week or -month voyage to reach their destination in the boats of that time would seem adventurous, but such ocean voyages were a matter of course. Some travelers didn't venture much beyond the British enclaves once they got to their destination. Others traveled to learn and were keenly interested in exploring and learning about the culture, history, flora and fauna, and people who made up their surroundings.

Few women who stayed in one place for a long period of years are included in this book, and it focuses on women who did some significant travel before 1900.

Most of the women were British, for several reasons. As Britain was a seafaring nation, women had traveled from early times. In the 1800s, women of the emerging middle class often had the means, typically family money, to travel. Because of the long reach of the British Empire, women could travel the globe. It was quite acceptable to do so. And, once at the far reaches of the Empire, why not go farther?

As an affluent and educated middle class developed, there was a certain tolerance (and often admiration) of eccentricity in Britain — as long as the behavior and opinions fell within what were deemed to be allowable parameters. Ironically, the higher ranks of nobility, and of course royalty, were allowed less flexibility.

Other European women tended not to travel. They didn't have the independence, or independent money, that British women did. Also, without membership in a global empire, travel was far more difficult for these women.

Stringent social (and financial) restrictions were a significant factor. Women from Italy and Spain had no independence and in general had no control over "their" money, even when widowed or unmarried. Travel was also problematic for German women. French women may have had fewer restrictions, certainly fewer than Italian or Spanish women, but they tended not to travel, in part because adventurous travel wasn't "done" to any extent. American and Canadian women didn't travel abroad in significant numbers, except to Europe. They had adventurous travel right at hand in North America.

Many of the women were interested and involved in the natural sciences. The later 1700s and 1800s were a time of great exploration and discovery in the natural world. Travel, for many of the women in the book, was directly associated with exploration and scientific investigation.

Entries in the directory include biographical information and an excerpt from the travel writing of each woman — when available. There are gaps.

Some source books were too rare or too fragile to be loaned and weren't available locally. In a few instances an anthology of travel writing supplied an excerpt.

Regrettably, there is a dearth of information about some of the women, and some entries are scanty. For some women there is no information, except the fact that the woman traveled and wrote a book about it. I hope that future scholars will undertake research on these women.

They should not be lost.

Part I

Women Adventurers

Harriet Chalmers Adams,

1875–1937. American.

Harriet Chalmers grew up in California. When she was a girl, she and her father traveled on horseback throughout California, spending a lot of time in the Sierra Nevadas.

She married Franklin Pierce Adams, an electrical engineer, in 1899. The following year they went to Mexico, where he had a job assignment. The trip whetted their appetite for travel, and the next year they embarked on a three-year trip throughout South America. They visited every country and traversed the Andes on horseback. Harriet wrote articles about this trip both for newspapers and for *National Geographic.*

Those were long days in the saddle, with little food and less water. We knew the river water to be impure ... and the brooks are also contaminated as they pass through the villages. At night we slept on the ground, wrapped in our blankets, at times finding shelter in a ruined temple. We met no travelers save the highland Indians, and picked up a few words of their tongue. I felt that we had left civilization far behind.... To know a country and a people, one must leave the highway and live near to nature. We traveled much in the saddle on this great elevated plateau ... and gradually my standpoint changed. I started out as an outsider.... In time I grew, through study and observation, but more through sharing the life, half–Andean myself, and find, in looking back over years of travel in South America — years in which we visited every country — that my greatest heart interest lies in the highlands of Peru and Bolivia [In Netzley, *The Encyclopedia of Women's Travel and Exploration*].

After they returned to the United States, Franklin took an editing job that made lengthy travel difficult. Harriet continued to travel on her own. In 1910 she crossed Haiti on horseback; she visited the Philippines in 1912. At some point she visited every Indian nation in the United States. She traveled from Siberia to Sumatra to study traces of early man. She was in Libya and the Near East in 1929; in 1930 her African trip included Ethiopia and Egypt. The list goes on.

Between 1907 and 1935 she wrote twenty-one articles for *National Geographic* magazine; during World War I she served as a European correspondent for *Harper's*. She also was a lecturer.

In response to the fact that women were barred from becoming full members of the National Geographical Society, Harriet helped found the Society of Woman Geographers and was its first president. She never really stopped traveling — she is said to have traveled more than a hundred thousand miles.

Harriet died in France in 1937. Franklin died in 1940.

SOURCES: Netzley, *Encyclopedia of Women's Travel and Exploration*; *Who Was Who in America*; Wikipedia, November 2006.

BOOKS ABOUT OR INCLUDING HARRIET CHALMERS ADAMS

Netzley, Patricia D. *The Encyclopedia of Women's Travel and Exploration*. Westport, CT: Oryx, 2001.

Elizabeth Cabot Cary Agassiz,

1822–1907. American.

Elizabeth was an American author and educator. She was born in Boston, Massachusetts, the second of seven children. The Carys were an old New England family with close ties to other early families; several of

Elizabeth's close relatives lived in neighboring houses, so that the immediate neighborhood was a complex of family residences. Her maternal grandparents, the Perkinses, were a mercantile family; Mr. Perkins was benefactor of the Perkins Institution for the Blind.

Lizzie, as she was called, grew up surrounded by family; she was educated by governesses, but she alone was not sent to school, for her health was "delicate." She studied languages, drawing and music; she read widely. She took part in family pastimes of music and amateur theatricals.

When she was older she participated in upper-class Boston society. Her older sister's marriage in 1846 to Cornelius Felton, professor of Greek at Harvard, introduced Elizabeth to the circle of Cambridge intellectuals. It was at one of the Feltons' parties that Elizabeth met Louis Agassiz, who had come to America on a scientific mission but stayed to accept a professorship in Harvard's Lawrence Scientific School. In 1849 Elizabeth went to live with the Feltons, which brought her into more frequent contact with Agassiz. His wife had died the previous year.

Louis and Elizabeth were married in 1850. Louis had three children from his first marriage, who ranged in age from nine to fourteen at the time of his marriage to Elizabeth. Elizabeth was an excellent mother to the children and they remained close throughout their lives. She and Louis did not have any children. Elizabeth also managed the family finances (and often expedition finances as well), dealt with much of Louis's mail and business, and took notes on nearly all of Louis's lectures, which provided him with much material for publication. Although Elizabeth always thought of herself as without scientific knowledge and ability, she was excellent at presenting "second-hand knowledge" accurately and interestingly. She published two introductory guides to marine zoology, the second with her stepson Alexander.

In 1854 she and Louis built a large house in Cambridge; Elizabeth decided to found a school for girls on the third floor. This would help with household expenses and lessen the need for Louis to do public lecturing, thereby allowing him more time for his research and writing. Louis enthusiastically took up the idea and extended it, so that students were taught by leading Harvard professors, with Agassiz the main teacher. There were eighty students, age fifteen to eighteen. By 1863 the family finances had improved substantially and the school closed.

In 1865-66 Elizabeth accompanied Louis on an expedition to Brazil. The purpose off the expedition was to travel up the Amazon, observing, collecting, and investigating the flora and fauna, particularly the fishes. *A Journey in Brazil* recounts that trip. In the introduction Mr. Agassiz relates how the book came about. "One word as to the manner in which this volume has grown into its present shape, for it has been rather the natural growth of circumstances than the result of any preconceived design. Partly for the entertainment of her friends, partly with the idea that I might make some use of it in knitting together the scientific reports of my journey by a thread of narrative, Mrs. Agassiz began this diary. I soon fell into the habit of giving her daily the more general results of my scientific observations, knowing that she would allow nothing to be lost which was worth preserving. In consequence of this mode of working our separate contributions have become so closely interwoven that we should hardly know how to disconnect them, and our common journal is therefore published, with the exception of a few unimportant changes, almost as it was originally written."

Travel up the Amazon was comfortable. Elizabeth's accommodation consisted of a stateroom, with dressing room and bathroom. Others in the party had less luxurious accommodations but were still very comfortable. Everyone slept in hammocks on the deck for coolness. The trip was not without its inconveniences; Elizabeth was stalwart, however.

> I have said little about the insects and reptiles which play so large a part in most Brazilian travels, and, indeed, I have had much less annoyance from this source than I had expected. But I must confess the creature who greeted my waking sight this morning was not a pleasant object to contemplate. It was an enormous centipede close by my side, nearly a foot in length, whose innumerable legs looked just ready for a start, and whose two horns or feelers were protruded with a most venomous expression. These animals are not only hideous to look upon, but their bite is very painful, though not dangerous. I crept softly away from my sofa without disturbing my ugly neighbor, who presently fell a victim to science; being very adroitly caught under a large tumbler, and consigned to a glass jar filled with alcohol [*A Journey in Brazil*, pp. 326–327].

The steamer in which they traveled on the Amazon was in a channel known as the river Aturia as Lizzie wrote:

> It gives an idea of the grandeur of the Amazons, that many of the channels dividing the islands by which its immense breadth is broken are themselves like ample rivers, and among the people here are known by distinct local names. The banks are flat; we have seen no cliffs as yet, and the beauty of the scenery is wholly in the forest.... We have sometimes heard it said that the voyage up the Amazons is monotonous; but to me it seems delightful to coast along by these woods, of a character so new to us, to get glimpses into their dark depths or into a cleared spot with a single stately palm here and there, or to catch even the merest glance at the life of the people who live in the isolated settlements, consisting only of one or two Indian houses by the river-side [*A Journey in Brazil*, pp. 155–156].

In September 1869, Agassiz had a cerebral hemorrhage that incapacitated him until late November 1870. Elizabeth shared fully in the two remaining ventures: the Hassler Expedition through the Strait of Magellan, and the planning and administration of the (coeducational) Anderson School of Natural History in Buzzard's Bay, a summer school and a marine laboratory.

Louis died in December, 1873. Elizabeth was fifty-one. Eight days after Louis's death, his son Alexander's wife died leaving three young sons. Elizabeth became a mother to the three children, as Alexander lived with her during the winter. She also prepared the manuscript of *Louis Agassiz: His Life and Correspondence*, which was published in 1885.

But perhaps her most notable role was as one of the founders of Radcliffe College. Mr. and Mrs. Arthur Gilman originated the idea; they were Cambridge residents with a daughter approaching college age. They enlisted the help of seven women, none of whom were noted as feminist crusaders or advocates of coeducation; Elizabeth Agassiz was the seventh woman chosen. The college opened in September 1879 as the "Harvard Annex." In 1882 it became a corporation, and Elizabeth was president. In 1894 it became a degree-granting institution, and Elizabeth was the first president of Radcliffe College, a position she held from 1894 until 1903.

In 1892 she visited California. She also made a trip to Europe that included a tour to English women's colleges. In 1904 she suffered a stroke, which made her an invalid. Three years later she had another stroke and died.

MARIANNE NORTH MEETS ELIZABETH AGASSIZ

> I enjoyed my expeditions with him [James T. Fields] and his wife. He invited me to

meet Mrs. [Louis] Agassiz at a picnic one day, and called for me in his pony carriage, picked her up at the railway station, and drove us to one of the many beautiful high headlands on the coast; then we walked over the cliffs to find a most curious old cedar-tree, perfectly shaved at the top like an umbrella pine by the sea winds, with its branches matted and twisted in the most fantastical way underneath, and clinging to the very edge of the precipice, its roots being tightly wedged into a crack without any apparent earth to nourish it. It was said to be of unknown antiquity, and there was no other specimen of such a cedar in the country; it looked to me like the common sort we call red cedar. We sat and talked a long while under its shade.

Mrs. Agassiz and I agreed that the greatest pleasure we knew was to see new and wonderful countries, and the only rival to that pleasure was the one of staying quietly at home. Only ignorant folks think because one likes sugar one cannot like salt; those people are only capable of one idea, and never try experiments.

Mrs. A was a most agreeable handsome woman; she had begun life as a rich, ball-going young lady, then, on her father losing his fortune, she had started a girls' school to support her family, and finally married the clever old Swiss professor, whose children were already settled in the world. She made an excellent stepmother as well as traveling companion, putting his voyages and lectures together in such a manner that the Americans had a riddle, "Why were *Agassiz's Travels* like a mermaiden?" "Because you could not tell where the woman ended and the fish began!"

The Professor was a great pet of the Americans, who were then just fitting up a new exploring ship for him to go on a ten months' voyage to Cape Horn and the Straits of Magellan to hunt for prehistoric fish in comfort. She told me much of the wonders and delights of her famous Amazon expedition, and promised me letters there if I went....

She made another visit to the Agassiz household.

I found her and the Professor even more to my mind; he spoke funny broken En-

glish, and looked entirely content with himself and everybody else. They showed me photographs and told me of all the wonders of Brazil, and what I was to do there, then gave me a less poetical dinner. Then Mrs. Agassiz took me to the Museum and made Count Pourtalez take us up to the attic to see the most perfect collection of palms in the world (all mummies), intensely interesting as illustrating the world's history. Mrs. Agassiz showed me the great sheath of one of the flowers, which native mothers use as a cradle and also as a baby's bath, it being quite water-tight. The flowers of some of the palms were two to three yards long. She said, though she had wandered whole days in the forests, she had never seen a snake nor a savage beast. One day she heard a great crashing through the tangle and felt rather frightened, when a harmless milk-cow came out [*Recollections of a Happy Life*, pp. 48–50].

SOURCES: *American National Biography.*

WORKS

Agassiz, Elizabeth. *Louis Agassiz: His Life and Correspondence.* 1885.
_____, with Alexander Agassiz. *Seaside Studies in Natural History.* 1865.
_____, with Louis Agassiz. *A Journey in Brazil.* Boston: Tichnor & Fields, 1868.

BOOKS ABOUT OR INCLUDING ELIZABETH AGASSIZ

North, Marianne. *Recollections of a Happy Life: Being the Autobiography of Marianne North.* Ed. Catherine North Symonds. London: Macmillan, 1892.
Paton, Lucy Allen. *Elizabeth Cary Agassiz: A Biography.* Houghton Mifflin. 1919.
Tharp, Louisa Hall. *Adventurous Alliance: The Story of the Agassiz Family of Boston.* Boston: Little, Brown, 1959.

Henriette Ashmore

Henriette, her husband, the remainder of the regiment, and their wives sailed for

India early in 1833 and arrived at Madras on September 3. They landed at Calcutta and prepared to march to Cawnpore. Henriette traveled in a palanquin. Although this was not a dangerous or particularly adventurous trek, Henriette's account, *Narrative of a Three Months' March in India*, is one of the earlier accounts of a military wife in India:

> Arriving at our encamping ground on the banks of the sacred stream [*the Ganges*], what a scene presented itself! Wide as an inland sea, so wide that we could only discern a streak of land on the distant horizon, and smooth as glass, it formed a strange contrast to the busy scene on shore. Thousands, I may safely say, of the black natives were seated in groups, preparing and eating their dinners, their fires made on the ground in little mounds of mud, whilst hackeries, elephants, camels, bullocks, tents, horses, and tattoos, to say nothing of the soldiers of the regiment completely covered the open space near the river. The boats of the ladies, and the fleet belonging to the regiment, were below us, all laggo'd on the banks of the Ganges; most of the ladies were in camp; in fact every body was alive, and all were enjoying the beauty and variety of the picture [pp. 133–134].
>
> Wednesday, 25th.— Yesterday we marched to Nullah-Wah, ten miles; here the heat was considerably increased during the middle of the day; but in the evening several heavy showers, with thunder and lightning, cooled the air, and rendered our march of this morning to Aaing very agreeable. We are once more encamped in a thick mangoe top, and the face of the adjoining country presents rich fields of barley and Indian corn. After two more marches, we shall reach Cawnpore, and anxiously do we now look forward to the termination of our march. At Maharajapore our next encampment was formed, and on the morning of the 28th of February we entered Cawnpore [p. 211].

Later in the book, she reflected on camp.

> One would not readily imagine how much comfort may be enjoyed under can-vass during the cold season, either when the tent is closed against the external air, and cheerfully lighted for the evening's repast; when the brilliance of its painted cotton walls are fully displayed, and the servants spread the table with every usual and oft-times elegant appendage; or, when opened on each side to admit the cooling breeze, the occupant sits in a thorough draught, with no fear of rheumatism before his eyes, and reads, or lounges, or sleeps, as taste or inclination may dictate....
>
> Once I recollect being astonished to discover a multitude of sand-hills, from four to six or eight feet in height which had been thrown up by those busy little operatives the ants; and on more than on occasion, when unwilling to forego our evening's stroll, we had rambled forth without considering that the light of day was not to be immediately replaced by a tardy moon, we were compelled to retrace our steps to the camp, guided only by the distant watch fires, and when arrived, had to enter upon a difficult search after our own tent; stumbling every moment over tent pegs and ropes, or narrowly escaping too close contact with the slumbering camels and bullocks.
>
> True, that every one would not extract happiness from the obligation to rise each morning, in weather fair or foul, at the untimely hour of two or three [pp. 289–291].

Henriette and her husband were in India for four years.

WORKS

Ashmore, Henrietta. *Narrative of a Three Months' March in India*. London: R. Hastings, 1841.

Mary Atkins, 1819–1882. American.

Mary grew up in Ohio where her father, strongly abolitionist, was a sheriff and then a judge. She graduated from Milan Institute, then, after teaching in several schools, she went to Oberlin, now Oberlin College, the only place where women could get standard collegiate training in the 1840s.

She greatly desired to do missionary work in the Orient, but her father persuaded her to stay at Oberlin. Finally, in 1849, after further teaching in Columbus, Ohio, she went to Benecia, California, to teach and to be principal of the Benicia Seminary. Judge Atkins encouraged his daughter to write, and in 1855 he congratulated her on an article that appeared in the Ohio *Columbian*.

She bought the Young Ladies' Seminary at Benicia, California, in 1855. Her students included the daughters of bankers, merchants, ship captains, miners and ranchers as well as girls who were Spanish-speaking and Native American. Despite her abolition background, she included students with both southern and northern sympathies; tensions ran high at the school during the Civil War.

The school was in the midst of pioneer California, a rough environment. Mary stood up to the violence. She taught the girls music, dancing, and table manners as well as academic subjects, so that they could move in any society.

She took on more responsibility, and her various projects included acquiring land for the school and overseeing the building of a house, including the well, cistern, and fence.

In fall of 1863 she began a well-earned sabbatical to the Sandwich Islands (Hawaii) and to China. Her diary recounts the trip until her arrival at Shanghai. She found the trip long and boring, and was not entirely comfortable being at sea. There were fierce storms.

> Friday, March 4, Woosung River. We weighed anchor at 10½ A.M. and sailed slowly up the river. The banks are very low and the whole country would be under water after heavy rains were it not for a levy or bund on both sides. It is a rice soil and Chinamen could be seen all along the banks hoeing, and all along the bund stood coffins, some of simple boards, while others were covered with bamboo. Hundreds of coffins were standing on the bund. Here it seems the last house is above the ground, as well as those they have spent their lives in. All along in this section of the country the dead are placed above ground on account of the moisture of the soil. All along the river were junks, cargo boats and sampans, a small shallow boat sculled by one person. The Chinese junks are singular structures, but are all furnished with eyes, for the Chinaman says, "If the ship have no eye, he no can see." ... Thus ends my trip to Shanghai [*They Diary of Mary Atkins*, pp. 45–46].

The ship spent about three weeks at Japan, Yedo Bay and Yokohama, and then sailed around Japan before heading to the Yangtse River and Shanghai.

During her year abroad, enrollment in the school declined, and soon after her return she sold the school.

She then traveled in Europe and England observing different school systems. In 1869, when she was fifty, she married John Lynch. He was prominent in the Reconstruction in Louisiana, and they lived in New Orleans for six years. They then moved to Philadelphia and then to California.

Mary and John purchased the Benicia Academy in 1879; the core of the establishment had been moved to Oakland, where it became the Mills Seminary, then Mills College. Mary ran the school until her death.

SOURCES: *American National Biography*; *Diary of Mary Atkins*.

WORKS

Atkins, Mary. *The Diary of Mary Atkins, A Sabbatical in the 1860s*. Mills College, CA: Eucalyptus, 1937.

Lucy Sherrand Finley Atkinson, fl. 1820–1863. British.

Lucy Atkinson came from a large family and was obliged to support herself. Consequently, in about 1838, she went to St.

Petersburg, where for eight years she lived with the family of General Mouravioff and was charged with the education of his only daughter. In 1846 she met Thomas Atkinson, who was about to go to Siberia.

Thomas Atkinson was an architect with a successful practice in England. In 1842 following the devastating fire in Hamburg, Thomas competed unsuccessfully to be the architect of St. Nicholas's church. He was inspired by the accounts of Siberia as related by Alexander von Humboldt, and moved to St. Petersburg. In 1846 he left the profession of architecture and became an explorer and topographical artist. He traveled to the Urals, the steppes, and the Altai Mountains. A year later when he returned to Moscow, he and Lucy married with, she tells us, the consent of the general's family.

In February 1848 she and her husband left Moscow for Siberia, the land of exile. Before they left, many families asked them to deliver messages to their husbands, fathers, and brothers who had been in exile for over twenty years.

They traveled by sledge. The trip was arduous, with thieves and adventures. Lucy learned to shoot both a rifle and a pistol and practiced until she was a good shot. There was terrible cold, heat, and thirst, but her spirits remained high. She became pregnant. She expected the child in December or January, but their son was born prematurely in early November. Remarkably, he survived all the travel and hardships. By the end of that first year she had traveled about 6800 miles.

> On rising on the morning of the 13th we saw for the first time the snowy peaks of the Alatau shining like silver against a deep blue sky.... About four o'clock, I being very thirsty, we stopped for a few moments, having been persuaded by Mr. Atkinson to try the water melon given to us by the sessedatal at Aiagooz. This was the first time I had ever tasted one; my thirst was so parched

ing that it appeared to me the most delicious thing I had ever tasted in my life. I enquired of the Cossacks how much farther it was to our resting-place, and was told ten versts; hour after hour I got the same answer, till, being tired of this, I said, "I now insist on knowing the truth. How far are we from the aoul?" his answer was, "We do not know." I then bid him ask a Kirghis. After some talk, he turned to me and said, "You see yonder blue mountain?" "Yes!" "Well, it is a little farther than that." Mr. Atkinson being an excellent judge of distance, to my extreme horror, said that it was between forty and fifty versts. It would have been useless to have complained, so we cheered up and on we went [*Recollections of Tartar Steppes*, pp. 99–100].

They were gone from 1848 until 1853. During that time Atkinson produced over 500 watercolors of the landscapes and people. When they returned to Britain he held an exhibit of his Siberian and Chinese Tartar paintings. Some were lithographed and printed in his narrative: *Oriental and Western Siberia: A Narrative of Seven Years' Explorations and Adventures in Siberia, Mongolia, the Kirghis Steppes, Chinese Tartary, and Part of Central Asia*. He also published a second book of his travels in northern India and on the Amur. This book was well received, but questions arose about its authenticity, and there was evidence that at least part of the book was a plagiarism of a book by Richard Maak.

After Thomas's death in 1861, Lucy applied to the Treasury for money owed to him, only to learn that Thomas was already married when he married her and his wife was still living in Britain. Nonetheless she continued to be referred to as "Mrs. Atkinson." After her book was published she received a pension.

Lucy later returned to Russia.

SOURCES: *Recollections of Tartar Steppes and Their Inhabitants*; *Dictionary of National Biography* (S.V. Thomas Witlam Atkinson).

WORKS

Atkinson, Lucy Sherrand Finley. *Recollections of Tartar Steppes and Their Inhabitants.* London: John Murray, 1863. Reprint, New York: Arno/ New York Times, 1970.

Lucy Seaman Bainbridge,

1842–1928. American.

Lucy Elizabeth Seaman was born in Cleveland, Ohio. She attended the Cleveland Female Seminary for one year, then transferred to a seminary at Ipswich, Massachusetts.

In 1864 while on a visit to Washington with her mother, she was attending a public dinner. One of the speakers spoke of the urgent need for nurses at the war front. Lucy immediately joined the Ohio Soldiers' Aid Society and was sent to Fredericksburg, Virginia. Her job was to care for the wounded soldiers as they were being transported by boat to Washington, D.C. She did the work well and was asked to go to the front of the Union armies. Conditions and supplies were deplorable, but she did her best with what she had.

She met William Bainbridge during her war service. He had graduated from Rochester University and was working his way through the Rochester Theological Seminary. During his war service he was with the Christian Commission, working with the solders.

After the war he had a position at a church in Erie, Pennsylvania; Lucy went back to Cleveland, not far from Erie. The two were married in September 1866. William was then appointed pastor of a church in Providence, Rhode Island.

Their first child was born in 1868 but died before she was two. A son was born in 1871. Lucy then adopted a second daughter, who had been born in 1872.

The Bainbridges apparently were in Cleveland during this time. They returned to Providence, then several years later moved to Brooklyn. William was in charge of the New York City Mission society; Lucy was appointed superintendent of the woman's branch of the organization. In that position, which she held for 18 years, she managed fifteen nurses, fifty missionaries, and forty trained workers. She lectured constantly and wrote four books.

Lucy Bainbridge and her husband began their first trip around the world from Providence, Rhode Island, on New Year's morning, 1879. During the trip Lucy sent letters back to *The Providence Daily Journal*, and these letters are collected in *Round the World Letters*.

The Bainbridges traveled to learn about different countries and the customs of the people. "There is nothing like travel to teach one to appreciate the right of opinion in others and bring one to realize what a mote he really is in the vast shifting sands of the humanity of our great world," Lucy wrote [*Round the World Letters*, p. 14]. They planned to spend two years traveling. They first went to Cleveland to leave their six-year-old with her grandmother, then stopped in Chicago, where Lucy apparently spent some of her growing-up years, crossed the country, and sailed for Asia.

> Singapore is the bazaar of the world. There is here a little everything, and people from everywhere. This is the meeting-place of the coffee and spices from Java and the South, with the tobacco and fruits of Sumatra and Malacca; the silk and carved ivory from China, and the lacquer and fans of Japan, with the cottons and prints of England and France. Here are trinkets and beetle jewelry from Siam, rice from Burmah, opium from India, and the celebrated cloisonné work from Pekin, China.... The island is richly clothed in brilliant greens. Nature throws out her covering of grass and trees, and the drapery of ferns and vines and feathery bamboo in bewildering

abandonment of growth. Monkeys run wild and chatter and chipper in the tangled woods. Not many years ago elephants and tigers had a home in the jungle. The surface of the island is slightly undulating; each little hill near the city is occupied by one or more bungalow houses, and receives a fanciful name [*Round the World Letters*, pp. 206–207].

Lucy and her husband were particularly interested in the "extreme East"; they spent two months in Japan. Lucy wrote about seemingly everything, from the state prison to sponge cake. They left reluctantly to go on to China then traveled to Burma and India. After traveling in India for several months, Lucy and her son sailed — Mr. Bainbridge may have gone overland — to Egypt via the Suez Canal. (Apparently Lucy and her husband had visited Egypt thirteen years earlier.) Next was a visit to the Holy Land, then travel through Europe to England, and the voyage home.

As the trip — and the book — progressed, Lucy became more critical and less exploratory. Perhaps the trip lasted too long or there were so many new experiences and sights that she couldn't appreciate the novelty as much. Nonetheless, there was a second trip around the world.

In her later years Lucy became almost blind. She died at the age of 83. William had preceded her in death.

SOURCES: Maggie MacLean, 2006, in website "Civil War Women." Http://civil warwomen.blogspot.com/2006/10/lucy-seaman-bainbridge; *Round the World Letters*.

WORKS

Bainbridge, Lucy Seaman. *Jewels from the Orient*. New York and Chicago: Revell, 1920. This is the account of her second trip around the world.

_____. *Round the World Letters: Five Hundred and Forty-Two Pages of Charming Pen Pictures by the Way, a Graphic Portrayal of Scenes, Incident, and Adventures of a Two Years' Tour of the World*. New York: Blackall, 1882. Boston: Lothrop, 1882.

Florence von Sass Baker,
c. 1841–1916. English.

Florence's life prior to meeting Samuel White Baker in 1858 is clouded in mystery and legend. Baker was traveling with the Maharajah Duleep Singh party to Hungary. Ice blocked their boat in a Turkish town where many Hungarian refugees had taken shelter, among them Florence Barbara Mary Finnian Von Sass, who was seventeen. As the story goes, Baker visited a slave market where Florence was about to be sold, and he purchased her, outbidding the pasha for her. Consequently he and Florence had to race on horseback for the border and cross to Bucharest.

However they met, Baker became managing director for a railway that was being built in Rumania. When it was completed he decided he would follow John Speke and help with the exploration for the discovery of the sources of the Nile River. Richard Burton and Speke were already in Africa on the pursuit, but they were disagreeing about the potential outcome of the discovery. Baker also hoped to meet Grant, who was a partner with Speke. Baker, unlike the others, financed his own exploration and received no support from the Royal Geographical Society or his publisher. He had considerable wealth to draw on.

Florence insisted on accompanying Baker on the journey, which began in 1861. The trip was arduous and lasted far longer than anticipated. The British public believed that Florence and Baker had died.

They returned to England in 1865. There, Florence worked on learning English and tried to be a "good" Victorian wife when in England. She was strikingly beautiful; the fact that they were not married, however, worked against her in the eyes of many people. They never had children, but Florence became close to Baker's children from his first marriage.

In 1870 she went with him on his expedition to Gondorko to suppress the slave trade, another very arduous trip. They returned to England in 1873.

Africa, White Nile, Gondokoro, May 19, 1871. At last we arrived here — after a fearful struggle and weary journey in dragging a flotilla of 59 vessels including a steamer of thirty-two horse power over high grass and marshes.... The Bahr Giraffe, now the only route to the Upper Nile, was more or less un–navigable for about 48 miles alternately blocked up by floating marsh of high grass and mud through which we had to cut canals. Having overcome these obstacles the stream divided into numerous channels all of which were so shallow as to be utterly impassable.

Our vessels drew four feet of water but in many places the depth of the river was only two feet. These terrible shallows extended over about twenty miles with intervals of deep water.

[*Navigation was made possible only by using bundles of grass and mud and sacks of sand to fashion dams that created a channel.*]

We arrived at Gondokoro on 14 April and it appeared really quite like heaven to us after the horrible country through which we had been struggling for four months and 10 days. Nevertheless we found great changes since we last saw this spot. The whole of the villages are destroyed — not a dwelling is left and the country is strewn with the skulls and bones of the inhabitants.... The whole country is in a state of the wildest anarchy owing to the acts of the ivory and slave raiders.

We have great anxiety respecting the supply of provisions. We are cut off from all communication with Khartoum for twelve months until re-inforcements shall arrive with the North Wind next season. With many mouths, about 2,000 including sailors and camp followers, this is a serious matter and Papa is driving all hands forward in the work of cultivation as the rainy season has commenced and

we shall be entirely dependent upon our crops of corn [*Morning Star*, pp. 85–87].

Several years later they were ready to travel again. This time they set out for Cyprus, arriving in January 1879. They went on to India, then Hong Kong, Canton and Shanghai. Subsequently they visited the United States and finally completed their world tour in 1882. Their remaining travels were their annual trips way from England during the winter.

Samuel Baker died in 1893. Florence lived for twenty-three more years and died in 1916.

SOURCE: *Dictionary of Literary Biography.*

WORKS

Baker, Florence von Sass. *Morning Star: Florence Baker's Diary of the Expedition to Put Down the Slave Trade on the Nile, 1870–73.* Ed. Anne Baker. London: William Kimber, 1972.

BOOKS ABOUT OR INCLUDING FLORENCE VON SASS BAKER

Hall, Richard. *Lovers on the Nile: The Incredible African Journeys of Sam and Florence Baker.* New York: Random House, 1980.
Shipman, Pat. *To the Heart of the Nile: Lady Florence Baker and the Exploration of Central Africa.* New York: Morrow, 2004.

Alice Blanche Balfour. British.

Travelers made their way through various parts of Africa using all sorts of conveyance. For Alice Balfour and her four fellow travelers in 1894, their mode of travel from the Cape was wagons — "waggons." The group included her brother, the Right Honorable A. J. Balfour, later prime minister of Great Britain. They began with a good adventuring spirit. "In the spring of last year our party of four started for the

Cape, intending to travel through Matabeleland and Mashunaland by waggon. We were in happy uncertainty as to how this was to be accomplished, but as regarded both the route to be pursued and the mode of conveyance to be employed, two things only were certain — that no two people gave the same advice, and that each person was convinced that his plan was the only one that was practically possible" [*Twelve Hundred Miles in a Waggon*, p. ix].

That spirit carried them through the entire trip. Alice, and apparently her companions, find everything interesting. The discomforts, inconveniences and occasional perils were all part of it and literally, taken in stride. In her bits of spare time she sketched and wrote. Her letters form the basis for the book; in editing it she omitted personal information and news as well as political discussions. She recounted what they saw and their adventures in a fresh breezy style. One of the highlights of the trek was the Zimbabye (Zimbabwe) Ruins.

> To the north of us was the high steep kopje, on the top of which are the ruins of the ancient fortress. You climb up the kopje by a winding path, and it is not until you turn round the western shoulder of the hill that you see the native kraal, and to the right of that the gigantic smooth granite rocks, piled one above the other, which form the natural defenses on the north side of the fortress. The chinks between these boulder-like rocks were once all carefully walled up; and having squeezed through one of them, we found ourselves in the fortress itself, in the midst of a perfect labyrinth of half-ruined walls, with narrow winding passages, crumbling stairways, curved buttresses, and all sorts of devices for defense, the whole overgrown with tangled vegetation, and the rocks covered with lovely creepers and trees with long hungry snake-like roots lodged in the crevices.... From here you see the country spread out before you, fantastic kopjes and exquisite blue hills in the distance, and at your feet, on the yellow grassy plain, the Zimbabye

temple enclosure, filled, as the circle of a coronet is with velvet, with luxuriant vegetation [pp. 155–156].

They took their wagons as far north as Beira (Mozambique), where they continued their journey to Zanzibar, then to the Red Sea.

SOURCE: *Twelve Hundred Miles in a Waggon.*

Lady Mary Anne Barker,
1831–1911.

She is sometimes listed as Mary Anne Broome (formerly Lady Barker).

Mary Anne Stewart, who would become Lady Barker and then Lady Broome, was born in Jamaica, where her father was island secretary. She was the oldest of her siblings and traveled five times between school in England and holidays in Jamaica. By her own admission she was poorly educated, but she had a strong interest in literature and writing and could read French and German.

She married Captain George Barker in 1852. They had two sons, and for most of their married life Mary Anne lived in England. George was away much of the time. He served in the Crimean War and in the Indian Mutiny. In 1860 Mary Anne joined her husband in India. George died eight months later, and she returned to England, but apparently left at some time.

Five years later she married Frederick Napier Broome, who was eleven years younger than she was. He, too, had a colonial background. Mary Anne and Broome went to New Zealand shortly after their marriage; Mary Anne's two sons stayed in England. Broome bought a sheep run, where the couple lived until 1868; they had to give up the venture when a severe winter storm killed over half their herd. They returned to England, where they both took up writing to support themselves.

Broome was known as a minor poet; he began also to write articles. For her first book Mary Anne drew on the letters she wrote her sister while they were sheep farming in New Zealand. The success this book encouraged her to write other books based on her earlier travels, as well as essays on books written by other travelers.

Wednesday, June 3, 1876

Dust and the Bazaar; those are the only topics I have for you. Perhaps I ought to put the Bazaar first, for it is past and over, to the intense thankfulness of everybody, buyers and sellers included; whereas the dust abides with us for ever, and increases in volume and density and restlessness more and more. But still here is a little bit of bracing, healthy weather, and we enjoy every moment of it, and congratulate each other upon it, and boast once more to new comers that we possess "the finest climate in the world." This remark rather died out in the summer, but is again to be heard on all sides, now, and I am not strong-minded enough to take up lance and casque and tilt against it. Besides which it would really be very pleasant, if only the tanks were not dry, the cows giving but a tea-cupful of milk a day for want of grass; whilst butter is half-a-crown a pound, and of a rancid cheesiness trying to the consumer. Still it is bright and sunny and fresh all day, too hot indeed in the sun, and generally bitterly cold in the evenings and night.... About this season prudent people burn strips around their fences and trees to check any vagrant fire, for there is so little timber that the few gum trees are precious things not to be shriveled up in an hour by fast traveling flames for want of precautions.

I daresay in England you think that you know something about bazaars, but I assure you you do not; not about such a bazaar as this, at all events. We have been preparing for it, working for it, worrying for it, advertising it, building it — of zinc and calico, — decorating it, and generally slaving at it for a year and more....

Everybody from far and near came to the bazaar and bought liberally. The things provided were selected with a view to the wants of a community which has not a large margin for luxuries, and although they were very pretty, there was a strong element of practical usefulness in everything. There were contributions from London and Paris, from Italy and Vienna, from India and Australia; to say nothing of Kafir weapons and wooden utensils, live stock, vegetables, and flowers. Everybody responded to our entreaties, and helped us most liberally and kindly, and we are all immensely delighted with the financial result. Some of our best customers were funny old Dutchmen from far up-country, who had come down to the races and the agricultural show which were all going on at the same time. They recklessly bought the most astounding things, but wisely made it a condition of purchase that they should not be required to take away the goods. In fact they hit upon the expedient of presenting to one stall what they bought at another ... [*A Year's House-keeping in South Africa*, pp. 221–223; 225].

She and Broome spent five years in London, during which time they had two sons. Mary Anne broadened her writing interests. Broome received a series of government appointments, which included various colonial residencies in Natal, then Mauritius; he was then governor of Western Australia and eventually Trinidad in 1891, experiences that Mary Anne again utilized for her books. Broome died in 1896.

Mary Anne's last years were spent in England, where she continued to write. She died in London in 1911.

SOURCE: *Dictionary of Literary Biography*.

WORKS

The author is sometimes listed under Mary Anne Stewart Broome (formerly Lady Barker).

Barker, Lady Anne. *Colonial Memories*. London: Smith, Elder, 1904. Lady Mary Anne Barker also wrote stories and books for children.

_____. *Letters to Guy*. London: Macmillan and

Co., 1885. Also published in a new edition as *Remembered with Affection*. Melbourne and New York: Oxford University Press, 1963.

_____. *Station Amusements in New Zealand*. London: Wm. Hunt, 1873.

_____. *Station Life in New Zealand*. London: Macmillan and Co., 1870.

_____. *Traveling About Over Old and New Ground*. London: George Routledge, 1872.

_____. *A Year's Housekeeping in South Africa*. London: Macmillan and Co., 1877. Also published as *Letters from South Africa*. New York: Macmillan, 1877; and *Life in South Africa*. Philadelphia: Lippincott, 1877.

Frances Hornby Barkley,

1769–1845. British.

Little is known about Frances Barkley's early life. She married Mr. Barkley, a fur trader and ship's captain, in 1786. Four weeks later they left for a trading expedition to the Pacific Northwest. They reached western Canada the following year. Frances Island and Hornby Peak are named after her; Barkley Sound was also named by the Barkleys. They then sailed to China where they traded otter skins from Canada for trade goods to take to Mauritius.

Barkley's business partners took over the ship at Mauritius, stranding the Barkleys. During that time Frances had a child. An American ship was to take them to England, but the ship ran aground on the coast of France. Finally, in November 1789 they reached England, only to start out seven months later on another trading expedition, this time from Denmark to India. During that voyage Frances had another child. They then went to Micronesia, Japan, Russia, Alaska, Hawaii, Vietnam, then to Mauritius. One of the children died during the voyage.

Frances and her husband returned to England in 1794. Frances never traveled again.

SOURCE: Netzley, *Encyclopedia of Women's Travel and Exploration*.

WORKS

Barkley, Frances. *Among Boers and Basutos*. London: Roxburghe Press, 1893.

_____. *From the Tropics to the North Sea, including Sketches of Colonial Life*. London: Roxburghe Press, 1890.

BOOKS ABOUT OR INCLUDING FRANCES HORNBY BARKLEY

Hill, Beth, ed. *The Remarkable World of Frances Barkley, 1769–1845*. Sidney, B.C.: Gray's Publishing, 1978.

Lady Anne Lindsay Barnard,

1750–1825. British.

Lady Anne Lindsay's father was sixty years old when he married Anne's mother, a Miss Dalrymple, who was nearly forty years younger than he was. Anne was their oldest child. In the next twelve years there were ten more children. As Lady Anne once said, "Our excellent parents, having nothing else to do in the country, desisted not from their laudable sin of populating the castle of Balcarres, till their family consisted of eight boys and three girls" [*South Africa a Century Ago*, p. 5].

After her father died Anne went with her mother to Edinburgh, where she much enjoyed the literary society. This is likely also when she met Henry Dundas, a rising young Scottish politician. When Lady Anne's sister Margaret was widowed, Anne went to London to live with her. The two lived together for many years, enjoying the society of politicians and literary men. Meanwhile, Dundas had become one of the most powerful men in Scotland.

Dundas had been deserted by his first wife, and they were divorced. He and Lady

Anne became close friends, but when he re-married it was to someone else. In 1793 she surprised her friends by marrying Mr. Andrew Barnard, who was fifteen years younger than she was.

Barnard was the son of the Bishop of Limerick; he had little money and many debts. Lady Anne had little money of her own, but she was optimistic of obtaining a government appointment for her husband through her many friends and connections. She appealed to Dundas several times. Finally, after several years, Dundas offered Barnard the appointment of secretary of the South African colony. Lady Anne let Dundas know that he might have made Barnard a better appointment, to which Dundas essentially replied that she should take it or leave it. However, they reconciled before the Barnards left England. Barnard, for his part, was delighted with the appointment.

In March 1797, the couple sailed for the Cape, arriving in May. Lady Anne's letters, which form her book, were all written to Dundas, who kept them.

> I never saw the force of prejudice more apparent than in the way Englishmen here turn up their foolish noses at the Cape wines because they are Cape wines. They will drink nothing but port, claret, or Madeira, pretending that the wines of the country give them bowel-ache! It may be so, if they drink two or three bottles at a time, and that very frequently, but Cape wine will not do so if used in moderation. Mr. Barnard drinks nothing else himself, though we have every other good wine at table, champagne, and burgundy excepted. I must tell you, as an illustration, of what happened one day with us after dinner. We had a little hock on board ship, two bottles of which remained over, and we keep them for Lord Macartney when he is ill and wishes for a bonne bouche as they happen to be very fine. After dinner I thought myself drinking up one of this hock, and said to Mr. Barnard, "O fie! Why do you give us this to-day — it is some of our fine hock." A

certain lieutenant-colonel, who shall be nameless, on this filled his glass. "Lord bless me, what fine wine this is!" said he; "I have not tasted a glass such as this since I came here." I then found, on asking, that it was Steine wine, a cheap Cape wine, which Mr. Barnard had not liked, and had ordered for common use in the household. In a moment the colonel found fifty faults in it [pp. 114–115].

> We now arranged another party which promised to be still pleasanter — namely, to Paarl, a village at the bottom of mountains so called from two enormous stones being at the top of them of a size so immense that it took a friend of mine half an hour to walk around one of them. They are, however, each entire stones, somewhat shaped like imperfect pearls, and awful from gigantic and unique singularity; they are of granite and one of them is hollow. It is supposed it could contain 20,000 men, but this must be nonsense — let us call it 1,000 and then I shall have a better chance of being believed. The valley beneath is rich, fertile, and pretty, being tolerably wooded, watered by the Bergh river, and could produce anything and everything, was it tried. Almonds, walnuts, and oranges grow in plenty, but wine is also the chief article here [p. 121].

Lady Anne returned to England in 1802; Barnard followed a few months later. Lady Anne set about securing another government appointment for Barnard but was unsuccessful. Dundas (who had become Lord Melville) had resigned his office. Anne traveled to Ireland, where new trouble awaited. Barnard's father, the Bishop of Limerick, had, at the age of seventy-six, decided to marry a young girl, causing much scandal, talk and annoyance.

In 1806 the English again conquered the Cape, and Barnard again went out as secretary of the colony. Lady Anne was against his accepting the appointment, but with no other prospects there was no choice. He left for the Cape, and she made plans to follow him later. This changed, though, when Barnard died soon after his arrival at the Cape, in 1807.

Now a widow, Lady Anne returned to London to live with her sister Lady Margaret. Once again she enjoyed the company of literary men and politicians. Lady Margaret remarried in 1812, but died two years later. Lady Anne continued to live in the London house. She was well liked and known as a great raconteur. She died in 1825.

She has another claim to fame as the author of the ballad "Auld Robin Gray."

SOURCE: "Memoir" by W. H. Wilkins, in *South Africa a Century Ago: Letters Written from the Cape of Good Hope (1797–1801).*

WORKS

Barnard, Lady Anne. *South Africa a Century Ago: Letters Written from the Cape of Good Hope (1797–1801).* Edited by W. H. Wilkins. London: Smith, Elder, 1901.
Also published as *The Letters of Lady Anne Barnard.* Cape Town: A. A. Balkema, 1973.

Emily A. Beaufort (Viscountess Strangford), 1826–1887. British.

She is sometimes listed as Emily Anne Smythe.

Emily Anne married Percy Ellen Frederick William Smythe, Lord Strangford (1826–1869), in 1862. He had been educated at Oxford, where he studied languages. His spoken languages included Persian, Arabic, Turkish, Greek, and Sanskrit.

Prior to her marriage, Emily had traveled widely with her sister, visiting Egypt, Asia Minor and Syria. From this trip she wrote *Egyptian Sepulchres and Syrian Shrines.* Lord Strangford reviewed the book, which led to their meeting; eventually they married.

In her preface Emily Beaufort tells us,

"Circumstances having rendered change of scene and climate imperatively necessary for my sister and myself, we hastily determined, at the close of the year 1858, to leave England for Egypt." The two women hoped to find "an endless store of deeply interesting subjects for thought and study, unfatiguing traveling, and no society...." Their expectations were met on the first two aspects, but not on the third "on the now fashionable and crowded Nile."

In addition to providing an account of her travels, she tried to give other travelers useful information and tips regarding their trip; consequently the book contains many insights into the considerations of travel at that time.

Their first destination was Egypt, where they traveled up the Nile on a dahabeeyah. She was intrigued by the ruins and pyramids. From Egypt they went to Damascus. The ruins of Palmyra were difficult to reach and they had not planned to see them, but learning there was a group of travelers wanting to go to Palmyra, they joined. Visitors were allowed to remain in the ruins no more than twenty-four hours; the long day in the Palmyra combined with a strenuous trip there and back was fatiguing to everyone who made the journey. Emily and her sister found it a grand adventure in spite of the fatigue and some discomfort. Returning to Damascus they rested and explored, then continued traveling late in the afternoon to escape the heat.

> ... then we descended into a lovely winding glen, full of thick foliage and the rushing tumbling stream of the Barrada, and emerged from it on to the Desert and the desolate Sah'ra mountains just as darkness fell upon us. The country was scarcely light enough to show it in its dreary loneliness and silence, when — voices called us to stop. The dragomans immediately fell back to ask what they wanted, and we soon guessed they were the robbers or Syrian banditti which, as we afterwards learned, infest this

road. Fortunately we were, everyone one of us, dressed in the white mash'lah of the country, and we believe that they mistook us in the dim light for men; at all events they seemed to think we were too strong a party for them, and let us alone and we made the best of our way on. Of course, as contretemps always come together, one of the horses was lame from a bad shoe, and we could only go at a walking pace; and the fun of the thing was that, though we all showed our pistols and revolvers, not one of us, even the dragomans, had remembered to reload them on leaving Damascus [p. 273].

She found Syria fascinating.

But the grand object at Banias is the noble Castle of Subeibeh, which stand[s] on a cliff something more than 1000 feet above the town. It took us nearly two hours to reach the top, partly on foot, for the way is very steep. It has been an enormous castle; but its chief merit is in the splendid workmanship of the masonry. The stones are very large, and nearly all of the Phoenician bevel.... At the eastern end the castle expands into almost a second castle, mounted on much higher rocks. There are some remarkable cisterns hewn in the rock, one so vast that it must have been able to supply a large garrison for a year or two; this is finely vaulted over, and has two stone staircases descending to the bottom. Altogether this has been, I suppose, not only the finest fortress in Syria, but probably was one of the most ancient strongholds in the world.... Some peasants were cultivating tobacco in the light soil on the summit, and in the turned-up earth we found bits of ancient pottery and glass, some of fine colour and delicate texture, with the iridescence of time very beautifully marked upon them. The slopes of the rocky hill are now thickly wooded, and the whole place was spangled with flowers [p. 289].

From Syria they went to Israel, where they visited many Biblical sites. They then began their trip home, spending time in Crete and Greece. However, they postponed starting for home so that they might visit Turkey and Constantinople. Then, reluc-

tantly, she "took my last sad look of Asia and the Eastern world" [p. 546].

She and her sister had been traveling for about two years.

In 1863 Strangford and Emily traveled in Austria and Albania. He died suddenly in 1869, in London.

After his death Emily trained as a nurse for four years in a hospital in England. She began the National Society for Providing Trained Nurses for the Poor, later publishing a book on hospital training. In 1876 she helped organize a relief fund for Bulgarian peasants. The next year she went to Turkey to oversee a hospital she established for Turkish soldiers.

She continued her hospital and relief work, establishing an ambulance association, working with women emigrants, and founding a medical school in Beirut. She also prepared her husband's papers for publication and wrote a novel. She died en route to Port Said, where she was to open a hospital for British seamen.

SOURCE: *Dictionary of National Biography.*

WORKS

Beaufort, Emily A. *Egyptian Sepulchres and Syrian Shrines.* Two volumes. London: Longman, Green, Longman and Roberts, 1861.

Princess Cristina Trivulzio di Belgiojoso, 1808–1871. Italian.

Cristina Trivulzio was born in 1808 in Lombardy; her family was an old, aristocratic family. When Cristina was four her father died, and her mother soon remarried. Cristina had an excellent education, especially so for a girl of that time. At the age of fifteen she fell in love with Prince Emilio Barbiano di Belgiojoso d'Este; he was twenty-three. They married the following year. Emilio gambled, drank and womanized. In addition the two had very little in common, and they separated three years after the marriage.

Cristina was active in Italian politics, and after a time the government began to take note of her activities and actions. The crisis came when Cristina traveled to Switzerland to celebrate the new democratic constitution. Prince Metternich ordered her to return to Milan. Cristina refused, and a warrant was issued for her arrest. Cristina then fled to France. She was ordered to return to Italy within three months and surrender to officials, or she would be declared civilly dead and her property and sources of income would be sequestered. Returning was out of the question.

Cristina contributed political articles to local French newspapers while she painted fans and portraits to earn her living. She reunited very briefly with her husband, and in December 1838 she had a daughter.

Italian cities began to revolt against Austrian jurisdiction, and Cristina decided to get actively involved. She recruited and commanded a troop of two hundred men to fight in Milan. The next year, 1849, she was asked to organize and direct the military hospitals. Cristina created the first voluntary corps of military nurses, and she prepared twelve hospitals in forty-eight hours.

The revolution failed, and the Austrian government stringently fined nobles who had been involved. They also investigated those who had helped the revolution, and Cristina felt threatened. She decided to travel to the Orient, as the Middle East was called, hoping to find a new life there.

She bought a tract of property in Turkey, where she and her daughter and other refugees could live. While she was there she traveled to Jerusalem. On her return, she found that her farm needed expensive repairs. Her assets in Italy had been confiscated, and she didn't have the means to make the needed repairs. Matters worsened: she was attacked and stabbed by one of her employees, a man from Lombardy who had been having an affair with her companion. Cristina never recovered her health or her will to stay on. After four years in Turkey she returned to Paris.

In December 1855 the Austrian government proclaimed a general amnesty for exiled Italians and restored confiscated estates. Finally, in 1861, Italy was officially unified, and in 1870 French troops withdrew from Rome.

Cristina died in 1871 at the age of sixty-three, having seen her life's goals for the unification and independence of Italy realized.

In addition to her travel writing, Cristina published books on a variety of topics, including the history of Lombardy and the House of Savoy, the Catholic Church, and the political condition of Italy and France. She founded and financed journals and newspapers, as well.

WORKS

Belgiojoso, Princess Cristina Trivulzio di. *Asie Mineure et Syrie, souvenirs de voyages.* Paris: M. Lévy, 1858.
_____. *Oriental Harems and Scenery.* New York: Carleton, 1862.

BOOKS ABOUT OR INCLUDING PRINCESS CRISTINA TRIVULZIO DI BELGIOJOSO

Gattey, Charles Neilson. *A Bird of Curious Plumage: Princess Cristina di Belgiojoso, 1808–1871.* London: Constable and Company Ltd., 1971.
Whitehouse, Henry Remsen. *A Revolutionary Princess, Cristina Belgiojoso-Trivulzio, Her Life and Times, 1808–1971.* London: T. F. Unwin, 1906.

Gertrude Bell, 1868–1926. British.

Gertrude Bell was born on July 14, 1868, into a family of privilege and wealth, a family of prominent English industrialists. Her mother died when she was two, and Gertrude later took responsibility for the baby, Maurice. Five years later her father remarried. Three more children completed the family. Gertrude's parents traveled frequently, and Gertrude continued in her position of responsibility for the younger children.

The typical schooling for gentlewomen was not to Gertrude's liking; she became one of the first women to study at Oxford, earning highest honors in modern history. At her oral exams she challenged some of her professors in their premises and assumptions.

She clearly didn't fit into the marriageable mold. When she was twenty she was sent to Bucharest where her uncle was British Ambassador to Romania. Gertrude was interested in politics from an early age, and with her family's connections she had access to royalty and people in the public life. The trip to Bucharest was intended — or hoped — to change her into a polished (marriageable) young lady, but she was too outspoken for that. Instead she relished the political surroundings; on one occasion she told a visiting French statesman (in front of other diplomats) he had no understanding of the German people. The visit may have been a failure in the marriage aspect; however, the experience of living in a different place gave her a passion for travel.

Her first independent trip was to Switzerland. Gertrude, always a vigorous, athletic woman, enjoyed the rigorous outdoor life and climbed several unexplored peaks. In 1892 she went to Persia, a trip that changed her life and orientation. She fell in love with the Middle East, and for the rest of her life she identified herself with that part of the world. She also fell in love with Henry Cadogan, a young diplomat. He was ten years older than she was, and the two shared many interests. They spent much

time together, riding in the desert and going on picnics. Her father refused to let Gertrude marry Cadogan, who had some reputation as a gambler and a wastrel. Undeterred, Gertrude returned to England to change her father's mind. To pass the time she began writing a book about experiences in Persia, *Safar Nameh — Persian Pictures: A Book of Travel*, her first travel narrative.

Word came that Cadogan had died. Gertrude was devastated.

She began to travel again for consolation and distraction. Her first trips were more traditional, to France, Italy, and Germany, then a round-the-world trip with her brother. But the desert was in her blood, and by 1900 she had returned, going first to Jerusalem, then (after asking permission of her father) making a solo trip in the desert. This trip reinforced her passion for the desert and desert peoples. She studied Arabic, explored Baghdad and Damascus, rode (sidesaddle) across the Arabian Desert. Arabs said she was a "daughter of the desert." Gertrude, a striking woman, attractive, tall and with red hair, must have been a sensation in the desert. She must also have attracted interest for her mode of life when traveling; she continued to receive the London *Times* whenever possible, and she carried cutlery, china and fine linen.

Her trips home grew shorter and further apart. She often traveled alone or with just one or two Arabs, but in 1909 she embarked on an expedition to Mesopotamia, with an entourage of male servants, trunks, equipment, and a set of Wedgwood china, crystal and silver for proper dining. As she headed toward Baghdad she met and visited sheiks and Arab leaders, winning their respect and confidence. The journey was rough, but Gertrude seemed to thrive on it.

Toward the end of March she found the ruin of Ukhaidir. Nothing had been published about it, and Gertrude was very excited about the "discovery." She was determined that this would make her name as an archaeologist, and she photographed, sketched and drew the plan of the castle to scale. When she left the site she crossed to Babylon to explore the archaeological remains of the city. She then continued on to Constantinople. There, while at a dinner at the French Embassy, she was shocked to learn that a French archaeologist had beaten her to publication of the "discovery" of Ukhaidir. However, she was the only one who had actually drawn plans of the castle. Her name is linked with the discovery.

She returned to the desert eighteen months later, this time visiting the site of Carchemish where David Hogarth was excavating for the British Museum. There she met T. E. Lawrence ("Lawrence of Arabia"). The natives thought she had arrived to be his bride.

In 1913 she fell in love with Richard Doughty-Wylie, whom she had met on a trip through Turkey. He was an adventurer after her own heart, but he was married.

She went to northern Arabia, to cross the Nejd. By May 1914 she was back in Damascus.

My objective that day was the village of Umm Ruweik on the eastern edge of the Druze hills. Remembering the vagaries of the map, I took with me one of Muhammad en Nassār's nephews as a guide. Fāiz was his name, and he was brother to Ghishghāsh, the Sheikh of Umm Ruweik.... We had not ridden very far along the lip of the hills, I gazing at the eastern plain as at a Promised Land that my feet would never tread, before Fāiz began to develop a plan for leaving the mules and tents behind at Umm Ruweik and making a dash across the Safa to the Ruhbeh, where lay the great ruin of which the accounts had fired my imagination. In a moment the world changed colour, and Success shone from the blue sky and hung in golden mists on that plain which had suddenly become accessible.

Our path fell rapidly from Sāleh, and in half an hour we were out of the snow and ice that had plagued us for the last day and night; half an hour later when we reached the Wādi Busān, where the swift waters turned a mill wheel, we had left the winter country behind. Sāneh, the village on the north side of the Wādi Busān, looked a flourishing place and contained some good specimens of Haurān architecture — I remember in particular a fine architrave carved with a double scroll of grapes and vine leaves that fell on either side of a vase occupying the centre of the stone. It was at Sānh that we came onto the very edge of the plateau and saw the great plain of the Safa spread out like a sea beneath us. The strange feature of it was that its surface was as black as a black tent roof, owing to the sheets of lava and volcanic stone that were spread over it [*The Desert and the Sown*, pp. 107–108].

... I could scarcely stay while my men assembled here, so eager was I to see the Kal'at el Beida — Khirbeh or Kal'al, ruin or castle, the Arabs call it either indifferently. I left the Druzes to pay such respects as were due to Zeus Saphathenos or whoever he might be, and cantered off to the edge of the lava plateau. A ditch lay before the lava, so full of water that I had to cross it by a little bridge of planks; Habīb was there watering his mule, that admirable mule which walked as fast as the mares, and, entrusting my horse to him, I hastened on over the broken lava and into the fortress court. There were one or two Arabs sauntering through it, but they paid as little attention to me as I did to them. This was it, the famous citadel that guards a dead land from an unpeopled, the Safa from the Hamīd. Grey white on the black platform rose the walls of smoothly dressed stones, the ghostly stronghold of a world of ghosts. Whose hands reared it, whose art fashioned the flowing scrolls on door-post and lintel, whose eyes kept vigil from the tower cannot yet be decided with any certainty [pp. 124–125].

Whether you ride to Damascus by a short cut or by a high road, from the Haurān or from Palmyra, it is always further away than any known place. Perhaps it is because the traveler is so eager to reach it, the great and splendid Arab city set in a girdle of fruit trees and filled with the murmur of running water [p. 133].

When World War I broke out, Doughty-Wylie was sent to Gallipoli to lead the troops. Gertrude was in London when she learned he was one of the first to be killed.

The British, determined to keep their influence in the Middle East, wanted to utilize the Arab factions to revolt against the Turks. Gertrude's knowledge of the area and her influence were now considered valuable. She had mapped uncharted areas, noting the location of wells and railway lines, and she'd learned which tribes were allies and which were enemies. She could figure out who would be friends and who would be foes of English. She also helped Lawrence by supplying him with information that would lead to his fame as Lawrence of Arabia.

Gertrude was the only woman to serve as an intelligence agent in the Arab Bureau in Cairo. The man in charge of the Bureau was her old friend, David Hogarth. Gertrude was sent to India to convince the viceroy to put up men and money to support the Arab revolt against the Turks.

In 1916 she was working, first from Basrah, then in Baghdad. She reported directly to Sir Percy Cox; they had good rapport, but many of the men resented her presence and her opinions. Tired of the war and of what she was doing, she was reaching a personal crisis.

She regained her balance after the war, but she was often rude and edgy in her dealings. She was irritated at the British lack of interest in anything Arabic, and she resented their preoccupation with British ways while they were in the Middle East. Instead of making colleagues (she was never very good at that), people avoided her. She was perceived as having friends in high places who protected and allowed her meddlesome ways.

In 1918 she was invited to discuss the "Arab Question" at the Paris Peace Conference in 1919. Gertrude returned to Baghdad, which was then in the midst of a rebellion against the British.

Her involvement in politics and political decisions continued. At times she used her influence on tribal leaders and local dignitaries. She was instrumental in helping determine borders of Iraq. When Faisal was installed as King, Gertrude was one of his advisors. But as the Arab government of Iraq became more independent, her relationship with Faisal became less that of an advisor and more of a social secretary. Bored and restless, she turned to archaeology. She wrote Iraq's first antiquities laws and founded the first archaeological museum.

By the time she was 58 she felt she had lost all her importance. Iraqis didn't need her; her family had lost much of its huge wealth; the last of her loves had left her. In 1926 she took an overdose of sleeping pills, perhaps by accident, perhaps by design.

Arab crowds lined the streets to say farewell. The British gave her a full military funeral and buried her in Baghdad.

SOURCE: *Dictionary of Literary Biography*, Volume 174.

WORKS

Gertrude Bell also was the author of several articles.

Bell, Gertrude. *Amurath to Amurath*. London: Heinemann, 1911.
_____. *The Arab of Mesopotamia*. Basra, Iraq: Government Press, 1917?
_____. *The Arab War: Confidential Information for General Headquarters from Gertrude Bell,*
_____. *Being Despatches Reprinted from the Secret "Arab Bulletin."* London: Golden Cockerel Press, 1940.
_____. *The Desert and the Sown*. London: Heinemann, 1907. Republished as *Syria: The Desert & the Sown*. New York: Dutton, 1907.
_____. *Notes on a Journey through Cilicia and Lycaonia*. Angers: Burdin, 1906.
_____. *Palace and Mosque at Ukhaidir: A Study in Early Mohammadan Architecture*. Oxford: Clarendon Press, 1914.

_____. *Review of the Civil Administration of Mesopotamia.* London: H.M. Stationery Office, 1920.

_____. *Safar Nameh — Persian Pictures: A Book of Travel.* London: Bentley, 1894. Republished as *Persian Pictures.* London: Benn, 1928.

_____, with Sir William M. Ramsay. *The Thousand and One Churches.* London: Hodder & Stoughton, 1909.

BOOKS ABOUT OR INCLUDING GERTRUDE BELL

Bell, Lady Florence, Ed. *The Letters of Gertrude Bell.* Two volumes. London: Benn, 1927.

Bodley, Ronald Courtenay. *Gertrude Bell.* New York: Macmillan, 1940.

Burgoyne, Elizabeth, Ed. *Gertrude Bell, from her Personal Papers.* Two volumes. London: Benn, 1958–1961.

Goodman, Susan, *Gertrude Bell.* Leamington Spa, England: Dover, U.K., 1985.

Kahn, Josephine. *Daughter of the Desert: The Story of Gertrude Bell.* London: Bodley Head, 1956.

Richmond, Elsa, Ed. *The Earlier Letters of Gertrude Bell.* London: Benn, 1937.

Tibble, Anne. *Gertrude Bell.* London: Blank, 1958.

Wallach, Janet, *Desert Queen: The Extraordinary Life of Gertrude Bell, Adventurer, Advisor to Kings, Ally of Lawrence of Arabia.* New York: Doubleday, 1996.

Winstone, H. V. F. *Gertrude Bell.* London: Cape, 1978; revised London: Constable, 1993.

Gertrude Bell's correspondence is at several repositories, including the British Library, the Bodleian Library, the Cambridge University Library, and the Oriental Society of the Durham University Library. Additionally the University Library of Newcastle upon Tyne has more than two thousand items. Additional notes and papers are at the Royal Geographical Society, London. Official government documents are in the Foreign and Commonwealth Office, the India Office, and the Public Record Office, London.

Sarah Belzoni, 1783–1870.

Sarah's life, travel, writing and research tend to be overshadowed by that of her husband, Giovanni Belzoni. Her writing is part of Belzoni's larger book and is often overlooked.

Little is known of her before she married Belzoni. Her family name is not known, and it's not certain whether she was English or Irish. She and Belzoni met and married soon after his arrival in England in 1803.

Giovanni Belzoni was a strong personality, eccentric, an Italian theatrical performer turned adventurer. He discovered the tomb of Seti I in the Valley of the Kings and cleared the entrance to the large temple at Abu Simbel, among other contributions to archaeology. He is also known for his propensity to carve his name on various artifacts and for his somewhat destructive "methods" of excavation, recognized as inappropriate even in those very early days of archaeology.

Sarah was with Belzoni on his voyage to Egypt in 1815; travel and life in Egypt during that time were difficult. She often dressed as a Mamluk youth, particularly when she was on her own on an excursion. She frequently was left behind, to stay in Cairo, Luxor, or Aswan, or at a base camp while Giovanni went in search of antiquities. On her own she studied the life of the women around her, making friends with many of them.

Her contribution to Giovanni's book *Narrative of the Operations and Recent Discoveries in Egypt and Nubia* is a short chapter of forty-two pages, based on her own observations and contacts with local women. She spoke some Arabic and was admitted to houses where men would not have been able to go, giving her unique opportunities to observe and talk with the women.

> During Mr. B.'s absence, I took up my residence on the top of the temple of Osiris in that island [*Philoe*], and with the help of some mud walls, I had enclosed two

comfortable rooms. It was rumoured about there were thieves on the island opposite, though I rather think it was a trick to see what effect it might have on me. I thought it proper to guard even against those Barabras that had been engaged by Mr. B. to guard me. I had a servant with me at this time who had been with us some years; we kept the fire-arms always ready, and made our guards see we were not afraid, and that they might inform their friends we had plenty of powder and ammunition for their reception. It is well known that the people fear you when they know you do not fear them. They knew there was a deal of luggage left with me, and saw some silver spoons and forks which were brought up for the use of Mr. Beechey; and the servant used to let the Arabs and Nubians see and clean them. These people, when they see trunks or boxes belonging to Europeans, judge they are full of gold and silver, particularly after having seen such unnecessary things as spoons and forks of that metal. I was visited every day by the women inhabiting the different villages on the other side of the Nile; they used to cross on a ramouse bringing sometimes one or two beads of cornelian antiques, or a little barley, some eggs and onions, getting in exchange glass beads or small looking-glasses [*Belzoni's Travels*, p. 301].

My wish was to arrive in the valley of Jericho before the great concourse of pilgrims. As I had no one but myself to depend upon, I wished to procure a spot where I could be out of the crowd; and, without putting myself under obligation to any one, I had arrived in time to take possession of two bushes. I made the man cover them over with Arab shawls to shade me from the sun, and remained there till our departure for the Jordan. During the afternoon, an European traveler we had known in Egypt, in his strolling about encountered me, and politely offered to render me any services he could in that place; but in those journeys I made it an invariable rule to be independent of every one, that it might not be said, if it had not been for me or for us, she could not have gone on; and indeed as it was, I could not escape petty hints from a countryman of mine, who, "for his part had no notion of people

being so romantic as to travel about, who had no fortune to support it" [p. 304].

She made a trip to the Holy Land, leaving Cairo in January 1818. When she returned in May she traveled by mule (she was in her customary disguise as a Turkish youth) accompanied only by a driver.

When they returned to England Giovanni had an exhibition in the Egyptian Hall in Piccadilly. The show was a success.

Giovanni died on a trip to Benin in 1823. Sarah undertook to continue exhibiting results of their work, mounting an exhibition in London in 1825. That show was not successful; the exhibition material was seized and Sarah was destitute. Friends launched an appeal to the government for aid, and she petitioned Parliament for help. Only in 1851 did she receive a civil list pension of one hundred pounds a year.

She lived in Brussels and the Channel Islands towards the end of her life. She died in 1870.

SOURCE: William H. Peck, in website "Breaking Ground. Women in Old World Archaeology," November 2006.

WORKS

Belzoni, Sarah. *A Short Account of the Women of Egypt, Nubia and Syria,* in *Narrative of the Operations and Recent Discoveries in Egypt and Nubia and of a Journey to the Coast of the Red Sea, in Search of the Ancient Berenice and Another to the Oasis of Jupiter Ammon.* London: John Murray, 1820.
Reprinted in: *Belzoni's Travels.* Alberto Siliotti, Ed. London: The British Museum Press, 2001.

Agnes Dorothea von Blomberg Bensly

Agnes Bensly, with her husband, accompanied Agnes Smith Lewis and Margaret Smith Gibson on one of their expeditions to the convent of St. Catherine.

WORKS

Bensly, Agnes Dorothea von Blomberg Bensly. *Our Journey to Sinai: A Visit to the convent of St. Catarina, with a Chapter on the Sinai Palimpsest.* London: Religious Tract Society, 1896.

Mabel Virginia Anna Bent.
British.

James Theodore Bent (1852–1897) was a well known scholar, historian, writer and archaeologist. Unfortunately little is known of Mabel Bent, and perhaps because her work and almost all her writing were in collaboration with her husband, she often is not recognized, both for her contributions and as the traveler she was. Little is known about her beyond what is told in the travel books.

Theodore and Mabel Virginia Anna Hall-Dare of Newtonbarry, County Wexford, married in 1877, two years after he graduated from Oxford.

Theodore traveled to excavate ruins. In 1883, the two went to the Cyclades Islands, the subject of their first travel book. In January 1891, accompanied by a cartographer, they left England for a year in southern Africa and Mashonaland. Their focus was on both the archaeological ruins and the people of the area. In 1893 the couple was in Abyssinia, where they hoped to study Aksum, the center of Christianity and the ancient capital. The area was very unsettled, and the Bents had to stay in Asmara before they could go on to Aksum.

The area they wanted to study included the grounds of a monastery — where females were barred from entering. Mabel was frustrated by having to wait while the men did the interesting explorations. So on a visit to another monastery she devised an outfit that made it impossible to ascertain whether the wearer was male or female. The jacket of her outfit had braiding on it, and the monks apparently thought she was a general. Consequently she was treated as a person of superior rank, taken into the church, and shown the pictures and treasures.

Between 1889 and 1897 the two traveled to southern Arabia and to the Sudan to explore and make archaeological investigations. They began by going to Bahrein to excavate sepulchral mounds near Ali. They were attracted by stories of mysterious mounds, and they hoped to excavate and find traces of Phoenician remains.

They were in the area of Mt. Erba, on the west bank of the Red Sea.

> We rested our camels and our men at Hadai, and drank of some fresh water from a little pool, the first we had seen in this barren country, which was supplied by a tiny stream that made its appearance for a few yards in a sheltered corer of the valley, a stream of priceless value in this thirsty land. Debalohp suggested to my husband that he knew of some ruins in a neighbouring valley to which he could take him, but it was not without considerable hesitation that he decided to go. A long day's ride in this hot country, supposed to be almost, if not quite, within the Dervish sphere of influence, was not lightly to be undertaken, more especially as he had been on so many fruitless errands in search of ruins at suggestions of the Bedouin, and returned disgusted, and when he mounted his camel next morning, without any hope of finding anything, and sure of a fatiguing day, had a reasonable excuse offered itself, he would probably not have gone. But the unexpected in these cases is always happening. His long ride turned out only to be one of three hours. Wadi Gabei was somewhat more fertile and picturesque than any we had as yet seen, and as a climax to it all came the discovery of an ancient gold-mine, worked in ages long gone by doubtless by that mysterious race whose tomb and buildings we had been speculating on.
> Diodorus, in his account of an old Egyptian gold-mine, describe most accurately what my husband found in the Wadi Gabit. For miles along it at the narrower

end were the ruins of miners' huts; both up the main valley and up all the collateral ones there must have been seven or eight hundred of them at the lowest computation. Then there were hundreds of massive crushing-stones, neatly constructed out of blocks of basalt, which had been used for breaking the quartz, lying in wild confusion amongst the ruined huts, and by the side of what once was a stream, but is now only a sandy, choked-up river-bed. On a high rock in the middle of the valley he found a trifle of a Greek inscription scratched by a miner who had evidently been working the rich quartz vein just below it....

There was no question for a moment that he had come across the centre of a great mining industry lost in these desert valleys behind the mighty wall by which Mount Erba and its spurs shuts off this district from the Red Sea littoral [*Southern Arabia*, pp. 318–319].

Mabel was very much a participant in the expedition and was especially active in the later expeditions. She was the photographer, often working under very difficult conditions. She had her own group of laborers to oversee in the excavations. She wrote that the laborers had a questioning look at first, but since the Persians had learned to respect her, the others became amenable to her giving orders.

In many of the areas where they worked, both men and women were amazed to see a woman with an exploration team, and they would ask to see her. Mabel also told of several incidents where her courage and resourcefulness came into play.

On the last trip both Theodore and Mabel became very ill with what she described as malarial fever. She had to be carried the last seventeen miles on her bed. Theodore died four days after they arrived home.

In the preface to *Southern Arabia*, Mabel wrote that her husband had intended to write a book of the information they had gathered in their series of expeditions in Southern Arabia. Since Theodore Bent had died immediately after they returned from their last journey there, Mabel had undertaken the task. The book was written to help others who might follow in their footsteps, and it was for them that Mabel included such helpful information as the price of camels and the payment of soldiers. The book is drawn from Theodore's notebook, her chronicles of the journey, and incorporated material from earlier journeys.

SOURCE: *Dictionary of Literary Biography*, Volume 174.

WORKS

Bent, Mabel. *Anglo-Saxons from Palestine; or The Imperial Mystery of the Lost Tribes*. London: Sherratt & Hughes, 1908.
_____. *A Patience Pocket Book*. Bristol: Arrowsmith, 1904.
_____, with James Theodore Bent. *Southern Arabia*. London: Smith, Elder, 1900.

Isabella Bird, 1831–1904. British.

The child Isabella was an unlikely person to be an adventurous traveler. She was frequently ill, and a spinal disease periodically confined her to a restricted life. Living a rather dull existence, she suffered from depression. When she got older, however, a summer in the Scottish Highlands changed her outlook. She discovered she could hike and climb as well as anyone, and her health improved remarkably. Upon returning home, however, she returned to her old life of semi-invalidism, and this was the pattern for several years. Finally, when she was twenty-three, a doctor suggested a long sea voyage. Her father agreed and gave her money for the travel.

Isabella crossed the Atlantic and traveled around eastern Canada and the northeastern United States. She perked up remarkably and stayed away as long as she could. On her return she wrote *The English-woman in America*, which was widely and enthusiastically read.

When her father died, she, sister Henrietta ("Hennie") and their mother moved to Scotland. Isabella's next major trip was in 1872, when she went to the Sandwich Islands, now Hawaii. She spent several months on the islands, often traveling on horseback exploring the countryside and villages; she even climbed Mauna Loa. Her health was good, although she occasionally had back aches.

Instead of coming directly home she spent several months in the Rocky Mountains, where she often traveled on horseback and explored remote areas of the mountains. Her book *A Lady's Life in the Rocky Mountains,* recounting her adventures, has always been one of her most popular.

Isabella was a good writer and made her travel accounts fresh and interesting. Most of her books were based on her letters to Hennie, which were in effect journals of her travels.

Her next trip was to the Far East. She spent eighteen months in Japan traveling to remote areas of the islands; many of those areas had never been visited by a European woman. Isabella even traveled to the far northern part of Japan to see and move among the Ainu. This was remarkable at that time. There was great curiosity about the Ainu, who were regarded as a very primitive tribe. Japan hadn't been open to westerners for very long, and it still was difficult to travel around in some of the more remote areas.

Isabella was a good ethnographer; her observations of Japan are astute. *Unbeaten Tracks in Japan* is particularly readable and interesting, an early observation of a culture that was very remote from England.

Sarufuto. The night was too cold for sleep, and at daybreak, hearing great din, I looked out, and saw a drove of fully a hun-

dred horses all galloping down the road, with two Ainos on horseback, and a number of big dogs after them. Hundreds of horses run nearly wild on the hills, and the Ainos, getting a large drove together, skillfully head them for the entrance into the corral, in which a selection of them is made for the day's needs, and the remainder — that is those with the deepest sores on their backs — are turned loose. This dull rattle of shoeless feet is the first sound in the morning in these Yezo villages [*Unbeaten Tracks in Japan*, Vol. 2, p. 39].

I was very happy when I left the "beaten track" to Satsuporo, and saw before me, stretching for I know not how far, rolling, sandy mechirs like those of the Outer Hebrides, desert-like and lonely covered almost altogether with dwarf roses and campanulas, a prairie land on which you can make any tracks you please. Sending the others on, I followed them at the Yezo scramble, and soon ventured on a long gallop, and reveled in the music of the sound of shoeless feet over the elastic soil, but I had not realized the peculiarities of the Yezo horses, and had forgotten to ask whether mine was a "front horse," and just as we were going at full speed we came nearly up with the others and my horse coming abruptly to a full stop, I went six feet over his head among the rose-bushes. Ito, looking back saw me tightening the saddle-girths, and I never divulged the escapade.

After riding eight miles along this breezy belt, with the sea on one side and forests on the other, we came upon Yubets, a place which has fascinated me so much that I intend to return to it, but I must confess that its fascinations depend rather upon what it has not than upon what it has, and Ito says that it would kill him to spend even two days there. It looks like the end of all things, as if loneliness and desolation could go no further [pp. 41–42].

There is something very gloomy in the solitude off this silent land, with its beast-haunted forest, its great patches of pasture, the resort of wild animals which haunt the lower regions in search of food when the snow drives them down from the mountains, and its narrow track, indicating the single file in which the savages of the interior walk with their bare, noiseless feet....

Birateri, the largest of the Aino settlements in this region, is very prettily situated among forests and mountains, on rising ground, with a very sinuous river winding at its feet and a wooded height above. A lonelier place could scarcely be found. As we passed among the house the yellow dogs barked, the women looked shy and smiled, and the men made their graceful salutation. We stopped at the chief's house, where, of course, we were unexpected guests; but Shinondi, his nephew, and two other men came out, saluted us, and with most hospitable intent helped Ito to unload the horses. Indeed their eager hospitality created quite a commotion, one running hither and the other thither in their anxiety to welcome a stranger. It is a large house, the room being 35 by 25, and the roof 20 feet height; but you enter by an ante-chamber, in which are kept the millet-mill and other articles. There is a doorway in this, but the inside is pretty dark, and Shinondi, taking my hand raised the reed curtain bound with hide, which concealed the entrance into the actual house, and leading me into it, retired a footstep, extended his arms, waved his hands inwards three times, and then stroked his beard several times, after which he indicated by a sweep of his hand and a beautiful smile that the house and all it contained were mine. An aged woman, the chief's mother, who was splitting bark by the fire, waved her hands also. She is the queen-regnant of the house [pp. 52–53].

... I have lived among them in this room by day and night, there has been nothing which in any way could offend the most fastidious sense of delicacy [p. 55].

From Japan she went to the Malay Peninsula, then returned to England. Shortly after she returned, Henrietta died. Isabella was devastated. Dr. John Bishop, who had known Isabella for years and had looked after Hennie while she was traveling, now looked after Isabella as well. Within a year of Hennie's death they married. Although Isabella and John agreed that Isabella should do whatever independent travel she wanted, John's health wasn't good, and Isabella didn't travel to any extent. He died five years after the marriage.

Isabella then embarked on one of her most adventurous trips. She'd decided to go to Asia, and she particularly wanted to explore China and Tibet. That trip lasted almost three years and was almost too adventurous; she got caught in political problems and at least once was in serious danger of being killed.

In 1897 she finally returned home. She was in her late sixties then, a much more advanced age at that time than it is today. Her book on China, published in 1900, attracted wide interest. She made one more trip, to Morocco, and she thought of making another trip to China someday. But her health gave out. She was an invalid for several years before she died in 1904.

SOURCE: *Dictionary of Literary Biography.*

WORKS

Some of her books were originally published under "Mrs. Isabella Lucy Bishop."

Bird, Isabella. *Among the Tibetans.* London: Religious Tract Society, 1894.

_____. *The Aspects of Religion in the United States of America.* London: Sampson Low, Son and Co., 1859.

_____. *Chinese Pictures.* London: Casell, 1900

_____. *An Englishwoman in America.* London: John Murray, 1856.

_____. *The Golden Chersonese, and the Way Thither.* London: John Murray, 1883.

_____. *The Hawaiian Archipelago: Six Months among the Palm Groves, Coral Reefs and Volcanoes of the Sandwich Islands.* London: John Murray, 1875.

_____. *Journeys in Persia and Kurdistan.* London: John Murray, 1891.

_____. *Korea and Her Neighbours.* London: John Murray, 1898.

_____. *A Lady's Life in the Rocky Mountains.* London: John Murray, 1879.

_____. *Unbeaten Tracks in Japan.* London: John Murray, 1880.

_____. *The Yangtze Valley and Beyond.* London: John Murray, 1899.

Anna Bishop, 1810–1884. British.

Ann Riviere was born into a family with artistic and musical connections. Her father was from a family of clockmakers; he had a successful career as a painter of miniature portraits. Ann — who later added an "a" to her name — was one of at least five brothers and five sisters. Anna's mother was an accomplished pianist; not surprisingly several of the children became noted artists and musicians, as well as writers. Anna, who could draw well and sing passably, was most interested in being a pianist, and her parents sought out professional teachers for her. Anna increasingly was drawn to a career as a singer. She had a sweet singing voice, and it was developing into a high soprano.

She entered the Royal Academy of Music, where, among other masters, she studied under Henry Bishop. He was an ambitious composer and had had some success with his compositions, operas and stage works. (Only his song "Home, Sweet Home," from one of his stage works, has endured.) He was twenty-four years older than Anna.

Anna eventually went from performing at amateur concerts to appearances in professional programs; she also began developing her abilities of stagecraft and performance. By 1831 her appearances were in more public venues, and she was attracting the attention of critics. That year, Henry's wife died. As soon as the funeral was over Anna announced that she was marrying Bishop, and the two were married less than a month after the death of his first wife. Anna's family had mixed feelings about this. They'd known and liked Henry Bishop for over twenty years, but the marriage seemed hasty, and there was a significant age difference.

Anna and Henry had three children, including twins. As Anna's fortunes rose Henry's declined. They had financial difficulties, and Anna wanted to expand into opera, where there was much more money to be made than by giving concerts. Henry objected, and she resented his (and to some extent her parents') control of her career.

Robert Nicholas Charles Bochsa changed her life. A child prodigy, he was a well known composer, teacher, inventor of instruments, and performer. He was also something of a rascal and very enterprising. Needing to flee his creditors (and people he'd more or less defrauded), he had arrived in England when Anna was seven.

Now, he offered Anna the opportunity to develop as an opera singer. He proposed a tour with the Bishops to the North of England, concluding with a series of concerts in Edinburgh.

Later, in 1839, Anna left Henry (and their three children) and went to the Continent with Bochsa. After several years there was a formal deed of separation spelling out custody and financial matters. Henry was specifically prevented from suing Anna for divorce. He relinquished all claim on Anna's earnings and property; she also gained legal custody of the children and undertook to support them. (Anna had sent money for the children throughout her time with Bochsa and would continue to do so.) The twins were to remain with Henry until Anna's return to England. Her banker and agent were to have free access to them; when they were old enough to live elsewhere, Henry retained perpetual right of access. Anna was legally free; her money was beyond Henry's reach, and she had ensured financial security for the children.

Anna never had a strong voice, but it was true and sweet; she was considered very beautiful, and she had a good presence on stage and off. Under Bochsa's guidance her career and artistic reputation developed, and she was making increasingly significant appearances in Europe. Soon she was a star, a sought-after prima donna.

In 1847 she and Bochsa sailed for a tour in the New World.

In 1849 the tour extended to Mexico. *Travels of Anna Bishop in Mexico* recounts the twelve months of tours and performances. The book has no stated author, but it is thought that Bochsa probably wrote it. The book describes Anna's triumphs, the wealth and poverty of Mexico City and other destinations throughout the countryside. Published in 1852, the book sold well and attracted even more attention to Anna and her career.

> Cuanaillan — and thence to Queretaro. Nothing could have seemed to the traveling party more desolately miserable than the insignificant town of *Cuantillan* — and the dingy little *meson* (the only one in the whole place) where Don Alvarado took them. Not a living body was to be seen in the large dismal court-yard....
>
> The room into which the guests were shown, lighted only by round holes in the doors, were much of the same description as those of the Mexican *mesons* before talked of, with the usual comforts of a rickety table and bench, and a deal or brick platform in a corner for a bed. Nothing else was visible that could add to the attraction of these dens, with the exception of a few lean distracted rats, trembling about in the greatest excitement, to know what the intruders were up to. This gave Bochsa a shock of nervous uncertainty as to the time it would probably take to make the place inhabitable for the night. But even while he pondered upon this, he little supposed that Anna had already given her orders; and before he could well turn round, the two coachmen and the rest, under command of Don Luis Cortes, having lent a shoulder to clear the vehicle of everything needful to general comfort, were rushing to and fro with incredible swiftness, and in less than ten minutes the four rooms selected had, each, its pleasurable bed and bedstead, with all the customary necessities for toilette; while to that of Anna was further added a carpet and two chairs, with four whole legs apiece. Cortes hereupon opened a large basket containing the dinner apparatus, and with the scrambling eagerness of a spider at his weft, spun it out piece by piece upon the table in the dining-room, and rubbing his hands with the greatest glee, desired Anna to have the kindness just to come and look at it — that was all [*Travels of Anna Bishop in Mexico*, pp. 158–160].

Anna and Bochsa returned to the United States and stayed for over three years, touring throughout New England, and crossing the country to California — touring and performing seemingly everywhere.

In 1855 Henry Bishop died, age sixty-eight. He did not mention Anna in his will. He didn't leave much money, and a collection was organized on behalf of the twins, then only seventeen years old. Anna was angry at the suggestion that the twins were destitute and that she had abandoned them; when she and Bishop parted, she had stated that she was tired of his wasting all of her money (which was true) and that she would always see to the well-being of the three children. She had kept her word. She wrote her brother asking him to intervene, which he did with an announcement in the newspapers that all benevolences concerning the children should cease; the children would be well taken care of, as they always had been.

Meanwhile, Bochsa's health was declining. Nonetheless he and Anna sailed from California to Australia for yet another tour. As usual they traveled with a small retinue, which this time included an American, Martin Schultz. It was clear when they arrived in Australia that Bochsa's health was worsening and he would be unable to conduct performances. He died in Sydney.

After a short period of mourning Anna fulfilled her performing obligations in Sydney. She stayed in Australia for two years, and then set out for South America. She was accompanied by Martin Schultz.

Her South American itinerary began in Callao and Lima, Peru, continued in Chile, crossed Argentina to Uruguay, and ended at Rio de Janeiro, where she sailed for London. This was a rugged itinerary, involving crossing the Andes. Travel was by horse or mule — and Anna wasn't an experienced rider. Furthermore, not all of her appearances were as successful as she was used to. Meanwhile the relationship between Anna and Schultz continued to intensify; before they left South America she accepted his proposal of marriage. They planned to marry upon their return to London.

Anna's return to London was only moderately successful; she'd been gone over ten years, and there were many younger singers in the operatic world. After a year in England, she and Schultz, now married, sailed for New York. For several years she gave concerts in the Northeast and Canada. In 1866 they decided to cross the country, sail from California to Asia (via Hawaii) — Japan, China, Australia, give a tour in India, make their way back to Britain and then to New York.

Two weeks after sailing from Hawaii, the boat stuck a rock. For seven hours the boat stayed afloat, then began to list. The passengers and crew abandoned ship for the lifeboats. They were able to make their way to a small island, but there was little shelter and no indications of fresh water. The little water they were able to retrieve from the ship was stringently rationed. After nearly three weeks on the island it became clear that they would die of thirst if they remained there, and they would have to take to the small lifeboats and try to reach the Marianas, 1400 miles to the west. The captain estimated they could possibly reach the islands in a little over two weeks. They spent three days on preparations then set off.

After thirteen days they felt there was no hope — then an officer spotted gulls and a landmass on the far horizon. It had been five weeks since they'd had to abandon ship, and they'd traveled 1400 miles in open boats. The island was small, with no store

and few materials for re-outfitting the passengers, who were all in miserable shape. They had to remain for several weeks on the island, until they could be taken to Manila, from where they eventually resumed their tour. Anna soon recovered her health and her good spirits. By the time she reached Cape Town, Anna was at the top of her form.

She retired on her return to England, but she was talked into giving one final public appearance. Her voice wasn't as good as it had been, but more importantly, her voice and style were no longer in fashion. Although there were many loyal supporters in the audience, most of the audience was indifferent at best, and there were jeers. Notwithstanding, she made several more appearances, but on a more modest scale, no longer attempting the great operatic arias. After several years in England, she and Schultz sailed to New York, where Anna again made several appearances. She died in 1884, in New York.

SOURCE: *Anna Bishop: The Adventures of an Intrepid Prima Donna.*

BOOKS ABOUT OR INCLUDING ANNA BISHOP

Boscha, Robert Nicholas Charles. *Travels of Anna Bishop in Mexico: 1849.* Philadelphia: Published by Charles Deal, 1852.

Davis, Richard. *Anna Bishop: The Adventures of an Intrepid Prima Donna.* Sydney: Currency Press, 1997.

Foster, C. G. *Biography of Anna Bishop.* New York: 1853.

Elizabeth Bisland, 1861–1929.

American.

She is sometimes listed as Elizabeth Bisland Wetmore.

Elizabeth was born in Louisiana. She began her writing career by writing for the

New Orleans Times-Democrat. She moved on to write and edit for *Cosmopolitan*, at that time a magazine that ran stories and covered news for general readers.

In the early 1890s *Cosmopolitan* was a new magazine and was looking for features that would attract readership. Elizabeth's editor, learning of the plans of *The World*, the newspaper Nellie Bly wrote for, to see if Bly could beat the record of Phineas Finn, the hero of *Around the World in Eighty Days* by Jules Verne, decided to compete. Nellie Bly had been planning her trip for months. *Cosmopolitan* made a decision quickly, giving Elizabeth Bisland two days' notice for leaving. Bly's itinerary was to travel east; Bisland's was to travel west.

Elizabeth didn't want to make the trip and referred to it as "endeavoring to complete the journey in some absurdly inadequate space of time." She also objected to the notoriety of the effort to outdo Jules Verne's hero. But she was persuaded, and off she went.

She was fascinated by Hong Kong.

Another day we go to the shops and turn over costly examples of Chinese art — coming home through the many-colored ways of the native town — steep streets that climb laboriously up and down stairs, and so narrow that there is hardly room for our chairs to pass through the multitudes who swarm there. Sixteen hundred residents to the acre they average in this part of the town, buzzing and humming like the unreckonable myriads insects bred from the fecund slime of a marsh. Two thirds of their life is passed out of doors in the streets, and all seem to be patiently and continuously busy. Children are as flies in number and activity. The place smells violently; smells of opium, of the dried ducks and fish hanging exposed for sale in the sun, of frying pork and sausages, and of the many strange repulsive-looking meals being cooked on hissing braziers in the streets and in doorways. There is no lack of color. The shops are faced with a broad fretwork richly gilded, and the long perpendicular signs are ornamentally

lettered with large black characters. Every house is lime-washed some strong tint, and the whole leaves upon the eye the color-impression one gets from Chinese porcelains — of sharp green, gold, crimson, and blue; all vigorous, definite, and mingled with grotesque tastefulness [*A Flying Trip Around the World*, pp. 106–108].

Her account was as hurried as the journey; she tells us much more about the first part of the trip than the second half. But then...

... The ship slides into dock. I can see the glad faces of my friends upon the pier. My journey is done. I have been around the world in seventy-six days [p. 205].

Nellie Bly completed her trip in 72 days.

After the publication of her book in 1891, Elizabeth married Charles Wetmore, a lawyer from New York. Several years later they moved to Washington, D.C. Elizabeth published several more books.

Charles died in 1919, and Elizabeth moved to a plantation in Charlottesville, Virginia. During World War I she helped care for sick and wounded patients in an army hospital in London. When the war ended she came back to the United States, where she became president of a clinic for young working women who didn't have much money.

She died at the age of sixty-seven.

SOURCES: *Dictionary of Literary Biography*, Volume 174; *It Can't Be Done, Nellie Bly!*

WORKS

She also wrote as B. R. L. Dane.

Bisland, Elizabeth. *A Flying Trip Around the World*. New York: Harper, 1891.
_____. *The Life and Letters of Lafcadio Hearn*. New York: Houghton Mifflin and Company, 1906.
_____, with Anne Hoyt. *Seekers in Sicily, being a Quest for Persephone by Jane and Peripatetica*. London and New York: Lane, 1909.

Books About or Including
    Elizabeth Bisland

Butcher, Nancy. *It Can't Be Done, Nellie Bly!*
Atlanta: Beachtree Publishers, Ltd., 2003.

Lady Anne Isabella Noel Blunt,
1840–1922. British.

Anne Blunt had a rather chaotic childhood; her mother was Ada Byron, the only legitimate daughter of Lord Byron, and her father was William Noel. Her mother was often ill, and she spent much time with her grandmother, who provided a more stable base for her.

In 1869 she married Wilfred Scawen Blunt, a poet and diplomat, who retired that same year from the British diplomatic service to write full-time. Their marriage was challenging. Wilfred had frequent affairs. Anne suffered several miscarriages; one child, Judith, survived.

The two began traveling soon after Wilfred's retirement. Their first trip was to Spain. In 1873 they went to Turkey, where they bought their first eastern horse. Horses would be an important focus of their life and travels. That trip was followed by travels to Algeria and Egypt, where they started to learn Arabic to prepare for more adventurous travel in Arabia. Anne traveled well. She loved to ride both horses and camels, she had some artistic ability and drew very well, and she kept a detailed journal.

They next set out to explore central Arabia with the intent of updating the maps of the Royal Geographical Society. They left in December, 1878. It was an adventurous journey; much went wrong. During the course of the journey Wilfred came down with severe dysentery; Anne regarded his recovery as miraculous. Also on the trip Anne had a vision of her three dead children. Both events played a part in her later Catholicism.

The desert tribes were almost always at war; to avoid attracting attention to themselves the Blunts dressed like the Bedouin and spoke Arabic. They ate whatever was available as the Bedouins did, which might mean roasted grasshoppers and wild hyena, and they slept on the ground. They had escort or interpreters, and occasionally no guide — but they relied on the mercy and hospitality of the local tribes.

Baghdad was their first destination, but once there they found they didn't like the luxurious surroundings of the official British residence where they were lodged, and they resolved to leave Baghdad as soon as possible.

Without official permission to leave, they left the city quietly and set off. They were arrested when the local chieftain, suspicious of foreigners searching for desert tribes, concluded they were spies. They finally convinced the chief they weren't spies, and he let them proceed.

Their next expedition was to the Nejd, which meant crossing the Great Nafud Desert. This was a difficult crossing; this desert was one of the worst to cross, and the isolation of the tribes they would meet worried the Blunts. As it happened, Lady Anne was the first Western woman to visit the area.

While they were camping one night they were attacked by mounted horsemen. One Bedouin knocked Wilfred out, and another attacked Anne with a spear. She tried to protect herself and cried out in Arabic, "We seek your protection." The raiders were astonished to hear a woman's voice, and when they found out it was a foreign woman, they were even more amazed. The Bedouin considered the Blunts carefully, then eventually rode away. Anne and Wilfred resumed their trip.

The fact is, the Euphrates is more of
a mystery to the general public than any
river of equal importance in the Old

World [*Bedouin Tribes of the Euphrates*, p. 7].

The river Khâbur, which is the only tributary the Euphrates receives during the whole of its course through the desert, is a considerable stream, and a difficult one to cross. It is about sixty yards wide, has a strong current, and is very deep; has only a thin fringe of brushwood to clothe its nakedness on either side, with here and there a willow struggling to look like a tree.

To one of these a cord had been tied and made fast to a tamarisk root on the opposite bank; and floating on the water, we saw the most rickety-looking thing ever people trusted themselves to on deep water. It was a square raft, made of eight goats' skins blown out to serve as bladders, and tied together with a slight framework of tamarisk boughs. It was at most four feet six inches square, and lay nearly level with the water's edge. On this we were expected to embark and I confess that I had no pleasant anticipation of the voyage. But first there was the baggage to be ferried, and the camels and mares to be swam across.

A camel forced to swim is a very ridiculous object. He hates the water sincerely and moans piteously when he is obliged to face it. Ours were, of course, unloaded, and then brought one by one to the river bank. A man on the back, and half a dozen others to push behind, were needed to get them down the bank, a steep slide of mud, down which the camels went, with all their legs together, souse into the water. The men, who were stripped, jumped in after them, and, shouting and splashing water in their faces, forced them on, till at last they were out of their depth, and everything had disappeared except the camels' noses. Then they seemed to resign themselves, and swam steadily but slowly to the opposite shore, where, fortunately, there was a better landing place [p. 245].

About an hour before sunset we came to a broad river, broader and deeper than the Tibb, and here Ghafil decreed a halt. If we had been a strong enough party to shift for ourselves, and if we could have crossed the river alone, we should now have gone on and left our persecutors behind; but in our helpless state this was impossible, and we had no choice but to dismount. It was an anxious moment, but I think we did what was wisest in showing no sign of distrust, and we had no sooner stopped than we gave one a horse to hold, and another a gun, while we called on others to help us unload the camels, and get out coffee and provisions for a general feast. This seemed to most of them too good an offer to be declined, and we had already distributed a sack of flour and a sack of rice amongst them, which the two women had promised to bake into loaves for the whole party, when Ghafil and the one-eyed man, who had been down to look for a ford, arrived upon the scene. They were both very angry when they saw the turn things had taken.... Still it was a terribly anxious evening, for even our friends were as capricious as the winds, and seemed always on the point of picking an open quarrel. Later they all went away and left us to our own devices, sitting round a great bonfire of brushwood they had built up, "to scare away lions," they said. We managed to rig up our tent, and make a barricade of the camel-bag in such a way that we could not be surprised and taken at a disadvantage. I did not shut my eyes all night, but lay watching the bonfire, with my hand on my gun. Hajji Mohammed once in the darkness crept out and got near enough to overhear something of their talk, and he assures us that there was a regular debate as to whether and when and how we should be murdered, in which the principal advocate of extreme measures was the one-eyed man, a great powerful ruffian who carried a sort of club, which he told us he used to frighten the lion, beating it on the ground. The noise, he declared sounded like a gun and drove them away. With this tale of horror Hajji Mohammed returned to comfort us; nor was it wholly a delusion, for in the middle of the night, Wilfrid being asleep, and Hajji Mohammed, whose watch it was, having fallen into a doze, I distinctly saw Ghafil, who had previously come under pretext of lions or robbers to reconnoitre, prowl stealthily round, and seeing us all as he thought sleep, lift up the flap of the tent and creep under on Wilfrid's side. I had remained motionless, and from where I lay I could see his figure plainly against the sky. As he stooped I called out in a loud voice, "Who goes there?" and at the sound he started back, and slunk away. This woke Hajji Mohammed, and nobody slept again, but I could see Ghafil prowling like an hyaena round us the best part of the night [*A Pilgrimage to Nejd*, Vol. 2, pp. 149–152].

After reaching their destination of Bushire, they went (by train) to visit the viceroy of India, then returned to England.

In 1880 they returned to Egypt, where they eventually bought an estate.

The marriage had long been uneven; Wilfred continued to have various affairs. In 1883 matters began to deteriorate. Nonetheless they remained together for a dozen more years. Wilfred became increasingly involved in English politics. In 1906 matters of the marriage came to a head; Wilfred was entangled with Dorothy Carleton, whom he had met six years earlier. To "justify" her continued presence, he adopted her as his niece. Anne and Wilfred separated. In 1915 Judith determined to reconcile her parents and end their separation. The two met and talked but did not reunite.

In 1917 Anne died in Cairo, where she was buried.

SOURCE: *Dictionary of Literary Biography*, Volume 174.

WORKS

Blunt, Lady Anne. *Bedouin Tribes of the Euphrates*. Edited, with a preface and account of horses, including a sketch of Arab horse-breeding and a genealogical table of the descent of the thoroughbred Arabian horse, by Wilfred Scawen Blunt. Two volumes. New York: Harper & Brothers, 1879.
_____. *A Pilgrimage to Nejd, the Cradle of the Arab Race: A Visit to the Court of the Arab Emir, and "Our Persian Campaign."* London: Kegan Paul, 1881.
Translated by Anne, rendered into verse by Wilfred: *The Celebrated Romance of the Stealing of the Mare*. 1892.

BOOKS ABOUT OR INCLUDING LADY ANNE BLUNT

Winstone, H.V.F. *Lady Anne Blunt*. London: Barzan Publishers, 2003.

Most of the Blunts' papers are at the Fitzwilliam Museum, Cambridge, England.

Nellie Bly (Elizabeth Cochrane Seaman), 1864–1922.
American.

"Nellie Bly" was the pen name for Elizabeth Cochrane Seaman. Her maiden name was Cochran; later she added the "e." As she is best known as Nellie Bly, that is the name under which she is usually listed.

Her father was a judge who also was a real estate speculator and owned a store and a gristmill. The judge had ten children by his first wife and then had several more by his second wife. Elizabeth/Nellie was the third child of the second marriage — the thirteenth in the family.

When Nellie was five her father died, leaving no will. The oldest son succeeded in having the estate distributed among the heirs, which left the widow to support herself and her remaining children on a small annuity. She married again, but her husband was threatening and abusive, and she divorced. Elizabeth testified in her behalf.

When Elizabeth was fifteen she entered the state Normal School for training teachers; at that time she added a final "e" to her surname. She had to leave school, however, because of lack of money. In 1895 she began selling occasional articles to the *Pittsburgh Dispatch*, having attracted the attention of the editor George Madden. It was Madden who decided that Elizabeth needed a pen name and adopted the name "Nellie Bly" from Stephen Foster's song.

Nellie had limited education, but she

had a knack of identifying interesting angles for her stories. She could talk with people and was personally interested in their stories. When she and her mother traveled to Mexico in 1886, her articles about the journey ran in the *Dispatch*. This was the basis for her book *Six Months in Mexico*, which was published two years later. In 1887 Nellie Bly went to New York City and tried to get a job with various newspapers, including the *New York World*. She continued to write about various issues for the *Dispatch*. For material on the treatment of the insane, she had herself admitted to the Women's Lunatic Asylum.

Her fame was spreading, as she continued her investigative journalism.

She began her famous race around the world, sponsored by the *World*, on November 14, 1889, traveling toward the east. Elizabeth Bisland [see her entry], writing for *Cosmopolitan* magazine, began her race the same day, traveling from east to west. Nellie won easily, setting a record of seventy-two days against Elizabeth Bisland's seventy-six and Jules Verne's Phineas Fogg's eighty days.

From *Chapter XV: One Hundred and Twenty Hours in Japan.*

If I loved and married, I would say to my mate: "Come, I know where Eden is," and like Edwin Arnold, desert the land of my birth for Japan, the land of love — beauty — poetry — cleanliness.

The Japanese homes form a great contrast to the bungalows [*where the Europeans live*]. They are daintily small, like play houses indeed, built from a thin shingle-like board, fine in texture. Chimneys and fire places are unknown. The first wall is set back, allowing the upper floor and side walls to extend over the lower flooring, making it a portico built in instead of on the house. Light window frames, with their minute openings covered with fine rice paper instead of glass, are the doors and windows in one. They do not swing open and shut as do our doors, nor do they move up and down like our

windows, but slide like rolling doors. They form the partitions of the houses inside and can be removed at any time, throwing the floor into one room.

They have two very pretty customs in Japan. The one is decorating their houses in honor of the new year, and the other celebrating the blossoming of the cherry trees. Bamboo saplings covered with light airy foliage and pinioned so as to incline towards the middle of the street, where meeting they form an arch, make very effective decorations. Rice trimmings mixed with seaweed, orange, lobster and ferns are hung over every door to insure a plentiful year, while as sentinels on either side are large tubs, in which are three thick bamboo stalks, with small evergreen trees for background [*Around the World in Seventy-Two Days*].

When she returned she left the *World* and began lecturing. She also wrote her book about the journey. By 1893 she rejoined the *World*, continuing her interviews and investigative reporting. She left the *World* again and joined the *Chicago Times-Herald*, a position she had for only five weeks, leaving to marry Robert Livingston Seaman, a seventy-year-old millionaire. The marriage did not go smoothly, and she returned to the *World* in 1896. Some of her articles pointedly were about what a good husband should be like.

She abruptly stopped writing and went to Europe with Seaman, who had become a more attentive husband. During the years in Europe she looked after Seaman. She convinced him to rewrite his will to leave her the bulk of the inheritance; he transferred property into her name to avoid the inevitable probate battle. In 1899 when they returned to America, Nellie became involved in the family business. When Seaman died in 1904, most of the property was in Nellie's name, and she was well involved in successfully running the business.

By 1911, the business was in trouble, in part because her employees had been embezzling. The ensuing legal proceedings lasted for years. In 1912 Nellie began writing for the *New York Evening Journal*. Although bankruptcy hearings were settled in early 1914, Nellie faced an arrest warrant for obstructing justice.

She left for Vienna just at the advent of World War I. She was in Austria throughout the war, often reporting from the front. Her return to America when the war ended was delayed because of suspicions of American officials about her warnings that the Bolsheviks would take over Central Europe and then America. She finally was allowed to return, however, at which point she sued her mother and brother for what was left of her company, a lawsuit she eventually won.

She died in January 1922.

SOURCE: *Dictionary of Literary Biography*, Vol. 189.

Website http://ere.lib.umn.edu/dyna web/travel, December 2006.

WORKS

Around the World in Seventy-Two Days. New York: Pictorial Weekly, 1890.

BOOKS ABOUT OR INCLUDING NELLIE BLY

Markes, Jason. *Around the World in 72 Days: The Race Between Pulitzer's Nellie Bly and Cosmopolitan's Elizabeth Bisland.* New York: Gemittarius Press, 1993.

Baroness Annie Allnutt Brassey, 1839–1887. English.

Annie Allnutt was born in London, an only child. She was still a baby when her mother died, and she went to live with her grandfather in the country. When she was older they moved to London. Annie was educated at home. Although her education might appear limited, she was a student of history, archaeology, geography, and literature. At age twenty-one she married Thomas Brassey, the son of a railroad developer. Thomas Brassey went into politics and served as a member of parliament, then later held office in the Admiralty. Annie Brassey was active in her husband's political life, participating in his election campaigns, entertaining, and managing the households.

She also actively pursued her own interests, including photography, and it is this pursuit that defined her legacy. She was a very knowledgeable botanist, which is often reflected in her letters. She was also interested in the newly emerging practice of emergency medicine and an active patron of the St. John Ambulance Association.

The Brasseys traveled throughout their marriage, often with their children. Lord Brassey sailed to the Baltic Sea the year the two were married; whether he was accompanied by Annie Brassey isn't clear. We know they went to Egypt in 1869 for the opening of the Suez Canal. Annie was very sick with malaria on that voyage, and the trip was delayed for several weeks while she was recovering. There were also trips to Canada and the United States, the Arctic Circle, the Bahamas and West Indies, and a voyage around the world.

> I was lying down, below, after breakfast, feeling very stupid, when Mabelle rushed into the cabin, saying, "Papa says you are to come up on deck at once, to see the ship on fire." I rushed up quickly, hardly knowing whether she referred to our own or some other vessel, and on reaching the deck I found everybody looking at a large barque, under full sail, flying the red union-jack upside down, and with signals in her rigging, which our signal-man read as "Ship on fire." These were lowered shortly afterwards, and the signals, "Come on board at once," hoisted in their place. Still we could see no appearance of smoke or flames, but we nevertheless hauled to the wind, tacked, hove to, and sent off a boat's crew, well armed, thinking it not impossible that a

mutiny had taken place on [words obscured] captain or officers, mistaking the yacht for a gunboat, had appealed to us for assistance. We were now near enough to the barque to make out her name through a glass — the "Monkshave" of Whitby — and we observed a puff of smoke issue from her deck simultaneously with the arrival of our boat alongside. In the course of a few minutes, the boat returned, bringing the mate of the "Monkshaven," a fine-looking Norwegian, who spoke English perfectly, and who reported his ship to be sixty-eight days out from Swansea, bound for Valparaiso, with a cargo of smelting coal. The fire had first been discovered on the previous Sunday, and by 6 A.M. on Monday the crew had got up their clothes and provisions on deck, thrown overboard all articles of a combustible character, such as tar, oil, paint, spare spars and sails, plants, and rope, and battened down the hatches. Ever since then they had all been living on deck, with no protection from the wind and sea but a canvas screen. Tom and Captain Brown proceeded on board at once. They found the deck more than a foot deep in water, and all a-wash; when the hatches were opened for a moment dense clouds of hot suffocating yellow smoke immediately poured forth, driving back all who stood near. From the Captain's cabin came volumes of poisonous gas, which had found its way in through the crevices, and one man, who tried to enter, was rendered insensible.

It was perfectly evident that it would be impossible to save the ship, and the captain therefore determined, after consultation with Tom and Captain Brown, to abandon her. Some of the crew were accordingly at once brought on board the "Sunbeam," in our boat, which was then sent back to assist in removing the remainder, a portion of whom came in their own boat. The poor fellows were almost wild with joy at getting alongside another ship, after all the hardships they had gone through, and in their excitement they threw overboard many things which they might as well have kept, as they had taken the trouble to bring them. Our boat made three trips altogether, and by half-past six we had them all safe on board, with most of their effects, and the ship's chronometers, charts, and papers.

For two hours we could see the smoke pouring from various portions of the ill-fated barque. Our men, who had brought off the last of her crew, reported that, as they left her, flames were just beginning to burst from the forehatchway; and it was therefore certain that the rescue had not taken place an hour too soon. Whilst we were at dinner, Powell called us up on deck to look at her again, when we found that she was blazing like a tar-barrel. The captain was anxious to stay by and see the last of her, but Tom was unwilling to incur the delay which this would have involved. We accordingly got up steam, and at nine P.M. steamed round the "Monkshaven," as close as it was deemed prudent to go. No flames were visible then; only dense volumes of smoke and sparks, issuing from the hatches. The heat, however, was intense, and could be plainly felt, even in the cold night air, as we passed some distance to leeward. All hands were clustered in our rigging, on the deck-house, or on the bridge, to see the last of the poor "Monkshaven," as she was slowly being burnt down to the water's edge.

The crew of the "Monkshaven" — Danes, Norwegians, Swedes, Scotch, and Welsh — appear to be quiet, respectable men. This is fortunate, as an incursion of fifteen rough lawless spirits on board our little vessel would have been rather a serious matter. In their hurry and fright, however, they left all their provisions behind them, and it is no joke to have to provide food for fifteen extra hungry mouths for a week or ten days, with no shops at hand from which to replenish our stores. The sufficiency of the water supply, too, is a matter for serious consideration. We have all been put on half allowance, and seawater only is to be used for washing purpose [*The Voyage in the Sunbeam*, pp. 110–115].

Lady Annie Brassey died on a voyage to India and Australia, in 1887.

Annie was a photographer throughout her travels. She put much effort into compiling photograph albums, often supplementing her photographs with those of others, or with commercial photos. Her albums, seventy of which are in the Huntington Library in San Marino, California, are a valuable and fascinating documentary of social history and her travels.

SOURCE: *Dictionary of Literary Biography.*

WORKS

Brassey, Anne. *In the Trades, the Tropics, and the Roaring Forties.* London: Longman, 1885. To the West Indies and Madeira.

_____. *The Last Voyage.* London and New York: Longman, 1889. Trip to India, Borneo, and Australia. She died on this trip.

_____. *Sunshine and Storm in the East: or Cruises to Cyprus and Constantinople.* London: Longman, 1880.

_____. *The Voyage in the Sunbeam, Our Home on the Ocean for Eleven Months.* London: Longman, 1878. Also published as *Around the World in the Yacht Sunbeam,* New York: Holt, 1882; and *Afloat and Ashore: or, A Voyage in the Sunbeam,* n.p. Juvenile Publishing, n.d. Lady Brassey's first voyage around the world in 1876–1877. Her cruise books appeared in a number of editions, under various titles, and were translated into several languages. Two privately printed books, *The Flight of the Meteor* and *A Cruise in the "Eothen,"* appeared in 186? And 1872, respectively. *Lady Brassey's Three Voyages in the Sunbeam,* London: Longman, 1887, consists of all except the privately printed books and *The Last Voyage,* published posthumously and edited by M. A. Broome.

BOOKS ABOUT OR INCLUDING LADY ANNE BRASSEY

Miclewright, Nancy. *Victorian Traveler in the Middle East: the Photography and Travel Writing of Annie, Lady Brassey.* Aldershot: Ashgate Publishing Limited, 2003.

Frederika Bremer, 1801–1865.
Swedish.

The daughter of an ironmaster, Frederika was well educated. After her schooling, she retired to her father's estate and a life of "good works" that included working as a nurse. In her spare time she wrote novels and stories which were translated into English and attracted some attention in England and America. In 1849 she visited the United States, perhaps her first travels. Among other notables she met Emerson, and she was the first to translate his writing into a foreign language. She wrote *Homes of the New World.* Several trips on the Continent resulted in additional books.

Brooklyn, November 5, 1849. The effect of my American journey, as far as myself am concerned, is altogether quite different to what I expected. I came hither to breathe a new and fresher atmosphere of life; to observe the popular life, institution, and circumstances of a new country; to become clearer in my own mind on certain questions connected with the development of nations and people; and in particular to study the women and the homes of the New World, and from the threshold of the home to obtain a view of the future of humanity, because as the river is born from the springs of heaven, so is the life and the fate of a people born from the hidden life of the home.

I came, in a word, to occupy myself with public affairs; and it is private affairs, it is the individual which seizes upon my interest, my feelings, my thoughts. I came with a secret intention of breaking myself lose from fiction and its subjects, and of living with thinkers for other purposes; and I am compelled toward it more forcibly than ever; compelled involuntarily, both by thought and feeling, toward fiction; compelled to bring into life forms, scenes, and circumstances, which, as dim shadows have for twenty years existed in the background of my soul. And in this so-called realist country, but which had more poetical life in it than people have any idea of in Europe, have I already *in petto,* experienced and written more of the romance of life than I have done for many years [*With Women's Eyes,* pp. 63–64, extract from *Holmes of the New World*].

But it was her travels in the Holy Land that were her most adventurous. At the time of her travel the Bedouins were hostile to Western men and women, roads were almost nonexistent, and travel was by saddlehorse. For a woman unable to speak Arabic, to make the trip alone was remarkable. Her book relates many days and nights of discomfort, but Frederika was too interested in the people, their daily lives, and the countryside to waste her time complaining.

Frederika continued her travels throughout her life. She also spent much of her time and resources on philanthropic causes.

SOURCE: Netzley, *Encyclopedia of Women's Travel and Exploration.*

WORKS

Bremer, Frederika. *Greece and the Greeks: A Narrative of a Winter Residence and Summer Travel in Greece and Its Islands.* Translated by Mary Howitt. London: Blackett, 1863. Original published in 1852?

_____. *Homes of the New World: Impressions of America.* Translated by Mary Howitt. London: Hall, Virtue, 1853. Extracts reprinted in Tinling, Marion. *With Women's Eyes: Visitors to the New World 1755–1918.* Norman: University of Oklahoma Press, 1993.

_____. *Life in the Old World: or, Two Years in Switzerland and Italy.* Translated by Mary Howitt. Philadelphia: T. B. Peterson, 1860.

_____. *Travels in the Holy Land.* Translated by Mary Howitt. London: Hurst and Blackett, 1862.

Note: many of her books were published under various titles.

Adela Breton, 1849–1923. British.

Adela traveled because she wanted to get away from what she called "the gilded cage of English civilization." She also traveled because she was interested in archaeology and geology. She wanted to see for herself the ruins and artifacts that ancient people had left behind and how land forms varied in different parts of the world.

She grew up in Bath, England. Her father, retired from the navy, was interested in antiquities and geology, interests Adela would pursue throughout her life. She also painted and was interested in art. The family traveled in Europe, and Adela and her mother spent periods of time there. Her mother died when Adela was twenty-four; she looked after her father for thirteen years until his death.

Her first trip was to the mountains of Western Canada, in 1887. She loved the scenery and the outdoor life. The railroad had just opened up the area, and it attracted many travelers, particularly women who liked the outdoor life in that part of the country. Adela made several paintings of the mountains, often recording information about the geology of the scene on the back of the painting. After several trips to Canada she decided to go to Mexico.

In 1893 she began her first major trip through Mexico. She and her guide, Pablo, traveled through Western and Central Mexico for over a year, riding horseback, camping, visiting isolated villages, and seeing every pre–Columbian ruin possible, as well as archaeological sites that were less dramatic and known only to local villages. Throughout this "Grand Tour" she painted and drew, recording details about the countryside, geological details, and antiquities.

On a hill above the little town of Tlaxcala stands the famous church of Santa Maria de Octolan, its white towers visible far and wide over the country, to remind the humble peasant that in his worst troubles he has a sure help and refuge within reach.

The modern tourist, superior to such fancies, toils up the hill, over the bare tufa rock, thankful for the cool breeze which makes the sun endurable, for even at 8000 feet a tropical sun is powerful enough. Pausing a moment, and looking back, what a view! Below, in its amphitheatre of hills, the quaint town — apparently nothing but walls and courts — the two churches with their domes and towers, and the mass of tall trees in the Plaza. Beyond, the wide plain, browner in parts than it should be, owing to the long drought this spring, but mostly green with growing maize and hedges of aloe and many trees. Strips of gold show where the barley is ready for the reaper, and here and there villages and churches lead the eye into the blue distance, where, Ixtic-cihuatl and far Popocatapetl rise magnificent in their glacier snows.

As the great doors of the churches are usually closed, the visitor enters through a little cloistered court, in itself a charming picture, the walls and arches in palest blue stucco, roses and geraniums growing in the centre and dark cypresses festooned with trails of the granadilla. Opposite the en-trance is a rounded flight of steps faced with dark blue and white tiles, leading to a door also framed in them, with gables and bits of white tower and yellow dome show-ing above against the blue sky. In a corner is the tiny cell, with earthen floor, where the old man who keeps watch and ward over the sanctuary lives, its only furniture and table and the scrap of matting which serves in Mexico for a bed.

Then down the hill by a steep path to the miraculous spring. No wonder Ocotlan has a reputation for cures. Its pure, light, dry air is the best tonic, and there is certainly something very invigorating in the agua Santa, though it has no especially mineral flavour. A glass of it will make a tired per-son quite fresh.

Tlaxcala is a quiet little town and seems to have been left on one side since the Spaniards built Puebla, about sixteen miles away. Few of the houses have more than one story, and they consist of some rooms built round a court, with just the window-door to each, for light and air. In the Mu-seum are a few relics of the old days — a ragged piece of embroidery that belonged to Cortés, a good miniature of Phillip II, attached to the illuminated charter which he gave to the town, and one or two stone idols and vases. The people of the neigh-bourhood seem mostly well-to-do, and the Indians are all clean and tidy. They are chiefly Aztecs, and nice in their ways and manners, always saying Good morning or Good evening in Spanish when meeting one [*Bath Chronicle*, May 1892].

Every one who goes to Mexico visits Xochicalco, riding down thirteen miles from Cuernavaca, by the Indian village of Tetlama, to the ruins. There one sees a number of shapeless mounds and some terraces, scattered over the hills, and a low, sculptured building which at first sight perhaps does not appear especially interesting, but which, when it comes to be thoroughly studied and understood, may prove to be of great importance. The reliefs must certainly record some striking event, just as on the façades of European cathedrals, the Biblical scenes and compa-nies of saints recall the traditions of past ages.

... The truth is that however careful an observer may be, there are always details which evade the eye, but can be seen by those who follow with the advantage of having drawings and descriptions, and in this way interesting facts may often be added even to the most careful descrip-tions.

In order to unravel the meaning hidden in every detail of the reliefs of Xochicalco, it is necessary to have them represented with absolute accuracy and so completely that they can be studied as a whole. In Central American art, things rarely match exactly, and there must be a reason for the difference which deserves consideration. It is most unwise to take for granted that any-thing superficially like another is so in real-ity, and the building under consideration il-lustrates the truth of this statement; for although the north, south, and east sides at the first glance appear the same (except that there are two chiefs on the east and four on each of the other sides), here are many minor differences which must have been intentional [*"Some Notes on Xochicalco"*].

Although she didn't realize it at the time, she also found her life's work.

She was an excellent copyist — a valu-able skill before the days of color reproduc-tion. She was accurate and careful.

She did her first copying at Teotihua-cán, a large ruin outside of Mexico City. Just before she visited the site, remnants of murals were discovered. Adela undertook to copy them; today they are a valuable record of paintings that quickly deteriorated when exposed to the air.

After a second extended trip through Mexico, she considered whether there was work she might do in Mexico. Alfred Maudslay, a noted archaeologist and explorer (and friend) asked her to go to Chichén Itzá to verify the accuracy of drawings he intended to use in an upcoming series of books on the Archaeology of Central America — and also, he said, she might copy the extensive and elaborate murals in one of the temples. This was the opportunity she'd been wanting. And so, age fifty, she took her first trip to Chichén Itzá to begin the project. Working a few months (the slightly cooler dry season) each year, the project spanned seven years. The work was hard and life at Chichén wasn't very comfortable.

Her work opened up a new world for Adela, the world of professional work with archaeology. She quickly became involved with professional organizations; she knew "everyone" who was working with Mexican archaeology at the time, and she corresponded with many. Her work was highly regarded, and colleagues sought her advice.

She persevered with her copying, recording not only the murals but other carvings and details of the ruins. As anticipated, the murals and carvings eroded rapidly. Today her copies are the only records we have — not to mention the only ones in color — of those all-but-vanished images.

The Mexican Revolution in 1910 made travel and work in Mexico difficult. Adela continued to travel, but she never went back to Mexico. She always continued her inerest in Mexico and spent much time studying the Maya dialects.

Mexico wasn't her only travel. She visited archaeological sites in Egypt and Greece. She visited museums throughout Europe and made a trip to Peru and Central America. She made at least two trips around the world.

She belonged to several international associations of science and research, including one that focused on prehistoric man, a subject that interested her greatly. Adela also began writing articles for professional journals and presenting papers at international conferences. Her work with the murals gave her insights into the world and ideas of the ancient Maya; she was a careful thinker and a good writer.

When World War I began she was in the United States. She spent most of the war in Canada, only returning to England in 1920.

She decided to take one more trip to attend a conference in Rio de Janeiro. Her health was worsening, but her attendance was important to the organization, and friends urged her to go. She did attend, but after the conference she needed to rest for several weeks before she could start home. She still wasn't strong enough to travel and had to stop at Barbados, where, after a few weeks, she died.

Even though she never returned to Mexico, her heart was there, especially at Chichén Itza. "I cannot tell you what a transformation came over Chichen with the heavy rains. Everything suddenly blossomed & turned green, the ticks mostly disappeared, & it has been really Paradise..." [*Adela Breton: A Victorian Artist Amid Mexico's Ruins*, p. 75].

SOURCE: *Adela Breton: A Victorian Artist Amid Mexico's Ruins.*

WORKS

Adela Breton wrote no books. She wrote numerous anthropological articles that were published in *MAN*, the journal of the Royal Anthropological Institute, as well as various professional journals. In the early 1890s she wrote at least two travel articles that were published in the *Bath Chronicle*.

Brenton, Adela. "Some Notes on Xochicalco." In University of Pennsylvania: *Transactions of the Department of Archeology, Free Museum of Science and Art*, Vol. II, Part 1. University of Pennsylvania, 1906.

BOOKS ABOUT OR INCLUDING ADELA BRETON

McVicker, Mary. *Adela Breton: A Victorian Artist Amid Mexico's Ruins*. Albuquerque: University of New Mexico Press, 2005.

Mrs. F. D. Bridges, British.

Mrs. Bridges and her husband decided to travel round the world "to read with our own eyes some of the marvels written in that great world-book, hoping not only to glance over its pictures, but to try, though perhaps in simple fashion, to learn something of its deeper meaning, and see not alone the things new and old, but the men and women who make up the story of life told in its wonder pages" [*Journal of a Lady's Travels Round the World*, p. 1].

Their intent sets the trip apart; as Mrs. Bridges's journal recounts, they held true to their intent, exploring, inquiring, and learning. They seemed to have been particularly interested in the arts and in the shrines and monasteries; they made friends readily and were interested in learning about the countryside and customs.

The book opens in Greece and the journey began as they sail to Egypt, then to the Red Sea. They had planned the trip to include extensive excursions on land, not only visiting the "tourist attractions" but spending time traveling throughout the countryside. In India they saw the magnificent paintings of the caves of Ajanta and admired the Buddhist shrines. They traveled to Kashmir and the Indus Valley.

They penetrated the mountain passes of the Himalayas and climbed, crossing the mountains, then descending to Yarkand (Shache) in western China. They then crossed back over the mountains and returned to Kashmir.

[*From Tibet:*] But now the miracle-play began. Out from the gloom of the deeply-recessed porch of the church and down the steps came five or six Lamas or rather figures off old playing-cards, clad in gorgeous Chinese satins, with large witches' hats on their heads, and religious emblems in their hands, slowly moving around in mystic dance, displaying to the greatest advantage the really lovely satin brocades, stiff with gold and silver dragons, of their quaint garments. Then they gradually twirled their way back into the church to emerge again, it seemed to us, in a few moments wearing entirely different costumes, more gorgeous and beautiful, if possible, than the former.... And how well the strange picture was set off by the background of swarthy red-clothed lamas (the red of their flannel robe is almost chocolate colour), and the rich tones of the dark wooden balconies lit up by the glorious sunshine pouring down over all. The choir clashed out again in wild music, and a group of grinning masks — mask painting is an ancient art and brought to great perfection in China — lions' heads and harlequins' bodies came down the church steps, and whirling slowly round, retreated again into the gloom, and came out dragon-headed. Then lastly, strangest sight of all, a band of skeletons, the skulls (masks) admirably painted, gnashing their hideous jaws and shaking their lanky limbs, rushed out into the sunshine and executed a real "Dance of Death" before us....

As the skeletons danced their way back into the church, we, with the head Lama, rose and followed them up the steps and into the gloom [pp. 100–101].

Burma was the next stop on the voyage; the heat was difficult. They sailed to the straits of Malacca, then to Java, where they spent Christmas. New Year's was spent at Canton, with friends. From there they went to Japan, where they stayed about four months, traveling throughout the islands and seeing the countryside. They enjoyed their time in Japan and were sorry to leave, but Mrs. Bridges gives the impression that the stay seemed rather tame compared to the exploration and exertions in the Himalayas and India.

They stayed in San Francisco only a few days then left for Portland. After a brief trip to Victoria, British Columbia, they returned to San Francisco. Where to go next?

> It is no easy matter to make out one's route in this country, which contains nearly half the railway mileage of the world; but at last we decided on our line of travel [p. 373].

The "line of travel" took them to Yosemite, Salt Lake City, the canyons, and Denver. The book ends at the Palmer House in Chicago, where, she finds, "books abound as well as Bacon ... a good omen, we may hope" [p. 411]. They spent "some months more" in America [p. 411], then went home, after traveling for nearly two and a half years.

She summed up the experience as being well worth the fatigues, fever fits and perils. "The weariness of the way is amply compensated for by the delight of realizing long-cherished visions, of mentally annexing vast territories which before were only a geographical expression, of experiencing the true kindness (in our case often destined to ripen into firm friendship) which we invariably found awaited the stranger..." [p. 412].

SOURCE: *Journal of a Lady's Travels Round the World.*

WORKS

Bridges. *Journal of a Lady's Travels Round the World.* London: John Murray, 1883.

Harriette G. Britten

Harriette was a missionary in Liberia; she tells us else little about herself and her background in her book. While her book focused on her missionary and educational activities, she also related information and incidents — as the title states — of her daily life and the people with whom she worked. Harriette seems to have liked her life and her work in Liberia, although she was often quite ill. She was committed to the value of education, as well as to spreading the gospel.

> Daily Fare. — Back to my school duties again. You wish to know our daily fare. Well, for breakfast we have boiled rice (that at every meal), and either Indian meal, rice, or wheat bread, always hot in the morning; and then we have it cold at tea-time. You know it will not keep long in this climate. The rice bread is very nice. The rice is grounded into very fine flour, so that it resembles our ground rice. This, with salt mackerel and excellent coffee, forms our breakfast. Our dinner: rice and palm-butter, daily. The palm butter I have described. We always have a chicken or two in it. Occasionally, too, we are able to have a variety; sometimes roast or boiled chickens; or, once in a great while, a little fresh fish; or in a very great while, a bit of fresh meat; but this is very seldom. Then we have ham, and corned beef, and pork, from America. They catch, sometimes, a species of oyster; it is good, though it is much larger and coarser than ours. We have quite a variety of vegetables; sweet potatoes, very good, but quite white; eddo, which, when mashed, is an excellent substitute for Irish potatoes; cassada, which the natives use in great quantities. This is a long, round root, larger than the largest parsnip, and quite white; but its taste is very like a tough stringy turnip. The natives eat it raw a good deal. Then we have egg-plant, plantains — a species of banana, which is either roasted or cut lengthwise, and fried. Sometimes bananas are cooked in the same way. Then we have ochre, cucumbers, stringed beans, tomatoes, cabbage (very rarely heads), lettuce, radishes, lima beans, squashes, and Indian corn. None of these come to the perfection they do at home, but still they are good. Thus much for dinner. For tea, we have bread, or wheat cakes, molasses, and salt fish. Such is our ordinary fare. We do not starve, you may depend. Puddings, pies, or cakes, are too expensive, as

all butter and sugar come from America; nevertheless, on any very great occasions, we can have them. Though we may often long for home fare, yet we make out very nicely, and our friends there do not forget us. They often refresh our memories, and appetites, too, by jars of canned lobster, or oysters, preserves, pickles, prepared mustard, &c., &c.; all things rather expensive for the missionary's pocket, but receiving additional relish when they come as tributes of affection, and often so reviving, when suffering from loss of appetite, consequent on fever [*Scenes and Incidents*, pp. 105–106, from reprinted edition].

WORKS

Britten, Harriette G. *Scenes and Incidents of Every-Day Life in Africa.* New York: Pudney and Russell, 1860. Reprint: (New York: Negro Universities Press, a Division of Greenwood Publishing Corp., 1969.

Mary Anne Stewart Broome
(formerly Lady Barker) *see* **Lady Mary Anne Barker**

Lady Isabel Arundell Burton,
1831–1896. British.

Isabel Arundell was born in London on March 20, 1831. She was the first child of her father's second marriage. Both parents came from old and distinguished families, and Isabel was always proud of her heritage. Isabel was very close to her family, which included her older step-brother and seven younger brothers and sisters. Following her coming out in 1850, her mother took Isabel and her siblings to Boulogne to stay. This was Isabel's first trip abroad. One day while the family was taking their habitual walk, a man approached. Isabel always said she'd conceptualized her "ideal man"—and here he was! She turned to her sister and said, "That man will marry me."

The man was Richard Burton, ten years older than Isabel. Richard was very outgoing, and Isabel frequently saw him at social events, often flirting with other girls.

They met again in 1856 and became engaged. In his proposal Richard asked Isabel if she would be prepared to give up civilization and go with him, "living the sort of life that Lady Hester Stanhope led. I see the capabilities in you, but you must think it over" [p. 211]. Without hesitation she accepted, although the decision rested on her family's approval—a chancy matter given Richard's religion (Isabel's family was Catholic; Richard was not), poor financial prospects and reputation.

At that time Richard was planning to go to Africa for three years, on a trip that was potentially dangerous as well as rough. Their engagement was kept secret. They were reunited in 1859, and Isabel then told her mother about her engagement to Richard. Mrs. Arundel informed Isabel that she would never consent to Isabel's marrying Burton.

Isabel and Richard were not to marry for two more years. The marriage was a civil ceremony; it took a considerable amount of time and effort for Isabel's mother to accept the situation. Seven months later Richard left for his position as consul in West Africa.

After two years he returned, and he and Isabel sailed to Tenerife in January 1863, finally able to spend a period of time together. Richard then returned to the consulate. At that time much attention was being given to the question of the source of the Nile, and an expedition was outfitted. John Speke, one of the main people involved in the expedition, was also the source of bitter controversies. John and Katharine Petherick (see the entry for her) were at the center of controversy, with the result that John's career and life were ruined. Richard was also embroiled in the mess; Speke was a bitter opponent of Burton. The matter dragged on for several years, ending with the death of Speke either by accident or suicide.

Finally in 1865 the opportunity came for Isabel's much hoped-for travel with Richard, and the two sailed for Brazil, where Richard was consul. They stayed for three years, returning to England the summer of 1868. Within six months they had left for Damascus.

[Isabel visited Palmyra.]

You may walk down the High Street till you reach the mountains, perhaps for a mile or more. It is so long and ruined here and there, that one has to take it up at intervals, but there is no mistaking its direct line. From the triumphal arch to a very marked *point de depart* in about the middle, the right side of the street is in ruins, but after that the left side is almost completely ruined, whilst on the right hand here and there the columns remain perfect. This street also terminates at a Temple, six columns supporting a façade. Here, on turning to look back, one perceives that the great Colonnade must have had two lesser streets of the same kind, like the aisles of a cathedral. Doubtless the large road would be intended for equestrians and carriages, and the two side paths for pedestrians.

You can stand on the top of a spacious arch which must once have formed a magnificent gateway; now it is buried in sand. In the particular instance of which I now write, a muleteer is singing upon that noble perch, unconscious of anything grand, and wonders what I am staring at. Whilst so engaged a flight of storks darken the air — one small white butterfly, which must have been the scapegoat of the butterflies, and charged with their sins, myriads of small black beetles burrowing in the sand, and the snakes in the bath underground, complete all the live stock of Palmyra the Old.

I can even to-day shut my eyes and walk all over Palmyra, and tell every column standing *in situ*. Being so near the mountains at the farther end of the High Street, it is as well to ascend to the castle, which is built on a little detached peak of the range which backs the city. It is cruised round, with an infinity to labour, to form a moat, and the ascent, steep and slippery, tears hands and knees, clothes and boots. On two sides of it are mountain ranges, and on the other two the Desert stretches away into the horizon. This is quite the best point from which to look down on the plan of the town, and this is the general view of the ruins at your feet [*The Inner Life of Syria*, pp. 177–178].

Isabel was interested in Syria and the Middle East, and she and Richard traveled and explored when they could. Controversy was a fact of life for Richard. In 1870–71 he crossed paths (and swords) with Mentor and Augusta Mott (see Mott). A complaint was raised that Mott's proselytizing stirred up the Muslim population. Richard sided with the complainant over Mott. The matter escalated and caused trouble for some time. There were also other complaints and controversies, and in summer 1871 Richard was recalled from his position. Isabel continued to maintain that Richard had not been treated fairly. Her campaign paid off and officials came to accept that this was the case. Isabel and Richard both looked back on their time in Damascus as one of the happiest.

Richard made a short trip to Iceland. While he was there he was offered a position in Trieste; Isabel and Richard took up residence there in 1873 and remained (with intervals of travels and visits to England) until 1890.

Their travel to India at the end of 1876 was sparked by a desire to see where her husband had been stationed for nineteen years. The trip was decided somewhat impulsively; having only about six months for travel they consulted a map and divided India in half, then decided to see the western half, leaving the eastern part for another trip.

This was an unusually social trip for them, with numerous dinners, parties, and other social events with fellow English. The Burtons traveled around "their" segment of India, but they did little adventurous traveling. Isabel's book *Arabia, Egypt, India* has much history and factual material; overall the book has a distinct tone of "report" to it.

Richard died in Trieste in October 1890. This was the thing Isabel had feared. After several months of finishing up, packing, and sorting out matters, Isabel returned to England.

At the time of his death Richard was (as he often was) amidst controversy and difficulties, this time over his translations. The Burtons' financial affairs were amiss, and Isabel was short of cash. More complicated, however, was Richard's literary estate; it remained embroiled in controversy for years, and Isabel spent the rest of her life working on some aspect or another of his estate.

Isabel died March 22, 1896. She was buried in the tomb shaped like a tent that she had designed for Richard.

SOURCE: *A Rage to Live: A Biography of Richard & Isabel Burton.*

WORKS

Burton, Lady Isabel. *Arabia, Egypt, India: A Narrative of Travel.* London: W. Mullan, 1879.

_____. *The Inner Life of Syria, Palestine, and the Holy Land.* London: H. S. King, 1875.

_____. *The Life of Captain Sir Richard F. Burton K.C.M.G., F.R.G.S.* London: Chapman and Hall, 1893.

_____. *The Passion Play at Ober-Ammergau* London: Hutchinson, 1900.

_____. *The Romance of Isabel, Lady Burton: The Story of her Life Told in Part by Herself.* Two volumes. London: Hutchinson, 1897. Also published in one volume, New York: Dodd Mead, 1904.

BOOKS ABOUT OR INCLUDING ISABEL BURTON

There are numerous biographies and writings about Richard Burton, and many of them contain information about Isabel.

Lovell, Mary S. *A Rage to Live: A Biography of Richard & Isabel Burton.* New York: W. W. Norton, 1998.

Frances Erskine Inglis Calderon de la Barca,
1804–1892. Scottish.

When Frances Erskine Inglis, who was always known as Fanny, was born, the family already had four children under the age of seven. Eventually there were ten children.

Her father was a member of Writers to the Signet, a specialized branch of the legal profession. Both parents were from old families and well-connected. All the children were well educated and traveled in Europe; Fanny apparently spent some time in Italy.

When Fanny was twenty-three her father was forced into bankruptcy. Several of the children had already married or left home; the remaining family moved to Normandy. Two years later, in 1830, Fanny's father died. The family decided that part of the family would move to Boston to establish a school. Nine went, all women: Mrs. Inglis, Fanny and three sisters, and several children.

At first everything went well. The school was well-received and prospered. Then trouble occurred. Fanny was rumored to be the author of an anonymous pamphlet that skewered the charitable efforts of some prominent Bostonians. Several of the people mentioned in the pamphlet had girls in the Inglises' school, and they promptly withdrew them. Additionally, there was increased competition from other schools. The school dwindled.

The family divided again, with most of the group going to Pittsburgh. Fanny and Mrs. Inglis stayed in Boston for a time before moving to Staten Island, then a fashionable retreat from the hot Washington summers.

Angel Calderon de la Barca (1790–1861) was born in Buenos Aires. He studied in Europe, then fought for Spain during Napoleon's Spanish invasion when he was taken prisoner. After the peace he studied science and botany at university then began his career in government, eventually joining the diplomatic service. In 1835 he was assigned to the United States as minister plenipotentiary. In spring 1838 he met William Prescott; Fanny had known Prescott earlier in Boston, and it may have been through him that Fanny and Calderon de la Barca met.

They married in the fall of 1838. Shortly after, Calderon was appointed the first envoy from Spain to independent Mexico. On October 27, 1839, the opening date of Fanny's *Life in Mexico,* the couple left New York for Havana.

They were in Mexico for two and a half years. Instead of just staying in Mexico City, Fanny and Calderon de la Barca traveled in Mexico, often going to more out-of-the-way places. Fanny was a good observer and writer, and her book is a remarkable account of life in Mexico.

Sunday: February 7th, 1841
Hacienda of Atlacomulco

The cave of Cacahuamilpa, whose actual wonders equal the fabled descriptions of the palaces of Genii, was until lately known to the Indians alone — or, if the Spaniards formerly knew anything about it, its existence was forgotten amongst them. But, although in former days it may have been used as a place of worship, a superstitious fear prevented the more modern Indians from exploring its shining recesses — for here, it was firmly believed, the evil spirit had his dwelling and, in the form of a goat with long beard and horns, guarded the entrance of the cavern. The few who ventured there and beheld this apparition brought back strange tales to their credulous companions and even the neighbourhood of the enchanted cave was avoided, especially at nightfall.

The chain of mountains into whose bosom it leads is bleak and bare, but the ravine below is refreshed by a rapid stream that forms small waterfalls as it tumbles over the rocks, and is bordered by green and flowering trees. Amongst these is one with a smooth, satin-like bark, of a pale golden colour, whose roots have something snakish and witch-like in their appearance, intertwining with each other, grappling as it were with the hard rock, and stretching out to the most extraordinary distance.

We arrived at the entrance of the cave, a superb portal, upwards of seventy feet high and one hundred and fifty wide, according to the computation of a learned traveller — the rocks which support the great arch so symmetrically disposed as to resemble a work of art. The sun was already high in the heavens, shining with intense brightness on the wild scenery that surrounded us, the rocks and trees and rushing waters. A sensation of awe came over us as we stood at the mouth of the cave, and, turning from day to night, strained our eyes to look down a deep descent into a gigantic vaulted hall, faintly lighted by the red embers of a fire which the Indians had kindled near the entrance. We made our way down a declivity of, it may be, one hundred and fifty feet, surrounded by blocks of stone and rock, and remained lost in astonishment at finding ourselves in this gloomy subterranean palace, surrounded by the most extraordinary, gigantic, and mysterious forms — which it is scarcely possible to believe are the fantastic productions of the water which constantly trickles from the roof.

I am shocked to confess it — I would prefer passing it over — but we had tasted nothing that morning, and we had rode for eight hours and were dying of hunger! Moreover we traveled with a cook, a very tolerable native artist, but without sentiment — his heart in his stewpan — and he, without the least compunction, had begun his frying and broiling operations in what seemed the very vestibule of Pharaoh's palace. Our own mozos and our Indian guides were assisting his operations with the utmost zeal; and in a few minutes — some sitting round the fire and others upon broken pyramids — we refreshed ourselves with fried chicken, bread, and hard eggs before proceeding farther on our exploring expedition. Unromantic as this proceeding was, we looked, Indians and all, rather awful, with no other light than the ruddy glare of the fire flickering upon the strange, gigantic forms in that vast labyrinth; and as to what we felt, our valour and strength of mind were increased sevenfold.

Twenty-four huge pine torches were then lighted, each man carrying one. To [Kate] and me were given lighted wax candles, in case by accident anyone should go astray from his companions and lose his way, as would too certainly happen in the different windings and galleries and compartments of the cave, and be alone in the darkness! We walked on in awe and wonder, the guides lighting up the sides of the cavern with their torches. Unfortunately, it is indescribable — as in the fantastic forms of the clouds, everyone sees some different creation of his fancy in these stupendous masses....

We passed on into the second *sala*, collecting as we went fragments of the shining stones, our awe and astonishment increasing at every step. Sometimes we seemed to be in a subterranean Egyptian temple. The architecture was decidedly Egyptian, and the strange forms of the animals resembled those of the uncouth Egyptian idols — which, together with the pyramids and obelisks, made me think that perhaps that ancient people took the idea of their architecture and of many of their strange shapes from some natural cave of this description, just as nature herself suggested the idea of the beautiful Corinthian pillar.

Again, we seemed to enter a tract of country which had been petrified.

I never saw or could have imagined so beautiful an effect as that of the daylight in the distance, entering by the mouth of the cave — such a faint misty blue, contrasted with the fierce red light of the torches, and broken by the pillars though which its pale rays struggled [*Life in Mexico*, pp. 386–389].

When they left Mexico they returned to Madrid, where they waited for information about Calderon's next assignment. In 1844 he was appointed Spanish minister to the United States. They stayed in Washington for nine years. Fanny and Calderon did not have children, but Fanny was close to her nieces.

In 1853 Calderon was named minister for Spain's foreign affairs, and they returned to Madrid. Calderon's position was difficult; this was an unsettled time for Spain. The next year the unrest continued, finally reaching such a point that Calderon had to flee to France disguised as a French wine merchant. Fanny followed, also using an assumed identity, with two of her nieces. They remained in France for two years. During this time Fanny wrote *The Attaché in Madrid* which was published anonymously. They finally returned to Spain in 1856. Calderon never resumed public service. In May, 1861, he contracted an infection and died.

Fanny was asked by the queen to take the responsibility of educating the ten-year-old Infanta Isabel. Following Isabel's marriage at sixteen, Fanny returned to the United States for a visit. While she was gone, Spain erupted in revolution, and the royal family sought refuge in France. When Fanny returned to the exiled court it was to be companion to Isabel. In 1874, following the installation of Isabel's son as king, the court — and Fanny — returned to Spain.

Her many years in Spain were not years of isolation. The Inglis family was split between the United States and Spain, and Fanny lived the last part of her life with various sisters, nieces and families in close proximity.

SOURCE: *Life in Mexico*; *The Letters of Fanny Calderón de la Barca*.

WORKS

Calderon de la Barca, Frances. *The Attaché in Madrid: or, Sketches of The Court of Isabella II*. Translated from the German. New York: Appleton, 1856. Published anonymously as by the attaché himself.

_____. *Life in Mexico During a Residence of Two Years in That Country*. London: Dent, 1843.

Numerous editions are available of *Life in Mexico*. The most comprehensive is *Life in Mexico: the Letters of Fanny Calderón de la Barca*. With new material from the author's private journals. Edited and annotated by Howard T. Fisher and Marion Hall Fisher. Garden City, New York: Anchor Books, 1970.

Lady Maria Dundas Graham Callcott, 1785 or 1786–1842.

English. She is often listed as Maria Dundas Graham.

Maria Dundas was born in Papcastle, England. Nothing is known of her mother; her father, George Dundas, was rear admiral and commissioner of the Admiralty. Maria had a strong interest in botany from an early age.

When she was twenty-two she sailed with her father on a mission to India. There, two years later, she married Captain Thomas Graham of the Royal Navy. Their tour of India resulted in her first book, *Journal of a Residence in India*.

They returned to England in 1811 and lived in London. Graham was appointed to the Foreign Service, and in 1819 Maria went with him on a tour of duty in Italy.

Then, in 1821, the couple sailed for South America. They were in Brazil for seventeen months, living in Pernambuco, Bahia, and Rio de Janeiro. During her time in Rio, Maria was the English tutor of Donna Maria, who became queen of Portugal in 1826.

Chile was their next destination. They encountered severe storms rounding Cape Horn. Thomas, who had not been well, died during the fifth week of the voyage. Maria arrived in Chile in April, 1882, a widow. While she was in Chile there was a devastating earthquake, with repeated shocks and tremors. The next January she sailed back around the Horn and arrived back in Rio de Janeiro in March.

Maria was very interested in Chile's struggle for independence from Spain and the aftermath of their triumph in 1818.

> The Introduction to the present volume is, perhaps, its most important part. Of the first six years of the revolution in Chile, no account is to be procured, either from the offices of the secretaries of state, or among the papers of the actors in the scene.... It was the writer's good fortune while in Chile, to become acquainted with several persons, who, having participated either as actors or spectators in the great event, were kind enough to allow her to write down, from their several accounts, the main particulars which she has detailed. What was related by those still royalists, agreed in all facts with what was told by the patriots, and all with the clear and spirited narratives of the supreme Director, O'Higgins; whose liberality and politeness on this, as on every other point, towards the writer, deserve her warmest acknowledgements [*Journal of a Residence in Chile*, pp. 2–3].

Maria was surprised by the extent of her interest.

> I remember the time when I should as little have thought of reading the reglamento of Chile, as I should of poring over the report of a committee of turnpike rods in a distant country; and far less should I have dreamed of occupying myself with the *Constitucion Politica del estado de Chile*. But, times and circumstances make strange inroads on one's habits both of being and thinking; and I have actually caught myself reading with a considerable degree of interest, the said Political Constitution [p. 201].

Her book was far more than a political history and documentary, however.

> 11th. May — This morning, tempted by the exceeding fineness of the weather, and the sweet feeling of the air, I set out to follow the little water-course that irrigates my garden, towards its source. After skirting

the hill for about a furlong, always looking down on a fertile valley, and now and then gaining a peep at the bay and shipping between the fruit trees, I heard the sound of falling water, and on tuning sharp round the corner of a rock, I found myself in a quegrada, or ravine, full of great blocks of granite, from which a bright plentiful stream had washed the red clay as it leaped down from ledge to ledge, and fell into a little bed of sand glistening with particles of mica that looked like fairy gold [p. 122].

Friday, 20th.— Some very slight shocks; none of which I felt, being on horseback at the time. Unless the shocks are very violent or the sound very loud, the horses and mules do not appear to feel them.

I rode to Valparaiso: the morning was dull and drizzling. I cannot describe the effect of such a day on the scenery between Quintero and Concon, by the long beach of nine miles: on one side the sandhills with not a sign of vegetation, on the other a furious surf; both seeming interminable, and being lost in the thick air; or if a breeze now and then blows the haze aside, the distant dreary points of land seem suspended far above the visible horizon, and one goes on with a kind of desperate eagerness to see what will be the end. I was in a fine humour for moralizing. Earthquake under me, civil war around me; my poor sick relation apparently dying; and my kind friend, my only friend here indeed, certainly going to leave the country, at least for a time. All this left me with nothing but the very present to depend on; and like the road I was traveling, what was to come was enveloped in dark clouds, or at best afforded most uncertain glimpses of the possible future.

In such cases the mind is apt to make a sport to itself of its very miseries. I more than once on the way caught myself smiling over the fanciful resemblances I drew between human life and the scene I was in; or at the fatality which had brought me, an Englishwoman, whose very characteristic is to be the most domestic of creatures, almost to the antipodes, and placed me among all the commotion of nature and of society [p. 334].

The "poor sick relation" was her cousin Glennie, who arrived on September 17, having broken a blood vessel at Callao. He accompanied her back to Brazil.

Maria returned to London in October, 1823. She married Augustus Wall Callcott, who was a portrait painter and musician, in February 1827. Augustus was knighted that year, and Maria became Lady Callcott. The couple traveled to the Mediterranean in 1828. London then became their permanent home.

In 1831 she became bedridden after rupturing a blood vessel; she continued writing, however. She died in November 1842.

SOURCE: A. Curtis Wilgus's Preface to *Journal of a Residence in Chile*.

WORKS

Maria Dundas Graham Callcott wrote other books, including a very popular child's history of England.

The titles and dates of her books can be confusing; the residence in Chile was sandwiched by two residencies in Brazil. Her South American travel books were translated into Spanish and French.

Callcott, Maria. *Journal of a Residence in Chile During the Year 1822, and a Voyage from Chile to Brazil in 1823*. London: Longman, 1824.
_____. *Journal of a Residence in India*. Edinburgh: Constable, 1812.
_____. *Journal of a Voyage to Brazil, and Residence There, During Part of the Years 1821, 1822, 1823*. London: Longman 1824.
_____. *Letters on India*. London: Longman, 1814
_____. *Three Months Passed in the Mountains East of Rome, During the Year 1819*. London: Longman, 1820.
_____. *Voyage of H.M.S. Blonde to the Sandwich Islands in the Years 1824–1825*. London: Murray, 1826. Published anonymously.

Amelia Cary (Viscountess Falkland)

Amelia Cary was the wife of Lord Falkland, the governor of Bombay. Amelia had recently traveled from Halifax to England and after a short stay had sailed to Bombay. While there she traveled, exploring the area around Bombay and going to the hills to escape the worst of the heat.

She was particularly taken with the Caves of Elephanta.

> The island of Elephanta, in which is the well known brahminical cave, should be visited after the Monsoon, during the month of November, when the vegetation is still rich and brilliant.
>
> The name Elephanta is derived from a stone elephant, which carried a tiger on its back, and which formerly stood near the landing-place on the south side of the island. It has now nearly disappeared, and can scarcely be recognized [*Chow-chow* Vol. 1, p.109].

The cave was impressive, 130 feet long and 130 feet broad.

> On each side as you enter are large columns and at the end is an enormous three-faced bust, which stands nineteen feet high. It is much injured but the faces are untouched. This bust represents Siva in his threefold character of Brahma, Vishnoo, and Roodra... [Vol. 1, p. 110].
>
> Nearly in the middle of the cave is a chapel, or shrine, approached by steps; gigantic figures, which lean on dwarfs, guard the entrance.
>
> In the different compartments are sculptures representing gods and goddesses, having reference to stories relating to the heroes and heroines of the Hindoo pantheon... [Vol. 1, p. 111].
>
> What interested me most in these representations was to observe among them scenes in domestic life, with customs and costumes that still exist in this country, and to see how completely unchanged they are since the formation of this cave... [Vol. 1, p. 112].
>
> We returned home by moonlight. In India the nights are always beautiful, but when the moon is at the full they are particularly so. She seems nearer the earth in the tropics than in Europe, and certainly has more power and influence, especially in fevers, — the invalid generally suffering more

> at certain of the moon's phases ... by her light the flowers seem to be of silver, and those parts of the shining foliage of trees which catch her rays appear dotted with pearls [Vol. 1, pp. 114–115].

Amelia and her husband left Bombay in December 1853, sailing on the *Feroze*, a ship she had christened several years earlier. They sailed to Aden, then on to Egypt, where they sailed the Nile before traveling to Alexandria. After their time spent in India, where they were so involved with learning about the country, Egypt provided a slight culture shock. For one thing, the nights were cold and they missed the tropical evenings of India.

But they were intrigued with Egypt, particularly by the antiquities, although those, too, were very different from what they'd been used to seeing.

> I forgot at first I was in Egypt, and thought Siva, Vishnoo, or the elephant-headed god, would greet me when I entered the portico: but none of "the old familiar faces" were there. Instead of Gunputty, there was a stranger with a ram's head, who, I learnt, is called Knepf, and who, although met with in other temples, was the presiding deity of ancient Esné [Vol. 2, p. 126].

From Egypt they traveled to Joppa and Jerusalem, then eventually to Marseilles,

> where our pilgrimage and wanderings of many years terminated; and from thenceforth no new wares were added to the diverse contents of "the Chow-Chow" basket. [Vol. 2, p. 287].

She explained the title of her book: "'Chow Chow'" comes from the "'Pedlars' [sic] in Egypt, who go from village to village carrying wares in boxes and baskets. There is always one basket called the Chow Chow basket —'Odds and Ends.'"

Works

Cary, Amelia. *Chow-chow: Being Selections from a Journal Kept in India, Egypt, and Syria.* Two volumes. London: Hurst & Blackett, 1857.

Baroness Elizabeth Berkeley Craven (Later Margravine of Anspach), 1750–?

Elizabeth was born in December 1750, the daughter of the fourth Earl of Berkeley. She was well educated. At age sixteen she was married to Lord Craven. They had two daughters in two years; eventually she had seven children.

Lord Craven fell in love with someone else. After some time, she confronted him with her knowledge. Lord Craven went to the Continent but then returned, having reached a decision to leave her after thirteen years of marriage. Elizabeth decided to travel.

She first went to France, then to Italy. After spending some time in Italy she traveled to Vienna, Cracow, and Warsaw, where she was presented to the King of Poland. Also on this trip she met the Margrave and Margravine at Anspach. She was warmly welcomed to their household and treated like a sister.

On her arrival at Constantinople:

> But I am certain no landscape can amuse or please in comparison with the varied view, which the borders of this famed Straight compose — rocks, verdure, ancient castles, built on the summit of the hills by the Genoese — modern Kiosks*, Minarets, and large platane-trees — multitudes of people, and boats swarming on the shore and on the water; and what was particular, nothing to be seen like a formal French garden — the Turks have so great a respect for natural beauties, that if they must build a house where a tree stands, they leave a large hole for the tree to pass through and increase in size, they think the branches of it the prettiest ornament for the top of the house; in truth, Sir, contrast a chimney to a beautiful foliage and judge if they are right or wrong [p. 199].

The Margravine died; Lord Craven also died about the same time. The Margrave and Elizabeth married and went to live in England.

SOURCE: *A Journey Through the Crimea to Constantinople, in a Series of Letters.*

WORKS

Craven, Elizabeth. *A Journey Through the Crimea to Constantinople, in a Series of Letters.* Dublin: H. Chamberlain, 1789.

Mabel Sharman Crawford. British.

Mabel Crawford probably is best known not as a traveler, but for the spirited defense she made of women travelers in her introduction to *Through Algeria.* She commented on the standard that though "masculine eccentricity or originality of character is to be admired, very few will allow that any departure from ordinary rule is approvable, or even justifiable in a woman. We can applaud our grandmothers for overstepping the conventional proprieties of their day, or we can recognize the right of Chinese and Turkish ladies to go about with uncrippled feet and unveiled faces. But, clearly as we can see the follies of our ancestors, or those of contemporary nations, we cling with unreasoning reverence to every restriction on feminine liberty of action imposed by that society amidst which we live."

She wrote that people travel for a love of sunshine, a roving spirit and thirst for adventure. There was also the matter of an inherited restlessness or a quest of health. "As for those tourists whose love of travel springs from desire for information — a wish to study life under varied aspects — their numbers are too insignificant to give them

Kiosk means a summer-house with blinds all round.

a class existence." She didn't question — at least in her introduction — the "woman's sphere," but she raised the argument about independent women.

In bygone days, the rule that no lady should travel without a gentleman by her side, was doubtless rational; but in a period of easy locomotion, and with abundant evidence to prove that ladies can travel by themselves in foreign countries with perfect safety, the maintenance of that rule certainly savours of injustice. For unquestionable as it is that woman's sphere, as wife and mother, lies at home, it is surely unreasonable to doom many hundred English ladies, of independent means and without domestic ties, to crush every natural aspiration to see nature in its grandest forms, art in its finest works, and human life in its most interesting phases; — such being the practical result of social law which refuses them the right of travel, save on conditions often wholly unattainable. And if the exploring of foreign lands is not the highest or the most useful occupation of feminine existence, it is at least more improving, as well as more amusing, than the crochet-work or embroidery with which, at home, so many ladies seek to beguile the tedium of their unoccupied days [*Through Algeria*, pp. xi–xii].

She thought readers might question why, in the autumn of 1859, she went to Africa. "In general acceptation, a winter in Africa signifies a voyage up the Nile, and an interview with the sphinxes; but in my case, and in that of a lady who accompanied me, the phrase implied a visit to Algiers, with the supplement of a journey through Algeria."

And so they went.

But prominently picturesque as is the valley of the Hydra, it forms only one of a thousand beautiful walks abounding in the neighbourhood of Mustapha Superieur. In whatever direction I might wander, beauty was ever present in varied forms; and until the month of February, every charm of scenery was enhanced by brilliant sunlight and warm skies. Up to that time there had been no winter but in name; for, though the wind was often very high, it was not cold, and the rain had been so trifling in amount that alarmists prophesied there would be a famine cry that year amongst the colonists of Algeria....

The prospects of the colonists did look bad, I thought, as I saw almond trees and beans in flower, hedges starred with bright yellow Jessamine, the thorn showing clusters of opening buds, and butter-flies fluttering across my path with a summer-like frequency. From a philanthropical point of view I wished for rain, but as, from a tourist's point of view, I was averse to it, I cannot say that my stock of philanthropy was sufficient in amount, to reconcile me altogether to the cold heavy sleety showers with which February almost entered in its existence. If February rained, it ought reasonably to have done so warmly, as befitted its position in an Algerian year.

But as the days passed on, February rendered itself still more obnoxious to my censure, for on the morning of the 15th I arose form my bed to see a snow-covered ground. For many a year, such a sight as that had not been visible at Algiers.... [T]he grievance assumed a still graver character for the melting snow insinuating itself through various small chinks in a flat roof unused to such visitations, innumerable cascades commenced to fall from the ceilings; and though cascades are undoubtedly agreeable sights amidst rocks and trees, they cannot but be considered an objectionable feature of scenery in one's bedchamber, or sitting room [pp. 82–84].

WORKS

Crawford, Mabel Sharman. *Life in Tuscany*. London: Smith, Elder & Co., 1849.

_____. *Through Algeria*. London: Bentley, 1863.

Constance Frederica Gordon Cummings, 1837–1924. British.

In many respects Constance spent more time as a tourist than as an adventurous traveler, but she was a good observer and writer, and she went a number of places that were off the usual tourist trail.

She came from a large family and boasted of having fifty first cousins.

Her mother died when Constance was four; two years later she went to live with a married sister. After her father's remarriage she went back home, then attended school in London for five years. After her father died Constance lived with various relatives.

She led a very active social life until the early 1860s. Then, five older brothers and a sister died within several years of each other, and her youngest half sister married. Constance began traveling and making long visits; this lasted for twelve years. Her first trip was to the Hebrides. She then traveled to India, spending several years there.

She returned to England, where she met Isabella Lucy Bird; Isabella read the proofs of *From the Hebrides* while Constance was in Fiji. Her travels to Tonga, Samoa and Tahiti — where she stayed five months — followed.

On Sunday we walked along the shore, and then by a path through the abandoned sugar-fields, till we came to the little native church, where, much to our amusement, the teacher told us that he regulates the hour of service by the opening of a Banhinia blossom. He has no clock, but when the flower opens he beats the wooden lali or drum, and then the people assemble. We watched this floral timepiece expand its blossoms to the early light; and then the congregation came trooping in to a quiet, earnest service, with singing, prayer, and preaching — all very devout [*At Home in Fiji*, p. 72].

I must begin a letter to you to-night, for the strangeness of the situation exceeds any I have yet happened on. I have left the Langhams at Nirukuruku, and am here quite by myself, very much at home in a Fijian hut, and surrounded by natives, most of whom were, till within the last two years, uncompromising cannibals, and who, moreover, have never before beheld the face of a white woman!

The way it came about was this. When we were going up the river in hot haste, and with no time to loiter by the way the village of Nakamerousi had attracted my especial admiration. It is perched on a steep bank, and looks right along a broad reach of the river to a beautiful mountain-range. Being anxious to secure a sketch from that point, it was agreed that I should take advantage of the return thither of Reuben, the native teacher, who, with the help of Joshua, one of the boatmen, accordingly paddled me down in a small canoe. Great was the astonishment of the villagers, and greater still that of Reuben's exceedingly fat wife, in whose house I am spending the night. We made great friends, though I could hardly utter a word of Fijian, and probably few of those around me had ever heard a word of English.

As seen from the outside, this house promised well, but on entering I perceived that the first effort of civilisation had not improved the ordinary home. For the teachers have been encouraged to show the advantages of a separate sleeping-room, by having a third of the house screened off with a reed partition, but so little do they appreciate the innovation that they generally convert the inner room into a storeroom for yams or lumber. So it is in this case. However, the kind fat old lady resigned the post of honour for my benefit, and here I have hung up my plaid-curtain and mosquito-net, thereby greatly interesting a crowd of spectators, who had previously watched the wonderful process of consuming chocolate and biscuits. One kind woman has brought water in a bamboo, and therewith filled my big brass basin (the old companion of my happy tent-life in the Himalayas).

Now a party of laughing brown children are holding up small torches of blazing bamboo, by the light of which I am writing, but the illumination seems to me so likely to end in a general blaze that I will not be responsible for it. And so good night. The girls are greatly delighted with my hair-brushes, especially my tooth-brush. I shall have to keep jealous guard lest they experiment with it! They themselves use wooden combs, sometimes ornamented with coloured string and beads.

Really these falling sparks are too dangerous. Good night again [pp. 107–108].

Of all the countries and regions she visited and traveled around in, it was China that captivated her the most.

Constance and Isabella Bird overlapped interests on two occasions. Constance went to Japan in 1878. She did not write about this trip, during which she stayed with wealthy friends, until years later when she wrote her autobiography. Isabella Bird's book talks of a much more adventurous trip and was published before Constance began to write up her travels. The two met in Tokyo, however.

Then, during Constance's visit to China, she sailed to Hong Kong in December 1878, arriving in time to witness a fire on Christmas that destroyed a large part of Victoria. She talks of spending the night watching the scene of the fire. Her account was published several years later. Isabella Bird arrived the same night, disembarked and walked through the smoldering ruins; her account was published in *The Golden Chersonese,* several years before Constance's.

Most of Constance's publications were in the 1880s and 1890s; Constance, however, lived until 1924; her books had brought her much attention, but that time had long passed, and she lived out many years in relative obscurity.

SOURCE: *Dictionary of Literary Biography,* Volume 174.

WORKS

Cummings, Constance. *At Home in Fiji.* Two volumes. Edinburgh: Blackwood, 1881.
_____. *Fire Fountains: The Kingdom of Hawaii, Its Volcanoes, and the History of Its Missions.* Edinburgh: Blackwood, 1881.
_____. *From the Hebrides to the Himalayas: A Sketch of Eighteen Months' Wanderings in Western Isles and Eastern Highlands.* London: S. Low, Marston, Searle & Rivington, 1876. A new edition of Part I was published as *In the Hebrides.* London, Chatto & Windus, 1883; and an expanded version of Part 2 was published as *In the Himalayas and on the Indian Plains.* London: Chatto & Windus, 1883 and 1884.
_____. *Granite Crags.* Edinburgh: Blackwood, 1884,
_____. *The Inventor of the Numeral-type for China, by the Use of Which Illiterate Chinese Both Blind and Sighted Can Very Quickly Be Taught to Read and Write Fluently.* London: Downey, 1898.
_____. *A Lady's Cruise in a French Man-of-War.* Edinburgh: Blackwood, 1882.
_____. *"The Last Commandment" A Word to Every Christian,* bound together with *Work for the Blind.* London: J. Nisbet, 1888.
_____. *Memories.* Edinburgh, Blackwood, 1904.
_____. *Notes on China and Its Missions.* London: Church Mission Society, 1889.
_____. *Two Happy Years in Ceylon.* Two volumes. Edinburgh: Blackwood, 1892.
_____. *Via Cornwall to Egypt.* London: Chatto & Windus, 1885.
_____. *Wanderings in China.* Edinburgh: Blackwood, 1886.
_____. *Work for the Blind in China.* London: Gilbert & Rivington, 1887.

Several of Cummings's letters and her diary of a visit to Fiji are in the National Library of Scotland. Correspondence of Cumming and her publisher Chatto and Windus are at the University of Reading.

Hon. Mary Georgiana Emma Dawson Damer

WORKS

Damer, Mary *Diary of a Tour in Greece, Turkey, Egypt and the Holy Land.* Two volumes. London: H. Colburn, 1841.

Koncordie Amalie Nelle Dietrich, 1821–1891. German.

Many of the adventurous women travelers were wealthy and well connected;

Amalie's circumstances were just the opposite. Her father was an artisan, her mother an herbal healer in a small village in Saxony. Amalie had very little formal education, but she learned about plants and their healing properties from her mother. Her husband, Wilhelm Dietrich, an apothecary, was also interested in plants, and the two of them decided to collect plants for botanists. Amalie did most of the traveling, going about the countryside with a cart pulled by her dog, Hektor, collecting plants, minerals and insects. One day Amalie returned from a collecting trip to find that she and her young daughter were being turned out of their house; her husband had fallen in love with another woman. Amalie was forty then, and had few resources; she sold her cart and her beloved dog.

She heard that a wealthy German collector who owned a shipping firm was looking for naturalists to travel to the South Pacific to collect for the private museum he was starting. One of the collectors for whom Amalie had worked wrote her a letter of introduction, which said, in part, that Amalie had "an unusual talent for her profession, a sharp well trained eye for everything nature has to offer, a great certainty for identifying the collected material. On her long and mainly difficult journeys she has constantly shown great perseverance and bravery."

The shipping magnate, Johann Godeffroy, offered Amalie a job, but at half what he paid his male employees to collect for him. Amalie was pleased to have a job with a steady income for the first time in her life; above all she could now educate her daughter.

She set out, age forty-three, on one of Godeffroy's windjammers for Queensland, Australia. Although the voyage was long and hard, she didn't seem to mind. For the first time she had a future.

She lived in the field and collected, preserved, and then shipped her specimens off to Germany. It was an adjustment; the life was solitary and she had to look after herself, as well as make the collections. But Amalie persevered and sent back a great amount of material and specimens. She lived in the outback, collecting for ten years.

From a letter to her daughter:

I have to learn to look after myself in solitude.... With a truly solemn feeling I equipped myself for my first collecting trip in the new continent. I hung the vasculum over my shoulder, put flour, salt, tea and matches in it, put on my big straw hat and set out on my wanderings. My heart was pounding as I undertook this first trip, I was also a little afraid, so I took note of the direction, in order that I would be able to find my way back to the settlement again. I cannot describe to you the feelings which I had on this first excursion; I felt indeed that I would like on this first day to be led by a familiar, loving hand, as if I would like to be taught about all the strange new phenomena. How large, mysterious and impenetrable the Zell Wood once seemed to me, there I would have been afraid to go collecting alone for hours, as a young woman I never liked to go botanizing without your father, oh — and now! I had to keep asking myself: "Is it really me who is wandering around alone in the Australian woods?"...

Then the collecting started. First I filled the vasculum. Everything is new, and a wealth of material is growing around here, so that one is in a dilemma where to start first [*A Woman in the Wilderness*, p. 113].

Amalie gathered the single largest collection of Australia's flora and fauna; she sent back trees, shrubs, mosses, algae, birds, beetles, butterflies, spiders, corals and marsupials. She sent back so much that Godeffroy printed an entire sales catalog of just her specimens. Eventually she settled in Bowen, a frontier town, where she had a small zoo for the animals she was going to take back to Germany.

When she returned to Germany she settled in Hamburg and gave most of the animals to the Zoological Gardens there. She settled in to catalogue her extensive collections. But disaster struck.

The Godeffroy Company went bankrupt, and the museum was sold to pay creditors. Amalie lost her home. She ended her days in a charitable home for elderly women. She was estranged from her family; her daughter had married well but saw very little of her mother when she returned from Australia.

Scientists respected Amalie, and sometimes she was invited to attend their meetings. But she felt marginalized.

Little survives of Amalie's collections. Many of her samples, as well as all her field notes and letters, were destroyed in the fire bombings of Hamburg during World War II.

BOOKS ABOUT OR INCLUDING AMALIE DIETRICH

Sumner, Ray. *A Woman in the Wilderness: The Story of Amalie Dietrich in Australia.* Kensington: NSW University Press, 1993.

Jane (Jeanne) Henriette Magre Dieulafoy, 1851–1916.
French.

Jane Dieulafoy was born in Toulouse in 1851, the daughter of a wealthy family of merchants. In 1870 she married Marcel Dieulafoy (1844–1920).

He also came from a distinguished family. He studied at the École Polytechnique, became was a civil engineer, and was employed by the French bureau of roads and bridges. His first assignment was in Algeria, where he was exposed to the Arabic-speaking Orient in association with Roman antiquities. This had a profound effect on his future interests and pursuits. The year of their marriage, Marcel was appointed to the navigation service, and during the Franco-Prussian War, 1870–71, he was an engineering officer.

Jane was with him in the army of the Loire during the war. It was at that time she adopted masculine dress and a short haircut, which she retained throughout her life, not only on her travels but in Paris as well. She studied drawing and sculpture. She was good at languages and in addition to speaking English and Spanish, could read Italian and Portuguese. During their stay in North Africa she learned some Moroccan Arabic and Persian.

Marcel was acquainted with Violet-le-Duc, and he worked for four years under him in the commission of historic monuments. He traveled widely in that assignment and Jane went with him: England, Italy, Spain, Upper Egypt, and Morocco.

In 1880 Marcel left his post and requested an unpaid assignment in Persia. There, he intended to investigate the question of a link supposed to connect Oriental and gothic art. Jane accompanied him, of course. She was fascinated by everything about Persia: history, handicrafts, ethnology, economics, archaeology — everything. She kept a diary of the expedition and photographed and processed the film on the spot.

Both of the Dieulafoys, but Marcel in particular, were intrigued by the site of the City of Shushan, or Susa, and when they returned to France they applied to the French government for money and supplies to provision an expedition to do archaeological research at Susa. They also sought international protection so that the Persian government wouldn't interfere with their the research. In 1884 they returned to Persia with an engineer and a naturalist. Marcel was more interested in the architecture of the ruins, particularly the great columned hall, than in collecting objects.

Mixed with a hard soil, stratified materials of a different nature are distinguished. First of all, bricks of terra-cotta appear.

On the face of some I fancy I recognize the striated horn of an animal of great size, and a foot provided with claws. Others, but very few, are covered with a friable enamel which comes off and falls into dust. The design, surrounded by a partition, remains incomprehensible. Are these flowers, are these animals which reappear under my eyes? What *decadent* law does this fantastic flora or fauna obey? The fragments of bas-reliefs are employed like common ashlars.

Behind the first layer I perceive, regularly ranged in line, rough blocks of faïence, fourteen inches long, seven inches thick and wide. Invisible fissures separate these materials; when they are touched they break and crumble. One, two, three *ashlars* are cautiously taken out; then there appear, on the surface in contact with the pulverized brick-pavement, blue and green triangles intersected by white triangles. The design is continued with perfect regularity.

The second line shows yellow bands, terminated by curls joined to the base of a white palm-leaf. Continuing our excavation, we reach the palm-leaves, which recall a well-known Greek ornament, then a new line of blue and green denticules surmounted by a double green and yellow fillet.

The whole forms a complete frieze, about twenty-eight inches high, but the length of which cannot be estimated, for the "vein" which extends, parallel or perpendicular to the façade of the palace, penetrates obliquely into the sides of the trench. Can we have hit upon the doors so long sought for? Marcel is radiant.

The excavation promises to be a long and difficult operation; the bricks are so jammed together as to penetrate into each other. The materials of terra-cotta are still taken out without injury; but when we get at the blocks of faïence, we do not know from what side to attack them; more especially as the enamel always presents itself face to the ground, as the white facing of the joints and the back alone appears, and as the design is shown at the moment when the material falls to pieces. Each attempt causes us fresh apprehensions, and the heart beats a tattoo as long as the restored block is not laid out in the basket [*At Susa*, pp. 100–101].

Marcel's great work, *L'art antique de la Perse*, five volumes in folio and illustrated with photographs, won him great recognition. Jane published a diary of the expedition in *Le tour du monde*, which also attracted significant recognition. Jane also prepared the exhibition of the monuments in the Louvre; two rooms were named for her. In 1886 she was given the Legion of Honor in recognition of her work.

In addition to being involved in publication of the results of their expeditions, Jane embarked on writing novels. Her first historical novel, *Parysatis* (Paris, 1890), inspired by the history of Susa, won the prize from the Académie Française. She wrote several other historical novels and a psychological novel.

The Dieulafoys were active in the cultural life of Paris, but they continued their interest in historical and archaeological research, making frequent trips to Spain and Morocco. Jane expanded her literary output to include historical, geographical, and biographical works on Spain.

In 1913–1914 she campaigned for women to be allowed to serve in military auxiliary services. In 1914 Marcel was assigned to public works in the corps of engineers at Rabat; Jane directed excavations at the 12th-century mosque near Rabat.

She died in 1916.

SOURCES: *At Susa*; Internet Articles: "Jane Dieulafoy" by Jean Calmard; "Marcel Dieulafoy" by Pierre Amiet. Both at www.iranica.com/articles.

WORKS

Dieulafoy, Jane. *At Susa, the Ancient Capitol of the Kings of Persia: Narrative of Travel through Western Persia and Excavations Made at the Site of the Lost City of the Lilies, 1884–1886.* Translated by Frank L. White. Philadelphia: Gebbie & Company, 1890. A translation of *A Suse,* 1888.

Charlotte Anne Albinia Disbrowe

The storm continued to increase as the day wore on, yet no one as far as I knew anticipated any danger for the vessels in the harbour. We retired to bed, but at about ten o'clock the noise of the wind and waves became terrific. I was sleeping in the stern cabin with my governess and the maids, the rest of the family being in the saloon. The first warning I received of any danger was when the nurse rushed in and said, "You must all get up and dress, for we are all going to the bottom." I scrambled into my clothes as best I could and joined my mother in the saloon. She was sitting in her berth with her two baby boys in her arms, one seventeen months old, the other only three months. She was nursing them both as calmly and tranquilly as if in her own house. My sister, a very little girl, was lying half-asleep in the next berth, my aunt with her. I lay down on the floor at my mother's feet, our governess and the nurse sat by the table. My mother's maid was helping everybody. She was wonderfully courageous when there was any danger, but full of needless alarm when there was no cause for it. She was engaged to our butler, and in the middle of the night he rushed into the saloon in small attire, threw his arms round her neck, and said, "Harriet, my dear, good-bye for ever." Her touching retort was, "You old fool, go to bed, and leave me to take care of the children," which speech had the desired effect, for he returned to his own berth. We passed many a weary hour in hoping and fearing. My father looked in upon us every now and then, but did not dare to leave the deck for long at a time.

The sailors were in open mutiny, and he alone was able to keep some order. They had proclaimed him captain, and he told them his first order was for them to obey Captain Allen. Part of the time was spent by him and the French cook and English footman with their backs to the spirit-room door, each with a pistol in his hand, because the crew had threatened to break in and die drunk....

During the storm the captain had been seen close to the last remaining hawser, apparently in the act of cutting it, having quite lost his head. Whether the lurch of the vessel was the cause of his falling overboard, or whether he was pushed over will never be known, anyway, overboard he went, and was rescued by two of our gallant tars without being recognized. It was not until they had got him down to the cabin that they found out who he was, and then some regrets were expressed that it was not known sooner whom they were saving!...

Thinking of it now, I must say it was wonderful that of all our large party only one should have lost his presence of mind — the love-sick butler. I am proud to say *his*, for *all* the women were calm and collected [*Unsuitable for Ladies*, pp. 76–78].

WORKS

Disbrowe, Charlotte. *Old Days in Diplomacy: Recollections of a Closed Century.* London: Jarrold & Sons, 1903. This recounts Disbrowe's experiences in the earlier 1800s; her father was in the diplomatic service.

BOOKS ABOUT OR INCLUDING CHARLOTTE DISBROWE

Robinson, Jane, ed. *Unsuitable for Ladies: An Anthology of Women Travelers.* Oxford: Oxford University Press, 1994.

Mrs. Anne Disbrowe

WORKS

Mrs. Anne Disbrowe & Charlotte Anne Albinia Disbrowe. *Original Letters from Russia 1825–1828.* London: Ladies' Printing Press, 1878.

Lady Florence Douglas Dixie,

1857–1905. British.

Florence and her twin, James, were the youngest of six children of Archibald William Douglas, the seventh Marquis of Queensbury, and Caroline Margaret Clayton, who was from a distinguished military family. The Marquis had a notable history, and the Douglas clan was an old Scots family.

It was Florence's nephew Alfred Douglas who was Oscar Wilde's lover; her brother John Sholto, the eighth Marquis of Queensbury, was Wilde's opponent in the infamous lawsuit.

When she was three, her father fatally shot himself while cleaning a gun. Subsequently, her mother converted to Catholicism, which so angered the children's guardians that they threatened to take the children away from Lady Douglas; women at that time had no legal rights with respect to their children. Lady Douglas fled to France, taking Florence and James with her. They stayed in France for two years, and then returned to England, where Florence was enrolled in a convent school.

Florence always had a strong streak of defiance; she hated the school and missed her twin. Within a year she and James joined her mother for an extended tour of the Continent, and the family moved about for the next five years. At some point during this time one of her brothers (not James) was killed in the first English attempt to scale the Matterhorn.

Florence began writing poetry when she was about ten and completed her first volume, *Songs of a Child,* by the time she was seventeen. She continued to write throughout her life, publishing novels, poems, plays, travel books, political books, articles, and pamphlets.

She met Alexander Beaumont Churchill Dixie when she was eleven. He was seventeen, a tall, handsome young midshipman, and he promised to marry her and travel with her around the world. And he did! They married in 1875.

They had two sons; George Douglas was born in 1876 and Albert Edward Wolston Beaumont in 1878.

Marriage and motherhood exacerbated Florence's — Lady Dixie's — anger and resentment of the position of women in Britain. Shortly after her marriage, Lady Dixie published a blank verse tragedy *Isola; or the Disinherited: a Revolt for Woman and All the Disinherited,* published in 1902. Clearly Lady Dixie was not going to settle into a conventional pattern of marriage and motherhood.

Wanting adventure and an escape from civilization, Florence organized a trip to Patagonia, selected for its isolation and lack of visitors. Beau, two of her brothers, and J. Beerbohm, a naturalist and author of *Wanderings in Patagonia,* went with her. It was an adventurous trip, camping, riding, hunting for food, and Lady Dixie relished all of it. They were gone for six months.

> Accordingly ... we said goodbye-to the plains, and fording the stream which flowed down the valley, we entered on the winding ravine, full of curiosity as to what kind of country we were now to break in upon.
> The ravine is in itself a fit preparation for something strange and grand. Its steep slopes towered up on either side of us to an immense height; and the sunlight being thus partially excluded, a mysterious gloom reigned below, which, combined with the intense, almost painful silence of the spot, made the scene inexpressibly strange and impressive. Its effect was intensified by the knowledge that since these gigantic solitudes had been fashioned by nature, no human eye had ever beheld them.
> We hurried on, anxious to reach the mouth of the ravine, and behold the promised land as soon as possible, but several hours elapsed before we at last reached its farther end, and emerged from its comparative gloom into the sunshine of the open. A

glance showed us that we were in a new country. Before us stretched a picturesque plain, covered with soft green turf, and dotted here and there with clumps of beeches, and crossed in all directions by rippling streams. The background was formed by thickly-wooded hills, behind which again towered the Cordilleras — three tall peaks of a reddish hue, and in shape exact facsimiles of Cleopatra's Needle, being a conspicuous feature in the landscape.

Numerous small lagoons, covered with wild-fowl of strange and novel appearance, frequently came in our way, and by their shores basked hundreds of the lovely white swans whose species I have already mentioned. Unlike their comrades of the plains they appeared perfectly tame, merely waddling into the water when we approached close up alongside them, and never once attempting to fly away. I was greatly struck by the thousands of ducks and geese that covered these lakes [*Across Patagonia*, pp. 163–165].

We were in the saddle early the next morning, and, plunging into the woods, pursued our way through the same difficulties which had hampered our progress the day before. After a time, however, we came to a region evidently much frequented by wild horses, and eventually we hit on a path worn by them right through the woods, and following this, we jogged along at a very fair pace. Soon our horses began to neigh and prick up their ears as we advanced towards a clearing. Their cries were answered from somewhere beyond us, and pushing forward into the open, we came upon a herd of wild horses, who, hearing our advance, had stopped grazing, and now they stood collected in a knot together, snorting and stamping, and staring at us in evident amazement. One of their number came boldly trotting out to meet us, and evidently with no pacific intentions; his wicked eye, and his white teeth, which he had bared fiercely, looked by no means reassuring. But suddenly he stopped short, looked at us for a moment, and then, with a wild snort, dashed madly away, followed by the whole herd. They disappeared like lightning over the brow of a deep ravine, to emerge again

on our view after a couple of seconds, scampering like goats up its opposite side, which rose almost perpendicular to a height of six or seven hundred feet. They reached its crest at full gallop in the twinkling of an eye, and without pausing an instant disappeared again, leaving us wondering and amazed at their marvelous agility. I had often seen their paths leading up hill-sides which a man could scarcely climb, but till now that I had witnessed a specimen of their powers with my own eyes, I had scarcely been able to believe them possessed of a nimbleness and cleverness of foot which would not discredit a chamois [pp. 196–197].

When they returned she wrote *Across Patagonia*, recounting the trip; once she finished the book she was ready for new adventure as well as a serious outlet for her energy and convictions. Within a year she was planning a trip to cross the Bering Straits and spend the winter on the Arctic shores. This time she thought she would study the people of the Arctic.

Before she could leave, though, war broke out between the British and Dutch settlers in Southern Africa. With Florence Nightingale in mind, Lady Dixie decided instead to go to South Africa, where she would nurse the wounded on the field of battle. The editor of the *Morning Post* asked her to serve as a special correspondent. Consequently she, Beau, and a servant sailed to South Africa, arriving at Cape Town in March 1881 only to learn of the third British defeat in the war. They spent four days sightseeing, during which time Lady Dixie met the captive Zulu king Cetshwayo. He had been portrayed in the press as bloodthirsty and a tyrant; Dixie did not find those characteristics in him, and when he urged her to visit his land and consider his people vis-à-vis the British, Dixie agreed.

This was a turning point for her. Dixie and Beau began their trip to the war front, with Dixie sending dispatches of their travels across South Africa. They were startled by the news that the British had signed a peace agreement with the victorious Boers, which left Lady Dixie a war correspondent without a war. Regardless, Lady Dixie began her trip to Zululand, a rough, difficult journey.

In the course of her travels in South Africa, she became a passionate advocate of Cetshwayo and the Zulu. Her articles advocating Cetshwayo's reinstatement as king were published as *A Defense of Zululand and Its King: Echoes from the Blue Books* in 1882. The book was controversial and Lady Dixie was criticized for not presenting all the facts, but instead presenting a plea similar to that of a defending lawyer. She saw and presented Cetshwayo as a tragic figure; many others continued to see him as a brutal tyrant.

Cetshwayo came to England in August 1882 for two months of meetings with the Queen, various officials and the British public. Meanwhile, Florence was writing *In the Land of Misfortune* about her trip and about her increased involvement in the issues of South Africa.

Her political activism became the center of her life. She was involved with suffrage, animal rights, legal reform, and Irish Home Rule. Although in her early days she was proud of her hunting prowess, later she spoke out against "any sort or form of sport which is produced by the suffering of animals."

She was particularly interested in women's rights and changes in laws governing property, child custody and inheritance. She wanted absolute equality of the sexes, with the same occupations and professions open to both boys and girls, and she felt strongly that schooling should be co-educational. To illustrate and further her views on this matter, she wrote a novel, *Gloriana, or the Revolution of 1900*, which was published in about 1890. With respect to the throne, peerage, and estates, she felt that inheritance should go to the eldest child, not the eldest son.

Her views provoked strong reactions. She received a letter bomb, and one day when she was walking her dog behind her home in Windsor, she was physically attacked by two men. One of them stabbed her, but the steel stays of her corset helped protect her. She was only saved by her dog pulling off one of the attackers.

In the mid–1880s, Beau, who had always gambled on horses, sustained a severe loss that changed the couple's financial state and forced him to give up his extravagant lifestyle. Both Florence and Beau were in ill health during this time. Then, in 1891, James, her much loved twin, committed suicide.

To help their financial situation, Dixie wrote novels that drew on her childhood and life as a traveler. She also wrote children's books. Not surprisingly, the female protagonists in all her fiction defy gender stereotypes.

Florence Dixie died of diphtheria on November 7, 1905. Her last novel, uncompleted, was published the next year.

Her obituary in *The Times* of London had this to say about her: "Though evidently convinced of the truth and righteousness of her somewhat peculiar views, Lady Florence Dixie had an attractive and attaching personality, and a large circle of friends and neighbours mourn her premature death."

Beau died in 1924. He apparently remarried, as his obituary lists him as being twice married and survived by his wife and sons.

SOURCE: Stevenson: "*Victorian Women Travel Writers in Africa.*" The Times (London), Nov. 8, 1905; Aug. 22, 1924.

WORKS

In addition to her travel books, Florence Douglas Dixie wrote novels, books on political and social topics, and poetry.

Dixie, Florence. *Across Patagonia.* London: Richard Bentley and Son, 1880.

_____. *In the Land of Misfortune.* London: Richard Bentley and Son, 1882.

Lady Lucie Austin Duff Gordon, 1821–1869. British.

Lucie was born in Westminster, England, in 1821, the only child of John and Sarah Austin. Her father, John Austin, was known for his writing on jurisprudence, and if it hadn't been for poor health, he might have been a significant figure in law. Her mother, who was fond of society, had a keen intellect.

Lucie grew up in a house where her near neighbors were James Mill and Jeremy Bentham. Lucie's best friend was John Stuart Mill. The Austin home was a gathering for writers and radical thinkers. Lucie was a tremendously independent and courageous child, traits that stayed with her throughout her life. Her education was random, but she read avidly and traveled frequently with her family, first to Germany in 1826, where she absorbed the language. In 1833 the Austins, suffering from financial problems, went to live in Boulogne. When her father was appointed commissioner to Malta, Lucie was sent to boarding school. In 1838 her parents returned to England.

Lucie met Sir Alexander Duff Gordon at her first ball; they were married in 1840. Sir Alexander had little money, and Lucie had no dowry. Like her mother, Lucie was a notable hostess, and her guests included the leading literary figures of the day. She began to earn money by translating German texts. This, essentially her first writing career, lasted from 1844 to 1861.

Their first child, Janet, was born in 1842; Maurice was born in 1849. At some time during those years a black Nubian boy about twelve years old came to live with the Duff Gordons. A former slave, he was going blind. He was a much loved member of the household, where he lived until his death in 1850.

By this time Lucie was suffering from the effects of consumption. Financial difficulties were increasing, and in 1857 the family moved to Paris. Returning to England a year later, Lucie had a third child. In July 1861, Lucie went to South Africa, where she hoped the warm climate would improve her health. She returned to England in July 1862, but by the fall she was in Egypt, where she lived until her death in 1869. She is best known for her letters home, which were subsequently published by her family.

SOURCE: *Dictionary of Literary Biography.*

The cataract is very bad this year, owing to want of water in the Nile, and to the shameful conduct of the Maohn here. The cataract men come to me and pray me to "give them my voice" before the Mudir, which I will do. Ala Eddeen Bey seems a decent fellow, and perhaps will remove the rascal, whose robberies on travellers are notorious, and his oppression of the poor savages who pull up the boats odious. Two boats have been severely damaged, and my friend the reis of the cataract (the one I threatened to shoot last year, and who has believed in me ever since) does not advise me to go up, though he would take me for nothing, he swears, if I wished. So as the air is good here, and M — — is happy with his companions, I will stay here [*Last Letters from Egypt*, p. 181].

Yesterday was a real African summer's day. The D — — s had a tent and an awning, one for food and the other for drink, on the ground where the shooting [*hunting*] took place. At twelve o'clock Mrs. D — — went down to sell cool chickens, &c. and I went with her, and sat under a tree in the bed of the little stream, now nearly dry. The sun was such as in any other climate would strike you down, but here *coup de soleil* is unknown. It broils you till your shoulders ache and your lips crack, but it does not make you feel the least languid, and you perspire very little; nor does it tan the skin as you would expect. The light of the sun is by no means "golden" — it is pure white — and the slightest shade of a tree or bush affords a delicious temperature, so light and fresh is the air. They said the thermometer was at about 130° where I was walking yesterday, but (barring the scorch) I could not have believed it [*Last Letters*, pp. 252–253].

WORKS

Duff Gordon, Lucie. *Letters from Egypt, 1862–1863.* London: Macmillan, 1865.

_____. *Last Letters from Egypt. To Which Are Added, Letters from the Cape.* With a memoir by her daughter, Mrs. Ross. London: Macmillan, 1875. *Letters from the Cape* was first published in *Vacation Tourists and Notes of Travel in 1862–1863*, edited by Francis Galton, London, 1864.

Isabelle Eberhardt, 1877–1904.

Isabelle Eberhardt's childhood was chaotic. Her mother was married to a Russian general and had three children by him. The general employed a tutor, Trophimovsky. Eventually Isabelle's mother left her husband and fled Russia with the tutor, taking her three children with her. The household lived various places in Europe, Istanbul and Naples. Isabelle was born February 1877, in Geneva; she was Trophimovsky's child. She was given the surname Eberhardt, which was her mother's maiden name.

Trophimovsky was eccentric, erratic and a tyrant. The children were not allowed to leave the house and property and were compelled to labor on the farm. They came to hate Trophimovsky. Isabelle's sister escaped his tyranny by marrying a laborer. Isabelle's escape was travel.

Isabelle traveled through North Africa as a Muslim convert, dressed as a man and calling herself Si Mahmoud. The Arab world at that time was shifting from colonial attachments to national consciousness and independence. Isabelle apparently took no interest in these events. Her diary is meditative and explores her inner person rather than the countryside.

She made two trips to North Africa. From the first she was enchanted with the exotic lifestyles and the freedom from home and family obligations. She returned to Geneva, but soon left to go back to North Africa, too impatient to wait several weeks for a substantial inheritance.

> Once again the small train moves slowly through the desert. Stations pass after long stops. Djenien-bou-Rezg, the burning plain, a huge reddish fortress, several scattered huts.
>
> Now it is Duveyrier, the Arab Zoubia, in its amphitheater of hills, of black rocks.
>
> Not long ago the Saharan train used to stop there, and the new village, complete European, had grown from this traffic. Low houses, painted with grayish clay, multiplied with the songs of the Legion's exiles; canteens and bars opened, hovels made of planks and old gasoline drums; a courageous duenna had even brought several worn ladies of the night, rejects from the den of Saida and Sidi-bel-Abbes.
>
> Strings of camels knelt in the sandy streets before going to supply the remote outposts of the South.
>
> Duveyrier was the source of this river of abundance flowing toward the Sahara. An apparent prosperity reigned there for several months. People were getting rich, coming from just about everywhere, drawn by the lure of an easy if troubled traffic in goods....
>
> Then, one day, the stubborn little railroad — two iron rails that took off, gleaming and alone, across the desert — went beyond Duveyrier to stop farther on, across from the enchanting Figuig. Overnight another village sprang up, precocious as the grasses of the Sahara after the first winter

rains. And the short-lived existence of Duveyrier ended, displaced by the newcomer: Beni-Ounifof-Figuig.

Today, in the iridescent light of the morning, Duveyrier seems prematurely abandoned: houses with new walls, but no roofs, the black empty sockets of gaping doors and windows; the merchants have taken away all that they could — girders, boards, crossbeams, tiles — in their hasty exodus. The closed or disemboweled bars are already falling into ruin and filling up with sand. It seems like some calamity — fire or flood — has befallen this new-born market town and returned it to the silence of the desert.

There is poignant sadness to this corner of the world, an abandoned ruin [*Departures*, pp. 93–94].

Isabelle was an unstable woman. She spent her money on drugs and became a homeless addict who begged food. Her diary was written during her final months, when she was an outcast from both the expatriate European society that would not recognize her conversion to Islam, and the Arab society where posing as a man barred her from formal contact with women. She died at age 28 in a flash flood.

SOURCE: *Destiny of Isabelle Eberhardt.*

WORKS

Eberhardt, Isabelle. *Dans l'ombre chaude de l'Islam. La Tragique de la bonne nomade por Réné-Louis Doyon.* Paris: La Connaissance, 1923.

_____. *Departures: Selected writings / Isabelle Eberhardt.* Translated and edited by Karim Hamdy and Laura Rice. San Francisco: City Lights Books, 1994.

_____. *Notes du Route; Maroc-Algérie-Tunisse, publiées avec une preface par Victor Bairucand.* Paris: Librairie Charpentier et Fasquelle, 1923.

BOOKS ABOUT OR INCLUDING ISABELLE EBERHARDT

Kobak, Annette. *Isabelle: The Life of Isabelle Ebrhardt.* New York: Vintage, 1990.

Mackworth, Cecily. *Destiny of Isabelle Eberhardt.* London: Routledge and Kegan Paul, Ltd., 1951.

Amelia Ann Blanford Edwards,
1831–1892. British.

Amelia Edwards, an only child, was educated at home by her mother. She was always interested in art. She wrote and she studied music, not only the playing of music but its harmony and counterpoint. She did amateur acting as well.

In 1860, when she was 29, her parents died within one week of each other, and she was left to support herself. She'd already sold some of her articles and stories, and she'd translated an account by Fanny Loviot, a young French woman, of her captivity at the hands of Chinese pirates. Writing seemed the logical way to support herself, and Amelia wrote books of various types and subjects, including several romantic novels in the traditional three-volume form. One of her favorite narrators was a mid-century male traveler wandering around Europe. Her writing gave her enough money to finance some travel for herself.

Her first adventurous journey was in 1872, when she traveled with a female companion through the Dolomites in southeastern Tyrol. This was difficult terrain, and travel was only by foot or mule.

The next year she took her first trip to Egypt, and from then on Egypt was her passion. She traveled up the Nile in a dahabeeyah, stopping at ruins along the way where she drew and copied many of the paintings and hieroglyphs. She then crossed Syria and returned up the western Mediterranean.

When she returned to England she began her Egyptian studies in earnest, studying in libraries and museums and learning the hieroglyphic characters. Her purpose was to write knowledgeably about her experiences; *A Thousand Miles Up the Nile,* which took two years to write, was the result.

We found the new tomb a few hundred yards in the rear of the Ramesseum. The diggers were in the pit; the governor and a few Arabs were looking on. The vault was lined with brickwork above, and cut square in the living rock below. We were just in time; for already, through the sand and rubble with which the grave had been filled in, there appeared an outline of something buried. The men, throwing spades and picks aside, now began scraping up the dust with their hands, and a mummy-case came gradually to light. It was shaped to represent a body lying at length with the hands crossed upon the breast. Both hands and face were carved in high relief. The ground-colour of the sarcophagus was white; the surface covered with hieroglyphed legends and somewhat coarsely painted figures of the four lesser Gods of the Dead. The face, like the hands, was coloured a brownish yellow and highly varnished. But for a little dimness of the gaudy hues, and a little flaking off of the surface here and there, the thing was as perfect as when it was placed in the ground. A small wooden box roughly put together lay at the feet of the mummy. This was taken out first, and handed to the Governor, who put it aside without opening it. The mummy-case was then raised upright, hoisted to the brink of the pit, and laid upon the ground.

It gave one a kind of shock to see it first of all lying just as it had been left by the mourners; then hauled out by rude hands, to be searched, unrolled, perhaps broken up as unworthy to occupy a corner in the Boulak collection. Once they are lodged and catalogued in a museum, one comes to look upon these things as "specimens," and forgets that they once were living beings like ourselves. But this poor mummy looked startlingly human and pathetic lying at the bottom of its grave in the morning sunlight [*A Thousand Miles Up the Mile*, pp. 606–607].

It is fine to see the sunrise on the front of the Great Temple [*at Aboo Simbal*]; but something still finer takes place on certain mornings in the year, in the very heart of the mountain. As the sun comes up above the eastern hill-tops, one long, level beam strikes through the doorway, pierces the inner darkness like an arrow, penetrates to the sanctuary, and falls like fire from heaven upon the latter at the feet of the gods.

No one who has watched for the coming of that shaft of sunlight can doubt that it was a calculated effect, and that the excavation was directed at one especial angle in order to produce it. In this way Ra, to whom the temple was dedicated, may be said to have entered in daily, and by a direct manifestation of his presence to have approved the sacrifices of his worshippers [pp. 443–444].

The wanton destruction of antiquities disturbed her, and she decided the only remedy was scientific excavation. To this end she drew up circulars and appealed to the press. The result was the founding of the Egypt Exploration Fund in 1882, which sought to promote academic and scientific expertise. Amelia gave popular lectures, even touring the United States, to help the Egypt Exploration Fund.

The Egypt Exploration Fund was largely the result of her planning and promotion. Amelia became secretary of the fund. She didn't promote or suggest women archaeologists, but she focused on the professional interests of the fund. As the fund became established she was ousted from the decision-making process and relegated to doing most of the administrative work, which included much correspondence.

In 1889 she was invited by twenty-five college presidents and well known literary men to come to the United States on a lecture tour; she gave 120 public lectures. These were collected in *Pharaohs, Fellahs, and Explorers*, which she saw as a means of reaching more people and calling attention to the need for scientific inquiry and conversation on the antiquities. In recognition of her founding of the fund and her work with Egyptology, she received honorary degrees from several American universities, including the first doctor of laws given a woman in the United States. She received no academic recognition in Britain.

She died in 1892, a week after the death of a close female friend with whom she had been living. She bequeathed a chair of Egyptology to University College, London.

SOURCE: *Dictionary of Literary Biography*, Volume 174.

WORKS

Edwards, Amelia. *Pharaohs, Fellahs and Explorers*. London: Osgood & McLain, 1891. Also published as *Egypt and Its Monuments*. New York: Harper, 1891.
_____. *Sights and Stories. Being Some Account of a Holiday Tour Through the North of Belgium*. London: Faithful, 1862.
_____. *A Thousand Miles Up the Nile*. London: Longman, 1877.
_____. *Untrodden Peaks and Unfrequented Valleys: A Midsummer Ramble in the Dolomites*. London: Longman, 1873. Also published as *A Midsummer Ramble in the Dolomites*. London: Routledge, 1889.
Loviot, Fanny. *A Lady's Captivity Among the Chinese Pirates in the Chinese Seas*. Translated from the French by Amelia Edwards. London: G. Routledge & Co., 1858.

In addition to her travel books, Amelia Edwards wrote several novels, including *Barbara's History* (1864), *Debenhams's Vow* (1870), a history of France, ballads, and stories.

BOOKS ABOUT OR INCLUDING AMELIA EDWARDS

Moon, Brenda. *More Usefully Employed: Amelia B. Edwards, Writer, Traveller and Campaigner for Ancient Egypt*. London: Egypt Exploration Society, 2006.
Amelia Edwards left her Egyptological logical library and collections to University College, London, and her personal library to Somerville Hall, Oxford.

Anna Katharine Curtis Elwood, 1796–1873.

She is sometimes listed as Mrs. Colonel Elwood.

Anna was the seventh of ten children. Her father was a classical scholar, writer, and a member of parliament. She and Charles William Elwood married in 1824. At that time he was a major with the East India Company; he later became a lieutenant colonel. In 1825 Anna and Charles set out for India, where he had previously served. She was, she thought, "the first and only female who has hitherto ventured over-land from England to India" [*Narrative*, Vol. 1, p. vi]. However, Eliza Fay had preceded her in 1794.

The trip to India was leisurely. As they traveled through Europe they took time to view the sights. They sailed to Egypt in April 1826, and sailed up the Nile as far as Luxor. They then proceeded from Luxor to Bombay, traveling by land and sea, a trip that took over two months. They stayed in India until 1828, when they sailed for England via Ceylon, the Cape of Good Hope, and St. Helena.

Mrs. Elwood was travelling in her takhtrouan, which she described.

The body of it was about six feet long, and three broad, composed of a curiously-heavy-painted open wood-work, something like the Mameluke windows; and in this I lay as in a palanquin, which it a little resembled. This was placed upon shafts, and carried by camels, one going in front, the other behind, as in a sedan-chair; the latter having its head tied down, in order that it might see where it stepped; and when they were in harness, it was raised nearly six feet from the ground. Strange-looking creatures are camels to an English eye, and a fearful noise do they make to an English ear; they stretch out their long necks one way, and they poke them out another, and there is no knowing where one is safe from them; and I was to mount a litter conveyed by these singular productions of nature, probably the first and only Englishwoman that ever ventured in a native Egyptian Takhtrouan! My heart failed me terribly this instant, I cannot but confess, and I was nervously alarmed at the sight of my unwieldly vehicle [*Unsuitable for Ladies*, p. 142].

When she couldn't find any published biography of literary women, Mrs. Elwood wrote her own. *Memoirs of the Literary Ladies of England from the Commencement of the Last Century,* which appeared in 1841, included Lady Mary Wortley Montagu, Hannah More, Mary Wollstonecraft, Jane Austen, and Mrs. Radcliffe among its twenty-nine subjects. The book is a mixture of biography and personal commentary; given the period in which she wrote it, Mrs. Elwood probably knew some of the women or their relatives.

The Elwoods had no children. Charles Elwood died in 1860. Anne Elwood died in 1873.

SOURCE: *Dictionary of National Biography.*

WORKS

Elwood, Anne. *Narrative of a Journey Overland from England by the Continent of Europe, Egypt, and the Red Sea to India, Including a Residence There and Voyage Home in the Years 1825, 26, 27, and 28.* London: Colburn & Bentley, 1830.

BOOKS ABOUT OR INCLUDING ANNE KATHARINE ELWOOD

Robinson, Jane. *Unsuitable for Ladies: An Anthology of Women Travelers.* Oxford: Oxford University Press, 1994.

Anna Maria Falconbridge,
1769–? British.

Anna Maria was born in Bristol in 1769. In 1788 she married Alexander Falconbridge, a prominent abolitionist. As an agent of the St. George's Bay Company he was sent to Sierra Leone to reorganize the settlement of freed slaves in Freetown. In her book, compiled from letters, Anna Maria explained the reason for the first trip and incidentally gave us some curious infor-

mation about herself. She was reluctant to leave England.

> The thoughts of it damp my spirits more than you can imagine, but I am resolved to summon all the fortitude I can, being conscious of meriting the reproaches of my friends and relations, for having hastily married as I did contrary to their wishes, and am determined rather than be an encumbrance on them, to accompany my husband even to the wilds of Africa, whither he is now bound, and meet such fate as awaits me....
> Mr. Falconbridge is employed by the St. George's Bay Company to carry out some relief for a number of unfortunate people, both blacks and whites, whom Government sent to the river Sierra Leone, a few years since, and who in consequence of having had some dispute with the natives, are scattered through the country, and are just now as I have been told, in the most deplorable condition.
> He [Mr. Falconbridge] is likewise to make some arrangements for collecting those poor creatures again, and forming a settlement which the companies have in contemplation to establish, not only to serve them, but to be generally useful to the natives [*Two Voyages,* pp. 9–10].

They set off in January 1791, and by mid–February, a passage of eighteen days, they had arrived. The voyage didn't go well, and things didn't improve when they arrived. There were disagreements among the members of the company, with confusion and disarray. They resolved to leave as soon as possible, as matters seemed to be deteriorating, with much sickness and several deaths among the party. Few provisions were available for going to sea, but they were told that the rains would grow worse and that every day they delayed would only make it more dangerous to get off the coast. The trip back was a nightmare, with food a serious problem.

> Upon enquiring into the state of our provisions, we found they had been lavishly dealt with; there was not more than one

week's full allowance of meat, and scarcely four days of flour remaining.

These were alarming circumstances, for we had two thirds further to go, than we had then come, toward Saint Jago.... What would have been more dreadful, we should have wanted water, was it not for the rains; the worms having imperceptibly penetrated our water casks, all the water leaked out, except a small cask, which would not allow us more than a pint each, for three weeks.

My tea-cup of flour, mixed with a little rain water and salt, [boiled] to a kind of pap, when the weather would admit a fire, otherwise raw, was, believe me, all my nourishment for ten days, except once or twice, when some cruel unconscionable wretch robbed me of the homely morsel, I was forced to taste the beef [pp. 94–96].

By the end of September they were back in England.

The directors of the company increased Falconbridge's salary and gave the couple money in recognition for the services they had performed and as compensation for the loss of their clothes and goods.

They also wanted the Falconbridges to return to Sierra Leone. She resisted but felt so harassed by the company's continuing requests that she reluctantly agreed. They left in December and arrived in February 1792. Once again the voyage was miserable. They found their fellow passengers deplorable; worse, these were the representatives of the company who were to govern the colony. Then, after they arrived, Mr. Falconbridge received new instructions from the directors that reduced his authority and changed his assignment. The Falconbridges felt they had been enticed to Sierra Leone because he was the only person who could establish a footing for the company of Nova Scotia emigrants.

Falconbridge decided to pursue a "commercial career," that of a trader, and apparently had permission to do so. However,

when a ship from the company arrived at Sierra Leone, Falconbridge's appointment as commercial agent was annulled.

Falconbridge, although sick, was preparing for his trading voyage.

> I am certain it ("*the dismission*") proved a mortal stab to him; he was always addicted to drink more than he should; but after this by way of meliorating his harrowed feelings, he kept himself constantly intoxicated; a poor forlorn remedy you will say; however it answered his wish, which I am convinced was to operate as poison, and thereby finish his existence; he spun out his life in anguish and misery till the 19th instant, when without a groan he gasp'd his last!!!
>
> I will not be guilty of such meanness as to tell a fals[e]hood on this occasion, by saying I regret his death, no! I really do not, his life had become burthensome to himself and all around him, and his conduct to me, for more than two years past, was so unkind, (not to give a harsher term) as long since to wean every spark of affection or regard I ever had for him [pp. 169–170].

Matters in the area grow worse, with renegade seamen, slave trade, and great dissension among the members of the company and local officials.

Falconbridge died some time between September and late December 1792. In January 1793, Anna Maria remarried.

She and her new husband left Sierra Leone for Jamaica, where they stayed a short time. By October they were back in England, after a passage of nine and a half weeks from Jamaica.

WORKS

Falconbridge, Anna Maria. *Two Voyages to the Sierra Leone During the Years 1791–2-3, in a Series of Letters.* London: n.p., 1794. The second edition is entitled *Narrative of Two Voyages to the River Sierra Leone, During the Years 1791–1793 ... and Every Interesting Particular Relating to the Sierra Leone Company, also the Present State of the Slave Trade in the West Indies.* London: L. I. Higham, 1802.

Eliza Fay, 1756–1816. British.

Eliza may have been born at Black-heath. By 1783 her mother had died; her father, who may have been a sailor, died in 1794. Eliza had two sisters. We also know that her maiden name apparently began with C.

E. M. Forster, who wrote the introduction to Fay's *Original Letters from India,* speculated that her education may have been connected with dressmaking and France; she could speak some French; apparently she was adroit at picking up languages, as she spoke some Italian, Portuguese and Hindustani. She knew shorthand, and she liked music.

Her grasp of geography was less than rudimentary; she and her husband were horrified to find that crossing the Alps involved more than one mountain. But she wrote. Her grammar was eccentric at times, but she gave a vivid picture of her adventures, with little of the formality of much of the letter-writing at the time. There is much of Eliza in the letters. When she is telling her reader about the trip through France on the first voyage, she says that they have just arrived at Chantilly "where is a famous palace belonging to the Prince of Condé, but to my great mortification, I was through weariness [they had just traveled sixty miles without alighting from the coach] obliged to remain in the house while the rest of the party went to see it. Well never mind, you can read better descriptions of it, than mine would have been" [*Original Letters from India*, p. 37].

The book begins in spring of 1794; Eliza was twenty-three and recently married to Anthony Fay, of whom little is known. He had been called to the bar at Lincoln's Inn and was going to India to practice before the Supreme Court of Calcutta. The trip to India was a true adventure. When they arrived at Calicut, she and Fay were caught in the crossfire of politics and im-prisoned by Hyder Ali from early November until mid–February when they escaped. It was a grim, dangerous time, and the captivity was not a comfortable one — quite the contrary.

The fort must have been formerly a strong place, but is now in a dilapidated state — the walls are very thick and they mount guard regularly; which was one inducement for sending us here.... When I first arrived I was so extremely ill, as to be scarcely sensible of what passed for some hours; but I remember Hare burst into a violent flood of tears, declaring that we were all doomed to death by our removal to this wretched spot, which being completely surrounded by stagnant water, could not fail to produce some of those disorders so fatal to Europeans. We have not however hitherto experienced any complaint. The loft we sleep in is indeed disgusting beyond belief, and the Quelladar, I suppose at the suggestions of Fayres, has ordered the easier of the two ways of entrance, that discovered by Mr. F — to be blocked up. So that there is no way left but by means of a ladder placed almost in a perpendicular direction — there is a rope by which to hold, or it would be impossible for any person to descend, but even with this assistance, I have great difficulty to reach the bottom [p. 144].

Eliza was enterprising — more so than her husband.

I think I told you that, our watches were concealed in my hair, being secured with pins to prevent them from going; one of the pins however came out, at the very time I was set on shore. Never shall I forget what a terrible sensation the ticking of the watch caused! I think had it continued long, I must completely have lost my senses for I dared not remove it, from a fear of worse consequences; but happily it stopped of itself. When we were fixed in our prison Mr. Fay took these watches, (we had three you know) and all the money we had power to secure in chequins, which are of easy conveyance (about twenty-five pounds) and putting them into his glove, hid them in a snug place, as he thought about the Verandah. The day after we were taken prisoners, a most dreadful hurricane of rain and wind came in (it was the breaking up of the monsoon) and next morning we found to our extreme grief, that the place where Mr. Fay had concealed our treasure, to which alone we could look for the means of escape, was entirely blown down; and no vestige of our little property remaining. Mr. Fay was in despair from the first; but after he had told me, I searched diligently all round, but in vain. At length it struck me, from the direction in which the wind blew, that if I could make my way into an inclosure, at the back of he house, it might possibly be found there. The seapoys [sic] guarded the front, but there being only one door backwards, they seldom took the trouble of going round. I did not tell Mr. Fay of my scheme, as there was nothing he opposed so strongly, as the appearance of seeking to escape; but when he was completely absorbed in contemplating this new misfortune, I stole to the back door. There was a large lock and key inside and to my surprise when I had turned this, my passage was clear to the stairs, leading to the inclosure; and not a soul in sight. The grass was excessively high and wet, but I struggled to make my way through it and waded about, determined at least not to leave an inch unexplored. Imagine my joy when in the midst of a deep tuft I found the old glove with all its contents safe, and uninjured. What a treasure it seemed! [pp. 130–131].

Once they escaped and made there way to Calcutta, Fay eventually was admitted as an advocate and began to practice law. Matters did not go smoothly. Within two years he had run up considerable debt, alienated his professional colleagues and many of their friends, and produced an illegitimate child. Eliza left him, and with the help of friends, she supported herself by making mantuas.

Fay went back to England; by 1815 he had died.

In 1782 Eliza also went back to England. But in 1784 she was off again to Calcutta. She considered starting a semi-nary for young ladies, but that did not work out and she resumed her mantua and dressmaking trade. She was bankrupt in 1788.

In 1794 she returned to England, acquiring a financial interest in a boat, the *Minerva*, but the explosion of a bottle of aqua fortis set fire to the boat and it had to be scuttled.

The *Minerva* was repaired and Eliza went back to Calcutta, arriving in 1796, but only staying for six months. She acquired another boat, the *Rosalia*; her plan was to take expensive muslins to the United States — which would surely make her fortune. But almost immediately after the boat was launched (it didn't even reach the mouth of the river) it filled with water and the muslins were ruined.

By 1797 she was in New York; it's not clear how she arrived there.

Her letters then break off until 1815, when she was in Blackheath, probably living on her sister.

The next spring she went to Calcutta yet again. She died there in 1816.

SOURCE: Introductory notes by E. M. Forster and text.

WORKS

Fay, Eliza. *Original Letters from India, Containing a Narrative of a Journey Through Egypt, and the Author's Imprisonment at Calicut by Hyder Ally. To Which Is Added an Abstract of Three Subsequent Voyages to India.* Calcutta, India: 1817.

There have been several publications and editions, including:

Original Letters from India, 1779–1815. Calcutta, India: Thacker, Spink, 1908. Later, published London: L. & V. Woolf, 1925.

Also published with Introductory and Terminal Notes by E.M. Forster, author of *A Passage to India.* New York: Harcourt, Brace and Company, 1925.

Mrs. Bessie Knox Fenton,
?–1875. Irish.

Bessie Knox was born in Ireland, the daughter of a clergyman. We know little of her early life.

Her journal began in 1826 in India. At that time she was married to Niel Campbell. Her health was precarious, and Niel's death in the fall of 1827 devastated her. She mentions Fenton frequently in the journal as one of the party, a good friend who was very careful of her after Niel's death. Bessie married him in April or May 1828. By fall of 1828 they were preparing to leave India for Australia, where her brother lived.

They traveled to the Isle de France, present-day Mauritius. While there she met Robert Campbell, probably a relative of Niel, and she and Fenton made many friends.

Bessie was expecting a child and stayed at Government House at the Isle de France. They decided that Fenton would go on to Van Diemen's Land to convey their baggage and get settled, and Bessie would follow. Fenton left in mid–March 1829. Flora was probably born in early April. Bessie and Flora left Isle de France in June. After seven weeks they arrived at Hobarton, only to find that Fenton had left for the Isle de France to get her.

I had taken this miserable voyage in vain, and was alone in Van Diemen's Land, while Fenton was retracing the perilous sea I had just crossed [*Journal*, p. 341].

Fenton left a letter for her, in the event she arrived after he'd left, detailing arrangements for help, where she would live, money, and whom to rely on. A boat was sent after Fenton's ship — and because the ship had been delayed with bad weather, it reached the ship and retrieved Fenton, who returned to Hobarton soon after Bessie arrived!

They bought an estate, which they named Fenton Forest. The journal ends in mid December, 1830, with Bessie expect-

ing another child. Bessie died in 1875. Mr. Fenton had died several years earlier.

Bessie's extensive journal was considerably abridged for publication. The journal stops abruptly, with only a few additions. Bessie also kept a later journal for many years, but that has disappeared.

1st December [*1827*] . — On the Malda river. — I went to sleep on board my bamboo boat last night previous to my voyage, for I can call it nothing less.... I had to embark in a country boat so small I could hardly stand upright — indeed, I could not; but go I must, even in this boat, rather than wait. Besides my earnest desire to get to Calcutta, the inducement of Mrs. Grant being on the river at the same time was a great one; to have any recourse in case of sickness or accident, I regarded a most fortunate circumstance, being still dreadfully at a loss for the man George took with him to Calcutta.

I think I never before felt so low and heartsick as last night when I took possession of my floating habitation, for the first time in my life utterly alone, without a living soul who could understand one word I spoke. It was not in human nature to repress the sad remembrance and contrast of situation then with the time on which I first embarked on the Ganges accompanied by Niel and surrounded by every comfort [p. 146].

WORKS

Fenton, Bessie Knox. *The Journal of Mrs. Fenton, a Narrative of Her Life in India, the Isle of France-Mauritius-and Tasmania During the Years 1826–1830*. London: Edward Arnold, 1901.

Annabella Forbes (Mrs. Henry O.), Dutch? English?

Anna (as she refers to herself) made the journey to join her husband, who met her at Batavia. She liked the tropics from the beginning, and her letters are descriptive and convey her interest.

During their fifteen months of research they traveled from island to island, not staying long at any place. As the trip progressed she related,

> I am beginning to enter into the joys of a naturalist, and have grown quite learned in long names of birds and insects, and can help H. in labeling and arranging.... Strolling along the bay, on whose beach the east wind has been throwing a wealth of sponges, hydroids, and shells, we spend many hours examining them and watching the fields of shore-crabs, with their richly coloured pincer limbs and the curious fishes which come up out of the water and hop along the shore in their odd way [*Insulinde*, pp. 89–90].

They "settled" at the village of Ritabel and sought to build a house, but met with difficulties getting permission to build and disagreement about the location of the site. They had hoped to live outside the village, but found they could not do that. After almost three weeks they settled in their dwelling, which was close to the tide line and raised several feet off the ground, so that at high tide the waves could wash right under it. They then learned that their village was warring with neighboring villages.

> The Ritabel villagers seem perfectly well-disposed towards us, and without fear or suspicion, I was soon welcomed among them, and am allowed to carry the babies — good, interesting little creatures, profusely adorned with beads, and with their little limbs encased in a perfect buckler of shell bracelets: they wear a light shade of the chocolate skin which adorns their parents. I like to wander through the irregular paths intersecting the village, at sundown, when they are preparing the evening meal. Many of the mothers and maidens are stamping the Indian corn by the eaves, the fathers carry the infants, the young men dance on the shore, and the shouts of the children at play rings through the village [p. 155].

Fever then struck, and everyone in the party came down with it. Anna was the last to come down with it, and her case was particularly severe.

Several weeks after arriving in Ritabel, they left.

> I never seemed to realize until we were really off what a risk of life we have run; indeed I did not know it, for H. carefully concealed from me the reason of his nightly watches for the last six weeks. He professed that he slept in a chair to be ready to give me assistance while so weak, but the Kaleobar people had sent a threat that they were coming to attack our village, and it was to wait for them he sat. A small boat was hired and kept tied to the end of our house, and Lopez was instructed to take me across the strait, out of the fray, should the attack have been made before the steamer came [pp. 157–158].

Her health improved when they "settled" at Timor and she was able to join H. on the walks and collecting, but the fever would recur. Their house was in the hills, where the air was better. Anna stayed by herself for several weeks while H. went to the interior. She found the loneliness terrible — and the fever returned. The woman who had been hired to help her stopped coming, and she was isolated. She grew weaker and weaker. Finally someone came by and carried a message to the doctor, who came with a group of men to move her. They sent word to H., who rejoined her.

As the book ends, they are waiting for the steamer that will take them back to England.

SOURCE: *Insulinde: Experiences of a Naturalist's Wife in the Eastern Archipelago.*

WORKS

Forbes, Annabella. *Insulinde: Experiences of a Naturalist's Wife in the Eastern Archipelago.* Edinburgh: William Blackwood and Sons, 1887.

Margaret Fountaine, 1862–1940. British.

Margaret Fountaine was the second child and the oldest daughter of eight children. Her father was the rector of small parish near Norwich, and the family was comfortably well off. After her father died the family moved; Margaret and her sisters came out into society. When an unhappy love affair left her feeling depressed, Margaret decided to leave the cold climate (and the men who lived there) and go in search of blue skies and sunshine.

Her travels began in 1891, when she went to Switzerland. It was there that she began hunting and collecting butterflies, identifying her butterflies from a reference book. This became the focus of her life. For the rest of her life, with only occasional very short visits to family, she continued traveling and collecting, often in the company of gentlemen admirers. She loved the free life.

In 1901 when she was thirty-nine, she moved to the Middle East. There she hired an interpreter and guide, Kahlil Neimy. Kahlil, who was often referred to as Charles, had lived in the United States and spoke English. Kahlil/Charles fell in love with her; Margaret gradually came around and agreed to marry him. However, on a brief visit to England she found out that he already had a wife. She was disappointed and disillusioned, but she soon rejoined him.

Margaret's itineraries are wide-ranging. In 1903 she and Kahlil went to Asia Minor and North Africa, then Spain, Corsica, and the Balkans.

In 1908–09 they were in South Africa. The next year they went to America. They also went to Costa Rica, India, Ceylon, and the high passes of Himalaya, always in search of butterflies.

> We traveled inland to Stutterheim and a lovely forest clothing the greater part of a range of mountains. But a spell seemed to hang over it; the forest was haunted, I knew it from the first moment I entered it. Yet it was fascinating, with those dark silent kloofs rich in maidenhair fern where *Papilio Oppidicephalus*, the largest butterfly in South Africa, floated in majestic indifference up and down the watercourses. Then the cry of some wild beast (probably a baboon) would cause the creepy feeling to come back. It once gave Khalil such a fit of the scares that we both took to our heels and ran as fast as we could until we were both outside in the open meadows [*Love Among the Butterflies*, pp. 193–194].

> All the way, as the train crawled along through the darkness, Khalil was listening with big, frightened eyes to the farmer's lion stories, and I began to wonder if I had done right in compelling him to share these dangers; for myself I felt no fear. The empty farm was about half a mile from the station, and we walked through the starlit darkness over soft, sandy ground more or less on the edge of the bush, accompanied by the farmer, kaffir-boys, lanterns and dogs. The empty farm building was raised upon stone posts about six feet in height, leaving a space underneath. I passed a terrible night, lying on the floor, with nothing but the boards between me and the wild beasts that, when all was quiet and the farmer and his dogs were gone, came prowling under the house, grunting and growling all night. I longed to be with Khalil and as soon as there was the faintest indication of daybreak I put on my blue dressing-gown and went along the passage to his room, to find him wide awake; he had the additional terror of having no glass in his windows, so there was nothing to prevent a leopard from climbing the steps and jumping into his room. But now there was not a sign of wild animals to be seen. A heavy, white mist was enveloping the tropical world around us, while the dew was pouring from the roof of the house. I went back to bed and got two or three hours' sleep. That day we caught a fair amount of the much-coveted *Papilios* [p. 199].

The pair settled for three years in Australia, where they planned to buy land and raise horses while Khalil fulfilled his residence requirements for British citizenship.

Neither knew much about farming, and they didn't like the monotony and work. This was an unhappy time, and Khalil had periods of what appeared to be mental derangement.

In 1917 Margaret went to California by herself; in 1919 she was reunited with Khalil. Their last joint trip was an expedition to the Far East.

West Africa was Margaret's next objective, and she went on her own in 1926. Subsequently she received a commission to collect in the West Indies. While she was there Khalil, who was not with her, died.

Margaret kept traveling and collecting for another thirteen years. The story is that she died of a stroke in Trinidad while she was walking along a road, collecting, butterfly net in hand.

In her lifetime Margaret built up a useful collection of about 22,000 specimens, the Fountaine Neimy collection, now usually referred to as the Fountaine Collection.

Margaret began keeping a diary when she was sixteen, and she continued the practice until shortly before her death. Her will stipulated that her butterfly collection along with a large sealed lacquered box were to be deposited after her death in the Castle Museum, Norwich, with instructions that the box, which was thought to contain manuscripts and notes, not be opened until April 15, 1978. And shortly after that date, museum officials, along with one of the few surviving relatives of Margaret, opened the box. They were expecting to see unpublished notes on *Lepidoptera*. Instead, the box contained twelve volumes of diaries that were begun in April 15, 1878 and told a very private story. The diaries contained well over a million words.

WORKS

Margaret Fountaine wrote several articles for professional journals.

Fountaine, Margaret. *Butterflies and Late Loves: The Further Travels and Adventures of a Victorian Lady.* Edited by W. F. Cater. New York: Harper Collins, 1986.

_____. *Love Among the Butterflies: The Travels and Adventures of a Victorian Lady.* Edited by W. F. Cater. Boston: Casell, 1980. From Fountaine's diaries.

Rose de Freycinet, 1794–1832.
French.

Little is known of Rose's childhood. She was educated in Paris; her mother, a widow, was the head of a school for young ladies. Rose had one sister and a brother who had died in 1814, a prisoner of war. How the family fared during the Revolution, and the fate of her father, is unknown. When Rose was twenty she married Louis de Freycinet, a well known geographer and a veteran of naval service.

Louis was appointed commandant of a voyage around the world, a scientific expedition rather than a journey of discovery, that was expected to last three years. At that time Rose and Louis had been married about three years. The day of the sailing Rose visited the ship with Louis to say good-by. At midnight when the ship was boarded for sailing at dawn the next day, Louis was accompanied by a friend and a youth said to be the friend's son. The next morning the ship was blessed, then put to sea. Rose was that youth. She had determined she would not to be left behind for the several years the voyage would take, and she and Louis had planned carefully and secretly for her to accompany him.

Rose was on the tall side and in the style of the time made a passable appearance as a male youth. While the ship was in European waters she spent most of her time in the cabin and rarely came on deck. Finally, after the ship cleared Gibraltar, Rose and Louis allowed her identity to be known to the officers and gentlemen.

They first sailed down the west coast of Africa to Tenerife. They intended to continue on to the Cape of Good Hope, but they'd been delayed in the Mediterranean, and by then strong winds were blowing them west, so they crossed the Atlantic to Rio de Janeiro. This change of route would delay their return to France for eight months, which grieved Rose. From Rio they re-crossed the Atlantic and reached the Cape of Good Hope (previously known as the Cape of Storms) in thirty-five days. Rose was worried about rounding the Cape; the passage was difficult with high winds and huge waves.

After a welcome stop in Mauritius they sailed to Western Australia and Shark Bay, New Holland, a desolate land with only red or white sand.

> ... This time on shore was not at all agreeable to me, the country being entirely without trees or greenery, and the only place for a walk was on the burning sand where, when the heat had a little diminished, I amused myself collecting shells, of which I made a quite good collection [*Realms and Islands*, p. 92].

She — and perhaps everyone on the ship as well — was glad to leave for Timor, where they intended to stay for a while.

For most of the rest of the journey, which would last two years, de Freycinet was in parts of the world that were unknown to him. The expedition and explorations were going well; the naturalists were pleased by the results — one of which was the discovery of new species. One, *Colombe Pinon* or Rose's Dove, was discovered at Rawak and named after Rose.

Their next major stop was the Sandwich Islands, where their first priority was an interview with the king, in part to arrange for supplies. From there, they sailed to Sydney, New South Wales. To sustain them back across the Pacific, they took on board a hundred pigs, some goats, and kids.

> That is all we could procure. It was more abundant than choice. I could well have wished for a large number of chickens, but on the contrary we have very few: they do not know how to rear poultry in these islands. What we were able to find of fresh vegetable will not go very far.... We ought to be en route for Port Jackson but, to my great regret, this passage will be much lengthened by a prodigious deviation towards the east the dear commandment is having made with the object of conducting researches on the magnetic equator. I much respect science, but scarcely love it; it is not the way to reconcile us to each other to lengthen in its favour a passage that can offer me nothing very exciting [p. 173].

Cape Horn was stormy. Several times during the passage, everyone thought the boat, and they, wouldn't survive.

At the Falklands the boat was pierced by a submerged rock. They couldn't dislodge it, and it seemed inevitable that the ship would be engulfed. Everyone (except Rose) pumped, even the Abbé. Finally the corvette grounded on a sandy shore and keeled over, half full of water. The passengers and crew were stranded on a land of sandhills and treeless stretches. The weather worsened.

> The weather is horrible, it is raining and cold, and the storm keeps on lifting the ship; these movements are so violent that I feel them more and more alarming and I hold myself ready to leave at any moment, imagining that a catastrophe may happen suddenly and oblige us to make a quick escape.... I should have to get out by the window, for the door being on the side leaning into the water it would be impossible for me to leave that way [p. 206].

The ship was not repairable; they decided to dispatch the longboat with a party to seek help at Monte Video, a thousand miles away. The boat was named *Espérance*, or the *Hope*. Food was running short, and the weather was getting colder. Louis was ill.

Then, a boat was sighted, a sloop attached to a large vessel, a whaler. Contact was made. Several days later a three-masted ship came into the bay. (They had doubted the goodwill of the whaler.) Matters didn't go well; the ship needed repairs, which de Freycinet helped with, and there were questions of indemnity and arrangements. Their doubts about the goodwill of their rescuers were well-founded.

Eventually, they were taken on board an American ship and sailed to Rio de Janeiro.

They returned to France November, 1820, three years and fifty-seven days after leaving. De Freycinet faced a court martial on the wreck and loss of the ship — the matter of smuggling Rose on board was ignored. The court found unanimously that he had done all he could, and he was honorably acquitted. When Rose's adventures became known, she was considered a heroine.

Rose died at the age of thirty-seven, from cholera. She never regretted the voyage.

During the voyage she had kept a journal on almost a daily basis and had written letters that were posted on the way. The journal was for a young relative and close friend, Caroline, and the journal had been Caroline's idea. After Rose's death Louis considered publishing an account of the voyage, using Rose's letters which he had copied, and the journal, but it wasn't until many years later when a descendent of Caroline put together the journal and copies of the letters — by then the original letters had been lost — and published a book in 1927.

WORKS

Freycinet, Rose de. *Realms and Islands: The World Voyage of Rose de Freycinet in the Corvette Uranie 1817–1820, from Her Journal and Letters and the Reports of Louis de Saulces de Frey-*cinet, Capitaine de Corvette. Ed. Marnie Bassett. London: Oxford University Press, 1962.

BOOKS ABOUT OR INCLUDING ROSE DE FREYCINET

Riviere, Marc Serge. *A Woman of Courage.* National Library of Australia, 1996.

Margaret Smith Gibson

Material for Margaret Smith Gibson is with the entry for **Agnes Smith Lewis.**

Maria Dundas Graham *see* Callcott, Lady Maria Dundas Graham

Countess Ida Marie Louise Hahn-Hahn, 1805–1880. German.

Ida's father, the Graf Karl Friedrich von Hahn, was well known for his keen interest in the stage and for squandering much of his fortune on that interest. In 1826 Ida married her cousin Count Adolf von Hahn-Hahn. It was a very unhappy marriage, and the couple divorced in 1829.

Ida then traveled and wrote, at first poetry, later novels. She entered a convent in 1852 but soon left and moved to Mainz, where she founded a nunnery. Although she lived at the nunnery she did not join the order, and she continued writing. Her novels were popular in aristocratic circles.

Countess Ida clearly found her extended travels to be a wonderful adventure. In the preface to *Letters of a German Countess,* written to her mother (as the letters were), she said

I cannot sufficiently repeat to you how far the difficulties, dangers, disappointments and annoyances of this tour have fallen short of my expectation. I cannot forbear laughing to be everywhere received like one risen from the dead, to be questioned concerning extraordinary perils, which I never encountered, and to find the courage admired which I never had occasion to display. Neither accidents, nor troubles, nor illness, have befallen us — sometimes vexations and annoyances, such as sluggish people, vermin, and riding on camels through the Desert; but vexations are met with everywhere. Fear I have never felt for a moment, still less experienced the momentary desperation which causes us to exclaim, "Would that I had not undertaken it!" In the whole affair, I found but one difficulty — that was to make up my mind to travel [*Letters of a German Countess*, preface].

Such was the first day at Beyrout. Exquisitely beautiful, was it not? And such was the second, and the third, and the fourth day, and such would be every day, if one were to pass all one's days here. You sit in the liwan in the day-time, on the terrace, that is, on the flat roof, in the evening, and contemplate the sea and the mountains in sun-light and moon-light; and, at times, when it is not too hot, you take a ride to the palm-wood and admire the magnificent trees, and enjoy the scent of the acacia, the genuine, that is, which is almost overpowering. This wood is the pride of Beyrout. Palms form its crown; beneath their tall stems flourish large plantations of mulberry-trees, of which the greatest care is taken, because the breeding of silkworms is assiduously prosecuted [*pursued*]. Hence this is the predominant tree of the country, intermixed with carob-trees and fig-trees, with palms and pines. These latter lift their beautiful, tranquil, erect heads into the air, and the others form the underwood, so that a wood has a rich and magnificent character.

This, however, does not prevent you from sinking, just outside the gates, into sand a foot deep, which renders walking most fatiguing and unpleasant, especially as, the moment you leave the sea, you find yourself between cactus-hedges as high as houses, which surround the gardens. This plant needs little water, and therefore grows here to a monstrous size; every other vegetable production is reared by attentive irrigation. Every consideration gives way to that, and so the roads are turned into canals, and rendered impassable by banks, thrown up whenever water is more or less wanted here or there. Where no care is taken to irrigate, nothing grows; and where no plants grow sand grows. From year to year it spreads further and further; it advances insensibly but steadily, so that, after a series of years, large tracts are discovered to be inundated with sand. These encroachments might be prevented by plantations; but these are not made [Vol. I, pp. 300–301].

At half-past five o'clock we arrived at Saïda, the Sidon of Scripture, no longer celebrated as in the time of the Phoenicians for its purple dye, but for its bananas, which flourish in great profusion. The Arabs are so fond of the banana that they believe this to have been the fruit which tempted Eve in Paradise, and they even fancy that they can trace the figure of the serpent's head in the form of the blossom. We halted at the city gate and pitched our tents on the solid sand of the shore, between the Mediterranean and large gardens abounding in olive trees enclosed with tamarisks [Vol. II, pp. 89–90].

We passed by the silent city, which looked desolate and melancholy, and destitute of the verdant environs which usually surround the towns of Syria. I am ashamed to confess that a gazelle captivated me so much, that my attention was so riveted by this singularly beautiful animal, that Tyre received only a transient glance. The only excuse I can offer is, that it was the first time I had ever seen a wild gazelle....

We rode for an hour and half beyond Tyre and stopped at a village, the chief buildings of which were a large khan, and a water-mill turned by a beautiful limpid stream — a sight not often met with here. Perhaps it was from the bed of this stream that the sand was taken for the manufacture of the glass for which the Phoenicians were so celebrated. Foreign nations imagined that none but the sand from a river in the vicinity of Tyre could be employed for this purpose, till they discovered that any sand might be used [Vol. II, pp. 91–92].

WORKS

Hahn-Hahn, Ida Marie Louise. *Letters from the Orient*. London: J.C. Moore, 1845.
_____. *Letters of a German Countess Written During her Travels in Turkey, Egypt, The Holy Land, Syria, Nubia, &c. in 1843–44*. Three volumes. London: Henry Colburn, 1845.
_____. *Travels in Sweden*. London: H.G. Clarke and Co., 1845.

Margaret Hunter Hall,

1799–1876. British.

We know little about Margaret's early years. She began traveling early. In 1815 she and her sister Jane — there's no mention of her mother — traveled to Spain to join their father, Sir John Hunter, who was the British consul-general in Spain. Both girls enjoyed their life in Madrid, making many friends and learning, among other things, to valse or waltz.

We don't know how she and Basil Hall (1788–1844) met. He was the son of Sir James Hall the geologist. Basil Hall had entered the navy in 1802. One of the early travelers to China and Korea, his account of the voyage of discovery was published in 1818. From 1820 to 1822 he sailed to the coasts of Chile, Peru, and Mexico; his account of that was published in 1825. He also spent some time in New York and Boston. He wrote a book for young people on his travels. In 1824 he retired on half pay, and in 1825 he and Margaret were married.

Basil had spent some of his early years at the naval bases in Gibraltar and Malta, and early on he'd made friends of the officers of the United States Navy while they used the British fortresses there. He and Margaret may have met during this time.

It wasn't surprising, then, that in 1827

Captain Hall suggested to Margaret that they, with their child Eliza, should tour the United States. (Eliza was about fifteen months old when the trip began; she proved to be an excellent traveler.) Margaret liked the idea very much. Her letters to Jane are the basis of *Aristocratic Journey*.

Una Pope-Hennessey, who wrote the preface to *Aristocratic Journey*, suggests that society and life in Spain set the standard for life abroad in Margaret's eyes. This seems likely. Certainly she was very patronizing about the United States, making unfavorable comparisons about manners, customs, people, education, and so on, to those found in Europe and particularly Spain. Both Margaret and her husband disapproved of everything America stood for, and Margaret has no interest in attempting to understand the basis of the United States. (Basil's account of the tour was soundly criticized by the American press.) Margaret wrote about all sorts of matters; her writing was often critical and disapproving, but her letters convey much about life at that time in America.

Inevitably there are comparisons with Frances Trollope, whose travels to America are better known. It is perhaps an open question who is the more patronizing. Yet both of them wrote vividly and in an entertaining style, and they both left a lively picture of America at that time.

The Halls were well connected, and they brought with them letters of introduction to "everyone." They made friends and received more introductions. The book is full of anecdotes and glimpses of prominent people. Captain Hall had learned the *camera lucida*, and the illustrations in the book are by him.

Their American tour began with their arrival in New York City. They next went up the Hudson to Albany, then across to Niagara, going by canal part of the way. From there they crossed over to Canada, where they stayed for nine weeks, then returned to Albany.

Captain Hall wanted to study a state legislature, so they stayed twelve days in Albany, which gave Margaret ample time to be sociable. They then spent several weeks in Boston.

Well, my good opinions of Boston and the Bostonians gain strength by seeing more of both. I am quite delighted with the town, which even in this wet, nasty day looked cleaner than any town I was ever in. The outward appearance of the houses is so handsome that I feel a wish to go into each one as I pass, and those that I have seen do not fall short of what they promise on the outside [*The Aristocratic Journey*, p. 87].

She met quite a round of Bostonians.

The person we have seen most is Mr. Daniel Webster, a very eminent lawyer and one of the Members to Congress from the State of Massachusetts. He is a very celebrated man in this country and well known by reputation to many persons in England. He is by much the most generally informed and cleverest man that we have seen in America. We dine with him and Mrs. Webster to-day [p. 86].

From Boston they went to New York, then to Philadelphia and Baltimore. They spent a month in Washington.

The first appearance of Washington is exactly what I expected, as unlike the capital of a great country as it is possible to imagine, excepting the very first building of all, the Capitol, situated on an eminence and looking very commanding and beautiful on the first impression, but except for that, one is tempted to ask even in the heart of the city, "Where is Washington?" [p. 165].

Yet, she thought it the best place she'd been, largely because it was quieter and they had nice accommodations. They found various amusements:

We took our usual three hours' dose of the Senate and House of Representatives yesterday, the tenth.

They then began their southern tour — Norfolk, Charleston, Savannah — with various stops along the way.

Savannah is a very pretty place, quite like an English village with its grass walks and rows of trees on each side of the street. The gardens, too, are in great beauty and I have actually seen sweet oranges growing [p. 226].

They stayed at several plantations, where they admired the comfort and graciousness of the houses. They were curious about slavery and the contrasts between the north and the south. Eventually they went into Alabama, crossing the area that had formerly been Creek territory, and then made their way to Mobile.

We drove out about five miles amongst our old friends the pines to a place called Spring Hill, which is the spot to which the inhabitants of Mobile fly for refuge during the season of yellow fever. They consider any place safe a little elevated, with a sandy soil and running water. This is not peculiar to this part of the States but all over the south, and going to the sand hills is reckoned a perfect security against the certain death that would probably be their portion not a dozen miles off [p. 247].

From Mobile they took a boat to New Orleans.

There is something in the short view I have yet had of Orleans that pleases me particularly. There is an air of cheerfulness and gaiety and, withal, an old Continental aspect which is peculiarly pleasing after being for so long teased with the newness and rawness of all American cities. The mixture of lively, French tone heard in the streets, too, adds to the interest, and the forests of masts all around beget a feeling of connection with more distant and far dearer countries. Then the appearance of the houses with their queerly-shaped high roofs and iron balconies instead of the pitiful wood thing universal elsewhere, for which I have not yet got over my contempt [p. 252].

They stayed in New Orleans for ten days. It was April, and the days were hot and sultry. The trip on the boat going up-river was no improvement on the discomfort of the climate.

> The heat was oppressive beyond anything I ever felt, the mosquitoes swarmed and made it necessary to kept the mosquito curtains down, which in those little berths increase the heat to an intolerable degree... [p. 260].

As they traveled up the Mississippi they were intrigued by the large rivers and their confluence with the Mississippi.

> The Missouri empties itself into the Mississippi eighteen miles above St. Louis. It has two mouths and the view up both is very striking, tho' neither of them of the imposing magnificence of the confluence of the Ohio. The most remarkable circumstance is the instantaneous change in the character of the water of the Mississippi below and above its meeting with the Missouri. I have often mentioned the muddy nature of the river all the way from the Balize, but that part of it from the mouth of the Ohio up to St. Louis is doubly dirty, indeed the mud accumulates so fast in the boilers of the steamboats that they were obliged to clean them out every day. The innumerable logs and other driftwood were also proportionately increased, and the strength of the current was such that we had the greatest difficulty in making way against it. All those circumstances arose from the approximation of the Missouri, and as we continued to paddle up from hence they increased, and when we got near the confluence the mixture of the two waters was very distinct. Had you been in the United States I could have told you what it resembled, but you have never seen a dish containing American gravy and, therefore, my simile is lost, but you must know that the said gravy is always of two colours, a lighter and a darker and of a thicker and a thinner substance, if liquid may be so termed. Such was the water of the Mississippi until we got about the confluence and then all at once it was as pure as the sea and quite the same colour [p. 276].

The trip up the Ohio to Cincinnati and Pittsburgh was monotonous, and they were glad to travel on to Philadelphia. They sailed from New York and arrived on the Isle of Wight on July 22, 1828, fifteen months after they left.

Frances Trollope was completing her travels around America when Captain Basil Hall's *Travels in North America* came out.

> Having now arrived nearly at the end of our travels, I am induced, ere I conclude, again to mention what I consider as one of the most remarkable traits in the national character of the Americans; namely, their exquisite sensitiveness and soreness respecting every thing said or written concerning them. Of this, perhaps, the most remarkable example I can give, is the effect produced on nearly every class of readers by the appearance of Captain Basil Hall's *Travels in North America*. In fact it was a sort of moral earthquake, and the vibration it occasioned through the nerves of the Republic, from one corner of the Union to the other, was by no means over when I left the country in July, 1831, a couple of years after the shock [*Domestic Manners of the Americans*, p. 313].

See entry for **Frances Trollope**.

As memorable as the journey to America was, Spain was perhaps the high point of Margaret's life. When she lay dying, her last words were of bells ringing in Madrid.

SOURCE: *The Aristocratic Journey: Being the Outspoken Letters of Mrs. Basil Hall Written During a Fourteen Months' Sojourn in America, 1827–1828.*

WORK

Hall, Margaret Hunter. *The Aristocratic Journey: Being the Outspoken Letters of Mrs. Basil Hall Written During a Fourteen Months' Sojourn in America, 1827–1828.* Prefaced and Edited by Una Pope-Hennessey. New York: G. P. Putnam's Sons, 1931.

Mary Hall, 1857–1912. British.

Little is known about her early life. She is best known for crossing Africa from south to north, beginning in South Africa and ending in Cairo. She traveled with servants and guides. When she began her cross-Africa trek, she'd already been in South Africa sightseeing for a year. This was not her first trip; as a young woman she had traveled for her health.

Mary Hall traveled throughout her life. Following the African trip she traveled extensively in New Zealand, Australia, the South Pacific, China and Siberia.

SOURCE: *Encyclopedia of Women's Travel and Exploration.*

WORKS

Hall, Mary. *A Woman in the Antipodes and in the Far East.* London: Methuen, 1907.
_____. *A Woman's Trek from the Cape to Cairo.* London: Methuen, 1907.

Alice Marian Rowlands Hart.

She is often referred to as Mrs. Ernest Hart. ca. 1850–after 1898. English.

Alice Marion Rowlands was born about 1850 in Lower Sydenham, England. She trained as a nurse, and in 1872 she married Dr. Ernest Hart (1835–1898). She was his second wife; his first wife was rumored to have died in suspicious circumstances. Ernest Hart was involved in the founding of the Medical Society of London, a group that encouraged discussions of medical subjects by medical students and recently qualified doctors. A surgeon and medical writer, he was also noted for founding (with Alice) the Cremation Society, a very controversial subject at that time. Alice also — with Ernest's help — established the Donegal Industries Fund to develop the home industries of Irish cottagers.

In 1894 the two went to Burma, China and India, possibly their first such trip. At that time most Westerners knew about Burma through Rudyard Kipling; traveling in Burma seemed very remote and difficult, especially for a woman. Nonetheless, Alice and her husband explored the Irrawaddy River, traveling on a three-deck mailboat.

On her return to England she published her first book, *Diet in Sickness and Health*, 1895; she also wrote several magazine articles about her impressions of Burma. She had found Burma to be interesting and beautiful. Struck by how little the English knew about Burma, she resolved to write a book about it. *Picturesque Burma* (1897) was published by both an English and an American publisher. Alice was a good observer of customs, and the book has straight-forward explanations of Burmese life, more that of a trained observer than an exuberant tourist.

> Amaurapoora exercised a strange charm over me, and I went again and again to explore and to sketch its ruined temples, to sit beside its great lake, and to reconstruct in imagination its gorgeous past. The scene even now from the shore of the lake is fascinating. Massive ruined temples standing among groves of tamarind, palm, and peepul trees are reflected in the placid water, and in the far distance are seen the graceful lines of the Ruby-mine mountains.
>
> The city stood on a wide plain. The outer walls and moat are easily made out. After crossing these, the road leads over open ground covered with jungle growth, from which rise the ruins of great buildings on either side. Some are square and of red brick, others bell-shaped; there are great gateways leading to ruins which recall the baths of Caracalla at Rome, tall silvered poles are still surmounted by the Brahminy goose, and monster griffins guard shapeless masses. Among the pagodas rises one taller and statelier than the rest; this is the great white Pato'-dau-gyi, the St. Paul's of Amaurapoora.
>
> The jungle throws its pall of green over

the site of busy streets and golden palaces, and is now the haunt of deadly snakes. On my going, the first day I was at Amaurapoora, into the vestibule of a ruined temple to see three statues of Buddha which stand under a canopy in solemn draperies of black and gold, I was warned to be careful where I trod, as the place was full of cobras. The idea was not pleasant, but being anxious to make some more sketches, I returned alone to Amaurapoora the next day. I had mounted my easel and was steadily at work sketching in pastels a group of pagodas and griffins, surrounded only, as I thought, by naked children, when I was startled by hearing a voice behind me say, "What for you photograph Burmese pagodas?" I turned round and saw a young Burman, dressed in a pink silk pasoh and turban.

"You speak English?" I said, glad to find some one who could answer questions about the ruins.

"Yes, I am one of Dr. Mark's boys."

After watching me draw for some time with great interest, he exclaimed, "How easy!" and then, "Would you like to go into the pagodas?"

"Yes," I replied, "I should like to very much, but I am told the temples are full of cobras, and I am afraid to go in."

"Ah! All English afraid of cobras; Burmans not afraid: Burmans charmed. I am charmed; I not afraid; you safe with me."

After packing up my sketching utensils I prepared to explore the ruins of what I was told was the temple of Kuji. I passed with my barefooted Burmese guide under the tumbledown roofs of a long passage, which conducted us into a spacious vaulted hall, at the end of which on a raised platform, sat a colossal statue of Buddha, with two kneeling figures in the attitude of adoration on either side. At a lower level was a beautiful statue, about nine feet high, of Buddha standing, with the right hand raised in benediction. The gold-leaf had been washed off by the rains, and the black lacquer underneath was exposed; the edge of the draperies was set with glass mosaics. We wandered through the halls and vestibules of the temple. In every nook were figures in alabaster and wood, but the standing statue

of Buddha beneath the altar in the great hall was still the finest. I returned to it.

I returned to Mandalay delighted with my day's work. I had made three sketches and had contracted to buy a genuine Buddha out of a ruined pagoda.

The temples still drew me with a strange fascination, and I went alone again the next day to Amaurapoora, determined to try and find Moung Tso and to further explore the ruins. I shrank from entering them without the protection from cobras vouchsafed by my charmed guide.

I told Moung Tso that I wished to explore the Kuji temple still more, and had therefore sent for him to be my guide. He was politely willing, so again we passed up the ruined passage into the hall under the dome, where the great Buddha sat on the raised altar, waiting for worshippers that never came. Aided by my guide, I explored every nook of the great mass of ruins, and for an hour or more we wandered from one spacious hall to another, down long corridors and into open courtyards. Again and again we pulled open creaking carved doorways, to be startled by the gleaming white face and uplifted hand of a Guatauma standing in the sacred recess. Indeed, in every hall, in every niche, sat or stood the solemn Buddhas, carved in marble, in alabaster, in wood, with gilt and glass bejewelled garments, twenty, thirty feet high, monoliths defying Time's decaying hand; or they lay prone, dying Buddhas, fifty feet long. The carved gables of the temples were falling down, the roofs were generally gone; the monster lion temple guardians started up suddenly with staring eyes and fierce faces from among the abundant green undergrowth; all was ruins except the silent steadfast Gautaumas, that seemed to bear passive witness to the desolation of the sacred places induced by the alien race which now possesses the ancient land of Buddha.

In the woods I came across a kioung with splendidly carved eaves and balconies falling into ruin. Outside an old monk was standing, fondling with evident delight and affection a little one-year-old baby — a foundling I was told, who would be brought up in the monastery. As I walked along to reach the gharry, I mused how kingdoms may rise and fall, how governing races may succeed one another, and stately religions with sumptuous temples may rise into power and fall into oblivion, but that human nature remains the same, and that the old monk fondling the little child among the ruins of royal Amaurapoora represents what is most real and lasting in life [*Picturesque Burma*, pp. 46–53].

The entry for Ernest Hart in the *Oxford Dictionary of National Biography* mentions that he traveled extensively, and his travels included trips to the Americas and the Far East. Alice likely accompanied him. The entry cites a collection of material from Japan. Alice Hart survived her husband.

SOURCE: *Picturesque Burma, Past and Present.*

WORKS

Hart, Alice. *Picturesque Burma, Past and Present.* London: Dent, 1897.

Ellen Julia Teed Hollond,

1822–1884. British.

Ellen's husband, Robert Hollond, was known for accompanying Charles Green on one of the earliest balloon flights; in 1836 they flew "The Great Balloon of Nassau" 800 kilometers, almost 500 miles, from England to Germany.

WORKS

Hollond, Ellen. *A Lady's Journal of Her Travels in Egypt and Nubia.* London: E. Faithfull, 1864.

Annie Boyle Hore

Annie Hore traveled to Africa for mission work. She, her husband, infant son, and eight missionaries from the London Mis-

sionary Society set out from London in 1882 to settle on the shores of Lake Tanganyika. Earlier, Captain Edward Hore had spent three years surveying the lake; there was great interest in the lake, as it was the longest freshwater lake in the world, with its own complicated weather system, but more than geography was involved.

He was also trying to determine where Europeans might live in interior Africa, both for mission work and commercial venture. He presented his conclusions in 1881 to the Royal Geographical Society:

> At Ugigi I resided over two years, and from it made my various voyages on the Lake. Here we lived out a character, which so recommended itself to the native mind, that after we had been there a year, they volunteered to give us a site for our station, and publicly recognized us as friends, in spite of all the opposition.... At this place, in its very stronghold, we struck a deadly blow at the slave traffic of Central Africa, so that from the day of our arrival the public exposure of slaves for sale ceased, and was only carried on as admittedly contraband [*Preface*, p. vii].

He concluded that the region around Lake Tanganyika was suitable, and the group set out. *To Lake Tanganyika in a Bath Chair* recounts their attempts to reach the lake. The "Bath Chair" in the title refers to a palanquin Captain Hore had designed for Annie and their son to ride in.

The plan involved putting a steamboat on Lake Tanganyika; the group of missionaries would carry it in parts to the lake and then assemble it. Captain Hore, an engineer, would be responsible for assembling and sailing the steamer and keeping it in good repair.

The group of eleven, including the Hores with their three-month-old son Jack, sailed in May 1882. After landing in Zanzibar and making extensive arrangements for the actual journey to Lake Tanganyika, the caravan set out. The first stage took them

150 miles inland, where Mrs. Hore and Jack stayed with an English couple while Edward returned to Zanzibar for the boat. There, Annie Hore had a sunstroke which laid her up for several weeks. At the same time, there had been a delay in the boat's arrival from England.

The rainy season, during which travel is virtually impossible, was too near at hand for the plan to proceed, so Captain Edward sent his family home and proceeded on with the missionaries to Lake Tanganyika. The plan was for the Hores to meet in a year to try the journey again, but taking a water route to Tanganyika. Meanwhile, though, the bath chair was made to fit on one of the carts, which allowed room for a cot for Jack. Annie and Jack returned to England.

The next attempt to reach the lake was to be by steamer, utilizing the Nyassa route, which would be less arduous and less expensive than the overland march to Ugigi. Annie was pleased with the prospect of a more comfortable trip with possibilities of stopping at various stations along the route. She and Jack set off to meet Edward, sailing around the Cape and arriving in July 1884 at Quillimane. Edward wasn't there, having been caught in the midst of an uprising against the Portuguese.

Finally, there was a telegram telling everyone to go to Zanzibar, that Captain Hore had made arrangements. Annie was excited by the news — at this point she and Edward had been separated almost two years, and Jack hardly knew his father.

They prepared to set out again, on foot and in caravan, as they had in the first attempt. Their route was through East Africa, a drought-stricken area with no comforts or amenities. Travel was slow, and water was a serious consideration. The heat was exhausting, and often there were long distances between stopping points. They carried water in galvanized tanks and rationed it carefully, never emptying it until they'd reached the new supply. Jack was ill, and the men were cheerless because of the weather and scarcity of food. The trip took ninety days.

On the 7th of January, 1885, we started on our last day's tramp, and perhaps the most terrible of the whole journey. The valley of the Luiche river, which we had to cross, spread out into a delta, some miles wide, covered with a dense jungle of reeds, grass, and bush, all in a tangle, some of it being short crooked thorns, and worst of all a bush bearing pods, covered with hairs and prickles, which at the slightest disturbance drop off, and irritate the skin fearfully.

In the dry season there is a proper path and crossing-place, but at the time we were traveling, all was overgrown and overflowed; and we had to penetrate the jungle, assisted only by the tracks of hippopotami, who had trodden the vegetation down here and there. To make it worse we had to make a wide detour to the north, so as to come upon the river where it was of fordable depth.

About seven o'clock we entered the mazes of this dreadful swamp, and nothing could be seen beyond a few feet distant, except now and then by myself, when the carriers lifted the chair above their heads. They were all knee-deep, and finally thigh-deep in a slimy black mud, and strive as they might and did, I got some heavy lurches, which threatened to give me a closer acquaintance with the mud. We could only proceed very slowly, sometimes standing still, while a few of our best men in front beat down the obstructions [*To Lake Tanganyika in a Bath Chair*, pp. 148–149].

We now passed over a smooth green ridge, and along well-trodden paths, and soon came in full sight of the lake in all its wide-spreading grandeur, while immediately before and below us, imbedded and dotted amongst a mass of deep-green oil palms, lay the settlement of Ugigi [pp. 152–153].

The Hore family finally arrived in Tanganyika and settled on Kavala Island, where they founded a school. The first year was particularly difficult. Annie was the schoolmistress. But overall matters didn't improve, and several missionaries died. Early in 1885 Captain Hore wrote to the London Missionary Society that he planned to retire from Africa. Other missionaries were struggling as well, and many were becoming convinced that Europeans could not live in the climate of that part of Africa. Finally, in June 1886, the mission's committee voted to abandon the station, although the Tanganyika mission survived. The Hores remained until 1888 when Captain Hore's continued ill health forced the family to leave Africa. He informed the London Missionary Society that he planned to move with his family to Tasmania and would use his engineering skill in industry. No more is known of his wife.

SOURCE: *Victorian Women Travel Writers in Africa.*

WORKS

Hore, Annie. *To Lake Tanganyika in a Bath Chair.* London: Sampson, Low, Marston, Searle, Rivington, 1886.

Mrs. (Alfred) Dora Hort

Mrs. Hort's trip from New York to San Francisco by boat took place in the first half of the 1880s. Mrs. Hort — and most people traveling by sea from the east coast to the west coast — made a land crossing on the isthmus connecting North and South America, hence the title *Via Nicaragua.*

The fact of there being no beaten track, no road by which to be guided, were startling facts that soon dawned upon us. As we could perceive nothing that at all resembled a path, we were constantly obliged to retrace our steps, having arrived at points from which there was no possible outlet. These incessant obstacles were not only aggravating, but they very considerably increased my consternation respecting my sis-

ter's absence, as in the fashion we were proceeding the chances of her overtaking us became less and less probable.

The route was through a vast labyrinth of dense forest, so somber and silent that it awed one; and I began to suspect from seeing no trace of any other passenger that we had strayed in a wrong direction....

It was, however, a grand old forest through which we were with so much difficulty endeavouring to make our way over masses of trailing foliage. The prolific parasites were entwined round the majestic trees, and drooped in graceful tendrils between branches; from decayed barks hung clusters of bright-hued blossoms, orchid no doubt, though I did not know them as such, my horticultural knowledge about the higher order of lichens being then very imperfect.

Brilliantly plumed birds twittered and fluttered overhead, startled into unusual activity by our unexpected approach. The gloomy solitude and grandeur of the scene became each moment more intensified, as precipitous ascents, with the probable descents on the other side, loomed before our eyes. We had gradually quitted the bush and luxuriant foliage to arrive at a far bolder description of scenery, when hills and deep glens intersected by waterfalls were charming to look at, but rugged to clamber over; however, so long as the animal I rode played no tricks to unseat me, and I was able to keep my extremely uncomfortable position on the Mexican saddle, I was quite prepared to endure, as well as admire the magnificent scene that surrounded us.

Some of these perpendicular eminences were thickly wooded, and sloped down to gloomy ravines over which we had to pick our steps with the greatest caution. I confess that with all my boasted courage, it was with a faint heart and trembling frame that I traversed such wild, weird defiles, spots which probably had never before been trodden by human feet, or the silence disturbed by the sound of profane language as was then the case! Fortunately for my nerves, the mule I rode was tractable, and condescended to steer clear of branches that threatened my face, and avoided passing close to the trunks of trees to the injury of my limbs; such pranks being the usual practice of the Nicaragua Isthmus donkeys and mule, whether with the object of unseating the rider, or the express purpose of doing him a cruel injury, it is difficult to determine [*Via Nicaragua*, pp. 216–218].

WORKS

Hort, Dora. *Tahiti the Garden of the Pacific,* London: T. Fisher Unwin, 1891.
_____. *Via Nicaragua: A Sketch of Travel.* London: Remington, 1887. Printed in Agosin, Marjorie, and Julie H. Levison. *Magical Sites: Women Travelers in 19th Century Latin America.* Buffalo, New York: White Pine Press, 1999.
She also wrote a novel, *Hena, Life in Tahiti.* London: Saunders, Otley and Co., 1866.

Mina Benson Hubbard (Mrs. Leonidas), 1870–1956. Canadian.

Mina was born on a farm in Ontario, the seventh of eight children. Before she married she worked as a teacher and then as a nurse. In 1901 she married Leonidas Hubbard, an American wrier. Two years later Leonidas, Dillon Wallace, and George Elson set out to map part of Labrador. On the second day of the expedition the team went up the wrong river. Leonidas died of starvation; three months later the other two were rescued. Wallace wrote an account of the journey that Mina thought made her husband look incompetent and responsible for the disaster.

Determined to finish his work and to honor Leonidas, Mina planned her own expedition. It took her two years to prepare, during which she learned navigation, surveying and canoeing. Finally she was ready. With the help of Elson and others, she set off.

Wallace also mounted an expedition to complete the trip that the earlier team had attempted. Both expeditions set off on the same day, paddling on opposite shores of Grand Lake.

Mina made the 576-mile trip in two months and was the first white woman to cross Labrador. In the course of the trip she charted river systems, recorded flora and fauna, made a record of the local Inuit, and showed that geographers were mistaken in their assessment of the river system.

Walking back along the point we found it cut by caribou trails, and everywhere the moss was torn and trampled in a way that indicated the presence of many of the animals but a short time since. Yet it did not occur to me that we might possibly be on the outskirts of the march of the migrating caribou.... Ptarmigan were there in numbers, and flew up all along our way.

The wind continued high, and squalls and heavy showers passed. Nevertheless, when lunch was over we pushed on, keeping close to the west shore of the lake. Little more than a mile further up the men caught sight of deer feeding not far from the water's edge. We landed, and climbing to the top of the rock wall saw a herd of fifteen or more feeding in the swamp. I watched them almost breathless. They were very beautiful, and it was an altogether new and delightful experience to me. Soon they saw us and trotted off into the bush, though without any sign of great alarm. George and Job made off across the swamp to the right to investigate, and not long after returned, their eyes blazing with excitement, to say that there were hundreds of them not far away.

Slipping hurriedly back into the canoes we paddled rapidly and silently to near the edge of the swamp. Beyond it was a barren hill, which from near its foot sloped more gradually to the water. Along the bank, where this lower slope dropped to the swamp, lay a number of stags, with antlers so immense that I wondered how they could possibly carry them. Beyond, the lower slope of the hill seemed to be a solid mass of caribou, while its steeper part was dotted over with many feeding on the luxuriant moss.

Those lying along the bank got up at sight of us, and withdrew towards the great herd in rather leisurely manner stopping now and then to watch us curiously. When the herd was reached, and the alarm given, the stags lined themselves up in the front rank and stood facing us, with heads high and a rather defiant air. It was a magnificent sight. They were in summer garb of pretty brown, shading to light grey and white on the under parts. The horns were in velvet, and those of the stags seemed as if they must surely weigh down the heads on which they rested. It was a mixed company, for male and female were already herding together. I started towards the herd, Kodak in hand, accompanied by George, while the others remained at the shore. The splendid creatures seemed to grow taller as we approached, and when we were within two hundred and fifty yards of them their defiance took definite form, and with determined step they came towards us.

The sight of that advancing army under such leadership was decidedly impressive, recalling vivid mental pictures made by tales of the stampeding wild cattle in the west. It made one feel like getting back to the canoe, and that is what we did [*A Woman's Way in Unknown Labrador*, pp. 109–110].

Later, while visiting England, she met Harold Ellis, and in 1908 they were married. Mina stayed in England and followed a career as a public speaker. She and Harold divorced in 1926.

In 1956 Mina was killed by an onrushing train as she crossed the railroad tracks.

SOURCES: Internet: *www.thecanadianencyclopedia.com*, December 2006; Internet: www.pikle.demon.co.uk/diary/junction December 2006.

WORKS

Hubbard, Mina Benson. *A Woman's Way Through Unknown Labrador: An Account of the Exploration of the Nascaupee and George Rivers*. London: Murray, 1908. New edition edited, and with an introduction by, Sherrill Grace. Montreal: McGill-Queen's University Press, 2004.

Mrs. Lucinda Hume-Griffith.
She is sometimes listed under Griffith.

Mr. and Mrs. Griffith had been in Ceylon for several years when it became apparent that her declining health made it necessary for her to leave. Her trip back to England had been much discussed between her and her husband, but they were both unwilling for her to make such a long journey by herself. She disliked the idea of his having to leave Ceylon so soon, but her health had declined to the point where he finally sent in his papers for half-pay and they departed in great haste to take advantage of the India steamer.

They sailed to Suez and prepared for their trip across the desert. The trip was broken up by "inns" or stations, at regular intervals. Travelers spent the heat of the day at a station, traveling in early morning and late afternoon. The quality of the food and water at these stations was generally dismal; insects were a serious problem.

Mrs. Griffith traveled by carriage. Even so she found the journey arduous. At the same time, she had a keen interest in what she saw.

By half-past four we were once more on our road. The afternoon sun was scorching hot, and it was impossible to prevent it from shining into the front of the van, as the curtains would not fasten.... G. got out and explored. He chased several lizards, and brought one to the carriage to shew me. It was of quite a different shape from any we had seen before, and of a light stone colour, like that of the desert, from which, when motionless, it is difficult to distinguish them. This peculiarity we observed in all the animals we met with. The wolf was of nearly the same hue, and even the larks partook of it.

He saw several beautiful flowers, different from those of the morning, and gaudy butterflies fluttering amongst them. The flowers faded, but G., even in this short time, made a collection of a great many different seeds; some had a very strong, pungent smell, so powerful that I could scarcely bear it when he came into the van again.

The most interesting specimens he found were several petrified shells. They are to be met with all over the desert, and in great variety. Those in question appeared to have been snail-shells; many of them were attached to a piece of stick, as naturally as if the snails were still in them.... Here and there we saw large blocks of petrified wood lying upon the sand. In fact, all seems to turn to stone in this truly "Arabia Petraea," whether by the action of the sun upon peculiar properties in the sand, or for other cause, I know not; but I suppose the learned could assign, or already have assigned, a reason [*A Journey Across the Desert, from Ceylon to Marseilles*, Vol. 1, pp. 122–124].

WORKS

As Hume-Griffith, M. E., & A. Hume-Griffith. *Behind the Veil in Persia and Turkish Arabia.* London: Seeley and Co., 1909.
_____. With Major George Darby Griffith. *A Journey Across the Desert, from Ceylon to Marseilles.* Two volumes. London: Henry Colburn, 1845.

Adelina Paulina Irby
see **Georgina Mary Muir Mackenzie (Lady Sebright)**

Anna Brownell Murphy Jameson, 1794–1860. Irish.

Anna Jameson was born in Dublin, Ireland. Her father was a miniature painter; her mother had been born in England. When Anna was very young, the family, which included several younger sisters, immigrated to England. Anna was educated at home and helped oversee the education of her sisters. She took a position as governess when she was sixteen, first with the marquess of Winchester and later with the Rowles family, who took her with them on their trips to Europe. She wrote her first book when she was a governess; some of her later works would draw on her travels on the Continent with the Rowles family.

She married Robert Jameson in 1825. The marriage was unhappy from the start. In 1829 Anna separated from Robert, who took a judgeship in Dominica. Anna traveled to Germany, a trip which led to more books. She became acquainted with German artists and intellectuals; her close friend was Ottilie von Goethe, daughter-in-law of Johann Wolfgang von Goethe.

Meanwhile, Robert had been appointed attorney general of Upper Canada in 1833. Throughout their separation he had supported Anna's work, travels, and writings and had assisted her in getting her first books published. With his appointment Robert assumed he would live the rest of his life in Canada, and he asked Anna to join him. In part because of financial pressures connected with helping her family, Anna joined him for nine months. She was too accustomed to her independent life and her traveling for that arrangement to work for very long. She did, however, enjoy her travels throughout parts of Ontario, and she was fascinated by the indigenous cultures.

The forest land through which I had lately passed was principally covered with hard timber, as oak, walnut, elm, basswood. We were now in a forest of pines, rising tall and dark, and monotonous on either side. The road, worse certainly "than fancy ever feigned or fear conceived," put my neck in perpetual jeopardy. The driver had often to dismount, and partly fill up some tremendous hole with boughs before we could pass — or drag or lift the wagon over trunks of trees — or we sometimes sank into abysses from which it is a wonder to me that we ever emerged. A natural question was — why did you not get out and walk? Yes indeed! I only wish it had been possible. Immediately on the border of the road so-called, was the wild, tangled, untrodden thicket, as impervious to the foot as the road was impassible, rich with vegetation, variegated verdure, and flowers of loveliest dye, but the haunt of the rattlesnake, and all manner of creeping and living things not pleasant to encounter, or even to think of [*Winter Studies and Summer Rambles in Canada*, pp. 91–92].

Anna was at the rapids of the River of St. Mary, Sault Ste. Marie.

But to return to my beautiful river and glorious rapids which are to be treated, you see, as a man treats a passionate beauty — he does not oppose her, for that were madness — but he gets round her. Well, on the American side, further down the River, is the house of Tanner, the Indian interpreter, of whose story you may have heard — for, as I remember, it excited some attention in England. He is a European of unmixed blood, with the language, manners, habits of a Red-skin. He had been kidnapped somewhere on the American frontiers when a mere boy, and brought up among the Chippewas. He afterward returned to civilized life, and having relearned his own language, drew up a very entertaining and valuable account of his adopted tribe. He is now in the American service here, has an Indian wife, and is still attached to his Indian mode of life.

[John Tanner was the author of *A Narrative of the Captivity and Adventures of John Tanner During Thirty Years' Residence Among the Indians in the Interior of North America.* New York, 1830.]

Just above the fort is the ancient burial-place of the Chippewas. I need not tell you of the profound veneration with which all the Indian tribes regard the places of their dead. In all their treaties for the cession of their lands, they stipulate with the white man for the inviolability of their sepulchers. They did the same with regard to this place, but I am sorry to say that it has not been attended to for in enlarging one side of the fort, they have considerably encroached on the cemetery. The outrage excited both the sorrow and indignation of some of my friends here, but there is no redress. Perhaps it was this circumstance that gave rise to the allusion of the Indian chief here, when in speaking of the French he said, "They never molested the places of our dead!" [pp. 205–206].

She continued to travel and write. Increasingly she was drawn to her interest in art and in cataloging art; she is perhaps best known as an art historian. She also worked for the betterment of women's lives, with particular emphasis on the need for equal opportunities in employment and education.

SOURCES: *Dictionary of Literary Biography*; *Encyclopedia of Women's Travel and Exploration*.

WORKS

Jameson, Anna. *Winter Studies and Summer Rambles in Canada.* London: Saunders & Otley, 1838. Reprinted in part as *Sketches in Canada and Rambles Among the Red Men.* London: Longman, 1852. Edited by James J. Talmar and Elsie McLeod Murray. Thomas Nelson and Sons, 1943.

Elizabeth Surby Justice, early 1700s.

For Winter, when they go on a Journey, they have what they call a travelling Waggon; in which they put their Beds, and Bedding. They can either sit upright, or lie along, as they shall think convenient. They generally take good Store of strong Liquor, tongues, Hung-Beef, or any thing that is potted; for there is but bad Entertainment upon the road: They travel Night and Day....

The Houses, which have been erected for many Years, are very low, and built with Wood. The Rooms are all on a Floor: But Houses of a modern Structure are very lofty. These are called *Perlots*, raised with Stone, very magnificent, but exceedingly cold. The Method they have in keeping their Rooms warm, is by a *Peach*, as they call it, in their best Rooms. They are built with fine *Dutch* Tyles; in others, only Brick. It is a Sort of Oven; and there is a Servant, whose Business it is to attend them; For they are very dangerous, if not rightly managed....

As I have given you a Description of their Winter, which is extreamly cold; I shall also of their Summer, which continues Four Months. *Viz.* May, June, July, and August: But *June*, and *July*, are the most severely hot. In these Two Months, they are very much troubled with what they call *Muskettoes*, or named *Gnats* by us in *England*; and when you are bit by them, your Flesh will be in bumps; which will be inflam'd, and itch violently. The Method the People there generally take to cure it, is, To rub the Part affected with Brandy; but that inflamed me the more. I used sour Milk; and that I found better [*Unsuitable for Ladies*, pp. 78–79].

WORKS

Justice, Elizabeth Surby. *A Voyage to Russia, Describing the Laws, Manners, and Customs of That Great Empire, As Govern'd, at This Present, by ... the Czarina, Etc.* York: G. Gent, 1739.

BOOKS ABOUT OR INCLUDING ELIZABETH SURBY JUSTICE

Robinson, Jane, ed. *Unsuitable for Ladies: An Anthology of Women Travelers.* Oxford: Oxford University Press, 1994.

Mary Kingsley, 1862–1900. British.

Because her father didn't believe in good education for girls, Mary was largely self-educated. Mary's father, an eccentric physician, married her mother, a servant, four days before Mary was born. One of her uncles was the novelist Charles Kingsley. To escape the situation — and the criticisms of it — Mary's father would leave the family for years at a time, traveling in Asia, the South Seas, and America. His absences allowed Mary a respite from his restrictions, and she made good use of his time away, reading her way through his extensive library. He did allow her to be educated to the extent of having German lessons so that she could translate articles for him.

At the death of her parents in 1892, Mary received a small inheritance, which she used to go to the Canary Islands. There, she heard about West Africa and the men who made money trading with the natives; this aroused her interest in visiting Africa. Charles Kingsley provided her with introductions to scientists, and she became interested in the possibility of researching and collecting West African fish.

West Africa was a difficult, wild place. Warned about the dangers, she carried a small dagger to use to kill herself should matters get desperate. She traveled alone, and she soon learned that traders provided a connection between the isolated places. She became convinced that England's involvement in Africa should be as trading partners, not as colonial rulers. She determined to collect fish, insects, and reptiles for the British Museum, and she collected several new species.

Mary always observed the proprieties, wearing long skirts and stays; after falling into a pit lined with pointed poisoned stakes, she remarked on the "blessings of a good thick skirt!"

Her first collecting trip so impressed the British Museum that they awarded her a collector's outfit for her next trip, which began in December 1894. That collecting trip was even more successful, and she studied the social organization and religion of a tribe known as the Fan, who were alleged to have practiced cannibalism.

My reasons for going to this wildest and most dangerous part of the West African regions [*Congo Français*] were perfectly simple and reasonable. I had not found many fish in the Oil Rivers, and, as I have said, my one chance of getting a collection of fishes from a river north of the Congo lay in the attitude Mr. C. G. Hudson might see fit to assume towards me [*Travels in West Africa*, p. 103].

I must say that never — even in a picture book — have I seen such a set of wild wicked-looking savages as those we faced this night, and with whom it was touch and go for twenty of the longest minutes I have ever lived.... [But] one by one I took my old ideas derived from books and thoughts based on imperfect knowledge and weighted them against the real life around me, and found them either worthless or wanting [pp. 105–106].

Well, just after we had leisurely entered a new reach of the river, round the corner after us, propelled at a phenomenal pace, came our fishing canoe, which we had left behind to haul in the net and then rejoin us. The occupants, particularly the big black A. B., were shouting something in terror stricken accents. "What?" says Obanjo springing to his feet. "The Fan! the Fan!" Obanjo then by means of energetic questioning externally applied, and accompanied by florid language that cast a rose pink glow smelling of sulphur, round us, elicited the information that about 40,000 Fans, armed with knives and guns, were coming down the Rembwé with intent to kill and slay us, and might be expected to arrive within the next half wink. On hearing this, the whole of our gallant crew took up masterly recumbent positions in the bottom of our vessel and turned gray round the lips. Bu Obanjo rose to the situation like ten lions. "Take the rudder," he shouted to me, "take her into the middle of the stream and keep the sail full." It occurred to me that perhaps a position underneath the bamboo staging might be more healthy than on the top of it, exposed to every microbe of a bit of old iron and what not and a half that according to naïve testimony would shortly be frisking through the atmosphere from those Fan guns; and moreover I had not forgotten having been

previously shot in somewhat similar situation, though in better company. However I did not say anything; neither, between ourselves, did I somehow believe in those Fans. So regardless of danger, I grasped the helm, and sent our gallant craft flying before the breeze down the bosom of the great wild river (that's the proper way to put it, but in the interests of science it may be translated into crawling towards the middle). Meanwhile Obanjo performed prodigies of valour all over the place. He triced up the mainsail, stirred up his fainthearted crew, and got out the sweeps, i.e. one old oar and four paddles, and with this assistance we solemnly trudged away from danger at a pace that nothing slower than a Thames dumb barge, going against stream, could possibly overhaul. Still we did not feel safe, and I suggested to Ngouta he should rise up and help; but he declined, stating he was a married man. Obanjo cheering the paddlers with inspiriting words sprang with the agility of a leopard on to the bamboo staging aft, standing there with his gun ready loaded and cocked to face the coming foe, looking like a statue put up to himself at the public expense. The worst of this was, however, that while Obanjo's face was to the coming foe, his back was to the crew, and they forthwith commenced to re–subside into the bottom of the boat, paddles and all. I, as second in command, on seeing this, said a few blood-stirring words to them, and Obanjo sent a few more of great power at them over his shoulder, and so we kept the paddles going.

Presently from round the corner shot a Fan canoe. It contained a lady in the bow, weeping and wringing her hands, while another lady sympathetically howling, paddled it. Obanjo in lurid language requested to be informed why they were following us. The lady in the bows said, "My son! My son!" and in a second more three other canoes shot round the corner full of men with guns. Now this looked like business, so Obanjo and I looked round to urge our crew to greater exertions and saw, to our disgust, that the gallant band had successfully subsided into the bottom of the boat while we had been eying the foe. Obanjo gave me a recipe for getting the sweeps out again. I did not follow it, but got the job done, for Obanjo could not take his eye and gun off the leading canoe and the canoes having crept up to within some twenty yards of us, poured out their simple tale of woe.

The Fans were after a runaway boy who was surmised to have joined Obanjo. Obanjo said he had joined him (as more armed canoes came round the corner) and that the mother could come and fetch her boy. He would not have dreamed of taking him if he had known his relatives disapproved. There were actually two boys involved, both wanting to see the world. One of the boys rejoined the Fans. After the Fans left the other was found hiding, and they took him safely to Gaboon.

> Really how much danger there was proportionate to the large amount of fear on our boat I cannot tell you. It never struck me there was any, but on the other hand the crew and Obanjo evidently thought it was a bad place; and my white face would have been no protection, for the Fans would not have suspected a white of being on such a canoe and might have fired on us if they had been unduly irritated and not treated by Obanjo with that fine compound of bully and blarney that he is such a master of.
>
> Whatever may have been the true nature of the affair, however, it had one good effect, it got us out of the Rembwé into the Gaboon, and although at the time this seemed a doubtful blessing, it made for progress. I had by this time mastered the main points of incapability in our craft. A. We could not go against the wind. B. We could not go against the tide. While we were in the Rembwé there was a state we will designate as C — the tide coming one way, the wind another. With this state we could progress, backwards if the wind came up against us too strong, but seawards if it did not, and the tide was running down [pp. 342–345].

Mary was matter-of-fact about danger and unpleasantness. Her collecting expeditions often took her into the mangrove swamps, where crocodiles were a real hazard.

Her observations ran counter to the allegedly prevailing European view that Africans hadn't developed past childhood. Notwithstanding the fact that some may have practiced cannibalism, Mary found most Africans to have belief systems equally as valid as those of Europeans, and furthermore to be less materialistic and more spiritual. She opposed missionary efforts to convert Africans to a white culture.

Her last trip to Africa was in 1900, when she went to nurse the Boers who had been captured by the English and were being kept in squalid detention camps. After four months she caught a fever and died.

SOURCE: *Dictionary of Literary Biography*, Volume 174.

WORKS

In addition to her books Mary Kingsley wrote articles.

Kingsley, Mary. *The Ascent of Cameroons Peak and Travels in French Congo.* Liverpool: Journal of Commerce Printing, 1896.
_____. *The Story of West Africa.* London: Marshall, 1899.
_____. *Travels in West Africa: Congo Français, Corisco and Cameroons.* London: Macmillan and Co., Limited, 1897.
_____. *West African Studies.* London: Macmillan and Co., Limited, 1899

BOOKS ABOUT OR INCLUDING MARY KINGSLEY

Birkett, Dea. *Mary Kingsley: Imperial Adventuress.* New York, Macmillan, 1992.
Campbell, Olwen. *Mary Kingsley: A Victorian in the Jungle.* London: Methuen, 1957.
Frank, Katharine. *A Voyager Out: The Life of Mary Kingsley.* Boston: Houghton Mifflin, 1986.
Gwynn, Sephen. *The Life of Mary Kingsley.* London: Macmillan, 1933.
Pearce, Robert D. *Mary Kingsley: Light at the Heart of Darkness.* Oxford: Kensal, 1990.
Wallace, Kathleen. *This Is Your Home: A Portrait of Mary Kingsley.* London: Heinemann, 1956.

Mary Kingsley's correspondence to Macmillan is in the Macmillan Papers at the British Library; letters to Alice Stopford Green and letters to Stephen Gwynn are at the National Library of Ireland; letters to Maj. Matthew Nathan are in the Rhodes House Library at Oxford University.

Sarah Wallis Bowdich Lee,
1791–1856. British.

Sarah married the naturalist Thomas Edward Bowdich when she was twenty-two. She, too, was very interested in naturalist studies. In 1814 Thomas was sent by the African Company on an exploring expedition to Ashantee. Sarah followed him, traveling alone to Cape Coast Castle, but when she arrived she found that he had already begun the journey home. The next year they set out together to Africa, again for exploring and naturalist studies.

Three years later she met Baron Cuvier, and she and Thomas spent almost four years studying Cuvier's collections.

In 1823 she and Thomas again went to Africa, this time to Sierra Leone to carry out, as she says in the introduction to *Excursions in Madeira and Porto-Santo,* "scientific researches." She herself was doing "botanical examinations and Arabic translations."

They sailed first to Madeira, leaving there in October 1823. The voyage was nightmarish.

The master of our vessel was then making his first voyage as Captain, and dearly did we rue his inexperience. He possessed little or no authority over his crew, consisting of two mates, and five men, the former of whom plundered our provisions at pleasure; and as he was extremely parsimonious, he not only shared in the spoil, but collected the remnants of our meals (thereby depriving his half-fed men) for his own

table. Our good friend had amply supplied us with delicious wine, and Mr. Bowdich had agreed with me, that the malmsey at least would be wasted; if broached at sea: reserving it, therefore, for better times we left the cask untouched: but, tired with the disagreeables attending the voyage, our resolution gave way, and we had recourse to our treasure. To our great dismay, however, not a single drop of malmsey, or any other sort, was left us. This disappointment entailed upon us suspicion in its fullest extent, and we feared for every part of our property which might be deemed valuable to another [*Excursions in Madeira and Porto-Santo*, pp. 176–177].

The geology, botany, and conchology of a place, may always be ascertained by the morning walks of an individual; but to catch fish, shoot birds, &c., it is frequently necessary to have recourse to others. This was our case, and we were obliged to leave the island without satisfying ourselves respecting its ornithology or ichthyology. We saw some large eagles, falcons, and boobies, and a few birds of a smaller kind flying about, but could only procure one or two of the latter.... The fishes seemed to be rare and beautiful, but neither money nor entreaty could prevail on any one to catch them.... I kept a troop of little ragged boys and girls in pay, to bring me shells, but they would go no further than the immediate precincts of the town, and they all deserted me when I refused to purchase the same shells four or five times over [p. 189]. *This portion may have been written by Mr. Bowdich.*

The gold of the Gambia is much softer, and said to be superior to that of the leeward coast. The gold merchants frequently come from great distances, even forcing their way through the country when it is covered with water. They never bring it in its native state, alleging as a motive, that the English would then sow it in their own country, and destroy their market [p. 209]. [*This portion may have been written by Mr. Bowdich.*]

Thomas Bowdich died on the Gambia River in January 1824. Sarah published an account of their last journey: *Excursions in*

Madeira and Porto-Santo, etc. In her introduction Sarah refers to herself as being left widowed with "three orphans" but tells us nothing about the children. The book has various listings of flora and fauna, and many wonderful plates.

Sarah revisited Paris, seeing much of Cuvier, with whom she became close friends. In 1829 Sarah married Robert Lee. She wrote many books, most of them devoted to popularizing natural science, often illustrated by her, as she was a very accomplished scientific artist. She wrote in several genres including science and travel; she also wrote for children. Her books are sometimes listed under Lee.

SOURCE: *Dictionary of National Biography*.

WORKS

Lee, Sarah Wallis Bowdich. *Stories of Strange Lands, and Fragments from the Notes of a Traveler*. London: E. Moxon, 1835.

Lee, Sarah Wallis Bowdich (Sarah Bowdich) with Thomas Edward Bowdich. *Excursions in Madeira and Porto-Santo, During the Autumn of 1823, While on His Third Voyage to Africa, by the Late T. Edward Bowdich ... To Which Is Added, by Mrs. Bowdich, I. A Narrative of the Continuance of the Voyage to Its Completion ... II. A Description of the English Settlements in the River Gambia*. London: G. B. Whittaker, 1825.

Anna Leonowens, 1831–1915.

English.

Anna's memoirs state she was born in Wales in 1834, and that her father was a British Army captain who died soon after her birth. Research by biographer W. S. Bristowe shows that she probably was born in India in 1831. Her father, a sergeant in the British Army, died soon after her birth. Anna's mother was part East Indian. Her mother then married an Irish corporal in Bombay. (Anna's sister Eliza married Edward John Pratt: their grandson, William Henry Pratt, was the film star Boris Karloff.)

Anna and Thomas Leon Owens married in 1849 — he was a civilian clerk. After their first child died they reputedly went to England and settled in London. They had two more children, Avis and Louis. However, W. S. Bristowe has suggested that the family moved throughout Asia.

Thomas Leon Owens was a hotel keeper in Malaya for a while. In 1859 he died in Penang, age 33. To support herself and her two children Anna opened a school for the children of officers in Singapore. She changed her surname to Leonowens, possibly because Thomas's name was written that way on his death certificate.

The school was successful but inadequate to support the family. When the Siamese consul in Singapore offered her the position of teacher of the children of King Mongkut, she accepted. (She was preceded by a teacher who was probably English.) Anna sent Avis to school in England but kept Louis with her in Siam.

When King Mongkut died, Anna had already left Siam and was in the process of negotiating her return to his court. The young king who succeeded him instituted many reforms; it's likely Anna's teaching had some influence on him. Meanwhile, Anna was writing articles based on her experiences in Siam. These were used as the basis for her memoir.

In 1867, following her departure from Siam, Anna went to Halifax, Nova Scotia. There she was involved in women's education and was one of the founders of the Nova Scotia College of Art and Design. Nineteen years later she moved to Montreal, where she lived until her death in 1915.

Some of the facts presented in Anna's memoirs were strongly disputed in Thailand. Dr. W. S. Bristowe, who regularly visited the Far East, was researching a biography of Anna's son Louis Leonowens, who had founded a company that still bears his name. In the course of his research it became apparent that there were many inconsistencies and fictions in Anna's memoirs. He located her birth certificate, marriage record, and other legal documents, on which he based statements in his biography. However, accounts of the life of Anna Leonowens vary.

Anna spent some time in India.

> After this the musicians struck up some lively Hindoo airs, and at length the heavy curtain from one side of the pavilion curled up like a lotus-flower at sunset, and there appeared a long line of girls advancing in a measured step and keeping time to the music. They stood on a platform almost facing us. Some of them were extraordinarily beautiful, one girl in particular....
> The Nautchnees, or dancing-girls, of whom there were no less than eighteen, were all dressed in that exquisite Oriental costume peculiar to them, each one in a different shade or in distinct colors, but so carefully chosen that this mass of color harmonized with wonderful effect....
> With head modestly inclined, downcast eyes, and clasped hands they stood silent for some little time, in strong relief against a wall fretted with fantastic Oriental carvings. The herald again gave the signal for the music to strike up. A burst of wild Oriental melody flooded the pavilion, and all at once the Nautchnees started to their feet. Poised on tiptoe, with arms raised aloft over their heads, they began to whirl and float and glide about in a maze of rhythmic movement, fluttering and quivering and waving before us like aspen-leaves moved by a strong breeze. It must have cost them years of labor to have arrived at such ease and precision of movement. The dance was a miracle of art, and all the more fascinating cause of the rare beauty of the performers [*Life and Travel in India*, p. 178].

Anna's memoirs were turned into a novel by Margaret Landon in 1944. The book was popular and was quickly made into a film, *Anna and the King of Siam*, which varied the plot. The musical by Rodgers & Hammerstein soon followed, with even more drastic changes.

SOURCE: Website: Wikipdia.org. December, 2006.

WORKS

Leonowens, Anna. *The English Governess at the Siamese Court: Being Recollections of Six Years in the Royal Palace at Bangkok*. London: Trubner, 1870. This, along with *The Romance of the Harem*, were the basis for Margaret Landon's *Anna and the King of Siam* and the film *The King and I*.
_____. *Life and Travel in India: Being Recollections of a Journey Before the Days of Railroads*. Philadelphia: Porter & Coates, 1884.
_____. *The Romance of the Harem*. Philadelphia: Porter & Coates, 1872. Also published as *The Romance of Siamese Harem Life*. London: Trubner, 1873; and as *Siamese Harem Life*, with an introduction by Freya Start. London: Barker, 1952.

BOOKS ABOUT OR INCLUDING
   ANNA LEONOWENS

W. S. Bristowe. *Louis and the King of Siam*. London: Chatto & Windus, 1976.

Alice Dixon Le Plongeon,
1851?–1910. British.

Alice Dixon met Augustus Le Plongeon (1826–1908) when she was nineteen. Augustus, twenty-five years older than she was, already had had several careers.

After finishing at the École Polytechnique in Paris, Augustus, along with a friend, had purchased a yacht and sailed to South America. Their boat was wrecked off of Chile, and the two managed to swim ashore. Augustus decided to stay in Chile for a while and taught drawing, mathematics and languages at a local college. He left to go to California and join in the gold rush. Instead, he became surveyor and engineer, and essentially city planner, for Marysville, for which he was given several land deeds.

He became interested in photography very early and continued his travels, going to Mexico, Australia, China, and the Pacific Islands. He returned to California, and by 1855 he had a successful photographic business in San Francisco. His continuing interest in science led him to acquire proficiency in medicine.

His initial interest in South America had never left him, and by 1862 he had a photographic studio in Lima, Peru. There, in addition to his photography business, he became involved in photographing the Peruvian ruins. He also established a medical clinic, and studied the use of electricity to help the healing of broken bones. This led him to study earthquakes. But increasingly, he explored and studied the pre–Hispanic sites. He returned to California in 1870, and the next year went to London to examine an old Spanish manuscript in the British Museum that he hoped would shed light on the pre–Hispanic civilization. It was on that trip to London that he met Alice.

They married in January 1873 and immediately left for New York. In July they sailed for Yucatan, Mexico, to study the Maya ruins. For the rest of their life together Alice and Augustus were partners in their work in Mesoamerican archaeology.

Yucatan at that time was uneasy; there were armed encounters between Mexican federal troops and Maya rebels. It was also unhealthy, with yellow fever that was unusually severe, particularly for people who were not acclimated to the country. Shortly after arriving in Merida, Alice came down with yellow fever; she was one of the fortunate ones who survived.

> We sailed all day, and toward evening saw in the distance some huts that we decided should be our hotel that night. We were lured on by what appeared to be a

massive and extensive wall; only after landing we discovered that what looked like a magnificent fortification was in fact millions of shells, principally conchs, that formed a high perpendicular bank. There was also a smaller shelf composed of thousands of tons of dry sponge and seaweed that might be utilized for commercial purposes. Nearby, on the top of a rock, was a small shrine and a stone snake-head. Afterward we found others of the same kind at intervals along the coast. They were altars, to which at the time of the conquest — according to the historians —fishermen went to make offerings and burn copal to their divinities of the sea.

Next morning we sailed to the end of the island, or as near as possible; it is an iron-bound coast that would afford no protection to any shipwrecked crew. We went back a little way, and hauled our boat up on the beach at the end of the bay where we had found shelter the night before. Near by there were turtle tracks, and soon we had transported one hundred eggs from the nest to our boat.

After examining the country around we launched the boat. When it was necessary to put it on the right course every member of the party wanted to be captain; we consequently stranded on the beach five times; each time the sails had to be lowered and the captains to get into the surf to shove off again. When tired of that fun the command was unanimously given to Dr. Le Plongeon. We then succeeded in starting homeward, and reached San Miguel village just in time to escape a tempest, for on entering our house we heard a small lizard making a noise in a corner of the roof; half an hour later a regular "norther" set in. This lizard is small and dark, subsists on insects, and is a veritable living barometer. It has a loud voice that is never heard except just previous to bad weather. This is so well authenticated that, even if the weather is fair, no sailor will venture out when warned by that lizard [*Here and There in Yucatan, Miscellanies*, pp. 37–39].

The Le Plongeons traveled about Yucatan, spending time in Maya villages to learn the language and customs, exploring the ruins, photographing villagers, and taking photographic surveys of various sites. Augustus was also asked by the governor of Yucatan to vaccinate for smallpox, although there was no money to pay any salary; Augustus agreed, and for a year he and Alice traveled around the site of Uxmal. Alice was an excellent ethnographer, and she wrote detailed accounts of the Indian customs and practices.

Augustus and Alice became convinced that civilization had arisen in the New World and spread east, back to the Old World. The Maya were key to this theory; Atlantis played a part. The Le Plongeons spent the rest of their lives developing and advocating their theory. They spent long periods of time in Yucatan, often living under difficult conditions, searching for links that would support their ideas.

They were always short of money. Both Alice and Augustus wrote and Augustus lectured, not only to educate people on their findings, but also to make money,

As Augustus became increasingly obsessed by his theories, he was increasingly marginalized by archaeologists and other Mesoamericanists. His archaeological accomplishments and his photography became obscured by his reputation. Alice's reputation suffered much the same fate.

After Augustus's death Alice devoted herself to bettering his reputation — and to providing some financial stability for herself.

She died in New York in 1910.

SOURCE: *A Dream of Maya.*

WORKS

Le Plongeon, Alice. *Here and There in Yucatan, Miscellanies.* New York: J. W. Bouton, 1886.
_____. *Queen Moo's Talisman.* New York: Peter Eckler, Publisher, 1902. Alice LePlongeon also published articles.

BOOKS ABOUT OR INCLUDING
  ALICE LE PLONGEON

Desmond, Lawrence Gustave, and Phyllis Mauch Messenger. *A Dream of Maya: Augustus and*

Alice Le Plongeon in Nineteenth Century Yucatan. Albuquerque: University of New Mexico Press, 1988.

Agnes Smith Lewis, 1843–1926, and *Margaret Smith Gibson,* 1843–1920. Scottish.

The twins were the only children in the family; their mother died three weeks after they were born. Agnes and Margaret were well educated by a governess and by their father, who placed particular emphasis on languages. He stipulated that when the twins studied a language, once they were fluent enough to speak it they would travel to the country of that language. Both twins had an aptitude for languages, scholarship — and travel. The family traveled widely in Europe.

When Agnes and Margaret were twenty-three their father died; they were left independent and wealthy. They decided to travel. At that time younger single women traveling alone would take an older woman along. The twins invited Grace Blyth, who had been their teacher and was about five years older than they were, to join them. Their first trip was to Constantinople and Egypt. After they returned home, Grace went back to teaching in London. The twins resolved to move to London as well. Once there, they knew they needed to stay busy; they needed work. They thought about pursuing science.

Agnes decided to write novels, which were moderately successful. Both of them, interested in travel, pursued private study. They learned Spanish, then Greek.

In 1883, at age 40, the twins, with Grace, went to Greece. Grace's cousin, James Gibson, who had long corresponded with the twins, joined them. He'd traveled in Jerusalem and Damascus and had spent three days in the Monastery of St. Catherine on Mt. Sinai. It was his enthusiasm that prompted the twins to go there later. On the way back from Greece he and Margaret married. The two lived in London, and Agnes lived with them.

Agnes, somewhat restless, studied Hebrew and wrote a book about their tour in Greece. Margaret translated "The Alcestis of Euripides."

After a year of marriage James took sick suddenly and died. Margaret was devastated. Agnes, desperate to find a way of helping Margaret, hit on the idea of going to Cambridge to live. In Cambridge with its libraries, manuscripts and scholars, they surely could find something for them. During a visit to Cambridge the librarian, Samuel Lewis, took them to see manuscripts and early printed books at the library. After much conversation they learned he had often visited the mid–East.

Samuel and Agnes fell in love and married. They took a honeymoon tour of Greece, with Margaret, whom Samuel had invited to live with them. Agnes saw very little of Samuel because of his University and clerical duties. There was some travel, and the couple built a house — Castlebrae. In 1891 Samuel became ill and died.

Again travel was the answer to assuage the sorrow, and they thought of St. Catherine's Monastery on Mount Sinai. A friend of Samuel's had visited it, and he'd reported finding some neglected manuscripts, possibly in Syriac. The twins decided that to prepare properly for the trip they needed to learn Arabic and Syriac; they already spoke Greek. They set off in January 1892.

The travel was difficult and rough, and there was a question of whether they'd be admitted to the monastery. But the twins were received by the prior and librarian, who showed them the library, and began

studies of library material. They stayed in their camp/tents.

It was on Saturday that we climbed the mountain....

A lay brother, clad in a blue frock, accompanied us as a guide. We climbed a very snowy path till we reached a spring of delicious water, called "The Fountain of the Shoe-maker," because St. Stephen, a cobbler of Alexandria, once dwelt there.... A little rain fell and dark clouds gathered about the mountain tops, but they passed off as we reached the little "Chapel of the Bursar." Then we mounted a flight of rock-hewn steps by the old way of pilgrims, and passing under an ancient arch turned back to gaze on a magnificent prospect of bare mountains and desert valleys extending to the horizon. Then we went under another archway and came in sight of a few cypresses near the Chapel of Elijah at the foot of the peak named "Jebel Mousa," the proper name for the mountain range being Horeb in its lower, and Sinai in its upper part. Within the Chapel is a cave, said to be that in which the prophet was fed by ravens.... We climbed amongst magnificent cliff pausing now and then to get a draught of delicious water, or to pick up a fine bit of granite graphites* till we reached the foot of the highest precipice: then began a very difficult ascent in which hands and knees had to be constantly used, and the ready help of the monk and Hanna accepted. The monk pulled sprigs of hyssop for us, and the Bedaween found pretty dendrolites for the Woodwardian Museum. Our eyes were much irritated by the dust thrown off by the ill smelling plant called Sphaka, which it was often necessary to grasp in order to get over some boulder. At length we reached the foot of the great inaccessible rock which crowns the summit, a rock which no human foot has ever rested on, and peering over a wind-swept ledge had a magnificent view of the extensive plain of Er-Rahah beneath us....

As I knew there were three roads by which we might descend, I asked Hanna three times which of these we were on saying we should prefer to return either by the

---

*Which was not the right thing after all.

path we had come up, or by a steeper and shorter one which led directly to the convent. Hanna, thereupon, directed Euphemios to lead us down the very longest way possible, by a path that brought us into a Wady on the side of Jebel Mousa, farthest from the convent, so that we had still five miles to walk over rough stones, in fact, to make a half circuit of Horeb at its base. I was very angry, and scolded Hanna for not consulting me. We were not consoled by being conducted through two little olive gardens belonging to the convent, in other Wadies, nor even being shown the genuine rock (a big boulder) which Moses struck in anger. I was so tired that I could hardly walk, and long after the moon had risen I was obliged to sit down on stones to rest. We reached our tents at eight o'clock, an Arab coming out with a lamp to meet us. Our excursion had occupied eleven hours, ten of which we had spent in quick walking and climbing over the roughest of rocks and stones — so it may be imagined we lost no time in retiring to rest [*In the Shadow of Sinai*, pp. 20–23].

On that first trip when the twins arrived in Cairo, they had an introduction to the Archbishop of Mount Sinai. He gave them permission to visit the Convent of St. Catharine on Mount Sinai, as well as a letter of introduction to the convent prior and the librarian.

They were delighted at being able to converse with us in their own tongue, and to read my descriptions of their own birthplaces in the Greek edition of my book Glimpses of Greek Life and Scenery and especially did they welcome us as friends of Dr. Rendel Harris. When I was asked "What do you wish to see?" I replied, "All your oldest Syriac manuscripts, particularly those which Dr. Harris had not time to examine, for I want to take a report of them to him."
A few minutes after this daring speech we were taken through a small room containing twelve boxes of MSS, into the dark closet which I had so often dreamt about, and from one of its two little chests some six or eight manuscripts were carried into the light of day. I first examined No. 16, which contained amongst other treatises the long-lost Apology of Aristides. Then I saw the palimpsest. It had a forbidding look for it was very dirty and its leaves were nearly all stuck together through their having remained unturned probably since the last Syrian monk had died, centuries ago, in the convent.

I had never before seen a palimpsest, but my father had often related to us wonderful stories of how the old monks when vellum had become scarce and paper was not yet invented scraped way the pages of their books and wrote something new on top of it; and how, after the lapse of ages, the old ink was revived by the action of common air, and the old words peeped up again; and how a text of Plato had come to light in this curious way [pp. 83–84].

The twins returned to the Convent of St. Catharine on Mount Sinai, where they were warmly greeted.

The many hints as to changes in the Convent which Father Nicodemus had given us in Cairo were more than justified. It fell to my lot that day, as it does to that of few people, to see the fulfilment [sic] of an object on which I had once set my heart [p. 110].

Unknown to the librarian, they examined the neglected manuscripts their friend had told them about. They found that these were palimpsests of great age. They photographed 110 pages of what was determined to be a Syriac Codex.

By accident they made another find. At meals the butter was served on vellum, which often was a palimpsest. Agnes would casually peruse the "butter dish" to see if the palimpsest was anything of interest. One morning she recognized a verse of the gospels. Tactful inquiries led her to a certain basket in the corner of a work room. There they found a complete Syriac palimpsest of 358 pages. None of the monks knew any Syriac, and they had no idea of the value.

The pages were stuck together by dirt and damp. Agnes and Margaret hit on the solution of separating the pages with steam from their tea kettle. (They traveled with tea, kettle, and spirit lamp for heating the water.)

Agnes dated the material on top to 700–800 C.E., which meant the underwriting was even older. The librarian was skeptical about their photographing the material, but he agreed.

The twins made six trips in all to Mount Sinai and St. Catherine's convent, the last in 1906, when they were sixty-three.

Agnes published her translation of the entire codex, and then published a final definitive work.

The discovery and the scholarship surrounding the codex caused considerable stir. Some scholars rate the discovery as significant as the finding of the Dead Sea Scrolls.

Their home, Castlebrae, was a center of a social, intellectual and religious circles. The twins still did some traveling (less adventurous) and they continued their scholarly research and work. They received honorary degrees from various universities — but not from Cambridge.

Mary Kingsley was among their friends. She reportedly wrote a friend that women have always gone where they have no business to go — her friends Mrs. Gibson and Mrs. Lewis "stroll to and fro in the Sinai desert as though it were Sauchiehall Street." The twins liked Mary very much. When Mary Kingsley died Agnes wrote *The Times*: "Her mind was like a finely-tempered sword which was forever wearing out its scabbard."

Margaret died first, in 1920, at the age of 77. Agnes, who became increasingly disoriented, lived six years longer.

SOURCES: *The Dictionary of Literary Biography*, Volume 2. Price, *The Ladies of Castlebrae*.

WORKS

Lewis also wrote several novels, a book of poetry, and a biography of Rev. Samuel Savage Lewis.

Lewis, Agnes Smith. *Eastern Pilgrims: The Travels of Three Ladies*. Illustrated by Gibson. London: Hurst and Blackett, 1870.
_____. *Glimpses of Greek Life and Scenery*. London: Hurst and Blackett, 1884.
_____. *In the Shadow of Sinai: A Story of Travel and Research from 1895 to 1897*. Cambridge: Macmillan & Bowes, 1898. Brighton, England: The Alpha Press, 1999.
_____. *A Lady's Impressions of Cyprus in 1893*. London: Remington, 1894.
_____. *Light on the Four Gospels from the Sinai Palimpsest*. London: Williams & Norgate, 1913.
_____. *Through Cyprus*. London: Hurst and Blackett, 1887.
_____. *Two Unpublished Letters*. Cambridge: Privately printed, 1893.

OTHER

Lewis, Agnes Smith, translator. *A Translation of the Four Gospels from the Syriac of the Sinaitic Palimpsest*. London: Macmillan, 1894.

Margaret Smith Gibson or Margaret Dunlop Gibson:

Gibson, Margaret Smith. *How the Codex Was Found, A Narrative of Two Visits to Sinai from Mrs. Lewis's Journals, 1892–1893*. Edited with an introduction by Gibson. Cambridge: Macmillan and Bowes, 1893.

Additionally both Lewis and Gibson wrote, translated, or contributed to numerous other publications and books including many on the Syriac texts.

BOOKS ABOUT OR INCLUDING AGNES SMITH LEWIS AND MARGARET SMITH GIBSON

Price, Whigham A. *The Ladies of Castlebrae: A Story of Nineteenth-Century Travel and Research*. Gloucester: Sutton, 1985.

The twins' papers, notebooks, photographs, and other material are maintained by Westminster College, Cambridge.

Emmeline Lott

Emmeline Lott's books are based on her position of governess for the grand pacha Ibrahim, who was the son of Ismael Pacha, the Turkish viceroy of Egypt. She arrived in Egypt in April 1864 to begin her duties as governess. A few months later she asked for a three-month sick leave, and she was told to resign. In August she left Constantinople for England. From that she wrote three extremely detailed accounts of her time and observations in Egypt.

In her books she refers to travels in Paris and to the fact she lived for a time in Bordeaux. Beyond that, except for information about the publication of her books, nothing is known about her.

SOURCE: *Dictionary of Literary Biography.*

WORKS

Lott, Emmeline. *The English Governess in Egypt: Harem Life in Egypt and Constantinople.* London: Bentley, 1866.
_____. *The Grand Pacha's Cruise on the Nile in the Viceroy of Egypt's Yacht.* London: Newby, 1869.
_____. *The Mohaddetyn in the Palace. Nights in the Harem: or The Mohaddetyn in the Palace of Ghezire.* London: Chapman & Hall, 1867.

Emily Lowe

Emily Lowe was a horsewoman.

Darkness soon came on; the twilight feebly penetrating the thick woods, and the hearty laughs of our guide were the only cheering sounds. He was in the highest spirit; my costume and attitude excited his warmest admiration. He was under the impression they were the last English fashion; and that great nation, which he knew swayed the world from somewhere, seemed to rise in his imagination in still more mysterious grandeur, and a stray cigar or two given him completed the illusion. What would one think of two French ladies, or two of any other nation, penetrating into the wildest recesses of Norway and finding out new roads for the natives? Who but English could do it? Madame Ida Pfeiffer has been rather active, but she confesses to being skinny and wiry and was able to wriggle about unmolested; the English or Americans are rarely of that make, and so generally blooming and attractive, that it must be a certain inborn right of conquest which makes them early always the first to penetrate into the arcane of countries triumphantly [*Unprotected Females in Norway*, p. 286].

WORKS

Lowe, Emily. *Unprotected Females in Norway, or The Pleasant Way of Travelling There, Passing Through Denmark and Sweden.* London: Routledge, 1857. Reprinted in Foster, Shirley, and Sara Mills, Eds., *An Anthology of Women's Travel Writing.* Manchester, England: Manchester University Press, 2002.
_____. *Unprotected Females in Sicily, Calabria, and on Top of Mount Aetna.* London: Routledge, 1859.

Georgina Mary Muir Mackenzie (Lady Sebright)
?–1874, and
Adeline Paulina Irby,
1831–1911.

Georgina and Paulina first traveled together in 1858, when they made a tour of Germany and the Austrian Empire. Neither woman was yet thirty; they were well-educated and at that time not politically active. Consumption was a factor in the Muir Mackenzie family, and Georgina's health was always a concern.

Their trip was leisurely, and there were frequent visits to spas. When they were to travel from Vienna to Cracow, they decided to cross the Carpathian Mountains instead of taking the usual route by train. They traveled alone and frequently rode in hay carts. They enjoyed the adventure — except for the fact they were thought to be spies and were even arrested, accused of "Panslavism." At the time they didn't know the term.

The incident heightened their interest in the political affairs of the region, and they became determined to undertake more serious travel and to learn more about the area of Slavonia. They learned Serbo-Croat and some Bulgarian. Over the next three years they made five trips to the area; they were always accompanied by guards and Dragomen.

Travel was arduous, and the countryside through which they traveled was isolated. They went from town to town, learning more about conditions under the Turks, the lives of the women, and education for girls. By the end of their travels they were strong champions of the South Slavs and determined to improve the condition of Christian Slav women through education.

The morning on which we entered Kóssovo was checquered by those alternations of cloud and gleam which usually herald a showery day. The wind blew fresh from the snow-wreaths on Liubatern, and swung aloft the boughs of the oak-copse, showing bright little lawns and dewy pastures, to which the grazing horses and cattle pushed their way through brushwood and fern: — we felt that we had exchanged the yellow plains of the East for the green mountain and watered valleys of Europe. Unhappily, the verdure and the breeze are all that now testify of Europe on the field of Kóssovo....

The large plain of Kóssovo, situated in a mountainous region and lying as it were before the odors of Danubian Serbia, Bosnia, and Albania, has in all ages been marked by its position as a battle-field, and it is still pointed out as the spot where combat may once more decide the fate of the surrounding lands....

[T]o this day it is scarcely possible for a traveller to converse for more than a few minutes with a genuine Serbian without hearing the name of Kóssovo.... We have ourselves been present when Serbians quarreling were quieted by the remonstrance, — "What, will ye strive among yourselves like your fathers before the battle of Kóssovo?" and we have heard a Serbian peasant answer, when praised for bringing in a large load of wood, say, "But it is time we Serbians should gather in our wood from the field of Kóssovo" [*The Turks, the Greeks, and the Slavons*, pp. 213–214].

The whole population of Roshaï turned out to see us, and a truly picturesque community they appeared: many wore turbans, and all wore white and red garments that well set off their stalwart forms.

The dwelling prepared for us belonged to a Mussulman. We were not a little surprised at its size, cleanliness, and the proportion of glass to paper in the window frames; above all, there was a regular fireplace, such as one still sees in mediaeval houses in England, with a peaked stone canopy for chimney-piece. The young mudir ushered us into the room, and then seated himself *à la Franca*, threw off his fez, and ran his fingers through abundant hair, which showed small sign of the Mussulman tonsure. He then began to talk at a great rate in Slavonic, and called to his counsels — not the master of the house, a dignified Bosniac, but the Christian kodgia bashi and pope, both of whom he introduced to us in a perfectly conventional style. In return those representatives of the rayah treated the mudir with ease; nor could we discern in their behaviour anything of the usual traces of fear.... Hereupon it appeared that the mudir had not the slightest knowledge of such a place as Détchani, although the far-famed monastery lies but thirteen hours from Roshaï....

... [A] fresh solicitude arose. Where was our luggage? We had not passed it on the way, and hence expected to have found it awaiting us, but no; and after the mudir was gone, some time passed without its appearance. At length, unpleasing ideas suggested themselves; either the drivers must have mistaken the road, or else some accident having happened, they had quietly resolved to wait where they were, counting that we should send to look after them. At last the mudir did dispatch some zaptiés, but not till it was already dark, and we had made up our minds to an uncomfortable night. However, about nine o'clock the wished-for tramp of horses was heard, and the drivers being called to account, explained that there had been no accident, nor had they lost their way, but they had taken a different road from ours, and in the middle of the day had indulged in a long rest [pp. 342–343].

Finally, suffering from ill health, they went home. *Across the Carpathians*, written by both of them, was published anonymously in 1862 (but with no serious attempt to hide the identity of the authors). They also began speaking publicly about their travels and observations.

Meanwhile, they were investigating how they might advance their ideas of providing education. In 1865 they had established The Association for the Promotion of Education among the Slavonic Children of Bosnia and Herzegovina, and they were making inquiries with the British consul in Sarajevo about setting up a girls' school.

It was an inauspicious start; the Association did not attract the attention they hoped for.

In 1867 *The Turks, the Greeks and the Slavons,* their major work which was primarily written by Georgina, drew significant attention. Georgina's health had worsened. Meanwhile, Paulina had become a close friend of Florence Nightingale and was becoming increasingly involved with her missions.

Finally, after considerable arranging, a school was opened in Sarajevo in 1869. By then, Georgina's and Paulina's lives were moving in different directions. Georgina had gone to Corfu for her health; while there she renewed her friendship with Sir Charles Sebright (begun when she and possibly Paulina had traveled to the Ionian Islands). He now was British consul in Corfu.

They married in 1871. Georgina died three years later. In her will she established a trust fund to provide for the training of Slav teachers.

The school in Sarajevo did not prosper, due to a variety of problems. The school was being run by Protestant deaconesses from Germany; in 1871 they withdrew from the school and Paulina took on the task of running the school. She was aided by a new companion, Priscilla Johnston, a family connection. Through the efforts of the two of them the school was firmly established.

Violence broke out in 1875, a revolt against Turkish rule. Paulina and Priscilla fled, taking some of their students with them to be placed in a school in Prague. The plight of the many refugees could not be ignored; when they returned to England, Priscilla and Paulina worked with the Bosnian and Herzogovinian Fugitives' Orphan Relief fund. They returned to Croatia and distributed food and blankets, working through the harsh winter in the midst of smallpox and typhus. They also established eight schools housing over four hundred refugee children. This would be their cause for years, aided by Florence Nightingale.

Paulina was increasingly outspoken about her pro–Slav, anti–Turk stance. Consequently after the Treaty of Berlin in June 1878, when Bosnia and Herzegovina came under Austrian jurisdiction, the Austrian authorities were reluctant to allow Paulina and Priscilla to return to Sarajevo. It took the intervention of influential friends to obtain permission. They were warmly welcomed in Sarajevo, and their school flourished.

Priscilla returned to England in 1885. Paulina stayed until her death in 1911. People came to her funeral from all over Bosnia and from Serbia. In 1934 celebrations were held in Sarajevo and throughout Yugoslavia to commemorate the centenary of her birth (although she was born in 1831).

SOURCE: Anderson, *Two Women Travelers in the Balkans in the 1860s: Georgina Muir Mackenzie, Adeline Paulina Irby*. Proceedings of the BRLSI, Volume 8, 2004.

WORKS

Mackenzie, Georgina, and Paulina Irby. *Across the Carpathians*. London: Macmillan and Co., 1862.
_____. *The Turks, the Greeks and the Slavons. Travels in the Slavonic Provinces of Turkey-in-Europe*. London: Bell and Daldry, 1867.

BOOKS ABOUT OR INCLUDING GEORGIA MACKENZIE AND PAULINA IRBY

Anderson, Dorothy. *Two Women Travelers in the Balkans in the 1860s: Georgina Muir MacKenzie, Adeline Paulina Irby*. Proceedings of the BRLSI, Vol. 8, 2004.

Susan Shelby Magoffin,

1827–1855. American.

Susan Shelby Magoffin was eighteen when she accompanied her husband on a trading expedition to Santa Fe and then to Old Mexico. She was born in 1827 at Arcadia, south of Danville, Kentucky, and was educated at home. She was the granddaughter of the first governor of Kentucky. She and Samuel were married in 1845. One of Susan's sisters, Anna, married Samuel's brother, Beriah, who was later governor of Kentucky.

For their honeymoon Samuel and Susan went to Philadelphia and New York, where Samuel bought various goods to take to Santa Fe. In the spring of 1846 they went to Independence, Missouri, to wait for those goods to arrive and to begin their trek.

Samuel and his brother James were partners in a trading enterprise that took goods overland to Mexico in exchange for specie or products. This was a very lucrative business, but not without its perils.

Friday [*February*] 5th. A la leguna del muerto. 2 O'k last evening we started into the jornado, traveled till 5 o'k and stoped [*sic*] two hours to rest the animals and get a little supper. The wind blew high all the evening and the dust considerable. A short time after we stoped or when the fire was made the scene reminded me of one described by Mr. Gregg in his Prairie scenes. The grass caught fire near to our baggage wagon and but for the great activity of the servants and wagoners all of whom collected around, we should have been now with out the wagon or any thing in it and perhaps worse off than that, the consequent explosion of two powder kegs in it might have caused [*cost*] the life of some of us. They beat it out with blanket, sticks, wagon-whips & in short every thing within their reach, half-dozen of the men pushed the wagon off as fast as the fire advanced towards them, till 'twas entirely extinguished. 'Tis singular how rapidly it will spread in the dry grass — before the alarm could be given yesterday it spread several yards [*Down the Santa Fe Trail*, p. 197].

Saturday [*August*] 29th. I have visited this morning the ruins of an ancient pueblo [*Pecos in New Mexico*], or village, now desolate and a home of the wild beast and bird of the forest.

It created sad thoughts when I found myself riding almost heedlessly over the work of these once mighty people. There perhaps was pride, power and wealth, carried to its utter most limit, for here tis said the great Montezuma once lived, though it [*is*] probably a false tradition as the most learned and ancient American historians report that great monarch to have resided much farther south than any portion of New Mexico.

At any rate these pueblos believed in and long looked for the coming of their king to redeem them from the *Spanish yoke*. And I am told by persons who saw it, that tis only within some two or three years since it was inhabited by one family only, the last of a once numerous population. These continued to keep alive "Montezuma's fire" till it was accidentally extinguished, and they abandoned the place, believing that Fate had turned her hand against them. This fire, which was kept in vaults under ground, now almost entirely filled in by the falling ruins, was believed to have been kindled by the king himself, and their ancestors were told to keep it burning till he returned, which he certainly would to redeem them, and it has been continued down to this time, or within a few years [pp. 99–100].

Friday, July 2nd. Wrote a long letter to mama this evening. I do wish I could have a letter from home; how lonely it is, week after week & month after month, and I hear nothing more than if I never belonged to their numbers. 'Twould indeed give new energy to my being to hear from them, quite a new creature I should feel but as it is I am perfectly isolated [p. 236].

Susan came down with yellow fever on the journey; while she was ill she had a son, who died soon after birth. She also apparently had a miscarriage at some time.

The expedition related in Susan's journal ended the trading enterprise, and Samuel and his family returned to Kentucky. Samuel bought a large estate, and the family lived there for about four years. Susan and Samuel had another son, who died young. In 1851 a daughter, Jane, was born.

In 1852 the family moved to St. Louis County, Missouri, where Samuel purchased land. Susan died in 1855. Samuel lived out the rest of his life as a country gentleman, dying in 1888.

SOURCE: Introduction to *Down the Santa Fe Trail and into Mexico.*

WORKS

Magoffin, Susan. *Down the Santa Fe Trail and into Mexico. The Diary of Susan Shelby Magoffin 1846–1847.* Edited by Stella M. Drumm. New Haven, Connecticut: Yale University Press, 1926.

Julia Charlotte Maitland,
?–1864. British.

Julia's mother was a niece of Fanny Burney, the novelist, and thus the granddaughter of Dr. Charles Burney, a traveler and music historian.

She was a young married lady when she accompanied her husband to India. Her husband's position was not made clear in the book, but as there are references to "A's Court," he may have been a magistrate. They settled at St. Thomé, near Madras, and during the hot summer Julia and their daughter Etta went to a cooler area. Julia helped set up a school. Although she was not one of the teachers, she sometimes lectured in astronomy as well as other subjects. She also worked at learning the local dialects. She studied the local botany and entomology and sent specimens home to the British Museum. Julia's book reflects the fact that she was a well-educated or well-read woman of wide interests, curious about her surroundings and with particular interest in science.

I have been trying to entomologize, as there [*is an*] abundance of curious insects. Mr. Spence himself told me, before I left home, that the insects of India were very little known; and that I could not fail to find many new specimens, especially among the smaller Colopteria [*Letters from Madras,* p. 71].

At times she was living in a rather isolated area.

Today I have had a specimen of the kind of company I am likely to see at Samuldavee. Three wild monkeys came to take a walk round the house and peep in at the windows: they were the first I had seen, and very fine creatures — what the natives call "*first caste*" monkeys," not little wizen imps like live mummies, such as we see in England, but real handsome wild beasts. They were of a kind of greenish-grey colour, with black faces and long tails, and their coats as sleek as race horse's. They were as large as calves, and as slim as greyhounds. They bounded about most beautifully, and at last darted with one spring to the top of a rock ten feet high, and sat there like gentlemen taking the breeze and talking politics [pp. 190–191].

Etta's health was difficult in the climate, and like many families would do, Julia and Etta left to return to England, probably in January 1840. Her husband accompanied them as far as the Cape.

She was widowed some time after her return home and subsequently remarried. She worked with her mother preparing the seven-volume edition of Burney's diary and letters. In addition to the publication of her letters from India, she wrote three books for children. She died in 1864.

SOURCE: Internet: *http://www.wood stckbooks.co.uk/vic/maitland.html,* Dec. 2006.

WORKS

Maitland, Julia Charlotte. *Letters from Madras in the Years 1836–1839.* By "A Lady." London: John Murray, 1843.

Kate Marsden, 1859–1931.

Kate was a traveler with a mission: to find an herb reputed to alleviate the suffering caused by leprosy. She heard of this herb while working as a nurse during the Russo-Turkish war. The herb could be found only in northern Siberia; the secret was so carefully kept that information might only be given to someone who could prove he or she was working to help those who had leprosy. At that time — as happens periodically — there was a general notion that shamans and plants that could work marvelous cures could be found in an exotic, remote place, this time in Siberia. (There is a Shangri-la aspect to this; at times the secrets lie with a mysterious tribe in Africa or the Amazon.) Kate decided that since some doctors didn't care enough to risk their life or health to get the herb, while others didn't have the time or the money to make the trip, and still others wouldn't or couldn't spend the years it would take to visit the lepers and test out the herb in a systematic way, it was up to her to get the herb and learn to work with it.

She decided to go herself to try to persuade those who knew about the herb to share the knowledge with her, a woman, and not a man who might want to use the herb for his own advantage. In 1890 she presented her proposal to Queen Victoria, who sought the assistance of the Empress of Russia to allow Kate to travel in Russia.

In preparation for the journey Kate visited the Middle East to learn about the conditions of lepers there. The trip strengthened her resolution to get the herb, and soon after she left for Moscow. The journey across Asia, primarily by sledge, was rugged and difficult, but finally, after several months, she reached Yakutsk, the capital of the Yakutia region in northern Siberia. From there she rode 2000 miles on horseback to Viluisk, then traveled around visiting the scattered groups of leprosy sufferers. She spent about three months searching out leprosy sufferers, whose living conditions appalled her.

Our experience of sledging along a road terribly broken up, owing to the immense traffic and almost endless string of sledges, carrying heavy loads of goods to the annual Siberian fair, held in February, will be repeated in your case, dear reader, if you ever undertake a similar journey to Siberia at a corresponding period. Bump, jolt, bump, jolt — over huge frozen lumps of snow and into holes, and up and down those dreadful waves and furrows, made by the traffic — such is the stimulating motion you will have to submit to for a few thousand miles. Your head seems to belong to every part of the sledge; it is first bumped against the top; then the conveyance gives a lurch, and you get an unexpected knock against the side; then you cross one of the ruts, and, first, you are thrown violently forward against the driver, and, second, you just as quickly bound. This sort of motion is all very well for a few miles; but after a time it gets too monotonously trying. You ache from head to foot; you are bruised all over; your poor brain throbs until you give way to a kind of hysterical outcry; your head-gear gets displaced; your temper, naturally, becomes slightly furled, and you are ready to gasp, from so frequently clutching at the sides to save yourself.... Night comes on apace, to soften your feelings with a low-ered temperature and the pleasing sugges-tions that darkness brings. Still on you mer-rily go — but, oh, for five minutes' peace! Bumping, jolting, tossing; heaved, pitched and thumped [*On Sledge and Horseback to the Outcast Siberian Lepers*, pp. 18–19.]

Sometimes we rested all day, and traveled at night to avoid the intense heat. We passed forests, where hundreds of trees had fallen. According to popular superstition, the Yakut witches quarreled, and met in the forest to fight out the dispute. But the spirit of the forest became so angry at this con-duct that he let loose a band of inferior spir-its and then, in a moment, a tempest began and rushed through the forest, tearing up the trees and causing them to fall in the di-rection of those disputants who were in the right. But the true meaning of those fallen trees is yet more interesting and singular than the superstitious one. Underneath the upper soil of these forests combustion goes on, beginning in the winter. The thaw of summer and the deluge of rain seem to have little effect upon the fire, for it still works its way unsubdued. When the tempest comes the trees drop by hundreds, having but slight power of resistance. I brought home with me some of this burnt earth, intending to send it to the British Museum, should no specimen be already there [pp. 102–103].

Apparently the bishop of Yakutsk did have specimens of the herb, but it's not clear what the herb was, or whether the specimens made it back to London. During her stay in Russia Kate became very ill and had to be taken back to Saint Petersburg.

After two years in Russia she returned to England. Her book, *On Sledge and Horseback to Outcast Siberian Lepers*, publicized their plight and raised funds, as did her lectures. She was largely responsible for the founding of the St. Francis Leprosy Guild in 1895.

Kate was elected a Fellow of the Royal Geographical Society, one of only twenty-one women to receive the honor between 1892 and 1894. (Subsequently some of the Fellows successfully challenged the Society making additional appointments of women, and membership was again closed to women until 1913.) Ironically, Kate was not allowed to at-tend the anniversary dinner in 1894; since she would be the only woman among 200 men and most of them would be smoking, her at-tendance was deemed to be unsuitable.

In addition to working on behalf of leprosy sufferers, Kate spent the rest of her life involved in a wide variety of charitable endeavors.

SOURCES: Internet: *www.stfrancisle prosy.org*, March 2006; *Ladies on the Loose: Women Travellers of the 18th and 19th Cen-turies.*

WORKS

Marsden, Kate. *My Mission in Siberia: A Vindi-cation.* London: E. Stanford, 1921.
_____. *On Sledge and Horseback to the Outcast Siberian Lepers.* London: Record, 1892.

BOOKS ABOUT OR INCLUDING KATE MARSDEN

Hamalian, Leo, ed. *Ladies on the Loose: Women Travellers of the 18th and 19th Centuries.* New York: Dodd Mead, 1981.

Harriet Martineau, 1802–1876.

Harriet was born in Norwich, England. Her father, a Huguenot, was a wine im-porter and a bombazine manufacturer. Harriet, the sixth of eight children, had an unusually good education in languages, the classics, rhetoric, and philosophy. She also had musical training. She was educated to be a governess; however, when she was twelve it became apparent that she was growing deaf. It was clear she would be unable to support herself as a governess; needlework was deemed to be her only option, and she was encouraged to pursue this avocation. She, however, had other ideas.

She attributed the development of her interest in writing to her brother James; in 1821 when he was leaving for college, he suggested that Harriet write something for a Unitarian periodical. Harriet's paper, signed with the initial "v," was published and, as it happened, read aloud and admired by her elder brother, Thomas. When she told him she was the author he told her: "Now, dear, leave it to other women to make shirts and darn stockings; and do you devote yourself to this."

She did, although at that time this was considered inappropriate for a woman of her social class. In just a few years, however, both her brother Thomas and her father died; this was followed by the failure of the family business and the bank and stock crises of 1825–1826. Harriet, declaring that they had lost their gentility, could now write openly. She continued writing for the periodical and became its only paid contributor.

In 1829 she moved to London to live with an aunt and uncle, in order to establish more literary connections. When her aunt insisted that Harriet should instead focus on her needlework, her mother ordered her to leave London.

Hearing of an essay contest, she entered an essay for each of the three categories and won in every category. This convinced her mother that Harriet should go to London every year for three months.

It was the publication of the *Illustrations of Political Economy* series, 1832–1834, that proved to be the turning point. Al-

though this focused primarily on British issues, she also wrote about other countries, finding much of her material in the travel accounts of others. Her study of these travel accounts led her to consider the possibility of traveling herself.

Her first trip outside England was to America in 1834–1836. She published three books based on her American travels.

All this morning we were passing plantations, and there were houses along both banks at short intervals; sometimes the mansions of planters, sometimes sugar-houses, sometimes groups of slave-dwellings, painted or unpainted, standing under the shade of sycamores, magnolias, live oaks, or Pride-of-India trees. Many dusky gazing figures of men with the axe, and women with the pitcher, would have tempted the pencil of an artist. The fields were level and rich-looking, and they were invariably bounded by the glorious forest. Towards noon we perceived by the number of sailing-boats that we were near some settlement, and soon came upon Donaldsonville, a considerable village, with a large unfinished Statehouse, where the legislature of Louisiana once sat, which was afterward removed to New-Orleans, whence it has never come back. Its bayou boasts a steamer, by which planters in the south back-country are conveyed to their estates on leaving the Mississippi.

We now felt ourselves sufficiently at home to decide upon the arrangement of our day. The weather was too hot to let the fatigues of general conversation be endurable for many hours together; and there was little in the general society of the vessel to make us regret this. We rose at five or a little later, the early morning being delicious. Breakfast was ready at seven, and after it I apparently went to my stateroom for the morning; but this was not exactly the case. I observed that the laundresses hung their counterpanes and sheets to dry in the gallery before my window, and that, therefore, nobody came to that gallery. It struck me that this must be the coolest part of the boat, such an evaporation as was perpetually going on. I therefore stepped out of my window, with my book, work, or writing; and sitting under the shade of a counterpane, and in full view of the river and western shore, spent in quiet some of the pleasantest mornings I have ever known.

We passed Baton Rouge, on the east Louisiana bank, on the afternoon of this day. It stands on the first eminence we had seen on these shores, and the barracks have a handsome appearance from the water. A summer-house, perched on a rising ground, was full of people, amusing themselves with smoking and looking abroad upon the river; and truly, they had an enviable station. A few miles farther on we went ashore at the wooding-place, and I had my first walk in the untrodden forest. The height of the trees seemed incredible as we stood at their foot and looked up. It made us feel suddenly dwarfed. We stood in a crowd of locust and cottonwood trees, elm, maple, and live oak; and they were all bound together by an inextricable tangle of creepers, which seemed to forbid our penetrating many paces into the forest beyond where the woodcutters had intruded. I had a great horror of going too far, and was not sorry to find it impossible; it would be so easy for the boat to leave two or three passengers behind without finding it out, and no fate could be conceived more desolate [*Retrospect of Western Travel*, pp. 9–10; 13].

Subsequently she traveled to Europe, but she became seriously ill and had to return to England where she lived with her sister, who was married to a doctor. She spent five years on bed rest. Her poor health hampered her writing and her income. Family and friends, some of whom were quite influential, helped out.

Eventually she felt well enough to establish her own home in the Lake District, where her neighbors were William Wordsworth and Matthew Arnold. She experimented with small, self-sufficient farming, and she wrote.

In 1846 she traveled to Egypt, Palestine, Syria and Lebanon with a group of other Europeans. She found traveling with a group trying.

Upon her return she continued her involvement with social reform. Never in robust health, she continued her lecturing and writing. She died at her home in June 1876.

SOURCE: *Dictionary of Literary Biography.*

WORKS

Martineau, Harriet. *Eastern Life: Present and Past.* London: E. Moxon, 1848.
_____. *Letters from Ireland.* London: J. Chapman, 1852.
_____. *Retrospect of Western Travel.* London: Saunders & Otley, 1838. *Society in America* was based on these diaries.
_____. *Society in America.* London: Saunders & Otley, 1837.

Anne Cary Maudslay, c. 1848–1926. American.

[Her name is variously given as Ann or Anne; she was known throughout her life as Annie.]

Anne Cary Morris was descended from many of the founding families of the United States — Randolphs, Jeffersons, Carys, and Morrises. She was also descended from Powhatan and Pocahontas through the Cary line. The Morrises had settled early in New York; Gouverneur Morris was Anne's grandfather, and her father has been named after him.

Alfred Percival Maudslay (1850–1931) was from a British family that had made a fortune in manufacturing. His early career had been with the British foreign service. In the course of his travels he became increasing interested in archaeology. Finally, in 1880, while on a trip around the world, he landed in Central America and began his famous explorations and surveying of the Maya ruins. From that point there was no turning back for him.

In 1872 Anne met Maudslay while on

a trip with her mother that included a stop at Yosemite. Alfred and his brother Charles were returning from Mexico, and had stopped in San Francisco. From there they planned to go to Yosemite by train to the end of the line, then by coach. The coach passengers included several ladies from the East, among them Mrs. Gouverneur Morris and her two daughters. The long coach ride gave them ample opportunity to get acquainted. When the trip was over Alfred and Anne parted, but kept in touch through letters and occasional visits. According to family tradition, however, theirs was no more than an ordinary friendship for the next twenty years.

However that may be, in 1892 they married in Rome. In 1894, Anne accompanied Alfred on another extensive trip in Central America. *A Glimpse at Guatemala*, written by both Anne and Alfred, resulted from those travels.

The Lake of Atitlan

Our tent was pitched so close to the precipice that even from my bed I had a grand view of the lake, and could watch the black masses of the volcanoes looming clear cut and solemn in the moonlight, or changing from black to grey in the early dawn; then a rosy flush would touch the peak of Atitlan and the light creep down its side, revealing for a brief half-hour every detail of the cinder ridge and chasm on its scarred and wounded slopes, until with a sudden burst of glory the sun rose above the eastern hills to strike the mirror-like surface of the lake far beneath us; then, almost before the sun had power to drink up these lees of the night, from the deep gap between the hills to the south, a finger of white cloud, borne up from the seaward slope, would creep round the peak of Atitlan only to be dissipated in the cooler air; but finger followed finger, and the mysterious hand never lost its grasp until, about noon, great billowy clouds rolled up through the gap and the outpost was fairly captured, although the crater itself often stood out clear above the cloudy belt [*A Glimpse of Guatemala*, p. 47].

Copan

I wish I could do justice to these imposing plazas, studded with strangely carved monuments and surrounded by lofty mounds and great stone stairways, moss-grown and hoary with age, broken by the twisted roots of giant trees, but very solemn and imposing in their decay. The huge mass of squared and faced building-stones, the profusion of sculptured ornament, boldly-carved human figures, strangely grotesque imps — half human and half animal, — elaborate scrolls, graceful and beautiful feather-work, the later especially crisp and delicate in execution, all combined to make it difficult to believe that no metal tools were used by the ancient Indian workmen. Yet the fact remains that no implements other than stone axes and obsidian flakes have ever been found amongst the ruins, and this adds to the wonder and mystery which enshrouds them, so that one almost fears even to guess at the number of centuries or the thousands of busy hands and brains which, under such conditions, must have gone to the accomplishment of the work.

I was always conscious of a longing desire to witness some great ceremony at Copan, such as one's imagination conjures up amid such surroundings, and the thought constantly recurred to me that possibly in the half-Christian, half-heathen rites of the Indian pilgrims and the strange dances they indulge in on certain festal occasions some echo might yet be caught of the ancient ceremonial [p. 126].

When they weren't traveling the two made their home in England. Alfred continued to be active professionally after his traveling years ended. Anne died in 1926.

SOURCE: *Alfred Maudslay and the Maya.*

WORKS

Maudslay, Anne Cary, and Alfred Percival Maudslay. *A Glimpse of Guatemala*. London: John Murray, 1899. Reprint: Detroit: Blaine Ethridge Books, 1979.

BOOKS ABOUT OR INCLUDING ANNE
CARY MAUDSLAY

Graham, Ian. *Alfred Maudslay and the Maya.*
Norman: University of Oklahoma Press,
2002.

Elizabeth (Nina) Sarah Mazuchelli, 1832—1914. British.

Little is known of Elizabeth's life before she married her husband, Francis, in 1853. No maiden name was given on the marriage record. Francis was an Anglican parish priest.

In 1857, after they'd been married four years, he joined the British Army as a chaplain. A year later they went to India. The Indian mutiny, which had taken place in 1857, was largely settled, but there was uneasiness about the illusion of British invincibility in India.

The heat was almost intolerable, and it was a relief when, after eleven years, Francis was ordered to serve in Darjeeling, in the Himalayas. Nina thrived in the mountains. She was a good artist; she rode everywhere in the area and took her easel with her, painting everything in sight. Increasingly she was attracted to the Himalayas. Finally, she proposed to Francis that they make a "grand tour" into the interior. Francis was reluctant — and skeptical, so he took her on a trial camping trip into the hills for two weeks. Nothing bothered Nina; she loved the outdoor life.

After several weeks of preparation, Nina, Francis, a friend only identified as C., and about seventy servants set off. Women's clothing at that time made physical movement difficult and climbing almost impossible. Nina made no compromise with her choice of wardrobe; instead she was carried either in a reclining chair suspended on a frame and carried by four men, or, when going up a steep slope, she was strapped into her chair and carried on a bearer's back up the slope.

The trip was arduous to the point of danger. The weather got worse; some of the servants deserted. Most worrisome, however, was the ongoing question of supplies. At one point the Soubah of Sikkim was several days late bringing the promised supplies.

The goal was Mount Everest. On they pressed.

At this elevation — 10,000 feet above sea level — we naturally expect wondrous views of mountain and vale; but to the north all is hidden in mist, whilst from the west we are completely shut out by the still greater heights of Nepaul. Nothing daunted, however, we all set off, after a short rest, to ascend them, and soon find ourselves standing upon the frontier of that country, overlooking its "Terai" — the almost boundless plains.

We had ascended the heights in a westerly direction and were struck speechless when, on turning round, we beheld a scene described by one who has visited the four quarters of the globe as "unequalled in grandeur and magnificence in the whole world of God's creation," the stupendous pile of snow seeming within a day's march.

In one long line stretching away as far as eye can reach, peak rises above peak in "spotless procession." In the centre, as if guardian of the whole, Kinchinjunga, with a dignity not of earth, rears its glittering crest, extending upwards, till there seems to be no separate earth or heaven, but both are joined in one [*The Indian Alps and How We Crossed Them*, pp. 224–225].

Whilst gazing on the snowy world around us, an indescribable something creeps over the scene — a something one feels, rather than actually sees — a kind of palpable silence.

It is the moment of the sun's farewell: he has this instant sunk below the highest peak, and Earth begins to mourn his departure. For one brief period colour fades; then gathering up her forces, she speeds him on his way with high festival of gorgeous colour, and the whole becomes one shimmering sea of crystal, in which are golden cities, with towers of jasper and onyx, and shining fortresses, and minarets, and "many mansions.".... [p. 226].

One of the very first things which we learnt on quitting our tent this morning was, that our Guide had decamped during the night, and having met in solemn conclave over the fire, C told us we must consequently relinquish all hope of ever reaching Yangpoong. None of our camp knew the way, and it would not only be a hazardous thing to endeavour to reach it in the absence of a guide, but in all probability our attempt would prove unsuccessful. Yet it was a fearful disappointment to us all, to give up the hope that had been leading us onwards for so many marches, and forego our intention of sacking the little village, in case supplies of food should not be awaiting us there.

To retrace our steps therefore, as quickly as possible towards Mount Singaleelah, was now our only alternative. Habjeh, a large village, lies within half a day's quick march of that mountain; and if it be looted — should things come to extremities, and food not reach us from any source before we get there — if we ever do — there would be enough live stock in it to keep them from starving, even if it contained a short supply of both rice and bhoota, as the old Soubah of Mongmoo had stated....

About ten o'clock we managed to strike tents and make a start, the coolies suffering from inflamed eyes being led blindfolded by those who were well, many of whom might often be seen carrying double loads....

... Sad was it to watch the progress of our pilgrim band throughout the day's march, and note their downcast, weary looks, and footsteps growing slower and slower each hour; the small quantity of food which C has it in his power to give them now, being barely sufficient to keep them alive in these inclement heights, with such fatiguing marches and comparatively heavy loads. Fortunately we had a little port wine with us, and this we administered to two or three, who had broken down completely on the way [pp. 444–445].

Francis believed strongly that irregular habits were demoralizing or worse, and he insisted on observing the conventions of proper dining. No matter what the weather, cold, altitude, or downpour, the table was set with a cloth, china and a lamp in the center.

Matters became more difficult the higher they climbed. Meals were simplified. The expedition was traveling through areas that were unmapped, or only sparsely so. They were at 14,000 feet, and the combination of cold and altitude was debilitating. Supplies didn't arrive. At that point the three of them, Francis, Nina and C., knew that the situation was dangerous. At almost the last minute, supplies finally arrived, enabling them to make their way to the Pemionchi monastery.

As difficult as the expedition turned out to be, the three were unhappy to see it end.

In 1875 Nina and Francis returned to England, and Francis returned to civilian life. Nina wrote one other book, about her travel in the Carpathian Mountains.

Francis served in several parishes then settled in Wales; Nina presumably was with him throughout. He died in 1901, age eighty-one. Nina died in 1914 at the age of eighty-two.

"I am seized with a spirit of unrest and long to be far away and once more in their [the Himalayas'] midst," Nina wrote in the introduction to *The Indian Alps and How We Crossed Them* [p. 5]. Life back in England may have seemed confining and dull to her.

SOURCE: *On Top of the World: Five Women Explorers in Tibet.*

WORKS

Mazuchelli, Elizabeth. *The Indian Alps and How We Crossed Them*. London: Longman, Green and Co., 1878.
_____. *Magyarland: Being the Narrative of Our*

Travels Through the Highlands and Lowlands of Hungary. Two volumes. London: Samson Low & Co., 1881.

BOOKS ABOUT OR INCLUDING ELIZABETH MAZUCHELLI

Miller, Luree. *On Top of the World: Five Women Explorers in Tibet.* London: Paddington Press, 1976.

Loretta L. Wood Merwin,

1818–? American.

Loretta Wood married George Merwin in 1838. They had two sons, who went to Chile with them, as did Loretta's parents. The Merwins' sojourn in Chile was due to Reuben Wood, Loretta's father. He was a lawyer, and had served as state senator, circuit court judge and justice of the state supreme court of Ohio. In 1850 he was elected governor; however, in early 1853 he resigned because of financial difficulties. He'd been very active in the Democratic party during the presidential election of 1852; as a result, it was said, Secretary of State William L. Marcy named him consul for Valparaiso, Chile. This was anticipated to be a choice appointment; ever since the discovery of gold in California, Valparaiso had had a very heavy volume of traffic. Unfortunately, by the time Wood and Merwin arrived, the volume of traffic through Valparaiso and Chile had plummeted. Living expenses, however, were still very high. Wood resigned and saw to it that Merwin was appointed consul. Merwin didn't fare any better in the position; he couldn't afford a clerk, and household expenses combined with the rent for his office exceeded his salary and fees.

Mrs. Merwin knew no Spanish when she went to Chile, but she learned Spanish quickly. She was curious about what she saw, and wrote with a quiet humor. By the end of the three years, her views had changed, and she enjoyed aspects of Chile that earlier she had dismissed.

May. On Friday, the 7th, a "norther" commenced blowing, which, increasing through the night, on Saturday morning was most terrific. The bay opening to the north receives the full force of the wind — the waves roll upon the beach in the center, and hurl themselves upon the rocks at the extremities of the city, with a force that is seemingly irresistible. The water is very deep, and if vessels are not securely anchored, they are inevitably dashed to pieces upon the shore. There were some eighty ships and steamers in the bay, all rolling and plunging fearfully, with sheets of spray flying over their masts. Early in the morning, an old ship loaded with coals sunk at her moorings; and soon after another old vessel pulled her bows out and sunk. Later in the day, we observed a large ship gradually drawing near the breakers: ten minutes after she reached the first line, she was tossing in the furious surf of the beach like a cork, while her crew were plainly seen clinging to the masts and rigging. Hundreds of people thronged to the shore to render aid, and succeeded in stretching a rope from a mast to the beach, and by this means saved the crew. In two hours not a vestige of the vessel was to be seen; and before night three others ships were wrecked — so close in sight of us that we looked down upon their decks [*Three Years in Chile*, p. 43].

Very few foreigners, beside the diplomatic corps of some four or five countries, reside in Santiago, and the streets present an appearance very different from that of the port of Valparaiso, where there is much of the bustle and activity of one of our American cities. Early in the morning the women, in their black dresses and montos — a large black shawl worn over the head and shoulders (no other color than black is ever worn to church) — throng the streets on their way to mass, and hundreds of peons from the country, noisily cry their wares. As noon approaches, the heat of the sun drives everybody within doors, where the people remain until its declining rays permit them to issue forth again. Night and day the clangor of church bells is incessant — as if it were a dogma of the mother church to make all the clashing possible, and to destroy the slumber of heretic foreigners [pp. 60–61].

In September 1856, Consul Merwin resigned, feeling that his health had suffered from his holding the position.

SOURCE: Introduction to reprint of *Three Years in Chile.*

WORKS

Three Years in Chile. Columbus, Ohio: Follett, Foster & Co., 1861. Reprint: Edited and with an introduction by C. Harvey Gardiner. Carbondale: Southern Illinois University Press, 1966

Jane F. Moir

Jane Moir was involved with missionary work. Her husband was Frederick Moir, a merchant and director of the African Lakes Company. Earlier he had run a steamer on Lake Nyasa hoping to use the ivory trade as a weapon against Arab traffic in slaves.

Jane found her trip through central Africa to be pleasant, interesting, and overall enjoyable. Hers was a more leisurely tour in 1890. She wrote with a sense of humor and apparently enjoyed the social scenes of the market, an Arab household, and harem women. While for many women associated with mission work the impetus for writing an account of their travels was to call attention to their missionary activities, Jane seemingly had no underlying reason for writing her narrative.

SOURCE: *Victorian Women Travel Writers in Africa.*

WORKS

Moir, Jane. *A Lady's Letters from Central Africa, a Journey from Mandala, Shire Highlands, to Ujiji, Lake Tanganyika, and Back.* Glasgow: J. Maclehose, 1891.

BOOKS ABOUT OR INCLUDING JANE MOIR

Stevenson, Catherine Barnes. *Victorian Women Travel Writers in Africa.* Boston: Twayne Publishers, 1982.

Lady Mary Wortley Montagu, 1689–1762. British.

Lady Mary was well-educated, in part because she had a good governess, but largely because she had access to a fine library and read well. By her late teens her essays and satires were appearing in broadsides. As was customary, her father selected a husband for her — to her horror. When financial negotiations with the intended husband broke down, she eloped with Edward Wortley Montagu; she was then twenty-three. Her father was appalled, but Montagu had money and a title, he was a member of parliament, and he was well placed in social and literary circles.

Mary had grown up around the eminent men of her time and — now Lady Mary — she fit readily into the social circles of the court of George I and with the writers and wits of the day. She knew "everybody," and she and Alexander Pope became particularly good friends. She continued her writing and became well known for her biting satires of court life and writers; she was also a poet.

When Montagu was made ambassador to Turkey in 1716, she accompanied him with their young sons and twenty servants. Her long, frequent letters to her friends back in England provided the basis for her book, *Turkish Embassy Letters.* Her letters are informative and interesting. An intelligent woman, when she arrived in Constantinople she immediately contacted the leading scholars to learn as much about the East as possible, and to learn the Turkish language and customs.

I was in my traveling habit, which is a riding dress, and certainly appeared very extraordinary to them, yet there was not one of 'em that shew'd the least surprise or unpertinent curiosity, but received me with all the obliging civility possible. I know no European court where the Ladys would have behav'd themselves in so polite a manner to a stranger [Letter 38].

I fancy you are now wondering at my profound learning; but alas! Dear madam, I am almost fallen into the misfortune so common to the ambitious; while they are employed on distant, insignificant conquests abroad, a rebellion starts up at home—I am in great danger of losing my English. I find it is not half so easy to me to write in it as it was a twelvemonth ago. I am forced to study for expressions, and must leave off all other languages and try to learn my mother tongue. Human understanding is as much limited as human power or human strength. The memory can retain but a certain number of images; and 't is as impossible for one human creature to be perfect master of ten different languages as to have in perfect subjection ten different kingdoms, or to fight against ten men at a time. I am afraid I shall at last know none as I should do. I live in a place that very well represents the tower of Babel—in Pera they speak Turkish, Greek, Hebrew, Armenian, Arabic, Persian, Russian, Sclavonian, Wallachian, German, Dutch, French, English, Italian, Hungarian; and what is worse, there are ten of these languages spoken in my own family. My grooms are Arabs; my footmen, French, English and Germans; my nurse, an Armenian; my housemaids, Russians; half a dozen other servants, Greeks; my steward, an Italian; my janissaries, Turks; [so]that I live in the perpetual hearing of this medley of sounds, which produces a very extraordinary effect upon the people that are born here; they learn all these languages at the same time, and without knowing any of them well enough to write or read in it....

As I prefer English to all the rest, I am extremely mortified at the daily decay of it in my head... [Letter 45].

Lady Mary traveled extensively in Turkey, often wearing native dress. Interested in almost everything she saw, she was particularly intrigued with seeing an inoculation against smallpox. The procedure seemed to be effective; when she returned to England she inoculated her daughter in the presence of doctors, to show them the technique. This was tremendously controversial. People were vehemently opposed to the practice or vehemently in favor of it. Pamphlets, either supporting or opposing, circulated widely. Clergy denounced the procedure. Even though a great outbreak of smallpox was occurring, the practice was condemned and abandoned. Not until Edward Jenner re-instituted the practice seventy years later did inoculation begin to be standard practice.

Mary resumed the social and intellectual life she'd left, but she fell out with Alexander Pope when he portrayed her as Sappho in the "Dunciad." At some point she separated from her husband, although they seem to have remained on friendly terms, so much so that when Lady Mary left England to pursue the man she loved, she was accompanied by her husband. The romance failed, but Mary stayed in Europe another twenty-two years, without her husband but often with an escort. Mary continued to send long letters of her travels to her friends. Italy attracted her, and she lived in several Italian cities, especially Venice, before she finally returned to England in 1762.

She obviously thrived on the travel and change of scene. Her travel letters, delightful to read, cover a broad range of subjects and are filled with insightful observations and descriptions.

After her death her daughter—who was appalled by her mother's eccentricities—burned whatever of her mother's writing she could get hold of. Fortunately, before Mary returned to England, she gave a copy of her letters to a friend in Holland and asked him to publish them. Her daughter tried unsuccessfully to prevent their publication. They have never been out of print since the original edition.

SOURCES: *Dictionary of Literary Biography*; *Dictionary of National Biography*.

WORK

Wortley, Lady Mary. *Letters of the Right Honourable Lady M—Y W—Y M—e.* London: n.p., 1763. These are frequently referred to as the *Embassy Letters*, or *The Turkish Embassy Letters*. There are several editions of these letters and of her general correspondence.

Lady Judith Cohen Montefiore, 1784–1862.

Lady Judith was the wife of Sir Moses Haim Montefiore (1784–1885), who was prominent as a financier and leader of the Jewish community. Lady Judith was educated and had well developed cultural and artistic tastes. She was a sister-in-law of Nathan Mayer Rothschild; Sir Moses became his stockbroker.

The journey Lady Judith recounts took place in 1827–1828, over a period of nine months. She and Sir Moses were traveling together. In Italy they toured the churches of Florence and Rome, observed Catholic religious ceremonies, and attended church during a mass in which the Pope participated. They were traveling during the time of the Greek Revolt, and sailing was dangerous in the eastern part of the Mediterranean. Consequently, the travelers had to stay longer than expected in Egypt, waiting for a ship that would reach the Holy Land.

Tuesday, August 28. Alexandria...

In the afternoon we took a most delightful ride to see Cleopatra's needles, which are situated in one of the most obscure and distant quarters of the city, but are well worth the attention they usually obtain from travellers. They are covered with hieroglyphics, and while they interest the specta-

tor by their connexion with remote antiquity, astonish him as specimens of that gigantic art which taught the Egyptians to hew such masses of granite out of the rock. In our way to Pompey's Pillar, we passed three other granite columns, which are said to have belonged to the Alexandrian Library; two of them were erect, but the other lay half-buried in the sands, which were continually beating over it, and will soon, it is probable, form its tomb, as they have done in regard to so many other monuments of this ancient land [*Private Journal*, pp. 132–133].

Friday, October 19. Jerusalem...

I commenced the journey on a mule, but finding its pace too heavy and fatiguing, I changed it for a donkey, which I found far more agreeable. We obtained, as we proceeded, a good view of the mosque built over the tombs of David and Solomon, and of the Mount of Olives. We also passed a ruin said to have been the tower of Simeon, and the monastery of Elias, which is now occupied by Greek monks. The road was rocky; but fig, olive, and mulberry-trees adorned many of the hills, and the declivities were covered with a gay harvest of the most beautiful wild flowers. After an hour's ride we came to Rachael's tomb, which stands in a valley on the right, near to which is a well at present without water. We dismounted to view this most interesting monument of sacred history. It is formed of four square walls, with Gothic arches bricked up, and is covered by a dome-roof. On entering I was deeply impressed with a feeling of awe and respect, standing, as I thus did, in the sepulcher of a mother in Israel. The walls of the interior are covered with names and phrases chiefly in Hebrew and other Eastern characters; but some few English are to be found among them, and to these I added the names of Montefiore and myself. My feelings of gratitude on this occasion were not a little increased by a knowledge of the circumstance, that only six European females are said to have visited Palestine in the course of a century [pp. 205–206].

Thursday, September 27. Alexandria...

There has been a dispute, we heard, between the Pacha of Damascus, Abdallah, and Lady Hester Stanhope, which required the interference of the British consul; his highness having prohibited her ladyship's Arabs from serving her on pain of death. The consul received some affront during the dispute; but I believe he succeeded in making an amicable arrangement between the parties. Lady Hester's estate is situated on a mountain called Sida, where there is no spring of water. It consequently becomes necessary to employ the Arabs in fetching a supply for her household of that essential article, and they have to go some considerable distance. Singular strength of mind and forbearance must be required in such a situation; and her ladyship must possess both spirit to resist tyrannical caprice, and eccentricity to make her abode agreeable [p. 171].

Lady Judith's journal was not published but was printed for private circulation. There is a published photocopy of the 1836 London edition, pages 128–234, with an introduction by I. Bartal. This was published in Jerusalem in 1975. These excerpts are from that edition.

Moses made other journeys; Judith accompanied him on a second visit to Palestine, and perhaps on his other journeys as well: to Russia in 1846 and 1872, the Middle East in 1840, Constantinople and Morocco in 1863–1864, and six additional trips to the Holy Land.

She was author or co-author of the first Anglo-Jewish cookery book, the *Jewish Manual,* 1846. In her memory, Moses founded the Judith Lady Montefiore College.

SOURCE: *Dictionary of National Biography; Encyclopaedia Judaica.*

WORKS

Montefiore, Lady Judith Cohen. *Notes from the Private Journal of a Visit to Egypt and Palestine.* London: Joseph Rickerby, 1844.

_____. *Private Journal of a Visit to Egypt and Palestine, by Way of Italy and the Mediterranean.* London: Rickerby, 1836.

Susanna Strickland Moodie,

1803–1885. British/Canadian.

Susanna Strickland Moodie and her sister Catharine Strickland Traill [see entry] were part of a British family that produced several important writers. When their father had financial reverses then died, all of the sisters determined to use their writing to alleviate the financial problems. Susanna wrote her first children's book in 1822, and then went on to publish other children's stories. Elizabeth Strickland became an editor in London; Agnes Strickland began by writing poetry and eventually published biographies, including the well known and successful series *Lives of the Queens of England.* Jane Margaret, Catharine, and Susanna wrote for children and adolescents.

In April 1831 Susanna married John Moodie, a retired officer. The next year they and their young daughter immigrated to Canada, where they settled on a farm near Peterborough. Susanna continued her writing throughout.

They never forget any little act of kindness. One cold night, late in the fall, my hospitality was demanded by six squaws, and puzzled I was how to accommodate them all. I at last determined to give them the use of the parlour floor during the night. Among these women there was one very old, whose hair was as white as snow. She was the only grey-haired Indian I ever saw, and on that account I regarded her with peculiar interest. I knew that she was the wife of a chief, by the scarlet embroidered leggings, which only the wives and daughters of chiefs are allowed to wear. The old squaw had a very pleasant countenance, but I tried in vain to draw her into conversation.... I administered supper to them with my own hands, and after I had satisfied their wants (which is no very easy task, for they have great appetites), I told our servant to bring in several spare mattresses and blankets for their use. "Now mind, Jenny, and give the old squaw the best bed," I said: "the others are young and can put up with a little inconvenience."...

Some weeks after this as I was sweeping over my parlour floor, a slight tap drew me to the door. On opening it I perceived the old squaw, who immediately slipped into my hand a set of beautifully-embroidered bark trays, fitting one within the other, and exhibiting the very best example of the porcupine quill-work.... "You remember old squaw — make her comfortable! Old squaw no forget you. Keep them for her sake," and before I could detain her she ran down the hill with a swiftness which seemed to bid defiance to years [*Roughing It in the Bush*, pp. 38–39].

The early part of the winter of 1837, a year never to be forgotten in the annals of Canadian history, was very severe. During the month of February, the thermometer often ranged from eighteen to twenty-seven degrees below zero....

The morning of the seventh was so intensely cold that everything liquid froze in the house. The wood that had been drawn for the fire was green, and it ignited too slowly to satisfy the shivering impatience of women and children; I vented mine in audibly grumbling over the wretched fire, at which I in vain endeavoured to thaw frozen bread, and to dress crying children....

I had hired a young Irish girl the day before. Her friends were only just located in our vicinity, and she had never seen a stove until she came to our house. After Moodie left, I suffered the fire to die away in the Franklin stove in the parlour, and went into the kitchen to prepare bread for the oven.

The girl, who was a good-natured creature, had heard me complain bitterly of the cold, and the impossibility of getting the green wood to burn, and she thought that she would see if she could not make a good fire for me and the children, against my work was done. Without saying one word about her intention, she slipped out through a door that opened from the parlour into the garden, ran round to the wood-yard, filled her lap with cedar chips, and, not knowing the nature of the stove, filled it entirely with the light wood.

Before I had the least idea of my danger, I was aroused from the completion of my task by the crackling and roaring of a large fire, and a suffocating smell of burning soot. I looked up at the kitchen cooking-stove. All was right there. I knew I had left no fire in the parlour stove; but not being able to account for the smoke and smell of burning, I opened the door, and to my dismay found the stove red hot, from the front plate to the topmost pipe that let out the smoke through the roof.

My first impulse was to plunge a blanket, snatched from the servant's bed, which stood in the kitchen, into cold water. This I thrust into the stove, and upon it I threw water, until all was cool below. I then ran up to the loft, and by exhausting all the water in the house, even to that contained in the boilers upon the fire, contrived to cool down the pipes which passed through the loft. I then sent the girl out of doors to look at the roof, which, as a very deep fall of snow had taken place the day before, I hoped would be completely covered, and safe from all danger of fire.

She quickly returned, stamping and tearing her hair, and making a variety of uncouth outcries, form which I gathered that the roof was in flames.

This was terrible news, with my husband absent, no man in the house, and a mile and a quarter from any other habitation....

The house was built of cedar logs; in all probability it would be consumed before any help could arise. There was a brisk breeze blowing up from the frozen lake, and the thermometer stood at eighteen degrees below zero. We were placed between the two extremes of heat and cold, and there was as much danger to be apprehended from the one as the other....

[The Irish girl was sent for help, which arrived.]

Beyond the damage done to the building, the loss of our potatoes and two sacks of flour, we had escaped in a manner almost miraculous.... Here were six men, who, without the aid of water, succeeded in saving a building, which, at first sight almost all of them had deemed past hope [pp. 159–165].

Susanna didn't particularly like life in "the bush," and in 1840 the family moved to Belleville, where there was more urban life. After her husband died she stayed in Belleville. She died in Toronto in 1885.

SOURCE: Internet: Celebration of Canadian Women Writers, December 2006.

WORKS

Moodie, Susanna Strickland. *Roughing It in the Bush*. Susanna Strickland Moodie. London: Richard Bentley, 1852.

Rachel Wilson Moore

Rachel Moore traveled for health. A Quaker, she was interested in — and very critical of— slavery in the various areas of the West Indies. She and her husband traveled throughout the islands of the West Indies, visiting and observing.

Nine o'clock. Sea-water light green, then it became muddy; at ten o'clock we descried a steamer to the south, also a brig. Saw with a glass the glad-ship. The tide being low, we steered on for an hour below the mouth of the river Demerara. We crossed the bar about three o'clock, and came to anchor opposite Georgetown, about four o'clock.

Little did we think, on leaving home, we should have extended our wanderings so far, and being about to land, with prayerful hearts, and in good health, looked forward to leaving the steamer. It was amusing to hear the crowing of fowls, cackling of chickens, and quacking of ducks from our deck, a goodly number always being carried, as if they really knew we had reached our destination, and they joined in hilarity with those on board. It seemed as if those in charge of clearing up and putting all to rights, moved everything capable of transit, while water was thrown in every direction, scrubbing, dashing over every part above us, so that it was not safe to venture on

deck, unless one required a general ablution....

We landed about four o'clock, after much difficulty, which arose from the turbulence and bad temper of the boatmen, who are more violent on these islands, as they come out with their boats, than any other class of people with whom we have met. Each seemed determined to get all the passengers in his boat. Their conduct amounted to desperation. We were afraid to go with them, and told them we would not, unless they would be quiet. The captain forbade them coming on deck, when one of those in whose boat we thought we should go, jumped on to the stairs, as if to come up; that moment the fourth officer had taken me by the arm to assist me down the stairs, while my dear husband was just behind us, with some of our baggage. The officer gave the man on the stairs a shove, which we feared would make trouble, throwing him back into his boat. He got up instantly, and with his fist or some instrument, knocked the officer down with great force; at the same time my dear husband was thrown with violence against the boat, producing considerable injury to his face. I fully believe he would have been overboard, and might have been drowned, had I not sprung and caught him as he was going into the water [*Journal of Rachel Wilson Moore*, pp. 165–166].

WORKS

Moore, Rachel Wilson. *Journal of Rachel Wilson Moore Kept During a Tour to the West Indies and South America in 1863–64*. Philadelphia: T. E. Zell, 1867.

Abby Jane Morrell, 1809–?

Happily, Abby Jane Morrell began her remarkable account by telling us who she was. She was born on February 17, 1809, the daughter of Captain John Wood, shipmaster. Her father died when she was very young. Her mother placed the family property in the hands of someone who either mismanaged or appropriated the property, leaving the Morrell widow and children in sorry straits. In 1814 Mrs. Morrell married Mr. Burritt Keeler. Abby was close to her step-father and held him in high regard.

Early in 1824 the Morrell family had a visit from Captain Benjamin Morrell, a cousin, who had returned from a long voyage in the Pacific. Abby, who hadn't seen him since she was five, was strongly attracted to him. She and Benjamin married that June; Abby was fifteen. Three weeks later Benjamin left for a two-year voyage. During the next four years he made several European voyages, and he and Abby had a son. In June 1828 he left again for the South Seas and was gone about 13 months.

When he returned he was prepared to leave on a longer voyage to the Pacific for two years; Abby resolved to go with him. Benjamin resisted at first but eventually gave in. The two sailed on September 1829, leaving their son with Abby's mother. One of Abby's brothers was also on the voyage.

She was a good sailor, and her husband ran a good ship. They were on a schooner, and the crew got along well. (Among other things Benjamin didn't allow "ardent spirits" on board except for medicinal uses.) They sailed to New Zealand and the Philippines, where Abby was left at Manila for about two months while the boat went to several islands. The voyage was considered dangerous, and in fact some of the crew were killed in fights with natives. Abby rejoined the schooner, which spent the next six months traveling around the islands, stopping at New Guinea, New Ireland and New Britain among other islands. After they returned to Manila, they started home, first stopping at Singapore to unload some of the cargo, as the ship was too heavily loaded. They traveled back to New England via the Cape of Good Hope.

We fell in with numerous islands, but I do not recollect that my husband gave them

a name, or that they had already had one given them. They lie low and are surrounded by coral reef. Here there is plenty of biche-de-mer, pearls, tortoise, and oysters. Of this place I had neither latitude nor longitude given me, and I have never inquired the cause, but I could easily conjecture it. From these islands the natives came off to us in great numbers in large canoes. They made an attempt to get us on the coral reef, by making their canoes fast to the schooner and paddling towards the shore; but the wind being brisk, they could not make any headway. Their lines soon parted, and in their rage they shot their arrows at the schooner.... [*The schooner did not fire.*] We had already had enough of blood and were unwilling to shed it [*Narrative of a Voyage*, pp. 81–82].

Abby returned home to find that in the two years she'd been gone her stepfather and an aunt she was particularly fond of had died. Her mother and son were well. Nine days after landing she gave birth to a second son.

In January 2000 the French Southern and Antarctic Territories issued the Abby Morrell Commemoration stamp.

SOURCE: *Narrative of a Voyage to the Ethiopic and South Atlantic Ocean, Indian Ocean, Chinese Sea, North and South Pacific Ocean in the Years 1829, 1830, 1831.*

WORKS

Morrell, Abby. *Narrative of a Voyage to the Ethiopic and South Atlantic Ocean, Indian Ocean, Chinese Sea, North and South Pacific Ocean in the Years 1829, 1830, 1831.* New York: J & J Harper, 1833.

M. Augusta Mott

Augusta Mott tells us little about herself and her travel, except that she had had a winter's sojourn in Beirut.

The month was April.

And now we are riding briskly across the plain towards the Dead Sea; it is not nearly so hot and scorching as we anticipated, nor is the scenery so utterly sterile and blasted. Nay, it is curious and interesting, and does not give the impression of a locality upon which the curse rests. The colour of the Dead Sea is extremely beautiful; the purest cobalt does not equal it; and the exquisitely pink and lilac, blue and green, and yellow-tinted mountains of Moab are enchantingly lovely: but it has this peculiarity — no wave, no ripple, disturbs its calm, unruffled surface; no tree, no flower, no shrub enlivens its banks: nor is the stillness broken by the hum of an insect or the song of a bird! We sat down on the shore and thought upon Sodom and Gomorrah, and Abraham and Lot, the cities of the plain, and the little Zoar on the other side. I dipped my fingers into the sea, and tasted the water, and indeed it was brackish and very nauseous [*The Stones of Palestine*, pp. 45–46].

WORKS

Mott, M. Augusta. *The Stones of Palestine*. London: Seeley, Jackson & Halliday, 1865.

Florence Nightingale, 1820–1910. British.

Florence Nightingale was born in Florence, which inspired her parents to give her that name. Her father was a wealthy landowner, and the family usually spent summers at the family estate in Derbyshire and winters in Hampshire. Florence and her sister, Parthenope, were taught at home by their father, who taught them modern languages, history, philosophy, and the classics, and by a governess who taught them music and art. Florence wanted to study math as well, but her parents ignored her wishes, so Florence studied with an aunt in secret.

When she was sixteen Florence, by her own account, experienced a "call" from God, who called her to his service. Just what the mission might be was not clear. In the mid–1840s Florence began traveling in Eu-rope. The first trip, which lasted for about 16 months, was with her family to France and Italy. She was a traveler with a wide range of interests; art, social conditions, and institutions of European cities were just a few of her several areas of focus. In Paris she visited hospitals and nursing sisterhoods, and there she met many of the reigning intellectuals. She also had a passion for opera. Florence enjoyed society and her social successes. But when she returned to England she increasingly vacillated between enjoying her social life and doubting just what she ought to do.

When family friends invited her to accompany them to Rome, she accepted. Her parents and sister hoped this would serve to distance Florence from her sense of vocation. And, while Florence enjoyed Italian society, she also visited hospitals, convents and orphanages. She returned home with a deeper belief of a calling and a mission, which increased the sense of estrangement with her family. When Richard Monckton Milnes proposed marriage in 1849, Florence agonized over the decision. She was very interested in him and found his offer tempting. Nonetheless, she turned him down, and determined that marriage could not satisfy her nature.

The friends she'd traveled with earlier invited her to join them on a trip to Egypt, Greece, and Germany, and Florence again accepted. Her family, particularly her sister, felt that this was another chance for Florence to return to family life and domestic orientation.

[*December 31, 1849*] Yet Karnak by starlight is not to me painful; we had seen Luxor in the sunshine. I had expected the temples of Thebes to be solemn, but Luxor was fearful. Rows of painted columns, propylaea, colossi, and — built up in the Holy Place — mud (not even huts, but) unroofed enclosures, chalked out, or rather mudded out, for families, with their one oven and broken earthen vessel; and, squatting on the ground among the painted hieroglyphs, creatures with large nose-rings, the children's eyes streaming with matter, on which the mothers let the flies rest, because "it is good for them," without an attempt to drive them off; tattooed men on the ground with camels feeding out of their laps, and nothing but a few doura stalks strewed for their beds — I cannot describe the impression it makes; it is as if one were steering towards the sun, the glorious Eastern sun, arrayed in its golden clouds, and were to find, on nearing it, that it were full — instead of glorified beings as one expected — of a race of dwarf cannibals, stained with blood and dressed in bones. The contrast could not be more terrible than the savages of the Present in the temples of the Past at Luxor.

But Karnak by starlight is peace; not peace and joy, but peace — solemn peace. You feel like sprits revisiting your former world, strange and fallen to ruins, but it has done its work, and there is nothing agonizing about it. Egypt should have no sun and no day, no human beings. It should always be seen in solitude and by night; one eternal night it should have, like Job's, and let the stars of the twilight be its lamps; neither let it see the dawning of the day [*Letters from Egypt: A Journey on the Nile*, p. 77].

[*February 6, Thebes*] Then we rode down again to the little temple of Kasr e Rubahk near the river. The sculptures in its chambers are beautiful; but I was weary, and while they went over it I sat down on the broken base of one of the columns in the colonnade in front, and watched the sun set.... The beauty of it was all new to our Egyptian eyes. Imagine, looking abroad through a grove of palm trees and acacias, and seeing under them the temples of Luxor on their promontory, brilliant with the setting sun (such a sun as only Egypt can show), so clear with gems of living light; and behind them those violet mountains (not purple) with a little border of gold — the whole western sky looking like a scene out of the revelations, so bright with "celestial jewelry," and the green plain, no longer hard and raw with this background, already in the darkness of twilight. No symptoms of ruin were here —

Luxor looked as she might have looked the day she was finished; in that sunset light all signs of decay disappeared... [p. 131].

I wish I could give you the least idea of the situation of this city, unparalleled in the world, I should think. Imagine a plain about ten miles diameter, surrounded by these lovely hills — a river, at low Nile, about twice as wide as the Thames at Westminster — the western mountains' rocky cliffs, with deep precipitous winding valleys, or rather ravines, between them, shaded by overhanging rocks, and without even the coloquintida, much less a blade of verdure among them, fit only for efreets and ghouls to live in the clefts of the rock — they look like the circle of mountains, the abode of the Jinn, which, we all know, surrounds the earth — and this within a mile of the city of temples and palaces. In these they buried their kings — surely there never was such a spot, by nature fitted for an imperial city [p. 131].

[*March 23*] I do not know why the desert of Gizeh is so much less striking than that of Sakhara. One can, in Egypt, seldom render an account to oneself of any impression. Perhaps it is that Sakhara looks like the burial-place of the world, it is so grand and desolate and lone, and so riddled with graves. Gizeh looks like what it is, the burial-place of a family of kings and their courtiers; the remains of buildings, too, about the place, give it the look of habitation, make one think of porters and sextons, and men and women; the utter loneliness of Sakhara, away from all that one is accustomed to see under the sun, makes one think of souls, not men — of another planet set apart to be the churchyard of this which is the dwelling place [p. 178].

After Egypt the group went on to Greece and Germany. Berlin provided a turning point. There, she visited hospitals that awoke her to the possibilities for providing clean, good care in facilities that were comfortable and well run. She observed training programs in nursing and childcare, and the day-to-day operations of a hospital, a penitentiary and an orphanage.

In 1854, Florence left for the Crimea, where she involved herself with nursing and rehabilitating the sick, as well as organizing, administrating and the medical facilities. Increasingly her duties were administrative, procuring clothing and equipment, and working with suppliers, but she always made a point of visiting the wards. She insisted on uniform, discipline, orderly procedures, and cleanliness, setting the standard for nursing.

She became terribly ill with "Crimean fever" in 1855 while she was inspecting the war hospitals. Her recovery was slow, but she resisted efforts to send her back to Britain.

The war ended in June 1856, and in July Florence returned to England. She had become a woman with a mission, resolving that the tragedy of so many deaths due to poor medical care and facilities must never be repeated. The Army Medical Services, and perhaps the army itself, must be reformed. She also worked for better health care for the poor. For the rest of her life she worked, campaigned, argued, and fought for changed conditions.

During her lifetime she received much recognition, and many honors. She worked for her causes as long as she could. When she died, her relatives declined the offer of burying her in Westminster Abbey.

SOURCES: *Dictionary of Literary Biography*; *Dictionary of National Biography*.

WORKS

Nightingale, Florence. *Letters from Egypt*. London: A. & G. A. Spottiswoode, 1854.

_____. *Letters from Egypt: A Journey on the Nile, 1849–1850*. Selected and introduced by Anthony Sattin. New York: Weidenfeld & Nicolson, 1987.

_____. *Florence Nightingale in Rome: Letters Written by Florence Nightingale in Rome in the Winter of 1847–1848*. Mary Keele, editor. Philadelphia: American Philosophical Society, 1981.

Marianne North, 1830–1890.
English.

Marianne traveled because she loved plants, especially the exotic plants, and she wanted to paint them in their natural settings. She was born in Hastings, England. Her father was active in politics, so the family often was in London, where she spent a lot of time at Kew Gardens. Sir William Hooker, the director of Kew Gardens, was a family friend. Marianne had little formal schooling, but she was interested in learning, especially about music and botany. She played the piano but was particularly interested in singing; however her voice wasn't strong and eventually she gave up music for art. She didn't have much formal training in art: a few lessons in flower painting, and instruction about painting in oil from a houseguest. Her younger sister Catherine married, but Marianne never did.

When her mother died Marianne promised she would look after her father. They often traveled together in Europe, and Marianne hoped that someday he would have time for them to take a more exotic trip — to the tropics. Her father's death while they were traveling in Europe hit her very hard. She was thirty-nine.

She knew she had to have a life for herself, and she was a determined woman. She continued her European travels and kept herself very busy, painting almost constantly, until she regained her balance and felt like seeing people again. She resolved that "painting from nature" would be the center of her life. And for her, "painting from nature" meant plants and flowers, painted in situ [*Visions*, p. 28].

A year later she went back to England and settled in London, and a year after that, in 1871, she started traveling again.

> I had long had the dream of going to some tropical country to paint its peculiar

vegetation on the spot in natural abundant luxuriance; so when my friend Mrs. S. asked me to come and spend the summer with her in the United States, I thought this might be made into a first step for carrying out my plan, as average people in England have but a very confused idea of the difference between North and South America [*Recollections*, p. 38].

Confusion, indeed! She asked a friend for letters of introduction to people he knew in Brazil and the West Indies. Marianne traveled in the northeast United States near Boston and in Eastern Canada, with a side trip to Illinois to see a former neighbor. Then Marianne did go to Jamaica, landing on Christmas Eve. She was excited about the trip, her first (finally!) to the tropics with their amazing, colorful plants and flowers.

Jamaica was enchanting to her. "I was in a state of ecstasy and hardly knew what to paint first" [*Recollections*, p. 83]. She rented a house.

> I painted all day, going out at daylight and not returning until noon, after which I worked at flowers in the house, as we had a heavy rain most afternoons at that season; before sunset it cleared again, and I used to walk up the hill and explore some new path, returning home in the dark. I found no difficulty in walking, and could see the plants far better than when on a pony [*Recollections*, p. 83].

That was the pattern for the rest of her life. She liked to go off by herself and paint. As much as she enjoyed people and friends — and she seems to have been congenial and well liked — she traveled to see and paint as much plant life as possible. After five months she left Jamaica and went back to London.

Back in London,

> I enjoyed the society of my friends in London, and then began to think of carrying out my original plan of going to Brazil, to continue the collection of studies of tropical plants which I had begun in Jamaica [*Recollections*, p. 113].

Less than three months after she'd returned from North America, she sailed for Brazil. Marianne made the most of her time there. Every day there were new sights — and new plants. She became interested in the fish, which looked like no fish she'd ever seen before, and she'd go to the market and get fish to paint. "Did I not paint? — and wander and wonder at everything?" [*Recollections*, p. 187].

She returned to England thirteen months later, where she stayed for almost a year and a half, spending part of the time learning how to etch on copper. Her next trip — Southeast Asia, Japan, Singapore, Borneo, Java, Ceylon (now Sri Lanka), then home, was an ambitious trip that took her around the world.

Japan! Marianne wasn't alone in being fascinated by the country and the people. Although Japan had been opened to Westerners, parts of it were still closed to foreigners. Marianne got permission from the Mikado, the ruler of Japan,

> to sketch for three months as much as I liked in Kioto, provided I did not scribble on the public monuments or try to convert the people [*Visions*, p. 91].

She wanted to stay in Japan over the winter, but her arthritis or rheumatism was getting worse, and the cold was intense, so she went south to Hong Kong.

When she finally returned to England she decided to have an exhibit of her sketches. The exhibition was well attended, and newspapers reviewed it. One reviewer suggested that her immense collection of paintings should eventually be given to Kew Gardens. Intrigued by the idea, Marianne wrote to her father's old friend, Sir Joseph Hooker, of Kew Gardens. Would he like her to give the paintings to Kew Gardens, and to build a gallery to put them in, along with a house for someone to be guardian of the paintings?

Sir Joseph liked the idea, so Marianne picked out a site in the Gardens, well in from the entrance gates and off the main paths, and hired an architect.

One of her friends was Charles Darwin's daughter; he was interested in Marianne's travels and work and asked to meet her. When they met he suggested she go to Australia, where she would see plants and animals she'd never seen before.

So, Australia it was, and many of the plants and animals and insects *were* different from anything she'd ever seen. She also went to New Zealand and Tasmania, then came home via the United States. She chose a route through the southwest so she could see the exotic desert plants and cactuses.

By then Marianne had been to every continent except Africa, so of course she decided she needed to go to Africa as soon as possible. After spending time in South Africa she wanted to go to Zanzibar or Mauritius, but there was transport only occasionally, and she'd have to wait several weeks to travel. She wasn't feeling well and she was homesick, so she decided to go back home.

Her health overall was getting worse. Her arthritis was becoming more of a problem, and Marianne often was tired. But she had one more trip she wanted to make. She'd drawn all the biggest tees in the world except one, so the only thing to do was to go to where the tree grew — and off she went to Chile to paint the monkey puzzle tree.

The Marianne North Gallery had already opened, in 1882, after an immense amount of time and work. Marianne had chosen the paintings to be shown and decided on their arrangement. She tried to group paintings from the same countries and same part of the world, to give people an idea of the geography of the plants and what plants grew in the same regions. After her trip to Chile she wanted to include those paintings, which necessitated a good deal of rearranging to fit the paintings in the appropriate place geographically. This was no small matter as the walls were (and still are) solid with paintings.

In 1886 she moved to a home in the country that had a good garden. The garden was a great center of interest, and people from all over sent her specimen plants. Four years later Marianne died, age sixty.

SOURCE: *Dictionary of Literary Biography*, Volume 174.

MARIANNE NORTH AND MISS CONSTANCE GORDON CUMMINGS MEET

There [the Gallery at Kew] also I first met Miss Gordon Cummings, who had so long haunted me (by name) in various corners of the world, and for whom I had often been taken. (We were both on a large scale, and both were sketchers.) I felt when I saw her that it was no small compliment to have been taken for her: she had a grand Scotch face and noble honest manner, with a deep toned voice and sweet smile. She was a thorough lady: genial and warm-hearted, but so strong and resolute that it might be quite possible she had walked certain limp Anglo-Indians to death before now. Were she chosen to lead they would follow unresistingly, as I did when she said she always went by the omnibus, it was so much cheaper than cabs, and she did not care what other people thought about it. So I was dragged over the muddy street and into a crowded omnibus, and then — she found it was a wrong one! I had a grand laugh at her, and treated her to a hansom next time. She took me to see her aunt, Mrs. C., a beautiful old Scotch lady, stone blind, yet seeming to see everything, all the family told her so exactly about everything. She felt over some Indian Ornaments, and told me the patterns she preferred, just as if she saw them [*Recollections of a Happy Life*, Vol. Two, p. 212].

MARIANNE NORTH MEETS ISABELLA BIRD

Miss Bird was a very different kind of woman from Miss Gordon Cummings. I had been told by a friend she stayed with in Ceylon, that she was so fragile and small that when he put up his hands to lift her down from a dog-cart they met in the middle as if he were lifting a bag loosely filled with fluff and about as light! But I found instead a very solid and substantial little person, short but broad, very decided and measured in her way of talking, rather as if she were reciting for one of her books. I saw her first at a party, given by some relations of hers, who sent out cards — "to meet Mrs. Bishop née Bird." I found her seated in the back drawing-room in a big armchair, with gold-embroidered slippers, and a footstool to show them on, a petticoat all over gold and silver Japanese-embroidered wheels, and a ribbon and order across her shoulders, given her by the King of the Sandwich Islands [the Hawaiian Islands]. She was being interviewed in regular Yankee fashion; and I was taken up to her the moment I came in. Miss Gordon Cummings put her great hand on my shoulder at the same time, on which Lady A. joined our three pairs of hands and blessed us — "The globe trotteresses all at once!" It was too much for the two big ones; and we retreated as fast as we could, leaving Miss Bird unruffled and equal to the occasion [*Recollections of a Happy Life*, Vol. Two, pp. 212–213].

See also Elizabeth Agassiz.

WORKS

North, Marianne. *Recollections of a Happy Life: Being the Autobiography of Marianne North.* Two volumes. Edited by Catherine North Symonds. London: Macmillan, 1892.
Some Further Recollections of a Happy Life, Selected from the Journals of Marianne North, Chiefly Between the Years 1859 and 1869. Edited by Symonds. London: Macmillan, 1893.
A Vision of Eden: The Life and Work of Marianne North. Graham Bateman, editor. New York: Holt, Rinehart & Winston, 1980.

Marianne North's letters are at the Royal Botanic Gardens, Kew. The North family papers are located at Rougham, Norfolk.

Countess Pauline Nostitz

She is listed variously, including Pauline, Grafin von Nostitz-Rokitnitz.

At the time she undertook the travel related in her book, the Countess Nostitz was married to Doctor Helfer. They'd met while they were traveling, separately, in a diligence to Dresden. As she related, this was a slow journey, so slow that passengers often walked instead of staying in the diligence, which provided much opportunity to talk and get acquainted. During this journey Doctor Helfer asked if they might continue their conversation by correspondence. She agreed, but thought this was just a social pleasantry after sharing so much time together. But he did write, and she replied. Their meeting took place about 1830; they married in 1834.

Dr. Helfer was an Austrian physician and naturalist. He died in 1840 (aged thirty) from a poisoned arrow off the Andaman Island in the Bay of Bengal. He loved to travel, and much of his travel involved gathering information and making reports back to the East India Company. The countess wrote the book as a memorial to her husband.

After spending over seven weeks on board ship the ride in the moonlight night, with so interesting an end in view, seemed like a party of pleasure. Childish reminiscences of the fairy tales concerning the city of the Khaliphs, about ministering spirits, dwarfs, and enchanted princesses, afforded subject of conversation till far into the night. Each looked forward to investigating the points which interested him most, and in comparing reality with fantastic fables.

But fatigue gradually stole over us, and we went on our way in silence, till we were revived by the dawning light. The hope of catching sight of the golden cupolas of the great mosque made us increase our speed. But when the sun at length lighted up the landscape there were no golden cupolas nor slender minarets in sight, but an immense marsh lay before us as far as the eye could reach. The Tigris had overflowed its banks and flooded the country for miles, and when it subsided it left a swamp, out of which there was but a narrow line of little hillocks distinguishable above the rest.

Our anticipations were not a little dampened by this prospect; and as, after the long ride, the stomach began imperiously to assert its claims, and there was no prospect of breakfast, even English stoicism gave way. I had taken care of Helfer and myself by taking provisions with me; taught by experience I never went on an excursion without, in spite of the comments of the English gentlemen, who, however, a scanty meal at table, had often thoroughly relished an Austrian "Jansen" [*afternoon coffee*] in my cabin.

The English are so accustomed to their regular meals that they think it unseemly to take a bit of anything between. Now, however, to my great satisfaction, one after another of the gentlemen came up to me with, "Mrs. Helfer, haven't you an egg left?" And before long the demands made upon my saddle-bag, the dimensions of which might have made Sancho Panza laugh, had completely emptied it.

It was soon evident that our exhausted steeds could not carry us through the bog; we had to dismount and proceed on foot, jumping, rather than walking, from hillock to hillock, and not seldom over the ankles in mud. We did not catch sight of Baghdad, on the other side of the Tigris, till noon.

From a little elevation we could see the river, and perceived that the ferry-boat, which connects the right bank with the city, was just pushing off. In vain we made signs that we wanted to cross; the more our Arabs called out to the ferry-men, the more haste they made to get away, and did not moderate their pace till they were in the middle of the river. As this was the last ferry for the day, there was nothing for it but to seek out the driest spot in the soaked ground for the night, and do the best we could. So we had

to spend the night, sleepless and famished, in sight of the wondrous city [*Travels of Doctor and Madame Helfer*, pp. 256–258].

We were told of a hill, said to be a long way off, which no one ventured to ascend, because the gnomes took possession of anyone who made so bold as to attempt it. Helfer was desirous to visit the place, and to investigate what could be the origin of this superstition, for there is generally some explanation of legends of this kind.

It was with great reluctance that an old Karen could be persuaded to be our guide, and not until his female relative had been propitiated with presents. Our way led through a tract of country which had once been cultivated and then abandoned. The spongy soil was overgrown with weeds of amazing strength, which had overpowered the products of cultivation and turned the land into a dense and thorny jungle. It is much more difficult to clear such spots again than to prepare a piece of the primeval forest for cultivation....

There were, however, fortunately for us, some well-trodden paths left, wider roads succeeded, and we conjectured that we were again nearing the habitation of men. But that was not so. Elephants, attracted by the bananas, their favourite food, had laid out these highways in accordance with the rules of art. We afterwards also had frequent occasion to admire the sagacity with which these giants lay out their roads, over mountains and through defiles, like intelligent engineers.

At this time of year they are mostly in the mountain regions, where, as they are less affected by drought they still find succulent food; but their occasional trumpet-like calls during the night, announced that they had not entirely forsaken the neighbourhood.

We contrived to make our way through the thicket without giving our tailor too much to do in the way of repairs, and at length entered a bamboo forest, a sight which was a great surprise to me; for notwithstanding the many forms under which I had seen this valuable product of the tropics, and much as a few isolated specimens had excited our admiration, we now beheld for the first time a whole forest of bamboos.

The stems grow up like reeds, from the roots, in regular rows at equal distances, like artificial avenues or plantations, to a height of from sixty to eighty feet, and are about a foot in diameter. These slender stems are bare about half way up, and shine as if washed with a bright yellow varnish. From the middle they branch off, with feathery green foliage, in all directions, and intertwine their boughs with wonderful regularity as if artistically arranged for vaulted roofing. The bamboo tolerates no underwood, but covers the firm ground with its own glossy fallen leaves, so that you see unhindered through the rows of stems, as through a pillared hall, and the feet glide over the ground as over a parquet floor....

Our cook had lost or forgotten his tinder box, searched everywhere for it, and was quite nonplussed at not finding it. A young Burmese looked on, evidently enjoying his perplexity. As he could only communicate with him by signs, he significantly tapped his forehead, took two pieces of bamboo, removed the outer rind, and rubbed the bark quickly together; in a few minutes there was a little smoke and sparks of fire.

And the bamboo served not only for striking fire but as vessels for cooking rice. The canes contain a fluid which is as good tasted as the purest drinking water. One side of the canes is opened, they are filled with rice, closed, and thrown into the fire. Before the cane is burnt through the rice is done, and is as delicious as the nicest boiled rice.

After a zigzag course — from which it was plain that our guide did not know the way — we reached a hill destitute of vegetation. Our followers halted, and could not be persuaded to go further; up there, according to them; you would be bewitched, and unable to get away. Fear and astonishment were depicted on their countenances when Helfer and I at once began to ascend the hill; some of the young people who had become attached to us, tried to dissuade us from the perilous enterprise, and followed us with anxious looks.

On the top Helfer at once observed large bare masses of pure lodestone, the magnetic effects of which may have given rise to the curious superstition [pp. 104–107].

SOURCE: *Travels of Doctor and Madame Helfer in Syria, Mesopotamia, Burmah and Other Lands.*

WORKS

Nostitz, Countess Pauline. *Travels of Doctor and Madame Helfer in Syria, Mesopotamia, Burmah and Other Lands.* Translated by Mrs. G. Sturge. Two volumes. London: Richard Bentley & Son, 1878.

Lady Maria Nugent,
1770/71–1834. British.

Maria was probably born in the colony of New Jersey. She was one of twelve children of Cortlandt Skinner and Elizabeth Kearny Skinner. Her father, the advocate general of New Jersey, was a loyalist during the Revolutionary War, and took his family to England when peace was declared.

In 1797 Maria married George Nugent, an army officer and member of parliament. In 1801 he was appointed lieutenant-governor and commander-in-chief of Jamaica, where he stayed until 1806. Maria recorded her experiences in Jamaica in her diary. She found the expectations and duties of her position tiresome, with endless traveling around, visiting, large dinners and breakfasts.

In the evening the conversation fell upon hurricanes, when many frightful stories were told. This reminds me of a strange circumstance, that was related to me by Mr. Shaw, Member for Kingston, when we were at Spring Gardens. Messrs. Grant and Murphy also attested the fact, therefore I will relate it. About six or seven months ago, Mr. Shaw saw from his window dark clouds arise from opposite points, accompanied by a sudden and violent wind. They seemed at first to have a conflict; at last they united together and came towards the house, in a great black column. The house was situated upon an eminence ... but as there were deep ravines on both sides, Mr. Shaw hoped the winds would be attracted by one of them. However, it made directly towards the house, and he and his servants had just time to escape with their lives, when the whole was carried away, scattered, and sunk in the sea, and now not a vestige remains. These columns of wind I have observed several times, but had no idea they were ever so serious in their effects... [*A Journal of a Voyage to, and Residence in, The Island of Jamaica*, p. 105].

Up at 4, and set off for the Decoy, Mr. Murphy's estate, in St. Mary's parish. — Arrive at Berkshire Hall at half past nine. Find a breakfast prepared, and Mr. and Miss Murphy waiting for us. — Proceed on our journey at 11. A dreadful hill to mount, and the heat beyond description. A tremendous thunderstorm met us, just as we were in a narrow road, with a great precipice on one side, and a hanging rock the other. The flashes of lightning, and the rain, beating in our faces, almost blinded the poor horses as well as ourselves. We were wet through, for General N. was obliged to throw away the umbrella to save our lives, as we were very near being down the precipice. The kittareen, that was driven by Captain Johnson, close behind us, was thrown down the precipice, and dashed to pieces, but he was active and saved himself.

Arrived at the Decoy about 2, but so stiff and heavy with the weight of water about me, my shoes even being full, that I was obliged to be lifted out of the carriage. My clothes were immediately taken off by the ladies of the house, who thought I was all over bruises; but soon found that the yellow and green stripes on my skin proceeded only from the dye of the umbrella having run in streams down my back. I was washed all over with rum, and then took some warm soup, and in two hours I was as well as ever and as gay [pp. 145–146].

While in Jamaica she had a son, and within eleven months she gave birth to a daughter. The children's health was a matter of concern, and Maria took the children back to England in 1805, leaving George to stay on another year.

The couple was in England for five years; during that time two other surviving

children were born. When George was made commander-in-chief in India in 1811, Maria had to leave the children behind. Grief-stricken at the separation from the children, she was ill and miserable. Matters improved slightly the next year when she left Calcutta and accompanied George on a year's tour of the areas around Delhi. This was in the earlier days of the British dominion, and her diary shows the uncertainty of that period as the British society and its relations with Indian ruling classes was being sorted out. Hers is a unique early record of British life in India at that time. But as interested as she was in her surroundings, the loneliness, illness and extreme heat took their toll.

In 1814 Sir George gave up his role as governor-general, and the following year the family moved back to England. Her diaries were published privately after her death.

SOURCE: *Dictionary of National Biography.*

WORKS

Nugent, Lady Maria. *A Journal from the Year 1811 Till the Year 1815*. Two volumes. Private, 1839.
A Journal of a Voyage to, and Residence in, the Island of Jamaica. Two volumes. Private, 1839.

Julia Pardoe, 1804–1862. British.

Julia Pardoe began writing as a child. In her early teens she published a volume of poetry, a book successful enough to go into a second edition. In her twenties she published a novel set during the time of William the Conqueror. Throughout her life she wrote and published, using a variety of subjects and genres.

Apparently afflicted with symptoms of consumption, she sought out warmer climates on the Continent; she drew on her travels for both novels and travel literature. In 1835 she traveled with her father to

Constantinople. Her accounts of Turkey were favorably compared with the writing of Lady Montagu.

It is impossible to write of the Bosphorus without enthusiasm, for both its historical and fabulous associations serve to deepen its actual beauty; while the endless variety of the perspective keep the eye and the mind continually on the stretch, never cheating either the one or the other of the anticipated feast. Could it be contemplated in its entire length, and swept from sea to sea by one long gaze, much of its charm would necessarily be lost with its novelty; but as it winds in graceful curves between its enchanting shores, it is like a chain of cunningly wrought gold, of which, as it uncoils, every link appears more beautiful than the last [*The Beauties of the Bosphorus*, p. 85].

There is, perhaps, no luxury throughout the luxurious East more perfect, or more complete, than the Baths. Those of the great and the wealthy in Constantinople embody the idea of a scene in the "Thousand and One Nights"— they are so bright and fairy-like in their magnificence — so light and gay with painted glass, white marble, brocade, and embroidery.

Every bath, however small may be its dimensions, consists of three apartments; the outer hall, in which the bathing-dress is arranged; the cooling-room, a well-cushioned and comfortable space, moderately heated, and intended for the temporary reception of the bathers before they venture to encounter the pure free air of the exterior apartment; and the bath itself, where the atmosphere is so laden with sulphuric vapour, that, for some seconds, the breath is impeded, and the suffocating sensation which ensues is positively painful.

The Imperial Bath at the summer palace of Beglier-Bey, is one of the most elegant and costly in the city or its environs: and as it can only be seen by the express permission of the Sultan himself, is well worthy of description. Passing a crimson door, surmounted by a crescent-shaped cornice of rich gilding, the visitor enters a small hall, in which stands a basin of fine white marble, occupied by two swans, wrought in the same material, and appearing to sport in the limpid water; which, escaping from this charming fountain falls through concealed pipes into the basins destined to supply the bathers. The cooling-room ... is hung with draperies of silk, richly embroidered; and the large mirror which occupies the wall at the lower end of the divan, is set in a frame-work of gold and enamel, surmounted by the Ottoman arms, skillfully executed; while the divan itself, formed of gay-coloured satin, is wrought in silks until it resembles a flower-bed; and the cushions which are scattered over it are of the same beautiful and costly description. The bath is a vast hall, of the most elegant proportions lined, and roofed, and paved with marble....

Here the fair Zibas and Heymines of the different palaces pass whole hours, folded in long scarfs of muslin, worked and fringed with gold, their dark hair streaming over their ivory shoulders; inhaling the sulphuric atmosphere, and enjoying the luxurious languor which it creates; sipping sherbets made of the most delicate conserves, or the finest fruits; and not unfrequently, enjoying a slumber which is nowhere deeper than amid the dense vapours of the bath-room [pp. 13–14].

The bath is the very paradise of Eastern women. Here they assemble to discuss every subject of interest and amusement, whether politics, scandal, or news; to arrange marriages, and to prevent them; to ask and to offer advice; to display their domestic supremacy, and to impart their domestic grievances; but, above all, to enjoy the noise, the hurry, and the excitement which form so great a contrast to the calm and monotony of the harem [p. 15].

The book she wrote based on her travels to Hungary in 1839–1840 had a significant impact on the British view of Hungary during the 1800s. She continued to write novels and nonfiction works; the list of her books, many of them the standard three-volume novel, is substantial. In 1860 the British government granted her a civil list pension "in consideration of thirty years' toil in the field of literature, by which she has contributed both to cultivate the public taste and to support a number of helpless relations."

She died in London in 1862.

WORKS

Pardoe, Julia. *The Beauties of the Bosphorus*. Illustrated with drawings by Wm. H. Bartlett. London: Published for the Proprietors by George Virtue, 1843
_____. *The City of the Magyar*. Three volumes. London: George Virtue, 1840.
_____. *The City of the Sultan*. Two volumes. London: Henry Colburn, 1837.
_____. *Pilgrimages in Paris*. London: William Lay, 1857.
_____. *The River and the Desert*. Two volumes. London: Henry Colburn, 1838.

Josephine Diebitsch Peary,

1863–1955. American.

Jo, as she was called, was born in Washington, D.C.; both parents had immigrated from Germany. Her father was an employee of the Smithsonian Institution. She met Robert Peary in 1882 when he was a civil engineer in the U.S. Navy. His trips to Greenland and Nicaragua made the courtship intermittent, but he and Jo were married in 1888. They moved to New York, and then to Philadelphia.

Peary aspired to be the discoverer of the North Pole. In 1891 he set out on an expedition to North Greenland, intending to winter in Whale Sound on the northwest coast of Greenland and then to cross the inland ice, and thereby solve the question of how far Greenland extended in the direction of the North Pole. The news that Josephine would accompany the small expedition stunned the nation. No Caucasian woman had ever wintered in North Greenland. In addition to the Pearys there were five members on the expedition — the smallest number ever for such an extended exploration in the upper Arctic.

The expedition sailed on the steamwhaler *Kite* on June 6, 1891. A year and three months later the expedition returned. One member had died. The expedition had required a relief party. But Peary had traversed northern Greenland from coast to coast.

Josephine Peary's book is the account of her experiences during a year spent on the shores of McCormick Bay. The Eskimos she came in contact with had never seen a white woman; in fact some had never seen anyone from such a different culture.

In the introduction to the book, Admiral Peary recorded two memories: one the first night they spent on the Greenland shore after the *Kite* had departed. They were in a little tent on the rocks. A furious wind blew. Peary had a broken leg and the two were alone. The second came later, while Peary still was subject to the broken leg. He and Josephine were in the stern of a boat that was being attacked by a herd of infuriated walruses. Josephine never faltered.

The book opens, in June, with Josephine's first sight of Greenland. She saw a mixed view of ice and mountain scenery, in brilliant sunshine. Several days later they were gathering and pressing wildflowers, sometimes crossing snowdrifts to get to the flowers. As they moved north, the ice became more formidable for the *Kite*. Shortly afterward Mr. Peary broke his leg in two places. The accompanying group returned home with the Kite, and the small party was left alone. On October 26 she noted that it was the last day the sun would be above the horizon until February 13.

The group lived in a wooden house with two rooms, which they named Redcliffe. At first Josephine was cook for lunch and dinner and general manager of the house until one of the men was trained to do all the cooking. Everyone was working to get the equipment and clothing ready for the long spring sledge trip across the inland ice; Josephine spent a lot of her time sewing and working on clothes, with native seamstresses helping.

The small group was not isolated, as there were natives near them; they all celebrated Thanksgiving, Christmas, and New Year's in style.

In February there was some light at midday. On St. Valentine's Day Peary, Astrup and Cook started for the mountain-top, planning to be gone for two days. A storm came up, and the temperature was 33 degrees, with heavy rain, wet snow, and wind. The partial thaw was dangerous. The group got back two days later, in the first sunlight any of them had seen for months.

At the end of April the expedition left for the inland ice; for the next three months Josephine and one of the men, Mr. Verhoeff, were by themselves — except for the numerous Eskimos who were near the house or who passed through on their way elsewhere. The whole expedition was successfully concluded, and the group returned to the United States.

Monday, May 30. We had a great excitement about 8.30 this evening. A black spot was seen out in the sound beyond an iceberg, over two miles away. With the aid of the glass we could see it was moving in our direction, and we thought it was Annowkah coming back from the other bay. Kyo, who was watching constantly, all at once became very much excited, declaring it was not an Innuit, and he could not tell what it was. Then, suddenly throwing down the glass, his eyes almost starting from his head, he exclaimed, "Nahnook, nahnook, boo mut toy-hoy, car, car, toy-hoy" (a bear! A bear!—the rifle, quick, hurry, hurry, quick). Matt and I rushed into the house for our rifles and ammunition, but by the time we came out the object was behind the berg, lost from view. It soon reappeared, however, and we then saw that it was a dog. Kyo, who had been watching it closely, immediately recognized it as one of Mr. Peary's pack, and said that it was in a starv-

ing condition.... The dog is the one which we had designated the "devil dog," and was in charge of the supporting-party. Can it be that the supporting-party had met with mishap, or are they returning by way of Smith sound? The incident brings up unpleasant foreboding, but I am utterly powerless in my position [*My Arctic Journal*, pp. 156–157].

On Thursday there still was no news, but on Friday some of the party returned with good news.

Saturday, June 11. The past week has been almost entirely without incident. Dr. Cook has assumed command of our establishment and I am therefore free of responsibility beyond that of taking care of myself. My thoughts wander constantly to the members of the inland ice-party, and I often wonder if they will return in time for us to go south still this summer. The doctor and Gibson do not expect them before the 1st of September, while our Eskimo friends cheerfully assure us that they will never return. My instinct revolts against this judgment, but it makes an impression upon me, nevertheless [p. 158].

The *Kite* returned from the south in late July, bringing letters from home. It would stay until the last of August before heading back south. Everyone urged Josephine to go back with the *Kite* even if Peary hadn't returned, but she was determined to stay on. The *Kite*, with Josephine, left with a relief party to plant stakes seven miles apart as guide-posts on the inland ice. Then, on August 6, early in the morning, Peary returned to the ship! Two days later they were back at Redcliffe.

Shortly before they were to leave, Verhoeff, who had been looking for minerals, failed to return to the two men who were with him. There had been a terrible storm while he was out, and he was long overdue. After a careful search, they found his footprints and followed them to a glacier — then nothing. He had been Josephine's companion for the three months alone in the spring.

Then, in late August, they sailed for home, arriving in Philadelphia on September 24.

> Amid a chorus of cheers and hurrahs, and the tooting of innumerable horns and whistles, we received the congratulations of the multitude that had assembled to await our arrival.
>
> I returned in the best of health, much stronger than when I left sixteen months before. The journey was a thoroughly enjoyable one. There were some drawbacks, it is true, but we meet with them everywhere, and were it not for the sad loss of Mr. Verhoeff, I should not have a single regret [p. 210].

Two years later Josephine, who was then expecting a child, returned to Greenland with Peary for another preliminary expedition before trying to reach the pole. She was criticized for her decision to go. Things started out well; in September Marie Peary, known as the "Snowbaby," was born, a healthy child. However Peary failed to cross the icecap and supplies ran short, and most of the expedition, including Josephine and her daughter, returned to the States. Peary remained. When she learned that no plan was in place to send a ship to retrieve Peary, Josephine worked to raise money to charter a relief ship, which was successful in bringing Peary home.

Peary's next attempt to return (with Josephine) to Greenland in 1896 was unsuccessful, but they were able to return in 1897.

In 1898 Peary got a five-year leave from the navy for a North Pole expedition. Josephine was pregnant again and decided to stay home. Her second daughter, born in January 1899, lived only six months.

Peary's attempt to reach the pole didn't go well. His feet froze and he lost most of his toes. Upon hearing about this, Josephine returned to Greenland with Marie in 1900, only to discover that Peary had not returned to Greenland but was in the far north of

Canada, more than 200 miles away. Furthermore, he had fathered a son with an Inuit mistress.

Ice entrapped the ship for the winter. In May 1901 Peary returned to the ship and reconciled with Josephine. His health was bad, but he was determined to stay another year and make another attempt to reach the North Pole. Josephine and Marie returned to Greenland in 1902 to meet him. On that attempt he'd gotten further north than ever before. Josephine and Robert returned to the United States. The next year Josephine had a son.

Robert reached the North Pole in 1909. He died in 1920.

After Robert's death Jo lived in Maine. She never returned to Greenland. In 1955 the National Geographic Society awarded her a gold medal for her contributions to her husband's expeditions.

SOURCES: *My Arctic Journal* and its preface; *American National Biography*.

WORKS

Peary, Josephine. *My Arctic Journal: A Year Among Ice-Fields and Eskimos.* New York and Philadelphia: Contemporary, 1893.
_____. *The Snow Baby.* New York: Frederick A. Stoke Company, 1901.

Annie Smith Peck, M.A.,

1850–1935. American.

Annie Smith Peck was born in Providence, Rhode Island, in 1850, the youngest of five children. After graduating from Rhode Island Normal School in 1872, she taught high school in Providence. She then moved to Saginaw, Michigan, and became the preceptress for their high school. Ambitious to do more, she enrolled in the University of Michigan. Three years later she graduated with honors, with a major in Greek and classical languages. She went on to earn her master's degree in Greek. She took a position at Purdue University as a professor of Latin and elocution — a rare position for a woman to hold at that time.

After spending two years in Europe, where she was the first woman student at the American School of Classical Studies in Greece, Annie accepted a position at Smith College. She was becoming increasingly well known for her teaching and speaking. In 1892, when she was forty-two, she resigned her position at Smith to support herself by giving public lectures.

After two years, she took up mountain climbing.

In the introduction to *A Search for the Apex of America* Annie Peck told of her attraction to mountains and climbing. "On my first visit to Switzerland, my allegiance, previously given to the sea, was transferred for all time to the mountains, the Matterhorn securing the first place in my affections. On beholding this majestic, awe-inspiring peak, I felt that I should never be happy until I, too, should scale those frowning walls which have beckoned so many upwards, a few to their own destruction."

But at that time she was on her way to Greece for study and had to turn away.

She climbed "the *little* mountains" that came her way, then Cloud's Rest and Mt. Shasta in California. She found the exercise "delightful and invigorating."

Although lecturing on Greek archaeology was still her vocation, it occurred to her that mountain climbing might be a more popular theme, and if she told audiences about her adventures she could continue her climbing. In 1895 she conquered the Matterhorn, to great acclaim. Her next goal was Orizaba in Mexico, at that time the highest point that anyone had reached in North America. The *New York World* sponsored her, and in 1897 she climbed it, a feat that gave her, temporarily, the women's world's record for climbing.

She had other peaks in mind, notably Peru's Mount Huascaran. It took her several years to get the funding she needed.

The persons who were sympathetic were most impecunious. Of those who had plenty of money, many regarded the scheme as foolish and unprofitable, some advised me to stay at home (I said I would if I had one), while others believe me insane, or ignorant of what I was planning and unable to carry it out; though the fact that I had, with little inconvenience, already surmounted over 18,000 feet was evidence that I had some ability in this direction. The attainment, without skilled assistance, of a height of 20,500 feet on Mt. Sorata in 1904 gave me confidence to ask for further aid in a matter that would seem of far more practical importance to the United States than Polar exploration, as extending our acquaintance with sections and peoples for commercial reasons most desirable to cultivate; yet the disheartening struggle continued to the last moment preceding the final triumph [*A Search for the Apex of America*, p. xii].

Her ascent, in 1908 at the age of fifty-eight, after six attempts, was a triumph.

Though the grade was slight, I was obliged to pause several times in the fierce wind, once leaning my head on my ice axe for a few seconds before I could continue to the goal. Gabriel stopped a short distance from the end, advising me not to go too near the edge, which I had no inclination to do, passing but a few feet beyond him. I should like to have looked down into the Llanganuco Gorge, whence I had looked up at the cliff and the thick overhanging cornice, such as impended above the east and west cliffs also. We had, therefore, kept in the centre of the broad ridge, at least 40 feet wide, it may have been more: it seemed wider than an ordinary city street. Had it been earlier in the day, being particularly fond of precipices, and this would have been the biggest I had ever looked down, I should have ventured near the north edge with Gabriel holding the rope; but now I did not care to hazard delay from the possibility of breaking through the cornice.

My first thought on reaching the goal was, "I am here at last, after all these years; but shall we ever get down again?" I said nothing except, "Give me the camera," and as rapidly as possible took views towards the four quarters of the heavens, one including Gabriel. The click of the camera did not sound just right, and fearing that I was getting no pictures at all, I did not bother to have Gabriel try to take a photograph of me. This I afterwards regretted, as I should like to have preserved such a picture for my own pleasure. But in later days I was thankful indeed that in spite of high winds and blowing snow the other pictures did come out fairly; for it is pictures from the summit that tell the tale, and not the picture of some one standing on a bit of rock or snow which may be anywhere [pp. 344–345].

In 1909 she climbed Peru's Mount Coropuna and planted a "Votes for Women" pennant on its summit. She traveled and climbed for the rest of her life. Her last ascent was New Hampshire's Mount Madison, 5636 feet: she was eighty-two.

SOURCES: *A Search for the Apex of America*; Dr. Russell A. Potter, Website: *www.ric.edu/rpotter/smithpeck.html*.

WORKS

Peck, Annie Smith. *A Search for the Apex of America: High Mountain Climbing in Peru and Bolivia Including the Conquest of Huascarán*. New York: Dodd, Mead and Company, 1911.

Katherine Petherick

John Petherick was British consul in Khartoum in addition to being a mining engineer, trader and author. In 1861 Katherine traveled with him from England to Africa. At first, life at Khartoum was pleasant and more or less relaxed. But the Royal Geographical Society had commissioned John to meet explorers John Speke and James Grant at Gondorko to re-supply their expedition. The two explorers had explored Lake Victoria and discovered where the Nile exited from the lake; the plan was for them to meet up with the Pethericks in summer 1862.

It was sunset ere we arrived at Khartoum. The firing had been incessant, and the shore was lined with people. As we stepped from the boat, Petherick was almost separated from me as his friends crowded to greet him. We could hardly force a passage to the consulate. I cannot even now recall my feelings. As I entered the courtyard I was fearfully agitated; and when an inner yard was reached, and the women set up a shrill zachareet of joy, the guns still firing, and when the threshold was crossed, and my husband embraced me and bade me "welcome home," I was fairly overcome [*Travels in Central Africa*, p. 61].

July 3rd. — Long before dawn we were roused by the disturbance incidental to the discovery of another leak. The boat was fortunately aground. Petherick was completely overcome: a man's silent grief is hard to witness. He did not rave, as was his wont, at the culpable negligence of the reis and crew, but said, "You were all drunk with meat." The boat was unladen, and when day broke the heavy loss sustained was apparent to all: nothing had escaped; books, stationery, powder, and stores of every description were alike saturated. A consultation was held, every one advising our return to Khartoum, to come back the following season — in November; but Petherick would not listen to the proposition so anxious was he to keep his engagement with Captain Speke and the Royal Geographical Society.

It was resolved, therefore, to march to Gondokoro, via the Aliab, Madar, Shyr, and the Bari territories — a most direct route, though Monsieur Poncet expressed great fear that such a proceeding would be found impracticable, in consequence of the alarming inundation then prevailing [p. 167].

September 1st. — A wretched night I have passed; the roar of lions, and the firing occasionally at hyaenas who come into the encampment, quite unnerve me. Rain at noon, then hot sun; the mists then rising I can see but a few paces before me — it is all so dismal [p. 197].

... From the men we heard that Captains Speke and Grant had arrived but four days previously at Gondokoro.

How great was our joy they were safe, and had accomplished their grand mission!

Eager to greet them, we pushed on, and in less than an hour were on board our dahabyeh the "Kathleen." We had not seen her since she sailed form Korosko on September 4th, 1861. The servants approached to kiss our hands and offer felicitations, their eyes full of surprise as they looked upon me, and a murmur of "Miskeen" (*"poor thing!"*) I heard. I knew not how great was the change in my appearance until I approached a mirror; it then was evident, startling even myself; "A woman clothed in unwomanly rags," skin red-browned, face worn and haggard, hair scorched crisp, and clad in a scanty dress of gaudy calico, purchased from one of the soldiers; this was the object reflected. How comfortable and home-like the cabins looked, with couches, tables, &tc.! Luggage of the travellers, Speke and Grant, writing and drawing materials were scattered about, as they had but just left the "Kathleen" for a stroll, when the summons arrived that the "Kathleen" was to be dispatched to meet us.... Arrived at the bank, and the *dahabyeh* moored, Captains Speke and Grant, accompanied by Mr. Baker, stepped on board. How much there was to relate, but how far out in their calculations both Captain Speke and Petherick had been as to the date of their probably meeting!...

It is evident Petherick is in ill favour here; the traders and their men are enraged in consequence of his efforts to put down the traffic in slaves.... Vengeance is vowed against Petherick, and they have sworn to shoot him. I was sadly troubled; and in addition to cares pressing heavily, a little cabin-boy of the "Kathleen" was shot when on board. A group of disorderly servants and other men, with menaces and shocking imprecations, kept up a discharge of musketry with ball cartridge, in the direction of our boat, from the shore. I was quite unnerved.

February 23rd. — The travelers and Mr. Baker dined with us last evening; but from the conversation which ensued, a painful presentiment oppressed me that it was the intention of Mr. Baker to supplant Petherick's expedition for the relief of the captains.

March 27th. — My fears proved not groundless; Mr. Baker did offer his boats, stores, &tc., to Speke, which were accepted in preference to Petherick's, and in his boat Speke and Grant sailed [pp. 311–313].

The Petherick expedition ran into inclement weather and bad luck, and what should have taken several months took a year — with Mrs. Petherick nearly losing her life. They finally met up with Speke and Grant in February 1863, only to be accused of stopping to trade ivory along the way instead of moving ahead to meet the expedition.

John Petherick felt dishonored by the accusations; he was removed from the position of British consul and also lost his right to trade on the Nile. He left Egypt, ill and disappointed.

As a result, *Travels in Central Africa* is a justification and vindication. More is involved in the book, though; Mrs. Petherick had kept a journal of the Nile trip and planned to publish it. However, illness prevented her from finishing the manuscript. *Travels*, written with John, utilizes Katherine's journal for most of the narrative; John also kept a diary, and that supplied details of events that occurred when she was ill.

SOURCE: *Victorian Travel Writers in Africa.*

WORKS

Petherick, Katherine, with John Petherick. *Travels in Central Africa and Explorations of the Western Nile Tributaries.* London: Tinsley, 1869.

BOOKS ABOUT OR INCLUDING KATHERINE PETHERICK

Stevenson, Catherine Barnes. *Victorian Travel Writers in Africa.* New York: Twayne Publishers, 1982.

Ida Pfeiffer, 1797–1860. Austrian.

Ida always wanted to travel, but was unable to realize that dream for many years. She was born in Vienna on October 14, 1797, the only daughter among seven children. Her father was a wealthy merchant. She had a Spartan upbringing and her education was idiosyncratic; according to her son, Ida was raised as tomboy and didn't wear dresses until she was thirteen. Her father died in 1806. When Ida grew older her mother pressured her to marry, but Ida refused the offers that were made.

Finally, in some desperation, she married Dr. Pfeiffer, a lawyer who was considerably older than Ida. One of the attractions to the marriage was that Ida would live in Lemberg, away from her mother. Her husband, who was committed to routing out dishonest officials, ran into trouble within his profession and could not get work. He left Lemberg for work in Vienna, but his reputation had preceded him. He relocated several times in search of work. By then there were two sons in the family. It was a time of bitter poverty, and Ida had to earn money to support them.

In 1831 Ida's mother died, and Ida inherited some money. She determined to use that to educate her sons. Ida moved to Vienna, but Dr. Pfeiffer stayed in Lemberg, where his son from an earlier marriage lived.

When her sons were finally settled in professions, she decided to carry out her childhood dream of exotic travel, and she decided to do it alone, which was unusual for that time. Her first trip, in 1842, was to Italy and the Middle East; she kept a diary of the trip. The idea of being an author bothered her, but a publisher made her an offer, and the copyright money was enough to fund another trip, this time to Iceland in 1845, to collect botanical and geological specimens. That also resulted in a book that earned Ida money for further travels.

My whole attention was still riveted by the lake and its naked and gloomy circle of mountains, when suddenly, as if by magic, I found myself standing on the brink of a chasm, into which I cold scarcely look without a shudder....

The scene is the more startling from the circumstance that the traveler approaching Thingvalla in a certain direction sees only the plain beyond this chasm, and has no idea of its existence. It was a fissure some five or six fathoms broad, but several hundred feet in depth; and we were forced to descend by a small, steep, dangerous path, across large fragments of lava. Colossal blocks of stone, threatening the unhappy wanderer with death and destruction, hang loosely in the form of pyramids and of broken columns, from the lofty walls of lava, which encircle the whole long ravine in the form of a gallery. Speechless, and in anxious suspense, we descend a part of this chasm, hardly daring to look up, much less to give utterance to a single sound, lest the vibration should bring down one of these avalanches of stone, to the terrific force of which the rocky fragments scattered around bear ample testimony. The distinctness with which echo repeats the softest sound and the lightest footfall is truly wonderful.

The appearance presented by the horses, which are allowed to come down the ravine after their masters have descended, is most peculiar. One could fancy they were clinging to the walls of rock.

[The ravine opens up and forms an outlet into the valley of Thingvalla.]

Thingvalla was once one of the most important places in Iceland; the stranger is still shewn the meadow, not far from the village, on which the Allthing (general assembly) was held annually in the open air [*Voyage to the Island of Iceland*, 1847, pp. 116–118].

The next year she began her most adventurous travels: a trip around the world. Her route took her through many unsettled regions of South America, China, India, Iraq, Iran and Russia. When the trip was over she decided it was time to stop traveling and settle down — but that didn't last long. She sold some of her collections, then wrote up and published her journal, and in 1851 she undertook a second trip around the world. This trip followed a different route than her previous trip; the itinerary included an area of Sumatra where no Western woman had ever been permitted to visit. In California she joined the gold miners and slept in wigwams of Yuba Indians.

In recognition of her travels Ida was elected to membership in the Geographical Society of Berlin and of Paris. The London organization wouldn't allow her to be elected to membership since she was a woman.

She always brought back biological specimens and ethnographical objects from her travels, and her trips around the world were no exception. While she was cataloguing material from her second trip, she decided to explore Madagascar, and she left off the cataloguing. While there she contracted Madagascar fever; she arrived home but could not get well, and in 1860 she died in Vienna.

SOURCE: Internet: *www.distinguished women.com/biographies*, December 2006.

WORKS

Ida Pfeiffer's books were translated and reprinted soon after their original publication in German. Titles sometimes varied. The following are early titles, translated, and publication dates.

Pfeiffer, Ida. *Journey to Iceland and Travels in Sweden and Norway.* Translated by Charlotte Fenimore Cooper. New York: G. P. Putnam, 1852.
_____. *A Lady's Second Journey Round the World: from London to the Cape of Good Hope, Borneo, Java, Sumatra, Celebes, Ceram, the Moluccas, etc., California, Panama, Peru, Ecuador, and the United States.* New York: Harper & Brothers, 1856.
_____. *The Last Travels of Ida Pfeiffer: Inclusive of a Visit to Madagascar: With an Autobiographical Memoir of the Author.* Translated by H. W. Dulcken. New York: Harper, 1862.

_____. *Visit to the Holy Land, Egypt and Italy.* Translated by H. W. Dulcken. London: Ingram, Cooke, 1852.
_____. *A Woman's Journey Round the World: From Vienna to Brazil, Chili, Tahiti, China Hindostan, Persia, and Asia Minor.* London: Office of the National Illustrated Library, [1852?].

Hester Lynch Piozzi, 1741–1821.
British.

Mrs. Piozzi is best known to many people as Mrs. Thrale, her claim to fame being the people she knew. Hester Lynch Salusbury was born in 1740 in Wales; her father was a squire without a fortune. She was sent to London to live with relatives, and while there she was tutored in languages. Many people sought out her company, as she was considered to be intelligent, cultivated, and well-read.

She married Henry Thrale, who was a member of parliament and a wealthy brewer. Their home was a center for the most accomplished people of the day: Oliver Goldsmith, Sir Joshua Reynolds, Mrs. Siddons and Fanny Burney, and most especially Samuel Johnson. Johnson lived with the Thrales intermittently and went with them to Brighton, Wales, and France. Mrs. Thrale was his patroness and closest confidante. When Mr. Thrale became ill she took over the running of the brewery, and when he died she sold it to Barclay's.

Her marriage to Gabriel Piozzi, an Italian musician, in 1784 was much opposed, and it harmed her close friendship with Johnson. The couple went to Italy, and Mrs. Piozzi began to travel and write extensively. She published a volume of material on Samuel Johnson, who had died in 1784, and a volume of their correspondence. Hester was a habitual journal keeper, and she always traveled with two notebooks. From these she wrote *Observations and Reflections*

Made in the Course of a Journey Through France, Italy, and Germany (1789).

Today that journey may not sound very adventurous, but Hester traveled before the time of tourists and the Grand Tour, and the places she visited were relatively unknown to the English at that time.

Her accounts and descriptions are fresh and personable. Her description of her arrival at Naples in the midst of a severe storm, accompanied by an eruption of Mount Vesuvius, is memorable.

> Our eagerness to see sights has been repressed at Naples only by finding everything a sight; one need not stir out to look for wonder sure, while this amazing mountain continues to exhibit such various scenes of sublimity and beauty at exactly the distance one would chuse to observe it from; a distance which almost admits examination, and certainly excludes immediate fear. When in the silent night, however, one listens to its groaning; while hollow sighs, as of gigantic sorrow, are often heard distinctly in my apartment; nothing can surpass one's sensations of amazement, except the consciousness that custom will abate their keenness: I have not, however, yet learned to lie quiet, when columns of flame, high as the mountain's self, shoot from its crater into the clear atmosphere with a loud and violent noise; nor shall I ever forget the scene it presented one day to my astonished eyes, while a thick cloud, charged heavily with electric matter, passing over, met the fiery explosion by mere chance, and went off in such a manner as effectually baffles all verbal description [*Observations and Reflections*, v. 2, pp. 4–5].

Vesuvius quieted down, and there was an expedition to climb the volcano.

> The connoisseurs here know the different degrees, dates, and shades of lava to a perfection that amazes one.... Bartolomeo, the Cyclops of Vesuvius as he is called, studies its effects and operations too with much attention and philosophical exactness.... The way one climbs is by tying a broad sash with long ends round this Bartolomeo, let-

ting him walk before one, and holding it fast [V. 2, p. 62].

Hester Lynch Salusbury Thrale Piozzi was one of the earliest female travel writers; her unconventional book inspired Ann Radcliffe to write about "marvelous Italy" in *The Mysteries of Udolpho.*

SOURCE: *Oxford Dictionary of National Biography.*

WORKS

Piozzi, Hester Lynch. *Observations and Reflections Made in the Course of a Journey Through France, Italy, and Germany.* London: Strathan & Cadell, 1789.

Miss Platt

Very little is known of Miss Platt, including her first name.

Miss Platt accompanied her stepfather, Henry Tattam (1788–1868), on his journey to the Holy Land in 1838–1839. Henry was a clergyman and Coptic scholar. He had married Eliza Platt, a widow, in 1830. Eliza died in or before 1855.

Henry was active in archaeological societies, and spent most of his time on his writing and studies.

SOURCE: *Dictionary of National Biography* [Tattam].

WORKS

Platt. *Journal of a Tour (of Henry Tattam and Miss Platt) Through Egypt, the Peninsula of Sinai and the Holy Land in 1838, 1839.* Two volumes. Private, 1841.

Sophia Lane Poole, 1804–1891.
British.

Sophia Lane was born in England in 1804; her father was the Reverend Theophilus Lane, and her mother was a niece of Gainsborough. She had three brothers, one who became a well known lithographer and another, Edward William Lane, a well known Arabic scholar. Her father died when she was ten.

When she was twenty-five she married Edward Richard Poole, a Cambridge barrister. He was a scholar and was known as a bibliographer and book collector. Their first son was born in 1830, their second two years later.

The date of Edward's death is unknown. By 1842 Sophia and her children were living with her elderly mother in Hastings. After the death of her mother that year, Sophia went to live with her brother Edward Lane, who had made his reputation as an orientalist and was preparing to return to Egypt. Sophia and her sons accompanied Edward and his wife on their return to Egypt in July 1842.

From the first Sophia planned to record her observations of Egyptian society for publication; she had the advantage of access to Egyptian women and learning about their lives, which would aid Edward. The book was to take the form of letters home, which Edward would edit or approve. He would also add some descriptions and observations, Sophia incorporating them from his notes.

The trip to Egypt was Sophia's first long voyage. The trip began inauspiciously, with Sophia seasick and homesick.

Sophia took readily to her new life. She adopted Egyptian dress, and learned the language and customs readily. Her letters ran until 1846, but she stayed for three more years. During their entire stay in Egypt the family was in Cairo and did not travel about.

My dear Friend   November, 1842

I have already attempted to describe to you my impressions of my first entry into Cairo. My ideas of it, for a considerable

time, were very confused; it seemed to me, for the most part, a labyrinth of ruined and half-ruined houses, of the most singular construction; and in appearance so old, that I was surprised at being informed that, only a few years ago, it presented a far less unhappy aspect.

... Though it has much declined since the discovery of the passage to India by the Cape of Good Hope, and more especially of late years, it is still one of the most considerable cities in the East. It is altogether an Arabian city; and the very finest specimens of Arabian architecture are found within its walls. The private houses are in general moderately large; the lower part of stone, and the superstructure of brick; but some are little better than huts.

The streets are unpaved, and very narrow, generally from five to ten feet wide. Some are even less than four feet in width; but there are others as much as forty or fifty feet wide, though not for any great length. I must describe the streets under their different appellations.

A shárë, or great thoroughfare-street, is generally somewhat irregular both in its direction and width. In most parts the width is scarcely more than sufficient for two loaded camels to proceed at a time; and hence much inconvenience is often occasioned to the passenger, though carriages are very rarely encountered. All burdens are borne by camels, if too heavy for asses; and vast numbers of the former, as well as many of the later, are employed in supplying the inhabitants of Cairo with the water of the Nile, which is conveyed in skins, the camel carrying a pair of skin bags, and the ass a goat-skin, tied round at the neck. The great thoroughfare-street being often half obstructed by these animals, and generally crowded with passengers, some on foot, and others riding, present striking scenes of bustle and confusion, particularly when two long trains of camels happen to meet each other where there is barely room enough for them to pass, which is often the case. Asses are in very general use, and most convenient for riding through such streets as those of Cairo, and are always to be procured for hire. They are preferred to horses even by some men of the wealthier classes of the Egyptians [*The*

Englishwoman in Egypt, Series One, pp. 140–142].

A darb, or by-street, differs from a shárë in being narrower, and not so long. In most cases, the darb is about six or eight feet wide, is a thoroughfare, and has, at each end, a gateway, with a large wooden door, which is always closed at night. Some darbs consist only of private houses; others contain shops [Series One, pp. 144–147].

With regard to a sojourn in Egypt, it is not an easy matter to give you the *pour et contre*. Of one thing I am convinced, that persons must remain a year in this country, that is, they must go the round of the seasons, or nearly so, before they can fully judge of the comforts it offers. I well remember the extreme annoyance I experienced, for some months after our arrival, from the unusually prolonged heat, of which I complained to you, and from the flies and musquitoes, which were really and constantly distressing; and I could scarcely believe what people told me, namely, that I should soon find myself very well contented with the climate of the country. As to the musquitoes, they interfere so much with enjoyment, that a traveller who visits Egypt only during the great heat may assert, with truth, that he has no comfort by day, nor by night until he enters his curtain. I confess that I often feared we could not remain here as long as I wished. No sooner, however, did the Nile subside, than my hopes revived; and finding that the most charming temperature imaginable succeeded the heat, I began to understand what travellers mean when they call this a delicious climate. November is a sweet month here — December and January are rather too cold, taking into consideration that there are neither fireplaces nor chimneys in any of the houses, excepting in the kitchens. February and March are perfectly delightful, the temperature then being almost as mild as that of summer in England. During April there occur some instances of hot wind, otherwise it is an agreeable month. In May the hot winds are trying, and then follow four months of oppressive heat [Series Two, pp. 10–11].

When she returned to England in 1849, Sophia and her family settled with her brother Edward. Sophia came to collaborate with her younger son, Reginald Stuart, writing the text that accompanied Francis Frith's photographs of Egypt, Jerusalem, Sinai, and the pyramids. The books were published in 1860 and 1861, with Sophia's name on the title page. For *The Englishwoman in Egypt*, her brother Edward's name had been on the title page, as he had the stronger reputation and name. This time, Sophia was well enough known through her book that her name carried some cachet.

Both of Sophia's sons became well known scholars, Edward an Arabic scholar and editor of Edward Lane's works, and Reginald an archaeologist and orientalist. Two of her grandsons also achieved eminence, one as an historian and curator of the Bodleian, and the other an orientalist and Arabic scholar.

After Edward Lane died, Sophia moved to her son's home in the British Museum, as he was keeper of coins and medals. She died there in 1891, eighty-seven years old.

SOURCE: *Dictionary of National Biography.*

WORKS

Poole, Sophia Lane. *The Englishwoman in Egypt: Letters from Cairo Written During a Residence There in 1842, 3, & 4 with E. W. Lane ... by His Sister.* Also a second series, from 1845 to 1846. London: C. Knight, 1844–1846.

Mrs. Marianne Postans, circa 1810–1897. British.

She is often listed as Mrs. Marianne Postans Young.

Little is known of her early life. In 1833 she married Thomas Postans, an officer in the infantry. She was well educated. She and her husband were both talented artists and enjoyed writing. Thomas also was interested in antiquities and was assigned to obtain copies of ancient Asokan inscriptions at Girnar in Junagarh. They both enjoyed traveling and exploring India. Marianne was a good linguist, as was Thomas, and she learned Hindustani, Persian, Cutchi and some Sindhi.

Her first two books, which drew on her experiences in western India, were well received, and her literary career was well launched when she returned to India in 1840. This time she was in Sindh and Balochistan, and the experiences were different from her earlier time in western India.

> ... Arrived at the garden, which was surrounded by a low wall, to keep out the wild hogs, who are sad destroyers of your pleasure-grounds, we found the rippling watercourses bridged over for the convenience of those whose horses could not leap, and the large parterres of rose-bushes, not denuded of their blossoms, as is usual at sun-rise, but imparting fragrance to all around.
>
> The people of Sindh delight in roses, and large beds of rose trees are cultivated entirely for the sale of the flowers; the sun robs them of their fragrance, and they are, therefore, clipped off before he rises; not being preserved in water, however, the stem is useless, and the blossoms are, therefore, closely cropped, thrown into large baskets, taken to the bazaar, and sold by the pound to people who scatter them about their rooms and beds, distil them as a perfumed water for their *hubble-bubbles* (water-pipe), or dry them to pound with ingredient of the *gracco* (smoking paste); they place them also in their turbans, and the women wear them as ear-ornaments. Ladies of character, however, seldom adopt this fashion, it being a favourite decoration of nâtch-women.
>
> The garden was crowded with people, and hundreds of horses and riding camel, with their holiday trappings, were picketed under the trees, contrasting well with the rich foliage that surround them; and people not entitled by invitation to the *entrée* had made all sorts of excuses for following the grooms and retainers of the guests. A little beyond these groups was a crowd of cooks, who, seated on the ground, smoking pipes, were in attendance on double files of kids, that, fixed on stakes between huge fires, were in preparation for the fête. An open space, between a perfect wood of lime and orange tress, was the spot destined for ourselves, and from opposite branches was suspended the fly of a handsome tent, which protected a table placed beneath it, heaped with fruit and flowers. A rich Persian carpet covered the ground, and on it were placed two richly-carved chapoys (bedsteads), on which, surrounded with cushions and velvet, sat our host and his immediate friends. The Shah-zadeh in full trowsers, pale-blue silk tunic, and black lambskin cap, with the European party in white jackets, contrasted oddly enough, in their gracelessly plain effect, with the rich attire of the gorgeous-looking Moslems; and as soon as we were all seated, salvers covered with heaps of roses were placed on the ground, with large silver trays covered with sweetmeats [*Travels, Tales, and Encounters*, pp. 27–28].

Her writing had changed. Earlier she had written books for the general public. Now, she wrote articles for the *Asiatic Journal*, a popular periodical.

The couple left India in fall of 1842 to return to England. Marianne continued to write articles, and she oversaw the publication of *Facts and Fictions*. They returned to India in fall of 1844, settling in Bombay. In 1846 Thomas was appointed to a special commission. He died two months later, in December, while on a mission.

William Young was the army surgeon who attended Postans in his last days. At that time Marianne was thirty-five and Young was a widower of nearly sixty. He had adopted his one-year-old granddaughter.

They married in England in 1848. Six years later Marianne accompanied Young to the Crimean war. She wrote one more book on India and Bombay, *The Moslem Noble*, which is "misleadingly titled."

Marianne and William retired to Somerset, England. Mary Anne, the adopted daughter/granddaughter, lived with them until she married in 1875. William died in 1879.

Marianne died in 1897.

SOURCE: Introduction to *Travels, Tales and Encounters in Sindh and Balochistan 1840–1843.*

WORKS

Postans, Mrs. Marianne. *Cutch; or Random Sketches, Taken During a Residence in One of the Northern Provinces of Western India; Interspersed with Legends and Traditions.* London: Smith, Elder & Do., 1839.

_____. *Facts and Fiction, Illustrative of Oriental Character.* Three volumes. London: Wm. H. Allen, 1844.

_____. *Travels, Tales and Encounters in Sindh and Balochistan 1840–1843.* Introduction by R. A. Raza. Oxford: Oxford University Press, 2003

_____. *Western India in 1838.* Two volumes. London: Saunders and Otley, 1839.

Young, Marianne Postans. *Our Camp in Turkey, and the Way to It.* London: Richard Benley, 1874.

_____. *The Moslem Noble, with Some Notices of the Parsees, or Ancient Persians.* London: Saunders and Otley, 1857.

Marguerite Agnes Power,

1815?–1867.

Marguerite was the daughter of Colonel Robert Power and Agnes Brooke. Agnes's aunt was Marguerite Gardiner, Countess of Blessington, who would play an important role in young Marguerite's life.

Little is known of Marguerite's early life; she probably spent her childhood in Ireland. Her father had an army career and later was agent for the Blessington estates in County Tyrone. In 1839 Marguerite and her sister Ellen moved to London to live with Lady Blessington.

Lady Blessington seemed to know everyone, particularly in the literary world. Through her aunt's connections Marguerite

became friends with many influential people, including Charles Dickens, William Thackeray, Benjamin Disraeli, Prince Louis Napoleon and Walter Savage Landor. In the 1840s Marguerite contributed writings to various annuals.

The Blessington household broke up in 1849, and Marguerite and Ellen went to Paris with their aunt. In June 1849 Lady Blessington died. Marguerite decided to remain in Paris and support herself as a journalist and novelist. The next year Marguerite's memoir of Lady Blessington was published as a prefix to Lady Blessington's novel *Country Quarters.* For six years she edited *The Keepsake,* an annual to which Dickens contributed.

When the annual folded, Marguerite's financial situation became precarious, and although she wrote for periodicals and annuals, she struggled financially. At Thackeray's recommendation she was given the job of Paris correspondent for the *Illustrated London News.* Her first novel was published in 1856 and was favorable received. Several more novels followed. In 1857 Dickens, Thackeray and John Forster raised a subscription of two hundred pounds among the friends of Lady Blessington.

Arabian Days and Nights, or Rays from the East, her only travel book, was based on a winter's residence in Egypt. She died in 1867 after a long bout with cancer.

SOURCE: *Dictionary of National Biography.*

WORKS

Power, Marguerite. *Arabian Days and Nights, or Rays from the East.* London: Sampson, Low and Son, 1863.

Mrs. M. A. Pringle

Mrs. Pringle's travels in Africa arose from the missionary work of her husband,

Alexander Pringle. In 1880 he was sent by the Established Church of Scotland to East Africa to view the conditions at the Blantyre Mission. Friction had risen between the missionaries and the local clans, and he was instructed to determine the cause of this. Mrs. Pringle was determined to join him, in spite of the reports that no woman could handle the travel. She was a persistent woman and possessed a remarkable amused detachment and a sense of irony. No official was any match for this: her personality and amused detachment to life and dangers also makes her book entertaining and interesting.

She had a respect and sympathy for the Africans and African cultures, and she was critical of missionaries who tried to eradicate the local culture and institutions and chauvinistically impose their own. She was convinced that had led to the failure of the Blantyre Mission.

When we left home, every one was afraid of our exposing ourselves to the heat in the Red Sea. They did not know that a much worse thing was to round Cape Guardafui, and that, too, in the month of July, the place and time at which the south-west monsoon blows the very strongest.

One often hears old Indians talking of the monsoon, but it is the coast of Africa that gets the whole force and fury of the storm. India gets only the tail of it; and there it ends in rain, for as it abates it deposits the water which it has taken up as vapour and spray on its journey across the ocean. This monsoon continues till about September, when there is quite a lull. After that there springs up the opposite (northeast) monsoon, which is called in India the "rainless one," and it reaches Africa in an exceedingly mild form. This is perhaps the reason why, in the country we are going to, the regularly rainy season is from October till March.

As we came up to Guardafui the weather was still hot and the sea tolerably calm. It was most difficult to realise that there could be a tremendous storm ahead of us. Nevertheless, our captain assured us that it must be so; and besides, we had been warned of

this before, because, while we were in the Red Sea, our captain there had told us he would not himself like to be here at this time, and expressed what we were to expect more by gestures than by words. Then we had the ominous sight of the Lascar crew taking away all our awning from the deck, and everything else that could catch the gale, and tying the seats with ropes.

For a little while we were tempted to grumble being thus exposed to the scorching sun; but just as we were turning the promontory, a most wonderful change happened, all in the course of two or three minutes. A wind got up that nearly blew us off the deck, and it was so cold, too, that it felt just like the shock of a heavy shower-bath. The ship both rolled and pitched tremendously, until we had all to hold on by ropes. Even the ship's cat rushed up on deck, and after some frantic movements, tried to climb the rigging.

Soon we were all obliged to go below, except the sailors, and Captain H — —, who was anxious to see what was going to happen to us. For the next forty-eight hours we lay perfectly helpless, listening to the roaring of the waves and the crashing of crockery. It is impossible to describe our outward and inward misery. The water came into the saloon and cabins below, and we got a great proportion of our clothes wet. Our boxes were floating about, while a poor old white-headed lascar was kept for several days constantly swabbing up the water at the door of our cabin.

By degrees, however, things became better. At last, when I was carried up on deck, and made secure by ropes, I thought it a most delightful change. The sea was covered with gigantic mountains of creamy foam, and looked inexpressibly grand. Sometimes these huge stormy waves seemed as if they were going to swamp us altogether, and many a time they broke over us, thoroughly douching us with spray [*Towards the Mountains of the Moon*, pp. 13–15].

Here I cannot but tell you, that as we approached Quillimane my heart beat faster and faster. A few hours, I knew, would decide my fate, but in what way it was impossible to foretell. Hitherto I had been sent on from port to port, until I had begun to hope that as nobody knew what to do with me, they would pass me on to their neighbours, who in their turn would do the same. But now we had arrived at the most critical point, and as Senhor N — — stood calmly scanning me from head to foot, I felt almost breathless. Fancy my relief when he turned to the gentlemen and said, "You cannot possibly leave the lady in Quillimane until your return from Blantyre, for she would be sure to take fever and die. Now she has come so far, it will be safer for her to go on [pp. 63–64].

WORKS

Pringle, Mrs. M.A. *Towards the Mountains of the Moon: A Journey in East Africa.* London: W. Blackwood and Sons, 1884.

Susie Carson Rijnhart, M.D.,
1868–1908. American.

Susie was born in Western Ontario, the daughter of a prominent Canadian educationalist. Her own education was under her father's direction. She studied medicine in Toronto, graduating at the age of twenty, the first lady in Canada to obtain first-class honors in medicine. She practiced in London, and at Newbury, Ontario, where she met and married Petrus Rijnhart in the fall of 1894.

A few months later Susie and Petrus left for Tibet, specifically Kumbum, which was one of the great lamaseries of Tibet and a center of Buddhist learning and worship. They intended to establish a medical station at Lusar, which was in the secular part of the lamasery, and they planned to enter Tibet from the Chinese side, where there seemed to be better access into "the forbidden land." Two years earlier Petrus had entered Tibet by going through China on the same route and had spent ten months in Lusar. He'd evangelized and used his limited medical knowledge as best he could, and

he'd been well received by the lamas and priests.

Theirs was a missionary trip. They intended to evangelize and give medical care. The Rijnharts were joined by a fellow-worker, Mr. Ferguson.

Susie readily admits that crossing northern China in mid-winter was not inviting, but they persisted. There was a great amount of unrest; China was at war with Japan. They had just arrived at Lusar when a Mohammedan rebellion broke out. They were invited to reside in the lamasery at Kumbum, which was regarded as a significant show of patronage. Meanwhile, Mr. Ferguson went back to Shanghai to take care of his business, leaving Susie and Petrus on their own. When peace was eventually declared, Petrus went to the Mohammedan quarters to treat the Mohammedan wounded, causing both amazement and consternation.

Life at Kumbum and Lusar fell into a comfortable pattern and the Rijnharts considered settling there permanently. They had made great friends, and had shared "months of terror, disease and slaughter" [*With the Tibetans*, p. 137] with everyone else. But they were restless for new challenges, and they determined to open a mission station at Tankar. The move was easily made; their good reputation had preceded them and they were welcomed by the officials and wealthy merchants as well as by the people of the village.

Charles — Charlie — was born in June, 1897. By the time he was one year old his parents were again on the move, this time to the northern parts to work and live among the nomads of Ts'aidam. They concluded that missionary work was possible among the nomads during the summer; during the winter the workers returned to Tankar.

They were traveling across very isolated country, a desolate area where no one lived. Trouble began.

O the bleak barrenness of that marshy district! Sand-hills, gravel and scrub! Not a sign of life in any place, not a drop of running water, only here and there in a little hollow in the bed of what had been apparently an irrigation stream, hidden in the shade of a bush, we would find a little, but not enough to refresh us and the horses. When it was nearly dark Mr. Rijnhart went ahead and found a camping-place among brushwood on the bank of a large stream of good water flowing towards Dsun, in a deep gully right at the foot of the mountain which towered in front of us. It seemed cruel to tether the horses, but there was not a blade of grass, and when such is the case animals will stray miles away in search of food unless prevented; so we gave them some barley, and all prepared for the ascent of the Burh'an Bota the following day. We started shortly after daybreak, beginning to ascend at once along a dry watercourse, where not an atom of green was to be seen, but strewn here and there were dead yak, many of them reduced to skeletons and others more recently dead. Of the latter we counted forty-two, and the sight made us pause to reflect on the name of the pass and wonder whether the explanation of its name, "Buddha's Cauldron," is not found in the fact that it claims so many sacrifices of these poor animals; or was the name suggested by the vapors that hang over it, which the natives call poisonous from the depressing effect they produce on travelers? [p. 234].

The desertion of these men [*two of the three Tibetans accompanying them*] left us in a quandary, but we rearranged our loads that they might be easily handled by two, fed some of the extra food to our horses, and continued our journey after a rest of four days. Storms seemed to be the rule, for it snowed and hailed at about twelve o'clock every day; but we pushed our way on past a lake called Uyan-khar, across a plain where the trail was scarcely visible and where quicksands were numerous, to a camp by the side of springs with plenty of wild onions, which were a great treat [p. 239].

Charlie was teething and ill. Amid the desolation and struggle of the journey, Charlie died.

The trek continued; one of the horses died, leaving only two, and Mr. Rijnhart and Rahim (the only man remaining) alternately rode and walked. They were accosted by a party of men who seemed to them to be spies, but the men rode away. As they proceeded they were under surveillance, and finally they were ordered to leave Tibet and go to China; their route was taking them too close to Lhasa. They sought permission either to winter in Hageh'uk'a or turn toward China and winter someplace on the road, but the officials wanted them to travel towards Ta-chien-lu; they negotiated for fresh horses and three guides who knew the road. Rahim had decided to make his way back and left them after a difficult parting. An attack by robbers killed several of their horses; the remaining horse was weak. The guides deserted.

They arrived at a river where there were tents and horses on the other side of the river. Being weak and exhausted they decided that

in the morning Mr. Rijnhart would swim over, hire animals, and at the same to find out our whereabouts in reference to the lamasery. How sore our faces were that night from the sun and snow, and how severely our eyes smarted!...

Wading half across, he put out his arms to make the first stroke, but suddenly turned around and walked back again to the bank where he had first entered the water. Shouting something up to me which I did not hear on account of the rushing river, he walked up-stream in the opposite direction to the tents he had set out for. Then he followed a little path around the rocks that had obstructed our way the day before, until out of sight, and *I never saw him again* [pp. 310–311].

She fell in with a party of Tibetans, whom she doesn't trust. After several days with them, when most of her few belongings were taken, she hired three guides to take her to Ta-chien-lu. The trek was long and difficult, but at long last she arrived and was welcomed at the China Inland Mission House,

I had arrived in Ta-chien-lu just two months after Mr. Rijnhart's disappearance. Could it be possible that I had survived that long and perilous journey alone over mountains and rivers, surrounded by hostile people and subjected to hourly danger from those who professed to be my guides.... Yes, at last, and the realization of it grew upon me when I saw myself delivered from the dirt and vermin of weeks, and lay down to rest once more on a clean bed [pp. 388–389].

She waited six months hoping to hear something about Rijnhart's fate. Friends in America supported her return. The minister for the Netherlands in China promised he would do all possible to find out the fate of Petrus Rijnhart, a Dutch citizen. The only response was vague rumors and suggestions of murder.

SOURCES: *With the Tibetans in Tent and Temple*; Internet: Celebration of Women Writers, December 2006.

WORKS

Rijnhart, Dr. Susie Carson. *With the Tibetans in Tent and Temple.* Chicago: Fleming H. Revell Company, 1901.

Emma Roberts, 1791–1840. British.

Emma Roberts was born in London, one of three children of Captain William Roberts and his wife Eliza. When her father died she and her mother lived in Bath. Her mother had literary interests and undoubtedly encouraged Emma to write. Emma's first book was *Memoirs of the Rival Houses of York and Lancaster*; while she was doing research in the British Museum she met the poet Laetitia Landon, who became a close friend.

When her mother died in 1828, Emma went to India with her older sister Laura, whose husband was in the Bengal infantry. This may not have gone well: she later

wrote, "There cannot be a more wretched situation than that of a young woman in India who has been induced to follow the fortunes of her married sister under the delusive expectations that she will exchange the privations attached to limited means in England for the far-famed luxuries of the East" [*Scenes and Characteristics*, Vol. 1, pp. 33–34].

While in India she published *Oriental Scenes*, a book of poetry.

Her sister died in 1830, and Emma's writing became her financial support. She moved to Calcutta, where she edited and wrote for the *Oriental Observer* in addition to writing articles for various periodicals. In 1832 she returned to London, where she wrote on a wide range of interests including history, biography, cookery, fiction, and poetry, but it was her writing on India that brought her the most attention.

Emma went back to India in 1839, using the overland route through France and Egypt. She wrote an account of her journey and her observation for the *Asiatic Journal*; the material was later turned into a book. In April 1840 she became ill. She moved to Poona, hoping the location would improve her health, but died there in September. The book *Notes of an Overland Journey* was subsequently published with a memoir.

She was well liked and known for her unassuming manner and good humor as well as her attractive appearance.

SOURCE: *Oxford Dictionary of National Biography.*

WORKS

Roberts, Emma. *Hindoostan, Its Landscapes, Palaces, Temples, Tombs.* London: 1845.

_____. *Notes of an Overland Journey Through France and Egypt to Bombay.* London: Wm. H. Allen, 1841.

_____. *Scenes and Characteristics of Hindostan.* Three volumes. London: W. H. Allen and Co., 1837. Written with George Francis

White. Emma may have been the editor and White the author.

_____. *Views in India, Chiefly Among the Himalayan Mountains.* London: Fisher, Son & Co., 1838.

Isabella Frances Romer

Isabella tells us little about herself, except for occasional comments, such as wanting all her life to behold the Egyptian Pyramids and daydreaming about being there, on the summit of the Great Pyramid. After she had seen them, explored their interiors, and climbed, she reflected and agreed with the American gentleman who remarked to her, "I have *realized* the Pyramids" [*A Pilgrimage*, Vol. II, p. 93].

In the preface to the two volumes of her 1846 book, *A Pilgrimage*, she laughed at herself for writing a book.

> Since the facilities of steam-navigation have brought the Nile within the scope of everybody's possibility, and rendered Constantinople an easier undertaking than the Giant's Causeway formerly was, so much has been published upon the East that the subject has been complete exhausted by minds of every caliber, and books of Oriental travel have become a mere drug. It therefore looks like a work of supererogation — a squeezing of the squeezed lemon — to endeavour to extract a new idea from so worn-out a theme, or attempt to add a word to that which has already been so often and so well said. But, such is the incorrigibility of human nature....
> ... and not a woman turns her face, Hadji-like, towards the far East that does not fancy she is bound to add her mite to the general fund of knowledge or entertainment to record some impression which may have escaped a mightier mind, or correct some mistake which may have been perpetrated by a more careless one. And, consequently, every fair wanderer who trusts herself to the Great Oriental at Southampton, or to the French steamers at Marseilles, for conveyance to the land of the Pharaoh,

> would as soon think of embarking without her *sac de nuit* as without a certain mysterious-looking little clasped volume, carefully closed with a Bramah lock, of which the tiny key is appended to her watch-chain, and whose blank leaves are destined to receive the "concentrated essence" of observations which are at a later period to be diluted into two or three respectable-looking octavo volumes.

She had promised herself not to do the same, and only write the family letters.

> ... yet no sooner was I on the move than I found the *cacothes scribendi* creeping upon me; and, unable long to resist the contagion, I began most vehemently to deface all the blank paper within my reach... [Preface, pp. v–vi].
> The interior aspect of Cairo is far more striking and original than that of Constantinople; it is purely an Arab city.... The houses are most picturesque in their construction, with large prominent windows of wooden lattice-work, elegant carved, the upper stories projecting over the lower ones so as almost to exclude sunshine from the narrow streets, in many of which the opposite houses nearly touch each other. Mosques and public fountains are numerous and beautiful; the shops are, like those of Constantinople, small, and presenting no outward show of merchandize; the owner sits crosslegged upon a carpet spread over his shop-board, which contains just space enough to accommodate one customer upon the cushion that occupies the other end. But the population of Cairo is the most striking feature of the place; for it has preserved its Oriental aspect both in men and things, free from those innovations which in the Turkish dominions have introduced the prose of European civilization into the wild and picturesque poetry of Eastern barbarism. None of the Frank mixture which neutralized the nationality of Stamboul is here to be seen — none of the *hybrid* Nizam uniform adopted by the most modern Turk! Here the turban flourishes in its pristine volume and integrity — the flowing Caireen robes of silk, or the elegant Memlook dress of cloth richly braided imparts a certain grace and grandeur to their

wearers; the dark face of the copt looks more somber surmounted by his black turban... [Vol. I, pp. 47–48].

She relished everything about her trip up the Nile and back, the glimpses of village life, the topography, and above all, the temples and ruins. On her return to Cairo she met Mrs. Poole and her "highly gifted brother Mr. Lane, author of *The Modern Egyptians*." The household, which included Mr. Lane's wife and Mrs. Poole's two boys, had adopted the customs and the dress, "keep strict hareem, and avoid meeting the many English travelers to Egypt" [Vol. II, p. 3].

From Egypt she went to Syria, and then to Palestine, visiting Biblical sites. The travel was rougher, and there was some danger from warring factions; a least once the guide mis-routed them and there was difficulty in getting to the correct route. She relished all of it, and at the end she rejoiced "that I have been permitted to see what I have seen, and to lay up for myself such treasures of thought — I dare not say of wisdom — as must be the result of time so employed, and as will prove a source of unalloyed satisfaction to me to the latest moment of my existence" [Vol. II, pp. 389–390].

WORKS

Romer, Isabella. *The Bird of Passage: or, Flying Glimpses of Many Lands*. London: Richard Bentley, 1849. Impressions of Europe and Turkey
_____. *A Pilgrimage to the Temples and Tombs of Egypt, Nubia and Palestine in 1845–46*. London: Richard Bentley, 1846.
_____. *The Rhone, the Daro, and the Guadalquivir: A Summer Ramble in 1842*. London: Richard Bentley, 1843.

Lady Florentia Sale, 1790–1853.
British.

Florentia was the daughter of George Wynch; little else is known of her early life.

She married Robert Henry Sale (1782–1845), a military man, in 1809. Their daughter, Alexandrine, married John Sturt; a granddaughter was born just before the time covered in Florentia's book.

The book recounts in part the experiences of a group who accompanied a military campaign and were taken hostage. The English hostages numbered 9 women, 20 officers, and 14 children; European hostages were 17 soldiers, 2 women, and 1 child.

I have not only daily noted down events as they occurred, but often have done so hourly. I have also given the reports of the day, the only information we possessed... [*A Journal of the Disasters in Afghanistan*, Introduction, p. 1].
... I believe several people kept an account of these proceedings, but all except myself lost all they had written; and had recourse to memory afterwards. I lost everything except the clothes I wore; and therefore it may appear strange that I should have saved these papers. The mystery is, however, easily solved. After every thing was packed on the night we left Cabul, I sat up to add a few lines to the events of the day, and the next morning I put them in a small bag and tied them round my waist [*Introduction*, p. 2].
A much better narrative might have been written, even by myself; but I have preferred keeping my Journal as originally written, when events were fresh, and men's minds were biased by the reports of the day or even hour.
It is easy to argue on the wisdom or folly of conduct after the catastrophe has taken place [*Introduction*, p. 3].

"The Retreat"
We commenced our march at about midday, the 5th N. I. in front. The troops were in the greatest state of disorganization: the baggage was mixed in with the advanced guard; and the camp followers all pushed ahead in their precipitate flight towards Hindostan.
Sturt, my daughter, Mr. Mein and I, got up to the advance, and Mr. Mein was pointing out to us the spot where the 1st brigade was attacked, and where he, Sale

&c. were wounded. We had not proceeded half a mile when we were heavily fired upon. Chiefs rode with the advance, and desired us to keep close to them. They certainly desired his followers to shout to the people on the height not to fire; they did so, but quite ineffectually. These chiefs certainly ran the same risk we did; but I verily believe many of these persons would individually sacrifice themselves to rid the country of us.

After passing through some very sharp firing, we came upon Major Thain's horse, which had been shot through the loins. When we were supposed to be in comparative safety, poor Sturt rode back (to see after Thain I believe): his horse was shot under him, and before he could rise from the ground he received a severe wound in the abdomen. It was with great difficulty he was held upon a pony by two people, and brought into camp at Khoord Cabul.

The pony Mrs. Sturt rode was wounded in the ear and neck. I had fortunately only one ball in my arm; three others passed through my poshteen near my shoulder without doing me any injury. The party that fired on us were not above fifty yards from us, and we owed our escape to urging our horses on as fast as they could go over a road where, at any other time, we should have walked our horses very carefully [p. 236–237].

[*February*] 19th. I heard from Sale. A friend writes me that there would be no relief before April. At noon I was on the top of the house; when an awful earthquake took place.... For some time I balanced myself as well as I could; till I felt the roof was giving way. I fortunately succeeded in removing myself from my position before the roof of our room fell in with a dreadful crash. The roof of the stairs fell in as I descended them; but did me no injury. All my concern was for Mrs. Sturt; but I could only see a pile of rubbish. I was nearly bewildered when I heard the joyful sound, "Lady Sale, come here, all are safe;" and I found the whole party uninjured in the courtyard. When the earthquake first commenced in the hills in the upper part of the valley, its progress was clearly defined, coming down the valley, and throwing up dust, like the action of exploding a mine.—I

hope a soldier's wife may use a soldier's simile, for I know of nothing else to liken it to [pp. 297–298].

After their stay at Kabul, Florentia and her husband spent time in England, then went to India. Robert was shot in 1845 during the outbreak of the First Anglo-Sikh War and died from his wound. Florentia stayed in India and received a pension. In 1853 she went to Cape of Good Hope for her health and died a few days after her arrival.

SOURCE: *Dictionary of National Biography.*

WORKS

Sale, Lady Florentia. *Journal of the Disasters in Afghanistan.* London: John Murray, 1843.

Helen Josephine Sanborn,
1857–1927. American.

Helen was born in Maine. Her father was an importer and distributor of spices and coffee; the family is the "Sanborn" of Chase and Sanborn Company. After her graduation from Wellesley College in 1884, Helen went with her father on a coffee-buying expedition to Guatemala, having learned Spanish so she could be his interpreter.

We very soon left the plains, and resumed our journey on a narrow mountain path, the precipice ever growing deeper and deeper as we wound around the mountain, and gradually ascended. At three o'clock we reached the very top, where there was a little village of three or four houses, and where we had planned to pass the night, but it was such a barren, lonely place, without a cabildo, or even "zacate" for the mule, that we felt as if we could not stay, and must try to reach another station before night. How anxiously I questioned the guide, but he said there was not even a hut between there and San Antonio, which was so far it could not be reached until very late, and that the road was too dangerous for traveling in the dark. So we reluctantly dismounted, and passed as best we could the long, weary afternoon, sitting on a hard bench, listening to the soughing of the wind in the pine trees, watching a drove of lean, hungry pigs trying to steal corn from our mules; or, as usual when we made a long stop, giving the guide a lesson in English, for he was very anxious to learn, and I was glad to help him, on account of his devotion and faithfulness.

The place where we were to spend the night was an open shed made of a few boughs bound together with vines, with no door, with no covering of mud or thatching for the roof, and with wide-open spaces where we looked out upon the sky. In fact, it was just the same as sleeping out of doors, and was so cold from the high elevation that all our wraps were not sufficient to keep us warm.... The mules never for a moment ceased champing corn all night; the whole drove of pigs were squealing, and grunting, and running about the shed; and all the dogs in the village, in numbers more than the inhabitants, were barking incessantly....

Finally, a little before three they determined it was useless to try to sleep and they should get up and start. However it was too dark, and they had to wait for dawn.

We went very slowly, in the dim light hardly able to see each other. The sunrise was entirely shut out by the great mountains surrounding us, but gradually the light of day came and revealed to us the awfulness of our situation. We were on a narrow shelf of rock overhanging a terrible precipice. Words utterly fail to portray the grandeur and awfulness of this great mountain gorge through which we were riding. The path, on the very side of a high mountain, was so narrow that two mules could barely pass, and the overhanging branches of the trees often brushed against us with such force as almost to throw us from our mules. On one side was a perfectly straight wall of rock, on the other a sheer declivity of hundreds of feet as straight as a plummet line....

What was more trying still, the mules would go on the very edge overhanging the precipice, and no amount of reining could prevent it. In fact if we reined them in toward the wall they would stop altogether; and as it was no place to have a tussle, we held our breath and let them have their own way.... Melesio went ahead very calmly, so well known and familiar a place having no terrors for him. In one spot where we bent sharply around the mountain, and the path was scarcely wide enough for the mule's feet, he turned around and told us to look down. Our heads fairly whirled at a mere glance [*Winter in Central America and Mexico*, pp. 98–105].

The ride across the Isthmus disclosed to us a miserable country — hot, swampy, unhealthy. There were frequent stations, but they were only wretched little negro villages, and all along the way were numerous graveyards and fresh graves; for the soil, composed of decaying vegetation, breathes out death as soon as overturned by the spade.

In building the railroad, it has been said that every sleeper cost a man's life; and without doubt as many if not more lives will be sacrificed in the digging of the canal.

Everywhere work on the canal was visible; but there seemed little connection between the different portions of the work, and nothing like more than a mere beginning. We were told by one of the engineers that so far only the "installation" was done, only ten million of the required two hundred and fifty million cubic metres of earth had yet been removed. The undertaking is a vast one, far exceeding that of the Suez canal, and every one there believed it would not be finished for many years.

At ten o'clock we arrived in Aspinwall, or, as it is always called there, Colon, this being the real name of the place, given by the people in honor of Columbus; Aspinwall is the name given by the Americans, but is not used on the Isthmus.

It is quite impossible to say which place is the worse, Colon or Panama. Everybody in Panama said, "It is not healthy here, to be sure, but not nearly as bad as Colon"; and in Colon they all said, "It is much healthier here than in Panama." From our own experience we concluded that both places were as bad as they could be [pp. 200–201].

Her travel had a significant impact on her; she became a dedicated "ambassador" of Hispanic cultures and strongly advocated the study of Spanish and Hispanic culture at academic institutions. She was instrumental in establishing the Instituto Internacional in Madrid, where young women from North America could learn Spanish.

SOURCE: *Magical Sites: Women Travelers in 19th Century Latin America.*

WORKS

Sanborn, Helen. *Winter in Central America and Mexico.* Boston: Lee & Shepard, 1886.

Janet Schaw. Mid-1700s.

Little is known of Janet Schaw's life. She was born in Lauriston, a suburb of Edinburgh, and she was about thirty-five or forty when she made the voyage to the West Indies and America. After she returned to Scotland she lived in Edinburgh, at least for a time.

Her journey took her from Scotland to Antigua and St. Kitts in the West Indies, then to Cape Fear, then to Portugal and Scotland. The Schaws had a brother Robert as well as other close family connections in North Carolina. "Schawfield" is a family property. The Scottish Schaws were in North Carolina just before the American War of Independence broke out, and Janet conveys the edginess of being a British traveler in America at that time.

> Schawfield. After I put my last packet into a safe hand, I left Wilmingtown and returned to Schawfield by water, which is a most delightful method of travelling thro' this Noble country, which indeed owes more favours to its God and king than perhaps any other in the known world and is

equally ungrateful to both, to the God who created and bestowed them and to the king whose indulgent kindness has done every thing to render them of the greatest utility to the owners....

> Nothing can be finer than the banks of this river; a thousand beauties both of the flowery and sylvan tribe hang over it and are reflected from it with additional luster. But they spend their beauties on the desert air, and the pines that wave behind the shore with a solemn gravity seem to lament that they too exist to no purpose, tho' capable of being rendered both useful and agreeable.... This north west branch is said to be navigable for Ships of 400 tons burthen for above two hundred miles up, and the banks so constituted by nature that they seem formed for harbours, and what adds in a most particular manner to this convenience is, that, quite across from one branch to the other, and indeed thro' the whole main branches of the river and every tide receive a sufficient depth of water for boats of the largest size and even for small Vessels, so that every thing is water-borne at a small charge and with great safety and ease.

> But these uncommon advantages are almost entirely neglected. In the course of sixteen miles which is the distance between these places and the town, there is but one plantation, and the condition it is in shows, if not the poverty, at least the indolence of its owner....

> I have just mentioned a garden, and will tell you, that this at Schawfield is the only thing deserving the name I have seen in this country, and laid out with some taste. I could not help smiling however at the appearance of a soil, that seemed to me no better than dead sand, proposed for a garden. But a few weeks have convinced me that I judged very falsely, for the quickness of the vegetation is absolutely astonishing [*Journal of a Lady of Quality*, pp. 158–162].

Janet was unmarried, and she traveled with her brother Alexander; Fanny, a girl of about eighteen; Jack, a boy of eleven; and Billie, who was nine. These were all relations of the Schaws. Also accompanying them was Janet's maid and an East Indian servant who proved to be invaluable in matters of food.

WORKS

Schaw, Janet. *Journal of a Lady of Quality, Being the Narrative of a Journey from Scotland to the West Indies, North Carolina, and Portugal in the Years 1774 to 1776*. Edited by Evangeline Walker Andrews in collaboration with Charles McLean Andrews. New Haven, Conn.: Yale University Press, 1923. From a manuscript in the British Museum.

Mrs. Mary Seacole, 1805–1881.

Jamaican.

Mary Jane Grant was born in Jamaica in 1805. Her father was Scottish, and an army officer. Her mother was a free black woman who ran a boarding house in Kingston. Many of the boarding house's guests were military officers and their families. Slavery was still a strong presence on the island; that, the fact that Britain was the center of the Empire, and the presence of military people and their values in her home, were significant to Mary's later aspirations and attitudes, particularly with respect to her service in the Crimean War.

From very early Mary was interested in learning about medicine. Her mother was one of the island's notable doctresses, who could diagnose and treat tropical diseases, as well as ailments and wounds. The traditional medicine had absorbed many of the practices of European doctors and both were respected. It was customary for patients to convalesce at a hotel, and the family's boarding house was well known.

Mary also loved travel and had a taste for adventure. While young she traveled to England twice and visited many of the islands.

She married Edwin Horatio Seacole, who was Viscount Nelson's godson. The marriage lasted only a short time as Mr. Seacole died young. Shortly after his death, her mother died also, and Mary suddenly found herself independent.

She rebuilt the hotel, which had been destroyed by fire. She was a well respected doctress herself, and the hotel became even more profitable than the old one. In 1850 when cholera broke out in Kingston, Mary was instrumental in dealing with the epidemic.

Shortly after she went to New Granada to join her brother Edward. This was an unprecedented move; she gave up her position and respectability in Kingston, but she also escaped the island life that she found claustrophobic. At that time New Granada was caught up in gold fever; anyone going to California or to South America passed through New Granada.

Mary was impressed by the substantial black community in New Granada, many of whom had fled the Southern United States. Her time in New Granada was somewhat nomadic; she moved around to some extent, always opening a business wherever she landed.

Cholera broke out in Cruces where she was living. Mary was the only person who had had any experience of dealing with cholera and knew what to do.

After the epidemic subsided she returned to Jamaica (in 1853) only to have her medical skills called into use to deal with a yellow fever epidemic. Not only did she care for patients at her house, but the medical authorities asked her to take charge of nursing at the military camp. She did an excellent job.

She went to England the next year. Bolstered by her experience and her field training, she volunteered her services to the army. She was unique in her knowledge and experience. This was at the same time that Florence Nightingale was fighting for the opportunity to be a nurse.

Mary's appeals to go to the Crimea and nurse were consistently rejected. Finally, she decided to go to the Crimea on her own, hoping to recoup the travel expenses by working with a relative as a sutler, or provisioner. With Mr. Day, a distant relative, she set up a canteen, the "British Hotel," where soldiers could get good food at very reasonable prices. Gambling and drunkenness were prohibited. The place was clean. The "Hotel" was very popular with the military men.

She often went to the front with her own medicines to treat the wounded. Within months she had organized an efficient establishment using only her own resources; she could get all the provisions, cook good meals, and dispense medicines that were much needed. The nutrition element was increasingly recognized as an important component of medical care: Mary provided both.

The war ended abruptly in March, 1856. Mary was left with expensive stock and no market for the goods and equipment. She returned to England impoverished, where she tried, unsuccessfully, to reestablish herself at Aldershot, a military town. She then went to London and took lodgings. By November she was in the London Bankruptcy Court with her former partner, Mr. Day.

There were many letters and testimonials in *The Times* on her behalf. She received many tributes, and well-placed people contributed to clearing her debts and enabling her to set up in business again. In early 1857 the court declared her no longer a debtor. Still the tributes continued. She was a celebrity. There were benefits, articles, and widespread recognition. She began to write her autobiography, which was highly recommended and sold well.

The major part of the population of Escribanos, including even the women and children, worked at the mine. The labour was hard and disagreeable. I often used to watch them at their work; and would sometimes wander about by myself, thinking it possible that I might tumble across some gold in my rambles. And I once did come upon some heavy yellow material, that

brought my heart into my mouth with that strange thrilling delight which all who have hunted for the precious metal understand so well. I think it was very wrong, but I kept the secret of the place from the alcalde and every one else, and filled some bottles with the precious dust, to carry down to Navy Bay.... You can imagine my feelings when he [*a gold buyer*] coolly laughed, and told me it was some material (I forget its name) very like gold, but — valueless [*Wonderful Adventures*, pp. 113–114].

I have never been long in any place before I have found my practical experience in the science of medicine useful. Even in London I have found it of service to others. And in the Crimea, where the doctors were so overworked, and sickness was so prevalent, I could not be long idle; for I never forgot that my intention in seeking the army was to help the kind-hearted doctors, to be useful to whom I have ever looked upon and still regard as so high a privilege.

But before very long I found myself surrounded with patients of my own, and this for two simple reasons. In the first place, the men (I am speaking of the "ranks" now) had a very serious objection to going into hospital for any but urgent reasons, and the regimental doctors were rather fond of sending them there; and in the second place, they could and did get at my store sick-comforts and nourishing food, which the heads of the medical staff would sometimes find it difficult to procure. These reasons, with the additional one that I was very familiar with the diseases which they suffered most from and successful in their treatment (I say this in no spirit of vanity), were quite sufficient to account for the numbers who came daily to the British Hotel for medical treatment.

That the officers were glad of me as a doctress and nurse may be easily understood. When a poor fellow lay sickening in his cheerless hut and sent down to me, he knew very well that I should not ride up in answer to his message empty-handed. And although I did not hesitate to charge him with the value of the necessaries I took him, still he was thankful enough to be able to *purchase* them....

Then their calling me "mother" was not, I think altogether unmeaning. I used to fancy that there was something homely in the word; and, reader, you cannot think how dear to them was the smallest thing that reminded them of home [pp. 166–168].

Mary hoped to go to India to work but could not find sponsors for the trip. The grueling work during the war had taken its toll on her health.

For the rest of her life Mary divided her time between England and Jamaica. Wherever she was, she had visitors, survivors, friends, relatives of people she had treated. She always stayed busy, helping anyone who could use her skills and knowledge. She died in 1881, in England.

Works

Seacole, Mary. *Wonderful Adventures of Mrs. Seacole in Many Lands*. London: James Blackwood, 1857.
_____. *Wonderful Adventures of Mrs. Seacole in Many Lands*. Edited by Ziggi Alexander & Audrey Dewjee. Bristol, England: Falling Wall Press Ltd., 1984.

Elizabeth Cochrane Seaman
see **Nellie Bly**

Lady Mary Leonora Woulfe Sheil

Concerning Persia, Lady Mary in her preface notes the "histories, the travels, and the novels" of various male British writers, that "have made the world acquainted with the literature, the geography, the commerce, and the antiquities of that country." Her book, she tells us, "is simply an attempt to describe the manners and the tone of feeling and society at the present day."

She began her trip in 1849, traveling with her husband and several servants. They traveled from England via Poland and Russia rather than through Turkish Armenia, the more usual route. She lived in Persia nearly four years.

The barren hills and nearly equally barren plains of Persia produce a most somniferous effect on the plodding wayfarer, particularly if he travels, as I did, in a carriage at a walking pace.... Even this was preferable to the ordinary mode of travelling among ladies, shut up in a large box, called a takhterewan, suspended between two mules, in which one creeps along with ambassadorial dignity, in a way that put one's patience to a severe trial. In a mountainous country this same box exposes the inmate to some danger and a great deal of terror. On a narrow road, with a deep precipice on one side without a parapet, and mules that neither prayers, blows, nor abuse will remove from the very edge, one sees the box hanging over the yawning gulf, and the occupant dares not move lest the balance be disturbed, and she willfully seek her own salvation before due time [*Glimpses of Life and Manners in Persia*, pp. 98–99].

We had now concluded our long journey of more than three months and a half. I was rejoiced at its termination; for although mixed with many pleasurable associations, many new ideas acquired, many wrong notions dissipated; I was tired of the constraint and the unceasing hurry from object to object. I was glad to rest and to be able to see the dawn and daylight appear with indifference. I felt inclined to do as an Indian officer I heard once did. After he left the army, he paid a man to blow a bugle every morning at daybreak, that he might have the satisfaction of feeling he need not get up [p. 121].

During that time her husband's health worsened, and in February 1853 they decided to leave Persia at once and avoid another hot, stressful summer. The trip back was difficult, with her husband virtually an invalid and with three young children to manage. Lady Mary had liked their stay in Persia and found it interesting; she was sad to leave.

WORKS

Sheil, Lady Mary. *Glimpses of Life and Manners in Persia, with Notes on Russia, Koods, Toorko-mans, Nestorians, Khiva, and Persia.* London: Murray, 1856. Reprint: *Glimpses of Life and Manners in Persia.* New York: Arno Press, 1973.

May French Sheldon, 1848–1936.
American.

She may be found under French-Sheldon in some listings.

Born in Pennsylvania, May French was educated in Europe and lived in England most of her life, when she wasn't traveling. Her father, a grand-nephew of Sir Isaac Newton, was a civil engineer. In 1876 she married Eli Sheldon, also an American. Eventually they settled in England, where Eli was a banker.

An author and journalist, she wrote a novel, *Herbert Severance*, and translated Flaubert's *Salammbo*. She and her husband founded a publishing house to publish her work.

In 1891 she traveled alone to Africa on an exploring expedition; her success in cir-cumnavigating Lake Chala attracted con-siderable attention. Some of the objects she collected on this journey won medals at the World's Columbian Exposition in Chicago in 1893.

May French Sheldon saw herself as an anthropologist, and on the voyage out she prepared herself for her study in East Africa.

Somehow the more I dispassionately con-templated my venture, reviewing the pros and cons, the more I was convinced that I should accomplish something worth the greatest hardships and indefatigable output of force and endeavor requisite. The voyage yielded an opportunity to acquaint myself with weak points, which had previously es-caped me. I could composedly formulate vague ideas into distinct shape, and prepare for possible emergencies, and fortify my health and strength. It was like gathering one's self up to enter an arena as a combat-ant. In making classifications for my future work, writing out leading questions, jotting down points for anthropological and ethno-logical observation in order to lose no op-portunity, when once in the field, of prob-ing every topic to the heart and thrashing out the subjects thoroughly, gradually I dis-covered in myself a latent gift for organiza-tion. Self-amazement awaited each effort in this direction, for every diverse avenue of thought revealed fresh tributaries, until the responsibilities of my project aggrandized beyond all the limits of original conception. After all, good work is an accretion of ideas put into effect [*Sultan to Sultan*, pp. 31–32].

The content of *Sultan to Sultan* reflects this aim; it contains very little about the travel and is primarily her ethnographic ob-servations.

Plains of Taro stretched out in vast, slop-ing, sandy lengths, defined by the clusters of hills on either side, and an isolated sand mound now and again looming up like a dome without apparent connection with the hills.

The rain had imparted an agreeable, smiling freshness to nature, veiling the burning red sands and tufted stubble with a generous verdure, which spared us all much discomfort. This portion of the route, how-ever, is generally conceded to be full of hardships, especially as the porters are scarcely broken in to their work, and their feet are soft and easily burnt. In making such a detour as the wait-a-bits and other natural obstacles provokingly compel in Africa, lengthening the journey to a given point at times immeasurably, my men be-came surly, evincing symptoms of insubor-dination. Suddenly the leaders wheeled around, halted the line of porters following, pitched their loads in wild disorder upon the ground, saying Bébé did not know the road, and refused to budge, and as the porters in the rear kept coming up they were incited to manifest the same spirit. The minor headmen made futile attempts to rally the men, and beat about in a lusty manner with their kibosh, all to no effect....

Then or never I realized I must demonstrate to these mutinous, half-savage men that I would be obeyed, and that discipline should be enforced at any cost. Only for one instant in perplexity I paused, a vulture flew overhead, I drew my pistols and sent a bullet whizzing after it, and brought it surely down at my feet, to the astonishment of the revolting men.

With both pistols cocked, suddenly I became eloquent in the smattering of the Swahali which I knew, without interpreter, inspired with fearlessness and strength I started through the centre of the rebellious throng, pointing first one, then the other pistol in quick succession at the heads of the men, threatening, and fully prepared, determined, and justified to shoot the first dissenter....

Then I had no fear; now I marvel how ever I had the temerity to take such extreme measures [pp. 173–175].

May traveled to the Congo again in 1903, and to Liberia in 1905. During World War I she gave lectures about the Belgian Congo and her travels in support of the Belgian Red Cross. She died in London.

SOURCE: Internet: A Celebration of Women Writers, December 2006.

WORKS

Sheldon, May French. *Sultan to Sultan; Adventures Among the Masai and Other Tribes of East Africa*. Boston: Arena Publishing Company, 1892. Reprint: Freeport, New York: Books for Libraries Press, 1972.

BOOKS ABOUT OR INCLUDING
MAY FRENCH SHELDON

Boisseau, Tracey Jean. *White Queen: May French-Sheldon and the Imperial Origins of American Feminist Identity*. Bloomington: Indiana University Press, 2004.

Felicia Mary Frances Skene

WORKS

Skene, Felicia. *Wayfaring Sketches Among the Greeks and Turks, and on the Shores of the Danube*. London: Chapman & Hall, 1847.

Emily Ann Smythe *see* Emily A. Beaufort (Viscountess Strangford)

Mrs. Sarah Smythe

In January 1860 Sarah Smythe and her husband, Colonel W. J. Smythe, left England for Marseilles. Smythe was to conduct an inquiry into Fiji, paying particular attention to the cotton crops. The finest cotton was from America, but that was in limited supply; as demand had risen the amount of land planted in cotton in America had not increased enough to keep up with demand. The expedition was also to make botanical and meteorological observations.

The trip to Fiji was via Alexandria and Cairo, then by train to Suez, then a long voyage to Australia and New Zealand. They arrived in July, and for ten months they explored, visited with chiefs, traveled, and made their observations. Mrs. Smythe was along for many of these sojourns.

Not long after we came to a second rapid, much more considerable than the one we had passed. Our canoe happened to be first. We landed, and having directed the baggage to be put on shore, were watching the approach of the other canoes, when our people, to save themselves the trouble of shifting [*the baggage*] made a dash at the rapid without unloading. They had got but a little way up, however, when they lost all command over the canoe, which was hurried by the torrent towards the opposite bank, a high perpendicular rock. In vain they put out their poles to prevent a collision. The canoe struck violently, turned over, and all our goods were thrown off into the water. Manoah managed to seize a portmanteau and heave it on a small sloping ledge of the rock, to which he himself clung. The other man, holding on by the broken canoe, was carried down the river.

He was soon obliged to let go his hold and swim ashore, bringing with him such things as he had caught. Among them was the portmanteau containing our stores. On opening it we had the satisfaction to find that the sugar was the only article seriously damaged. A canoe was sent across to bring over Manoah and the portmanteau from the ledge to which he was clinging.... The sun having just then kindly appeared from the clouds, we spread out our wet clothes to dry....

As there was an appearance of rain, the chief urged us to push on, so as to reach Nagadi, the town where we were to pass the night, before it commenced. We accordingly put up our wet things loosely in mats, of which the chief himself insisted on taking charge. The other crews, profiting by our misfortune, put ashore their loads, and even then had difficulty in getting up the rapid.

About 5 o'clock we arrived under the town of Nagadi, perched on a bluff at the junction of a small river with the main stream. We landed and commenced to ascend the very steep and difficult path that led up to the town, which we found enclosed with a reed fence, as hostilities were going on against a neighbouring tribe. As soon as our baggage was brought up we asked for an empty house in which we could have a good fire to dry our wet clothes. We ourselves took up our quarters at the *Bure ni Sa*, or strangers' house. In every Fijian town there is a house of this description, where strangers put up, and the men of the town pass most of their time. Round the floor are fire-places marked off by posts and rails. In the intervals between the fire-places mats are spread, on which the men sit and sleep. No time was lost in getting tea ready [*Ten Months in the Fiji Islands*, pp. 63–64].

You say in your letter to me that you like best to hear about the beauties of nature which surround us. Well, I will try to describe the fair scene on which we daily feast our eyes; but first you must have a rough sketch of the interior of our house....

It consists simply of two rooms, one of which is devoted to the magnetical and other instruments; the other answers as our bed and sitting-room, (a nice white curtain dividing it). The walls are lined with white calico, and the windows have neat white muslin curtains looped up with scarlet braid. A couple of long shelves contain our books, which between damp and sea air have got a fine old mouldy appearance; and a line of wooden pegs does duty as a wardrobe behind the curtain. The floor I covered with Fijian mats, and for seats we have a variety of cane chairs which we brought with us from Auckland. The house is clean, cool, and airy — no small luxuries after the close cabin of the "Pegasus."

But now to come to the rare picture beyond our walls. The frame is an open door, opposite to which I have seated myself to write to you. The horizon is the Pacific Ocean, beautifully blue and calm. Resting on it like a faint cloud is the distant island of Ngau; while a little nearer a soft purplish light falls on Wakaya, an island some seven miles off. About a mile from the shore beneath us, a varying breadth of different-coloured water marks where the reef lies, the passage through which is clearly distinguished by the deep blue sea interrupting the breakers on either side....

Between the reef and the shore the water is again of the same beautiful blue colour as the sea beyond, and so clear as it approaches the beach that I can see the stones at the bottom, though our house is some three hundred yards from the water's edge, and about a hundred feet above it [pp. 144–145].

They left Fiji in May 1861, returning to England via America and Panama. They arrived back in England in November 1861.

WORKS

Smythe, Mrs. Sarah. *Ten Months in the Fiji Islands*. With an introduction and appendix by Colonel W. J. Smythe. Oxford: John Henry and James Parker, 1864.

Lady Hester Stanhope,
1776–1839. British.

Lady Hester was the first Western woman to explore the ancient Arab world.

Throughout her life she was convinced of the rights of the aristocracy; for her that meant doing what she wanted and doing it well. Her parents were Lord Charles Mahon, an inventor, and Lady Hester Pitt, daughter of the "Elder Pitt."

Little is known of her early life. For a time she kept house for her uncle, the "Younger Pitt." On his death, she inherited 1500 pounds (a considerable amount of money then) and retired to Wales, working with the poor (and keeping an extensive diary). But she was ambitious, and by 1810 having decided that her curiosity and intellect needed more scope than England could offer, she went to the Middle East with her brother Henry and her doctor, Charles Meryon. He became her confidante, and eventually was the editor of her memoirs.

She met Lord Byron in Athens, not a propitious meeting, as they disliked each other. She went on to Constantinople, where she stayed for a year. At that time Napoleon was threatening the stability of Europe and Britain. Lady Hester devised a plan for beating him, but when she presented it to the British Embassy they rejected it. Angry, she left for Egypt in a temper, and she stayed more or less angry at Britain for the rest of her life.

En route to Egypt she was shipwrecked and cast up on the island of Rhodes. She emerged in Syria dressed as a Turkish gentleman, astride her horse. She bought a convent on the slope of Mount Lebanon and lived there until her death, entertaining visitors and writing indignant letters to family and friends. But most of all she traveled throughout the region, in spite of heat, primitive transport and civil wars, even crossing the Syrian desert alone, to go to Palmyra. She wore Arab clothes and made friends with the Bedouins.

The Island of Rhodes, January 2nd 1812
Dear Sir: [*her solicitor Mr. Murray*] — before this letter reaches you, you will have heard, in all probability, an account of my shipwreck from Mr. Coutts. That I am here to relate it is rather extraordinary, for I escaped not only a sinking ship, but put to sea in a boat when one could hardly have supposed it could have lived five minutes — the storm was so great. Unable to make the land, I got ashore, not on an island, but a bare rock which stuck up in the sea, and remained thirty hours without food or water. It becoming calmer the second night, I once more put to sea, and fortunately landed upon the island of Rhodes, but above three days' journey from the town, traveling at the rate of eight hours a day over mountains and dreadful rocks. Could the fashionables I once associated with believe that I could have sufficient composure of mind to have given my orders as distinctly and as positively as if I had been sitting in the midst of them, and that I slept for many hours very sound on the bare rock, covered with a pelisse, and was in a sweet sleep the second night, when I was awoke by the men, who seemed to dread that, as it was becoming calmer, and the wind changing (which would bring the sea in another direction), that we might be washed off the rock before morning. So away I went, putting my faith in that God who has never quite forsaken me in all my various misfortunes. The next place I slept in was a mill, upon sacks of corn; after that, in a hut, where I turned out a poor ass to make more room, and congratulated myself on having a bed of straw. When I arrived (after a day of tremendous fatigue) at a tolerable village, I found myself too ill to proceed the next day, and was fortunate enough to make the acquaintance of a kind-hearted hospitable Greek gentleman, whom misfortune had sent into obscurity, and he insisted upon keeping me in his house till I was recovered. At the end of a few days I continued my journey, and arrived here, having suffered less than any other woman would have done whose health was as precarious as mine has been for so long a time. Everything I possessed I have lost; had I attempted to have saved anything, others would have done the same, and the boat would have been sunk. To collect clothes in this part of the world to dress as an Englishwoman would be next

to impossible; at least it would cost me two years' income. To dress as a Turkish woman would not do, because I must not be seen to speak to man; therefore I have nothing left for it but to dress as a Turk — not like the Turks you are in the habit of seeing in England, but as an Asiatic Turk in a traveling dress — just a sort of silk and cotton shirt; next a striped silk and cotton waistcoat; over that another with sleeves, and over that a cloth short jacket without sleeves or half-sleeves, beautifully worked in coloured twist, a large pair of breeches, and Turkish boots, a sash into which goes a brace of pistols, a knife, and a short of sword, a belt for powder and shot made of variegated leather, which goes over the shoulder, the pouches the same, and a turban of several colours, put on in a particular way with a large bunch of nature flowers on one side....

Let those who envied me in my greatness alike envy me in rags; let them envy that contented and contemplative mind which rises superior to all worldly misfortunes which are independent of the affections of the heart. Tell them I can feel happier in wandering over wilds, observing and admiring the beauties of Nature, than ever I did when surrounded by pomp, flatterers, and fools... [*The Life and Letters*, pp. 92–93].

Her money ran low and she rarely left her garden, then her bed, although the house was crumbling about her. Virginia Woolf describes her as "arguing, scolding, and ringing bells perpetually."

Her correspondence was published in 1845 in three volumes.

SOURCES: *Dictionary of Literary Biography*; Internet: Wikipedia, December 2006.

See also **Lady Judith Cohen Montefiore.**

BOOKS ABOUT OR INCLUDING LADY HESTER STANHOPE

Bruce, Ian, ed. *The Nun of Lebanon: The Love Affair of Lady Hester Stanhope and Michael Bruce.* London: Collins, 1951.

Cleveland, Duchess of. *The Life and Letters of Lady Hester Stanhope.* London: John Murray, 1914.

Day, Roger William. *Decline to Glory: A Reassessment of the Life and Times of Lady Hester Stanhope.* Salzburg, Austria: University of Salzburg, 1997.

Gibb, Lorna. *Lady Hester.* London: Faber, 2005.

Hamel, Frank. *Lady Hester Lucy Stanhope.* London: Cassell, 1913.

Emily Ann Smythe Strangford see *Emily A. Beaufort*

Lady Emmeline Charlotte Elizabeth Manners Stuart-Wortley, 1806–? British.

Lady Emmeline was the daughter of the Duke of Rutland; the early part of her life was spent mostly at Belvoir. She was literary from childhood. Her first literary production, age eleven, was the account of a fire at Belvoir, which begins with maids rousing the nurseries by screaming, "Oh, for God's sake get up, the Castle is in a blaze, you will be burnt in your beds" [*Wanderers*, Introduction, p. 14].

Her mother died when she was nineteen. In February 1831, Emmeline became engaged to Charles Stuart-Wortley, who was a captain in the Light Dragoons and a "noted dandy." She traveled extensively — to Europe and Russia. In 1844 Charles died, and shortly afterward, her youngest son also died. Probably as a result of these deaths, her liking for travel intensified, and she traveled until she died.

Her daughter Victoria often accompanied her mother on her trips. (See following entry: **Victoria Stuart-Wortley.**) She was with her mother on the trip to the Americas. Both women kept a journal.

Lady Emmeline followed an extensive

itinerary on the trip she and her daughter made to the Americas. They arrived in New York in May 1849 and toured New England and Washington. They then went by river to Louisville and New Orleans, sailed to Mobile, then back to New York. From there they sailed to Vera Cruz, then toured overland to Mexico City, Puebla, Jalapa, and through the countryside. They then sailed to Havana, then to Panama where they crossed the isthmus. Their final major destination was Lima.

As to the extreme natural beauty we beheld during the almost magical journey from Vera Cruz to the capital, no words, I feel, can adequately describe it. We passed through every variety of climate, each with its own peculiar productions, with splendid snow-topped mountains crowning the scene, themselves crowned by the gorgeous magnificence of the resplendent tropical heavens. Such mornings! such sunrises! heaven and earth seemed meeting as it were, and mingling in glory without end. Such nights! heaving and blazing with stars. Those glorious masses of stars seemed almost coming down on our little world; nearer and nearer they seemed to shine, as if drooping under the weight of their immense glory and majesty, and sinking toward us!...

One morning, at sunrise, coming from Puebla, we saw the great mountain Orizaba, reflecting the light of the rising luminary, and looking as if it was literally made partly of gold and partly of fire, so gloriously was it beaming back those dazzling splendors from its huge crest of glittering snow. Between Jalapa and Peroté, and still more between Vera Cruz and Jalapa, the astonishing prodigality and unutterable magnificence of the tropical vegetation is perfectly overpowering!...

Nature seems like a perpetual miracle there. It made us think of the sumptuous Sultana in the "Arabian Nights" tales, who changed her regal dress twelve times a day. Just try to fancy in those marvelous regions endlessly-spreading colossal bowers, under a green overhanging firmament of towering trees, and such bowers, too! Myriads of flowers of a hundred colors, crowding coronal upon coronal; and these again intertwined and overtwined, and round and through, and sub and supertwined with others, and others still! It seemed as if there was really going to be a flood of flowers, and this was the first flow of the dazzling deluge; a gorgeous deluge indeed that would be its own rainbow. There were innumerable roses, interwreathed with convolvuluses, flowering myrtles, aloes, cherimoyas, floripundias (a magnificent sculpture-like bell-shaped flower), the verdant liquidamber, jessamines, and others, with creepers and parasitical plants, festooning and trailing themselves about with the very wildest luxuriance, so that often the coiled and heaped-together boughs and branches appear to bear hundreds of different sorts of leaves and flowers at once!...

But I have said nothing of the splendid birds, that like animated rainbows and winged sunbeams were darting about mid these transcendent scenes. But it is quite useless to attempt to describe these unimaginable regions — one might as well strive to convey in words a glorious strain of the most exquisite music [*Travels*, pp. 170–171].

If the truth is to be told, Lima itself, the regal and the aspiring, is very near being one huge colossal opera-scene. A great number of the princely-looking edifices that rear their haughty fronts as if they would defy the terrible temblor itself, are only built of stones and bricks (or often of gigantic adobes) up to the height of the belfries; above this all is lath and plaster, paste-board and rushes, reeds and stucco; a vast accumulation of architecturally arranged whips and wicker work, and whim-whams and walking-sticks; but the effect is as splendid as if all was built of granite and adamant.... But Lima is justified in placing her faith on a reed, and in thinking stability, or rather solidity, of construction not literally worth a rush here.

These light and fragile fabrics are the only edifices of any elevation that can withstand the shocks of the devastating earthquake.... No lofty structure could survive the assaults of frequent earthquakes, except those of such "leather and prunella" papery composition: they bend and quiver like a storm-shaken pine of the forest, but regain and recover their perpendicular position unimpaired....

... I should very much liked to visit the remains of the ancient Temple of the sun, about twenty miles from this city. This old edifice is said to have been about three hundred and thirty feet high; some writers state that it was at least six hundred feet above the level of the sea, raised on an elevation which was in part artificial. The ruins are scattered over three grand terraces, rising in regular gradations one over the other. The remains of an ancient and stately town lie mouldering around the fallen temple of Pachacamac, the life-bestowing deity [pp. 416–417].

Lady Emmeline died in Beirut while on a trip to the Holy Land. Her maid had died of sunstroke earlier on the trip. Lady Emmeline's death left Victoria, age eighteen, on her own and stranded.

SOURCE: *Dictionary of National Biography.*

WORKS

Stuart-Wortley, Lady Emmeline. *The Sweet South.* Two volumes. London: G. Barclay 1856.
_____. *Travels in the United States, etc. During the Years 1849 and 1850.* New York: Harper, 1851.
_____. *A Visit to Portugal and Madeira.* London: Chapman & Hall, 1854.

Victoria Stuart-Wortley, later *Lady Welby-Gregory,* 1837–1912. British.

Victoria was born to the Honorable Charles and Lady Emmeline Stuart-Wortley. She was christened Victoria Alexandrina Maria Louise Stuart-Wortley. As a child she had scarlet fever; she never fully recovered. She accompanied her mother on many of her trips.

These excerpts are from the journal Victoria kept when traveling with her mother to North and South America.

After landing in New York, they toured the area and traveled around New England. In Massachusetts they visited, among others, "M. Agassiz, the celebrated naturalist (a cousin, by the way, of mamma's former governess), and Professor Silliman, jun." They visited Cambridge "and attended a rather puzzling lecture, as I thought, about the relations of electricity with cholera." She added a footnote, "I dare say it was an exceedingly interesting one, only rather above my comprehension." They visited Professor Agassiz's house to see some "live coral insects."

October 18th. — We have lately had as fine weather as any mortal could wish for; it is the *l'été de Saint Martin* of America, and is here called the "Indian Summer."... [W]e went to the Greenwood Cemetery, which contains 242 acres, and which in itself is beautiful, but which is rendered far more so by the resplendent autumnal colours for which America is so famous. There was not a tint between crimson and primrose that [was] not there. The deepest purple, the softest rose-colour, the most dilate primrose, glowing scarlet, and shining gold-colour. What would Titian or Claude Lorraine have given for tints like those on their palette? [*A Young Traveller's Journal*, pp. 70–71].

Now the town of Jalapa does not even pretend, in the slightest degree, to light her streets, trusting, I suppose to the more primitive, as well as more beautiful mode of dispelling the darkness — namely to the moon and stars. But it so happened that on that same night on which they required us to start in such a tremendous hurry [*half-past four*] both one and the other had modestly retired behind a damp fog — not an uncommon occurrence at Jalapa, as they tell us at Vera Cruz — leaving the earth in utter darkness. But as our coachman did not choose to run the chance of running over half the houses of Jalapa, and against everything that happened to be in the streets at the time, he took a huge, blazing pine-torch, and providing his companion, a Mexican peasant, with another, galloped down the streets of Jalapa, in the same fierce way with which we entered it; and as soon as we left the last suburb of the town, we dropped the mozo with his pine-branches, and proceeded along a comparatively smooth road that led across the table-land.

Victoria, as well as Emmeline, was struck by the color and variety of plants, birds, and insect.

The splendid variety of flowers, all new to the eye, swarming with many-hued birds and butterflies, and glittering gem-like insects, almost bewildered me. One spot, only a few feet square, transported, just as it was, with all its living tenants to our cold climate, would form the proudest hothouse in England [pp. 198–200].

From Mexico they traveled to Peru, staying in Lima and traveling through the countryside.

The mistress of the house boiled our chocolate for us, and gave us a bowl of milk, which tasted sadly of garlic; and we started as soon as it was sufficiently light for the boat to make her way up the river. Thick, damp mists lay on the river, impregnated with millions of different rank perfumes from the massy vegetation on the banks of the river. These heavy fogs, frequent in the tropics morning and evening, though accompanied by delicious coolness, are, I believe, supposed to bring malaria and fever, from the noxious exhalations of the earth at that time. The river was very shallow and rapid the whole way from San Pablo to Gorgona, where we were not sorry to arrive, notwithstanding the magnificence of the forest scenery, for the motion the palankas gave to the boat, as I think I mentioned before, was very disagreeable and inconvenient. Once, as we were passing very near another cayuca, between whose boatmen and our own there was an evident race, propelled by an unusually vigorous pull, our boat made such a tremendous lurch to one side, that the water poured into the boat by hogsheads, almost setting everything swimming; and we must inevitably have capsized, had we not all, by one accord, clutched hold of the other boat

(a much larger one) and steadied the narrow cayuga again [pp. 236–237].

The houses of Lima are very picturesquely and Moorishly built. They generally, though not always, are of one story only, and are built round a court, or patio with mosaic or marble pavements, and often either a little bed of flowers or a fountain in the centre....

The walls of these one-storied houses are often painted all over with colossal pictures of sacred or mythological subjects, and these paintings are, in general more remarkable for brilliancy of colouring than for delicacy of touch or elaborate finish [pp. 257–258].

Emmeline died while on a trip through the Holy Land. The maid who accompanied them had already died from sunstroke, and on her mother's death, Victoria was left quite alone to deal with the death of her mother and make her way back to England.

Victoria didn't travel after the death of her mother. For several years she didn't have a home, but moved around from one relative's household to another. Two years before the death of Prince Albert she became Maid of Honour to Queen Victoria, who was her godmother and for whom she was named.

In July 1863 Victoria married Sir William Early Welby-Gregory (1829–1898). The couple had three children. At some point soon after her marriage, Victoria's life took a significant turn.

Her education had been sporadic. Now, she began a serious course of self-education. She read widely and well, corresponded with prominent scholars and intellectuals of the time, and invited them to visit. Her first studies were in theology focusing on the interpretation of Christian scriptures. From this came her first book, *Links and Clues*, in 1881. She began to specialize in more philosophical considerations, and she began writing scholarly papers that were published in leading journals. She wrote several more philosophical books and contributed an entry on "significs," the name she gave to her theory of meaning, to the *Encyclopedia Britannica.* She also wrote poetry and plays.

Victoria founded the Sociological Society of Great Britain and the decorative needlework society. She died in 1912.

Her materials are at several institutions, including the University of London and York University.

SOURCES: Introduction to *A Young Traveller's Journal of a Tour in North and South America During the Year 1850*; University of London Research Library Services.

WORKS

Stuart-Wortley, Victoria. *A Young Traveller's Journal of a Tour in North and South America During the Year 1850.* With numerous illustrations by the authoress. London: T. Bosworth, 1852.

Ella Sykes, ?–1939. British.

Ella Sykes traveled because her brother, Sir Percy Molesworth Sykes, was in the British army and spent much of his duty in Persia and Central Asia. He is in the *Dictionary of National Biography*; she has vanished into obscurity. Her travel suggests she wasn't married at the time.

Her first travel, which was through Persia, lasted from June 1894 to March 1897. Her brother was negotiating for territory, the establishment of a new Persian consulate, and rights of way for telegraph lines. The travel was not easy, and the two went throughout Persia. *Through Persia on a Side-Saddle* was received well and got good reviews.

> I can never forget my feelings of joy and exultation when I realized that I was at last in Persia, on the threshold of a new life, which I ardently trusted might have its quantum of adventure. I had been civilized all my days, and now I felt a sense of free-

dom and expansion which quickened the blood and made the pulse beat high. The glamour of the East penetrated me from the first moment of landing on its enchanted shores, and although many a time I encountered hard facts, quite sufficient to destroy the romantic illusions of most folk, yet they struck against mine powerlessly [*Through Persia on a Side-Saddle*, pp. 2–3].

> And through it all, with each fresh experience, the sense of a glad freedom is interwoven. The traveller knows that joy in living, a joy which our civilization has done its best to improve away.... Perhaps, however, I have not really hit upon what constitutes the glamour of the East. My love of it may be partly owing to the novelty of my experiences, partly to a longing for travel and adventure, never satisfied hitherto, and, it is possible, chiefly to the fact that I had never been so well in all my life before [p. 43].

> And while I am on the subject of gardens, it may not be amiss to say a few words about the system by which they are watered. As water is perhaps the most valuable property in Persia it is guarded with jealous care, and it is said to be a more fruitful and fatal cause of bloodshed than anything else. Our house, situated in the midst of several gardens, was supplied by an underground stream from the hills, and this was allowed to be used by the gardens in turn for so many hours at a time. Our landlord had only paid for twelve hours' water once in every ten days, and this was sadly insufficient, as our vegetable and flower-seeds from Sutton testified by withering up as soon as they had appeared above the ground. We had our compensations, however, as the stream which supplied the quarter was obliged to pass through our garden on its way to all the others, so that we were never without running water, which, nevertheless, it would have been little short of a crime to use for our plants, although it was allowable to take what we wished for purposes of washing and drinking [p. 109].

> The wives of one of the principal *Khans* sent a message saying they would like to call upon me, and I was nothing loth to be "*tashrif dared*," or "at home," as I was always much interested in Eastern women

and their restricted lives. Hashim did his best to lay out an elegant tea-table, although I had but little variety in the way of cakes and biscuits, and came to me later on to inform me that a great company of ladies and slaves was approaching, and that he was quite sure the room would be too small to hold them all. I confess to having felt a little nervous at this news, but ordered my *pishkidmet* to see that the coast was clear of our men-servants, and when my guests arrived, was relieved to find that only three ladies appeared with a few children, five women slaves, and two youths — these latter to guard the door of the room and the slippers which their mistresses had left there on entering.

I received the ladies with many a "*khosh amadid*" (you are welcome) and other polite expressions culled from my phrase-book, accepted with effusion their gift of a sour green apple, and ushered them to their seats at the table; while the slaves squatted on the floor, holding the pallid sickly-looking children in their arms. *Baji* served out tea in tiny glasses, putting four or five lumps of sugar into each, and helped on the conversation by giving a short biography of her mistress, expatiating largely on my accomplishments of riding and letting off a gun. They drank glass after glass of steaming tea-syrup — all Persians liking to swallow the beverage when almost boiling — and they sampled my European delicacies with much relish.

They answered with much politeness that the poor trifles they had brought me were unworthy of further notice, and thereupon produced various engraved seals, which they had brought knotted up in corners of their handkerchiefs. These were made of agate or cornelian, and were inscribed with Kufic characters, animals, and in a few cases, with figures, some of them being beautiful little works of art, and all dug up from the ruins of a certain buried city, mentioned by Marco Polo, near which the ladies dwelt during the winter months. My brother, who had visited this place on a previous journey through Persia, had told their husband, the Governor, how much he was interested in curios, and that he would be glad to buy anything found among the *debris* of what was once an important town.

So eager did the ladies become, when they saw how much I appreciated the seals, that they insisted on giving me some set as rings, which they were wearing, and even tore off others stitched on to the caps of their children in quite a frenzy of enthusiasm, until I felt ashamed of robbing them in such wholesale fashion, although as a matter of fact their gifts were of no intrinsic value....

I now began to wonder when my guests would take their departure, for the two hours of their visit had completely exhausted all the ideas that I could express in Persian. Conversation was flagging lamentably when *Baji* appeared, and with her most engaging smile remarked to the assembled company that the *Sahib* was just coming.

This announcement caused a general stampede: the cotton sheets were hastily adjusted, slippers put on, children and kalians snatched up, and with warm handshakes and "*khoda hafiz-shumas*" (good-byes) my visitors and their train went off in a great hurry. As soon as they were gone Hashim came in to clear away, and being surprised at not seeing my brother, who had been calling on the governor of Rahbur, I asked my waiter where he was. Hashim giggled, and became much confused, but finally confessed that, thinking my guests had stayed quite long enough, he had hit upon this means of sending them away. I felt that I ought to reprove him for conduct which in a European servant would have been most reprehensible, but could only feel grateful to him for having relieved me of the thirteen or fourteen persons who had crowded into my small room! [pp. 140–142].

She next wrote a children's book and two long articles, then a third book.

In 1911 the Colonial Intelligence League for Educated Women was seeking information on employment opportunities for educated, single English women throughout the dominion. She went to Canada posing as a woman seeking a position as a "home-help," a domestic servant for middle-class housewives. The mission and her pretense are not only condescending, but poorly thought out. The travel descriptions of the book are by far the best part.

Her last travels were in 1915, when she traveled through Chinese and Russian Turkistan; the book about that travel is co-authored with her brother. She wrote the first two-thirds of the book, about their journey. Some of the travel was rough, but she's as intrepid and enthusiastic as she was during the trip through Persia.

Her brother outlived her by six years.

SOURCE: *Dictionary of Literary Biography.*

WORKS

Sykes, Ella. *A Home-Help in Canada.* London: Smith, Elder, 1912.
_____. *Persia and Its People.* London: Methuen, 1910.
_____. *The Story-Book of the Shah; or Legends of Old Persia.* London: Macqueen, 1901.
_____. *Through Deserts and Oases of Central Asia.* With Sir Percy Molesworth Sykes. London: Macmillan, 1920.
_____. *Through Persia on a Side-Saddle.* London: Innes, 1898.

Annie Royle Taylor, 1855–c. 1909.
British.

Ann Royle came by her travel ambitions honestly; her father was a director of the Black Ball Steamship Line and a Fellow of the Royal Geographical Society. He continued to travel internationally through his life. Her mother, of French descent, had been born in Brazil.

Ann was the second of ten children. She was a frail child and wasn't expected to live long. She had little schooling. At the age of thirteen she decided to dedicate herself to a life of Christian work. At eighteen she and two sisters were sent to Berlin for schooling, but Annie became ill and returned home where, when she recovered, she visited the sick and did charitable work.

When the family moved to London she felt she had found fertile field for her charity, and she visited the poorest areas of London.

Her father disapproved of her charitable occupation, and eventually he ordered her to go back to her home duties and her social obligations. Annie was then twenty-eight years old. Instead of obeying him she sold her jewels, took cheap lodgings, and paid the fees for an elementary medical course that included midwifery.

At that time there was a strong appeal for women missionaries in China; Annie applied to be a missionary to the China Inland Mission and was accepted.

Annie's mother understood her daughter's commitment to her calling, and she worked towards reconciliation between Annie and her father. Mr. Taylor agreed to outfit her for the journey and pay her passage, but he stopped her allowance. He did, however, give her letters that would enable her to get return passage home. Annie sailed in September 1884.

She arrived in Shanghai about eight weeks later and immediately began studying the Chinese language and customs. The Mission emphasized that workers should minimize barriers between themselves and the Chinese by adopting Chinese dress and manners. Annie and a companion were posted at An'ching, up the Yangtze. Later she was sent further inland, to Lanchou, in the westernmost province, then known as Chinese Tibet or Outer Tibet. In her work she had occasion to go into Tibet, particularly to the festivals and fairs. (These were ideal for reaching large numbers of people.)

She contracted consumption (probably TB) and was sent back to the coast. Her parents, who were traveling in Australia, telegraphed her to visit them. She met with them and then went on to visit her married sister in Darjeeling. There, she settled where she could associate with Tibetans. She crossed the British-Indian border, but was ordered back by the Sikkimese authorities. But she held her ground and managed to get permission to lodge at the monastery. However, people were forbidden to sell her food and she nearly starved.

Annie's medical training was frequently of use. She treated a youth from Lhasa named Pontso, who was about nineteen, a runaway fleeing from the ill treatment he'd gotten from his master. Pontso became Annie's servant (and a convert); he served her for twenty years.

Her determination to go into Tibet persisted, and Annie returned to China where she and Pontso took up residence at the Tibetan border. After a year of working and waiting, they decided to make a dash into Tibet. Annie at that time was thirty-six with a history of pulmonary disease. She and five Asians formed a small caravan; their equipment was minimal.

The caravan was attacked shortly after they crossed the border, and everyone lost most of their belongings. One of the young men turned back to China. Another died on a snowy pass. The third Chinese was quarrelsome, a liar, and fearful of being killed by the Tibetans for bringing an Englishwoman into Tibet. Trouble escalated into violence. The problems continued — and so did Annie. Amazingly, she survived and returned to China in April, 1893, after a journey of about 1300 miles in seven months. And, in spite of everything, she had kept a daily record. It is thought that her diary was much edited by the gentleman who offered to transcribe it in later years.

It was a weary march up the mountain, and we halted at one o'clock in a glen just below the pass. Here we had tea, and let the horses graze. At four we started again, three of the men going in front and two behind. All went well until dusk. We were following the river, which here winds across a plain, with hills on our right. Noga and the lama, who were riding ahead, returned and made signs to hasten us on. We came as quickly as we could, driving on the horses with the loads. All got their guns ready, for the brigands had been sighted, sitting on a plateau, a little distance off. When they saw us, they jumped on their horses, for they had been drinking tea, and the lama, with three others, gave a shout and rushed towards them. Leucotze was behind, with two of the loads. Erminie, Pontso, and I drove on the rest, and tried to get past before the firing began. I counted the robbers. There were eight of them, while on our side were only five fighting men, but in the dusk we must have seemed a host.

One of the five had to go forward with us to show us the way, leaving four to fight. The firing commenced, and frightened the animals, so we had not much trouble in hurrying them on. We drove them as fast as we could, praying as we went. Darkness set in, and we could still hear the firing. After a while we stopped, fancying we heard Leucotze coming up behind. He brought the two missing beasts of burden, and also Noga's horse. We came to a river. It was very deep, but there was not much time to think. We went through it, driving the horses before us. The water came halfway up our leg. Then we hurried on. It began to rain, but we dared not stop to put on our wraps. Wet as we were, we still kept going on, till at last, to our great relief, Noga overtook us. He said the firing had ceased, and that none of them were hurt, but that three of the escort had stayed behind to prevent the robbers' giving chase. By this time, the rain was pouring in torrents. We struggled forward as best we could, with wet clothes and feet, in the cold mountain air. At one place the river had to be crossed again, and the strong current nearly carried away one of the horses with its load. It was past midnight when we reached a large encampment of black tents. There were about two hundred in all, and they belonged to the relatives of the lama. The dogs were troublesome, but we soon put our own tents up, and, taking off our wet clothes, went to rest. The people gave us some tea, mixed with butter and barley-flour, and it did seem so good, being hot ["Diary," in *Adventures in Tibet*, pp. 180–192].

Eventually Annie returned to England and left the China Inland Mission. She formed the Tibetan Pioneer Mission, a name that irritated supporters and others involved in Tibetan mission work. She was in great demand to speak.

In 1894 Annie returned to India determined once again to go back to Tibet. The British had a trading station at Yatung, permitted by the Tibetans; if Annie wished to reside there she had to become a trader. She worked this out, but matters worsened in Tibet, and Annie had to leave.

She returned to England sometime after 1907. Nothing more is known of her.

SOURCE: *On Top of the World: Five Women Explorers in Tibet.*

WORKS

Taylor, Annie Royle. "The Diary of Miss Annie R. Taylor's Remarkable Journey from Tau-Chau to Ta-Chien-Lu Through the Heart of the Forbidden land," In William Carey, *Adventures in Tibet, Including the Diary of Miss Annie R. Taylor's Remarkable Journey Through the Heart of the Forbidden Land.* Boston and Chicago: United Society of Christian Endeavor, 1901. Also published as *Travel and Adventure in Tibet, Including the Diary...* London: Hodder & Stoughton, 1902.

_____. *Pioneering in Tibet: The Origin and Progress of the Tibetan Pioneer Mission.* London: n.d. Ascribed to Taylor.

_____. *Tibetan Pioneer Mission, Together with Some Facts About Tibet. (My Experiences in Tibet, by Miss A. R. Taylor).* London: Morgan & Scott, 1894.

BOOKS ABOUT OR INCLUDING
ANNIE ROYLE TAYLOR

Miller, Luree. *On Top of the World: Five Women Explorers in Tibet.* London: Paddington Press, 1976.

Lady Louise Mary Anne Tenison, 1819–1892.

Lady Louse Tenison is perhaps best known for her wonderful drawings of Petra, made in the 1850s.

WORKS

Tenison, Lady Louise. *Castile and Andalucia.* London: Richard Bentley, 1853.

Susan Brewer Thomas, 1793–?
American.

Susan Brewer was born in Wilbraham, Massachusetts. The family home was a gathering place of preachers, as her father was one of the earliest Methodists in the area. At an early age Susan resolved to lead a life that was useful to others and to devote herself to the special education of young people. She was particularly interested in religious education but didn't limit her involvement to that area.

She began her teaching in New York by establishing a private school. She stayed there two years, then was selected to teach in the New York Wesleyan Seminary, the first Methodist institution in New York. She taught there for four years, then went to Baltimore, where she again established a private school. The school was very successful, and she stayed there for four years.

While she'd been away from Wilbraham, the Wesleyan Academy at Wilbraham had been built; Susan returned after an absence of ten years to be preceptress of the new seminary.

She had been there for two years when a call came for a teacher to take charge of the Alabama Conference Seminary at Tuscaloosa, and Susan Brewer was selected. Under her guidance the Seminary was soon thriving. As the school grew she sent north for two additional teachers. When the school was well established and sufficiently strong, she left to establish another school, this one in the southern part of Alabama, near Montgomery.

Then, after a year, she received a call from northern Alabama. She decided that the school was well enough established for her to leave it in the hands of a replacement, and she assumed the supervisory position at a large female seminary at Tuscumbia.

She stayed there a year; once again a school had become successful and well established under her direction. By that time she'd been in Alabama five years. Her reputation had spread through the region, and Mississippi asked for her aid.

She took charge of the Elizabeth Female Academy at Washington, and as was her usual practice, she sent north for assistants.

Two years later she married Captain David Thomas of Jackson, Louisiana. Her active career as an educator stopped, but she remained involved in education, in part because Thomas was a trustee of the State University at Jackson. Susan continued to receive requests for teachers from schools throughout the South, and she continued to place teachers from the North — about sixty in all.

By 1849 Captain Thomas had died, and Susan Thomas moved to New Orleans and to a more private life. She continued her interest and involvement in education, primarily through writing articles.

Her tour in 1857 must have been rigorous for her; at that time women of sixty-plus usually didn't undertake such travel. The tour lasted more than a year and included England, Scotland, Ireland, France, Belgium, Germany, Switzerland, Italy, Egypt, Palestine, Syria, Greece, and Austria.

> We crossed the Atlantic without seeing it. The voyage was very perilous — more so, the captain informed us, than he had experienced for twenty years. For many days we saw nothing but the dense fog which enveloped the ship and the spray which dashed over its side....
>
> The strong easterly wind and the dense fog lasted, without intermission, for five days and five nights [*Travels in Europe, Egypt, and Palestine*, p. 19].
>
> The Hotel, at which we stayed is as splendid as any dwelling in Damascus, although the approach to it is through a mean alley. It opens into a large court paved with mosaic, having in the center a beautiful colored marble fountain of cool, refreshing, flowing water. Around the walls of this wide court open to the fresh air, are orange, citron, and lemon-trees and flowering shrubs. Among them was the famous damask rose, an indigenous plant, in full bloom; but we have seen roses of equal beauty in Louisiana. A large lemon-tree shaded my window at the second story and filled the atmosphere with the rich perfume of its fruit and flowers. Citrons on the tall trees opposite were bursting with ripeness.
>
> The parlors, divided only by an arch with a gilded cornice on a ground of blue, were furnished with divans, the floors inlaid with colored marble, having a fountain in the center, over which was suspended a splendid glass chandelier ornamented at the top with small mirrors set in gilt. The walls, fifteen feet high, with double rows of gilded cornice, were set with mirrors ornamented with gilded filigree-work, like those described above. The blue ceiling was bordered with gilt, and the arches on the lower floor were elaborately ornamented.
>
> Another room, occupied by an Austrian prince, compared well with the parlors in beauty and splendor; but there are striking contrasts in these oriental palaces — some shades to these brilliant lights. Many of the streets and houses are mean, and the walls are falling down....
>
> The Environs of Damascus, which for miles around is one continuous garden, constitute its beauty. The "Abana and Pharpar" enrich it with its waters, which are conveyed along in every direction, either in natural or artificial courses. Such luxuriant grounds, fruit-trees, and walks amidst them, are seen only around Damascus; and so extensive are they, that they make in

reality an earthly paradise fragrant with the rose which breathes its perfume upon the air, and the orange whose blossoms send forth their unrivaled fragrance. These sylvan scenes, contrasted with the bold, rugged cliffs which crown the barren mountains surrounding them, heighten the beauty and freshness of the landscape... [pp. 352–354].

Balbec. — We rode up the valley between the two mountains, Lebanon and Anti-Lebanon, whose summits were still covered with snow, although at their base the valleys were beautifully green. We soon came in sight of Balbec, whose imposing ruins are the most magnificent moments of architectural grandeur in the world.

The Temple of the sun surpasses all description. It is utterly impossible to do justice to this noble structure, or to the beauty and grace of the designs which adorn it. The broken columns lying upon the ground, the fragments of sculptured cornices, and the capitals with delicately-carved frieze, are astonishing specimens of art and skill. The colonnade in front of the building, part of which remains, gives it an air of unequaled grandeur. What it must have been in its glory, may be perceived by what remains. In its ruins it surpasses all we saw in the palaces of the Caesars, or elsewhere [pp. 358–359].

Works

Thomas, Susan Brewer. *Travels in Europe, Egypt, and Palestine.* Philadelphia: Lippincott, 1860.

Alexandrine Petronella Francina Tinné, 1835–1868.
Dutch.

Like many people in the 1850s and 60s, Alexine, as she was called, was fascinated by travelers in Africa. Early on she decided to resolve one of the major geographical questions: the source of the Nile. At age nineteen she set out.

She was born in The Hague to a wealthy family. When she was young she traveled with her mother. At age sixteen the two traveled across Scandinavia on horseback. The expedition was so successful that they began looking for another adventure. The opportunity came three years later. Alexine needed a diversion as she was getting over a broken engagement, so her mother took her to Venice. When they learned that they could sail from Trieste to Alexandria, their minds were made up, even though family and friends — and the queen of the Netherlands — begged them not to go but to return home.

Alexine liked Egypt even more than she'd hoped, and she began learning Arabic while she and her mother were sailing up the Nile to Luxor. Once in Luxor, the two decided to ride camels across the desert to the Red Sea. Alexine decided to stay in the Holy Land for several months, then make a second trip up the Nile with her mother, hoping to reach the Sudan. The cataracts put a stop to their plan, and the two decided to return to The Hague to better outfit themselves for the lengthy expedition to the Sudan.

On that trip they were accompanied by Alexine's aunt and their servants. The women were not to travel in hardship; they outfitted their boats with a library, porcelain, silver, a photographic studio and plant-collecting equipment. They were highly optimistic; the reality of what they were facing was grim. Slavers, and the horror of slavery, were rampant. Throughout her travels Alexandrine would buy slaves and free them.

They sailed south (their boats were pulled over the cataracts) and finally loaded their belongings onto camels (102 of them) for the trek across the desert to Khartoum. Subsequently they sailed from Khartoum to Jebel Dinka, then up the White Nile. Alexine sent reports back to London that were passed on the Royal Geographical Society. Finally, though, they could go no further, and they sailed back to Khartoum to re-fit for another attempt. They set off again.

Finding their way blocked, Alexine left camp to scout for another route, only to return and find that her mother had died; two Dutch maids also had died. Alexine set off to return to Khartoum with the caskets; the party reached Khartoum only after several months of very difficult travel. Unhappily, Alexine's aunt, who had stayed back in Khartoum, had also died. Alexine was heartbroken.

She settled in Cairo, then bought a yacht that she sailed to Algeria with her Sudanese servants. Alexine had decided to cross the Sahara from the north to southeast and to travel with the Tuareg, and she learned Tamachek, the Tuareg language. In 1869 she left Tripoli. The Tuareg were feuding — and Alexine was caught in the middle. Alexine was killed to spite Ichnuchen, the Tuareg leader whom Alexine admired.

She left significant ethnological specimens, but her collections were destroyed in later wars. Alexine never had a chance to document her discoveries.

Dr. Livingstone wrote of her: "The work of Speke and Grant [previous explorers] is deserving of highest commendation inasmuch as they opened up an immense trace of previous unexplored country.... But none rises higher in my estimation than the Dutch lady, Miss Tinne, who after the severest domestic afflictions nobly persevered in the teeth of every difficulty" [in *Ladies on the Loose*, unattributed].

> There are Dutch ladies traveling without any gentleman.... They are very rich and have hired the only steamer here for a thousand pounds. They must be demented! A young lady alone with the Dinka tribe ... they must really be mad. All the natives are as naked as the day they were born. — Explorer Samuel Baker in Gladstone, Penelope. *Travels of Alexine*. London: Murray, 1970, p. 106.

She was a zealous collector of plants and had a number of camels loaded solely with blotting paper and immense collections of plants. The labor promised to be very valuable, for the flora of Soudan [sic] is almost unknown, and of previous African travelers only Dr. Vogel was a botanist, and all his papers were lost. — *New York Times*, August 30, 1869.

Lady Catherine Eflin Tobin,
British.

Lady Catherine tells us little about herself, her reasons for travel, or her three traveling companions. They left London in September 1853 and returned to London June 1854.

> ... A delightful walk of about a mile along the shore, brought us to the Baths of Emmaus; where a handsome building was erected by Ibrahim pasha. The *public* bath is circular, and surrounded by a colonnade of white marble: we gladly took possession of a private one for it was impossible to resist so tempting a luxury. The water has a salt, bitter, sulphureous taste; and oozes nearly boiling from the ground. Returning *homewards* we met a large party of women, some of whom were excessively pretty; the hands and arms of most of them were tattooed; and one was hideously disfigured by a blue stain round her eyes. Their demeanour was perfectly inoffensive; although they stroked us repeatedly, examined our clothes, marveled greatly at my note book, and made signs that we should accompany them to the *Bath*! — which proposal we of course declined. These females wore ornaments of coins, beads, and silver. The sun was oppressively hot; and we willingly jumped upon the donkeys, sent by Mr. T. for our use: they had neither saddles nor bridles, but merely pieces of carpet laid across their backs. It was a difficult matter to keep one's balance; for the animals — vigorously propelled from behind — trotted over the uneven ground at an alarmingly rapid pace! [*Shadows of the East*, p. 204].

I always found *some* amusement during the half hour that elapsed between breakfast and starting time. If any wild shrubs or tamarisk trees chanced to grow within reasonable distance, I loaded myself with food for my camel; and when *that* was impossible, I picked up bits of granite — of which there were such endless varieties! — or whatever else I could find. And then there was the *sunrise*! — upon which one never could gaze long enough — the naked rocks too, of every colour and fantastic form — and last of all, the busy scene of our encampment; where canteens were packing, camels growling angrily beneath their loads, Arabs lazy and grumbling — and Vincenzo with *coorbash* in hand and threatening gestures, storming furiously.

I quite agree with Miss Martineau, that one of the greatest nuisances in travelling is *keeping a journal.* One is far more disposed to lie down and rest, after a fatiguing ride of eight or nine hours on a camel, beneath a burning sun; than — having made a hasty *toilette* — to take out one's writing materials. I *persevered*, however, and rejoice that I did so [p. 101].

WORKS

Tobin, Lady Catherine. *The Land of Inheritance, or Bible Scenes Revisited.* London: Bernard Quaritch, 1862.
_____. *Shadows of the East.* London: Longman, Brown, Green and Longmans, 1855.

Catharine Parr Strickland Traill, 1802–1899. British.

Catharine Strickland Traill and her sister **Susanna Strickland Moodie** [see entry] were part of a British family that produced several important writers. When their father had financial reverses and died, all of the sisters determined to use their writing to alleviate the financial problems. Elizabeth Strickland became an editor in London: Agnes Strickland began by writing poetry and eventually published biographies, including the well known and successful series *Lives of the Queens of England.* Jane Margaret, Catharine, and Susanna wrote for children and adolescents.

Catharine Parr Strickland was born in Kent in 1802. Her father was an importer and manager but had become convinced of the advantages of living a rural life, and he relocated his business to Norwich. Eventually he bought Reydon Hall, a large manor house, where Catharine, her five sisters, and two brothers grew up. Her father died suddenly in 1818.

Catharine began writing about Canada before she herself moved there. A family connection had emigrated to Upper Canada, and Catharine drew on his letters in part for a book titled *The Young Emigrants: Or, Pictures of Canada: Calculated to Amuse and Instruct the Minds of Youth*, published in 1826. Her early writings also draw on her love of the natural sciences.

In the late 1820s she became attached to and perhaps informally engaged to Francis Harral. Francis, or Frank, was the editor of a London magazine and intended to study medicine. The Harral family was not in favor of the engagement, probably because of the financial difficulties of the Stricklands, and Catharine became increasing uncertain of the state of the engagement. Finally, Frank apprenticed to an apothecary in Dorset, giving up his medical plans. Apparently he ceased writing to Catharine, and by the end of 1831 she acknowledged that the relationship was over.

At some point, also during 1831, Catharine met Thomas Traill, a friend and fellow officer of John Moodie, who had married her sister Susanna. Thomas had been educated at Oxford. His first wife had died after a long illness, which had caused him to go into debt. Thomas felt he had been deprived of his patrimony and estates, but did not speak of the details.

Catharine and Thomas were strongly

attached to each other; in the eyes of Catharine's family, however, their decision to marry was hasty. Nonetheless, they married in May 1832. Their haste was due in part to their intention to join Susanna and John Moodie in emigrating to Upper Canada. Samuel and Mary Strickland had already gone to Canada and were settled north of Peterborough, and they had written back that there were opportunities and good land in the area.

The Traills went first to Scotland, staying for less than two months, where Catharine met Thomas's family and friends. They sailed to Canada from the Orkneys, landing in mid–August, 1832. They stayed for a while in Montreal, where Catharine, who had been seriously ill on most of the voyage, was diagnosed with cholera. When she had improved they traveled north to Peterborough and contacted Samuel Strickland.

Thomas purchased the lot adjacent to the Stricklands. In December 1833 they moved into the log house they'd built there. Shortly after, Catharine began to write "Letters from the Backwoods," later published as *The Backwoods of Canada*. James, their first child, was born during this time. Catharine worked on the manuscript between 1832 and 1834. Although the book appears to be a series of letters, it actually is drawn from letters and notes. It was accepted for publication in 1835 by Charles Knight at the Society for the Diffusion of Useful Knowledge. The book was well received and was reprinted and republished several times.

The waters of the Otanabee are so clear and free from impurity that you distinctly see every stone pebble or shell at the bottom. Here and there an opening in the forest reveals some tributary stream, working its way beneath the gigantic trees that meet above it. The silence of the scene is unbroken but by the sudden rush of the wild duck, disturbed from its retreat among the shrubby willows, that in some part fringes the banks, or the shrill cry of the kingfisher, as it darts cross the water. Or the eye follows the heavy noiseless flight of the grey heron, or crane, as it wings its way above the marshy borders of the river in pursuit of its fishy prey, sometimes darting with outstretched wings close to the surface, or alighting on some high stump or log to watch the favourable moment for its downward swoop [*The Backwoods of Canada*, p. 54].

This is the fishing season. Our lakes are famous for masquinongé, salmon-trout, white fish, black bass, and many others. We often see the lighted canoes of the fishermen pass and repass of a dark night before our door....

It is a very pretty sight to see the little barks slowly stealing from some cove of the dark pine-clad shores, and manoeuvring among the islands on the lakes, rendered visible in the darkness by the blaze of light cast on the water from the jack — a sort of open grated iron basket, fixed to a long pole at the bows of the skiff or canoe. This is filled with a very combustible substance called fat-pine, which burns with a fierce and rapid flame, or else with rolls of birch-bark, which is also very easily ignited.

The light from above renders objects distinctly visible below the surface of the water. One person stands up in the middle of the boat with his fish-spear — a sort of iron trident, ready to strike at the fish that he may chance to see gliding in the still waters, while another with his paddle steers the canoe cautiously along. This sport requires a quick eye, a steady hand, and great caution in those that pursue it [pp. 116–117].

Some few nights ago as I was returning from visiting a sick friend, I was delighted by the effect produced by the frost. The earth, the trees, every stick, dried leaf, and stone in my path was glittering with mimic diamonds, as if touched by some magical power; objects the most rude and devoid of beauty had suddenly assumed a brilliancy that was dazzling beyond the most vivid fancy to conceive; every frozen particle sent forth rays of bright light. You might have imagined yourself in Sinbad's valley of gems; nor was the temperature of the air at all unpleasantly cold [pp. 149–150].

In 1835 the Traills' farm was offered for sale. The region had not developed as quickly as hoped, and emigration had fallen off after the enthusiasm of the early 1830s. Thomas finally received a commission in the local militia in late 1837. By then there were four small children, and the family, Catharine in particular, was struggling.

They moved to Ashburnham, where Catharine attempted to open a school, but her health prevented her from continuing with the plan. Two of their children died. Finally, in 1846, they were given the use of a home on Rice Lake for a year. In 1848 they rented in the area, and the next year bought a farm near the lake. They remained there for eight years until August 1857, when they lost their home and almost everything in it by fire. They then lived with relatives and friends; the family was often split up.

Thomas died in June 1859, having been ill a short time. Samuel, Catharine's brother, and others, helped complete the house the Traills had intended to build. Catharine lived in this house until her death in 1899.

She wrote for publication throughout her life, and she produced a substantial number of books, articles, and stories.

SOURCE: Introduction to *The Backwoods of Canada*.

WORKS

Traill, Catharine. *The Backwoods of Canada*. London: Charles Knight, 1846.

_____. *Pearls and Pebbles*. London: Sampson Low & Marston, 1894.

There have been various reprintings and publications of *The Backwoods of Canada*, including:

Traill, Catharine. *The Backwoods of Canada*. Edited by Michael A. Peterman. Ottawa, Canada: Carleton University Press, 1997, from which the excerpts are taken.

Flora Tristan, 1803–1844. French.

Flora Celestine Therese Henriette Tristan was born in 1803. Her father was a Peruvian colonel in the service of the king of Spain. He had married her mother, a French émigré, in a religious service only, so that the union was not recognized and Flora was considered illegitimate. Flora went to Paris when she was fifteen. Six years later she married Monsieur Chazal, but they separated almost immediately.

In 1833 she traveled to Peru, anticipating a warm welcome (and largesse) from the relatives of her father. However, they opposed the irregularity of her marriage, and her expectations of welcome — and monetary help and support — were not met. She had to return to France in 1834.

Flora then began a literary career and published *les Pérégrinations d'une Pariah* in 1835.

Matters with Chazal, Flora's husband, had never been settled. She had not been able to get a divorce from him, in part because of a prolonged battle over child custody, and Flora had been campaigning for change in the divorce laws. Shortly after Flora returned to France, her husband shot her in the back. The divorce was granted.

Flora continued to write and work for her causes. She died in 1844. Flora's daughter married and had several children, one of whom was the artist Paul Gauguin.

That same Tuesday, a feast-day, the troops were paid, and in order to ingratiate himself with the soldiers Nieto gave them leave to enjoy themselves, a favour of which they took the fullest advantage. They went off to the taverns to drink chicha, sang all the songs I have mentioned above at the top of their voices, and spent the whole night in drunkenness and disorder. They were doing no more than following the example of their leaders who for their part had gathered together to drink and gamble. Thy were so sure that San-Roman would not dare to advance before he had received reinforcements that they made no preparations and took no precautions; the same negligence prevailed at the outposts. On Wednesday 2 April, while the defenders of the fatherland were still sleeping off the wine of the previous night, it was suddenly learned that the enemy was approaching, and everybody climbed onto the housetop. It was two o'clock in the afternoon; the sun was burning and a dry wind made the heat even more intolerable as it swept across the roofs of the houses blowing dust into the faces of the watchers. Only a person of my intrepid nature could have borne to remain there long. My uncle called from the patio that I would be blinded by the sun, that I was waiting in vain, that San-Roman would not come that day, but I took no heed of his advice. I had settled myself on top of the wall; I had taken a big red umbrella to protect me from the sun, and, armed with a telescope made by Chevallier, I felt very comfortable. As I contemplated the valley and the volcano I let my mind wander and forgot all about San-Roman until I was suddenly reminded of the reason for our being there by a negro who called out to me: "Here they come, madame!" I heard my uncle coming up; and training my telescope in the direction the man was pointing, I clearly saw, high on the mountain next to the volcano, two black lines, fine as a thread, winding their way through the desert in a series of unbroken curves, like flocks of migrating birds.

At sight of the enemy the whole town uttered a cry of joy. — *Peregrinations of a Pariah* in *An Anthology of Women's Travel Writing.* Shirley Foster and Sara Mills, editors.

SOURCE: *Biographie Universelle Ancienne et Moderne.*

WORKS

There are several editions and translations of Flora Tristan's *Peregrinations of a Paria 1833–1834* including the following:

Peregrinations of a Pariah 1833–1834. translated and edited by Jean Hawkes. London: Virago, 1986. The first English translation of

Tristan's *Mémoires et pérégrinations d'une paria.* (1838).

Peregrinations of a Pariah 1833–1834. Translated by Charles De Salis; introduction by Joanna Richardson. London: the Folio Society, 1986

Frances Milton Trollope,
1779–1863. British.

Frances Milton was born in Bristol, the daughter of a clergyman. Her father was also an inventor of gadgets, which perhaps held more interest for him than his clerical duties. Fanny's mother died when she was five or six; Fanny grew up a very self-reliant person. Her father remarried when Fanny was twenty-one. Fanny and her stepmother were never close, and several years after the marriage she and her older sister moved to London to keep house for their younger brother.

When Fanny was twenty-nine, she met Thomas Anthony Trollope; they married after a short courtship. The couple had seven children, one of whom died young. Fanny had a cheerful disposition and a delightful personality. Thomas Anthony's personality was just the opposite, and as time went on he became even more argumentative and erratic, likely due in part to medication he took that contained a mercury-based drug.

Thomas, who had never farmed, leased 160 acres and moved there with the family to establish a farm. He had always expected to inherit a significant amount of money from his elderly uncle. However, that uncle married and produced an heir in 1819, which ruined Thomas' expectations. The financial problems worsened.

In desperation Fanny, with several of the children, went to America to join a community in Tennessee; when the community turned out to be located in a malarial swamp, the Trollopes went to Cincinnati for the improbable purpose of establishing a department store. Three of her children were with her; Anthony Trollope, later the famous novelist, was left behind to manage on his own. After three years — before the store was completed — the venture was a failure. One of the children was sent home because of very poor health; Fanny and the two remaining children were stranded in America. They were very poor, and Fanny's already unfavorable impressions of America and Americans became even more negative. Fanny began to jot down her impressions and adventures in America, in the hope of making some money by publishing her writing when she returned to England. It was a move born of desperation, and it paid off.

At length we had the pleasure of being told that we had arrived at Memphis; but this pleasure was considerably abated by the hour of our arrival, which was midnight, and by the rain, which was falling in torrent.

Memphis stands on a high bluff, and at the time of our arrival was nearly inaccessible. The heavy rain which had been falling for many hours would have made any steep ascent difficult; but unfortunately a new road had been recently marked out, which beguiled us into its almost bottomless mud, from the firmer footing of the unbroken cliff. Shoes and gloves were lost in the mire, for we were glad to avail ourselves of all our limbs; and we reached the grand hotel in a most deplorable state....

The remainder of the day passed pleasantly enough in rambling round the little town, which is situated at the most beautiful point of the Mississippi. The river is here so wide as to give it the appearance of a noble lake; an island covered with lofty forest-trees divides it, and relieves by its broad mass of shadow the uniformity of the waters. The town stretches in a rambling irregular manner along the cliff, from the Wolf River, one of the innumerable tributaries to the Mississippi, to about a mile below it. Half a mile more of the cliff be-

yond the town is cleared of trees, and produces good pasture for horses, cows, and pigs; sheep they had none. At either end of this space the forest again rears its dark wall, and seems to say to man, "So far shalt thou come, and no farther!" Courage and industry, however, have braved the warning; behind this long street the town straggles back into the forest, and the rude path that leads to the more distant log-dwellings becomes wilder at every step. The ground is broken by frequent water-courses, and the bridges that lead across them are formed by trunks of trees thrown over the stream, which support others of smaller growth, that are laid across them. These bridges are not very pleasant to pass; for they totter under the tread of a man, and tremble most frightfully beneath a horse or a waggon; they are, however, very picturesque [*Domestic Manners of the Americans*, pp. 19–22].

One of the sights to stare at in America is that of houses moving from place to place. We were often amused by watching this exhibition of mechanical skill in the streets. They make no difficulty of moving dwellings from one part of the town to another. Those I saw traveling were all of them frame-houses, that is built wholly of wood, except the chimneys; but it is said that brick buildings are sometimes treated in the same manner. The largest dwelling that I saw in motion was one containing two stories of four rooms each; forty oxen were yoked to it. The first few yards brought down the two stacks of chimneys, but it afterwards went on well. The great difficulties were the first getting it in motion and the stopping exactly in the right place. This locomotive power was extremely convenient to Cincinnati, as the constant improvements going on there made it often desirable to change a wooden dwelling for one of bricks; and whenever this happened, we were sure to see the ex–No. 100 of Main Street, or the ex–No.55 of Second Street, creeping quietly out of town, to take possession of an humble suburban station on the common above it [p. 73].

In 1832, *Domestic Manners of the Americans* was published, and it was a great success. England was fascinated with the book;

America was indignant. The matter was international: France, not feeling friendly toward England in any event, took up the Americans' indignation at Fanny's depiction of them and their country. Fanny's writing career was launched. Although the book sold well, and Fanny quickly wrote three more books, the debts from the farming and the Cincinnati ventures were too great, and the family had to flee to Bruges to avoid debtors' prison. Thomas died, and Fanny's much loved son Henry died. Fanny returned to England, but didn't settle in one spot.

In 1843 Fanny visited Italy, where she remained the rest of her life. In 1850 her son Thomas and his wife came to live with her. They also were both writers, as, of course, was her son Anthony.

Fanny supported much of the family by her writing: six travel books and thirty-five novels. Her books were very popular, particularly her novels; at one time Dickens thought of her as a serious rival. Fanny thought of herself primarily as a travel writer.

Fanny died in Florence in 1863. Her son, Anthony, became one of the most famous English novelists.

SOURCE: *Dictionary of National Biography.*

WORKS

Trollope, Frances. *Belgium and Western Germany in 1833, Including Visits to Baden-Baden, Wisbaden, Cassel, Hanover, the Harz Mounts, &c. &c..* Philadelphia: Carey, Lea, & Blanchard, 1834.
_____. *Domestic Manners of the Americans.* London: Whittaker, Treacher, 1832; New York: D. Appletont Co., 1839.
_____. *Italy and the Italians.* London: Bentley, 1842
_____. *Paris and the Parisians in 1835.* London: Bentley, 1836.
_____. *Vienna and the Austrians, with Some Account of a Journey Through Swabia, Bavaria, the Tyrol, and the Salzbourg.* London: Bentley, 1838.
_____. *A Visit to Italy.* London: Bentley, 1842.

Note: Frances Trollope was in America when Captain Basil Hall's *Travels in North America* was published. See entry for **Margaret Hunter.**

Ethel Brilliana Tweedie (Mrs. Alec Tweedie), 1866–1940. British.

Ethel was the daughter of George Harley, a noted London physician. Her earlier trips were with her brother and sister, or with only her sister, but after that she traveled alone. Ethel wanted to become an actress, but her father wasn't keen on the idea. (She remained interested in theater throughout her life.)

She was distracted from her stage ambitions by a trip to Iceland, which instilled in her a life-long interest in travel. Her father suggested she keep a diary of the trip, since mailing letters wouldn't be practical. Travel in Iceland at that time was unusual and adventurous.

What a hard life is that of the poor Icelanders! When our ship arrived, they were on the verge of starvation, their supplies being all exhausted. Glad indeed they must have been to welcome the *Camoens*, and know that flour and other staple articles of food were once again within their reach [*A Girl's Ride in Iceland*, p. 39].

Akureyri is both famous for, and proud of its trees. There are actually five of them; these are almost the only trees in the Island. Miserable specimens indeed they appeared to us southerners, not being more than 10 feet high at most, and yet they were thought more of by the natives, than the chestnuts of Bushey Park by a Londoner.

The absence of wood in the island is to a great extent overcome by the inhabitants collecting their fuel from the Gulf Stream, which brings drift wood in large quantities from Mexico, Virginia, the Caroline Islands, and even from the Pacific Ocean [p. 42].

From here [*their stop*] we galloped merrily on for some distance; at last we called each other's attention to an extraordinary yellow haze, like a band of London fog, across the horizon. Thicker and thicker it became: and as it rolled towards us, we realized we had encountered a regular dust-storm. Into it we rode: so thick in fact did it become, that by the time we reached the Geysers all around was hidden in yellow sand, and our eyes were filed with dust, until the tears streamed down and we were nearly blinded. It whirled round and round in its storm fury, until we were half-choked, two of our party getting very bad sore throats produced by the irritation of the dust, as it filled eyes, nose and mouth. It powdered our hair to a yellow grey, but our faces, what a sight they were! The tears had run down, making little streams amid the dust, and certainly we were hardly recognizable to one another. These dust-storms are somewhat uncommon, but proceed, in certain winds, from a large sand desert.

We pulled up at some hot springs within a few feet of the lake, which were smoking and steaming to the height of several feet, and falling down again formed numerous boiling pools. In these we put our fingers, but pulled them out quickly. Next we inserted the handles of our riding-whips; but this pretty effect soon wore off. The colour of the water and deposit round the edges of this pool were very pretty, and the bubbles as they ascended took the most lovely colours — emerald, purple, etc., turning into aqua-marine before breaking on the surface; but the odour was like terribly bad eggs. These hot springs are a curious freak of Nature, boiling and bubbling up within three feet of a cold water lake; in fact we sat down and placed one hand in cold water and the other in hot. This was a very curious experience [pp. 118–119].

She was followed on that trip by Dr. Alec Tweedie. Soon after the two became engaged and married. They had two sons.

Her trip to Norway was made during an unusually severe winter, and Ethel and her sister found the travel arduous, even though much of it was by boat.

In 1896 Ethel lost both Alec and her father. She was left in poor straits with the two young boys; six months before Alec's death he had lost his fortune. Ethel turned to writing, specifically travel writing, to support the family. She had already written several books and articles.

Her trip to Mexico was her first trip alone. She went, in part, because when she told one of her friends she was thinking of the trip, the friend said she was too old! The trip was not particularly adventurous. Her trips to China and Russia in the 1920s were more exciting.

Ethel was elected a Fellow to the Royal Geographic Society.

SOURCE: *Dictionary of Literary Biography*, Volume 174.

WORKS

As Ethel B. Harley:

A Girl's Ride in Iceland. London: Griffith, Farran, Okeden & Welsh, 1889.

As Ethel Brilliana Tweedie, or Mrs. Alec Tweedie, or Ethel H. Tweedie.

An Adventurous Journey (Russia — Siberia — China). Hastings: Parsons, 1927.
America as I Saw It; or, America Revisited. London: Hutchinson, 1913.
Mexico as I Saw It. London: Hurst & Blackett, 1901.
The Oberammergau Passion Play 1890 . London: Kegan Paul, French, Trubner, 1890.
Russia as I Saw It. Hastings: Parsons, 1927.
Sunny Sicily: Its Rustics and Its Ruins. London: Macmillan, 1904.
Through Finland in Carts. London: Black, 1897.
A Winter Jaunt to Norway, with Accounts of Nansen, Ibsen, Bjornson, Brandes and Many Others. London: Bliss, Sands, & Foster, 1894.

She also wrote other books on a variety of subjects, memoirs, and numerous articles.

Mary Davis Cook Wallis

Mary's husband was a trader. Prior to the trip with Mary, he'd visited New Zealand

and the "Feejee" Islands on trading voyages and was familiar with the language and customs. Mary kept her journal for her own amusement and to pass the time.

Mr. W. believing that nearly all the male inhabitants of Vesonga were fishing on the reefs, proposed going on shore to see the "beech de mer" house. When the boat was ready, I expressed a wish to accompany him. "Perhaps it is not safe," said he. "If it is safe for you, it is for me," I replied, and we started with only two rowers and ourselves in the boat. When we reached the shore we were surprised to see Masella and twenty other men upon the beach. I observed that Masella held a hatchet behind him, as if trying to hide it. On looking around, I perceived the men were all armed; some with clubs, and others with muskets. Truly, thought I, we are not so formidable as to require such strength of arms....

Many of the faces of the men were painted a shiny black on one side, and a bright vermillion on the other. Others had the forehead, nose, and the upper part of their cheeks daubed with one color, and the lower part of their faces with another. An endless variety of tastes was displayed which did not in my view add to their beauty, although the house was well lighted from the red flames issuing from the trench, and well calculated to show their personal decoration to the greatest possible advantage. When we came from the house Mr. W. suddenly altered his mind about visiting Masella's house, and we immediately returned to the bark [Life in Feejee, p. 98].

We are obliged, while lying here, to send a long distance for water. To-day the boat was sent with four men, which left us rather short, as some of our people are with the schooner, and some at the houses on shore. Three men only, besides the captain, were on board after the boat had left. No sooner had it disappeared behind the island, than we observed two canoes put off, and sail for the bark; they were well filled with men. When we saw this goodly company approaching we felt in our very hearts that we would rather defer the reception of so many visitors in the absence of our crew. The captain told the few that were on board to leave their work, and each have some

weapon at hand, without seeming to be armed, and to let no one come onboard but the chiefs. He then put a small pistol in his pocket, while I, not caring to wield a broom-stick, took a pair of large scissors in my hand.

The chiefs came on board; one ordered an axe, one a hatchet, another a musket. This was a pattern for taking a vessel: coming on board without arms but arming themselves from the vessel. One of the chiefs came into the cabin and demanded three axes.

I was standing near, playing awkwardly with my scissors, when observing that he had possession of all the axes, I took one from his lap, and after remarking on its goodness and beauty, handed it to my husband.... As he [the chief] rose to go, he held he gleaming axe over my head and said, "Now, Marama, I will kill you with this hatchet." "It is very good for you to do it, and I will kill you with these scissors," I answered, pointing them to his heart.... "No, indeed; you are a good marama," he said, laughing, and left the cabin [pp. 140–141].

Works

Wallis, Mary. *Life in Feejee of Five Years Among the Cannibals.* By a lady. Boston: William Heath, 1851.

Margaretha Weppner

Fortunately for us, Margaretha Weppner began her book with a substantial account of her life. Without that, we might never know the rather Dickensian story that is Margaretha Weppner.

She tells us that she wasn't impelled by a desire to travel, but from a terrible grief and melancholy that she hoped to assuage by travel. She was left to her own resources early, and refers referred to a chain of circumstances that resulted in her tour.

Her family was affluent, but due to

"sad reasons" the affluence vanished. She speaks of the grief of her mother, and refers to her father, but doesn't explain. She had what she calls a common school education, but by hard effort learned several languages and music. She left home when young, a separation she found very hard, and went to Nancy, where she taught German in a private school. In return she was taught French and music and received her board. She then taught German and French in England, and learned English in the same way. Then, employing a similar arrangement, she learned Italian. She gradually saved some money and could help her mother and sisters. Margaretha's mother had had twelve children; eight survived.

She tells us her father was a Rhinelander and wished to purchase a vineyard. She helped with the installments of money needed to buy the vineyard.

Margaretha then discovered she had a disease of the eyes and left London to go to Paris for medical care, with good results. She went back to Nancy to enter a boarding school, and there she met a Miss F.

At this time Margaretha considered entering a convent to see if she might make it her permanent home. Miss F., who was "an extremely discreet and diplomatic Catholic," undertook to make her acquainted with the convent of the Angelic Sisters at Augsburg, where she was well known.

The initial introduction went well, but something went awry — Margaretha is mysterious on this point — and the decision to enter the convent became less clear-cut. Friends tried to dissuade her from entering the convent, but she was determined to try, and it seemed to her to be the only thing for her to do.

She found it difficult to make the trip to enter the Convent, and made stops along the way to put off arriving at Augsburg and the convent. After several months at the convent she left for Frankfort, where she'd been engaged to teach English at a convent school.

Her eyes again troubled her; she had to give up her teaching and undergo more operations. She stayed in the Eye Infirmary for three months. When she was finally discharged, her eyes seemed well, although needing time to strengthen, but her general health was poor and badly affected by the doses of chloroform she'd been given during the operations.

By this time she was out of money and unable to continue teaching for several months. She received some small amounts from friends, but didn't know how she'd provide for herself in the future.

The upcoming Paris Exhibition was much in the news, and it occurred to Margaretha that with her knowledge of languages she might be able to find occupation there. She wrote to friends in Paris, asking them to use their influence to help her. A friend advanced her the money to go to Paris. Finally, she was employed by the American commissioner as an interpreter. As part of her duties she had to learn the names of all the articles that had been sent from the United States. She liked her work. One of the pleasures was that the pianos of Steinway & Sons were being exhibited very near to her desk, and she heard many distinguished pianists and composers (including Verdi) try the pianos. Seven months later when the exhibition had closed, she left Paris in health, with her debts paid, and with savings. She went immediately home to see her family.

Some time later she became engaged to marry a Polish gentleman, "De L." She seems to have been reluctant to marry and was urged to make the commitment by her mother and friends. They were to be married in Paris; her sister accompanied her on her journey to Paris. The closer they came to Paris the more she dreaded arriving and felt she would make a terrible mistake. She could not bring herself to love De L. But she had given her word. She didn't let De L know she was in Paris until several days after her arrival.

French law required that De L's identity and origins be attested to by seven persons. Although the seven friends De L produced for the formality were nobility, Margaretha thought them a very suspicious lot, with not one respectable man among them. She became very suspicious of De L as well. He began asking her to advance him money for various bills, as his accounts had not yet cleared. She overheard remarks that referred to a swindle being perpetrated, and there was an encounter with a forger whom De L apparently knew.

Margaretha and her sister pressured De L to contact his firm in Frankfort and ask for money to repay Margaretha. A friend gave De L money; the bank notes were forged.

By this time Margaretha had made up her mind not to marry De L on any account, and in a superb scene she told him, "Leave me; you are a swindler." But the papers for the marriage had been filed, and in order to withdraw them she told the commissionaire about De L and his friends. There was a hearing, and De L was ordered to repay Margaretha at once; he was subsequently arrested on several charges.

She determined to leave France and go to America, and after much travail she departed. Her experiences and connections at the Paris Exhibition were useful to her both with her journey and on arrival in the United States; her health and finances were in terrible shape. Friends helped her, and she set out to cross the United States by railroad, periodically stopping for several days to rest. The plains interested her; she notes, "In America, every place consisting of a couple of houses is called a town" [*The North Star and the Southern Cross*, Vol. 1, 115].

At some point she'd decided to continue traveling, and she sailed from San Francisco for Japan. The voyage was long, and when she finally landed in Yokohama she found Japan difficult. She was even more negative about China, particularly Peking. Nonetheless she had friends in Peking, and there were a number of Germans in the city for her to meet. She stayed in China about ten months.

Canton and Hong Kong were her next stops, then Saigon, Singapore, and Java.

> I was now traveling in a new geographical line, and I missed the sky of my home. I raised my eyes to the horizon; the North Star was no longer there. The constellations were other than those above my beautiful Rhine; other than those above Europe or America; and yet I noticed something which in some sort compensated me for the loss of the North Star. I looked up, and for the first time I saw the Southern Cross [Vol. 1, p. 482].

Margaretha was rarely without an opinion of what she saw or, most particularly, the inhabitants of various places. She found the English customs of Hong Kong foolish and confining, particularly the custom of always being carried in a sedan chair, for to walk compromised the lady's character.

> The Dutch, however, I found more unconventional and reasonable than the English, and the highest in rank amongst them walk when they like, and the sun and weather permit it.
> These reasonable practical Dutchmen also enjoy the greatest comforts in their own residences, and their cool delicious baths are another custom worthy of mention. In short, they are a free and healthy people, not weak, fettered slaves of silly unreasonable rules and customs [Vol. 1, p. 490].

On her return to Singapore she had the good fortune to witness the phosphorescence. She then went on to India. Given her background, it's not surprising that

Margaretha visited various convents, monasteries and places of retreat, usually Catholic, but also of various faith groups. At a convent in India she came upon a young woman who was considered demented; she's referred to as Miss C. or "the lunatic." The woman was from Europe, and the convent very much wished her to be taken to their house in Germany. Margaretha undertook the task of delivering her to Germany. This proved to be troublesome and exhausting, but Margaretha seemed to feel some empathy for the woman.

The trip continued. Margaretha went to the Holy Land, then to Egypt, and finally to Trieste. Finally, she returned to Germany and attempted to take her companion to the convent, which was not without incident.

At the conclusion of the book she refers to boarding for two years in New York. She concluded the book by reflecting on her trip and on the extreme generosity she met with. And, in character with the rest of the book, the reader is left with ambiguity.

> We were quickly nearing Pekin; already we could discern the most prominent buildings of this once splendid but now decayed capital.
>
> Especially imposing to the eye of the stranger are the stately gate-buildings in conjunction with the colossal city walls, as well as the temples' pagodas towering high in their peculiar beauty. Pekin and its splendours give evidence of a rich and glorious past; now they look beautiful only from a distance. It was with a feeling of what the French call désillusion that later I surveyed the buildings of former rulers, all executed with the most lavish magnificence. The rich sheen of gold and silver ornaments is dimmed with thick dust; the costly damask hangings are being eaten away by dirt. No emperor of China does his predecessor the honour to keep up the ornaments of the capital which he may have either erected or beautified [Vol. 1, p. 277].

WORKS

Weppner, Margaretha. *The North Star and the Southern Cross.* Two volumes. London: Sampson, Low, Marston, Low and Searle, 1876.

Elizabeth Bisland Wetmore. *see* Elizabeth Bisland.

Mary Wollstonecraft, 1759–1797.
British.

While most of the women travelers were single, some were married. Of those, some husbands accompanied their wives — or were accompanied by them. Other couples, like the Blunts, traveled as a "team." Some husbands, like Isabella Bird's, knew that her independent travel was part of the marriage package. Mary Wollstonecraft had a male companion who had reasons of his own for encouraging her travel.

Mary began her professional life by keeping a school with her sister; when that failed she worked as a governess for Lord Kingsborough in Ireland. She also was a translator and reader for the publishing firm of Johnson. Her book, *A Vindication of the Rights of Men*, attacked Edmund Burke's conservative defense of the Establishment — the monarchy, church, and aristocracy. That book was well received, but it was the publication of *A Vindication of the Rights of Women* in 1792 that brought her success and immortality.

In late 1792 Mary went to France to see for herself the struggle against the establishment she had written about in the earlier book. Among the like-minded radicals she met in Paris was Gilbert Imlay, an American. The two fell in love.

Mary and Imlay were never married, although they were registered as man and wife at the American Embassy. Mary was working on her history of the French Revolution. As an Englishwoman, Mary was in a dangerous position, a danger that was exacerbated as Imlay was traveling and she was alone in Paris with her daughter. Fortunately she was able to return to London with her daughter — only to find out that Imlay was planning to leave her.

Thinking to divert Mary, Imlay sent her to Scandinavia for a summer as his business envoy. Her book from that summer, *Letters Written During a Short Residence in Sweden, Norway, and Denmark*, reflects Mary's interests and spirit. Not surprisingly, she wrote about prison reform, capital punishment, child care and the position of women. Her daughter Fanny and a nursemaid were with her, and Mary frequently took side trips on her own. For her, the capital was not the place to really see and meet the Scandinavian people.

Nothing, in fact, can equal the beauty of the northern summer's evening and night; if night it may be called that only wants the glare of day, the full light, which frequently seems so impertinent; for I could write at midnight very well without a candle. I contemplated all nature at rest; the rocks, even grown darker in their appearance, looked as if they partook of the general repose, and reclined more heavily on their foundation [*Letters*, pp. 43–44].

So far from thinking that the primitive inhabitants of the world lived in a southern climate, where Paradise spontaneously arose, I am led to infer, from various circumstances, that the first dwelling of man happened to be a spot like this which led him to adore a sun so seldom seen; for this worship, which probably preceded that of demons or demi-gods, certainly never began in a southern climate, where the continual presence of the sun prevented its being considered as a god; or rather the want of it never being felt, this glorious luminary would carelessly have diffused its blessings without being hailed as a benefactor. Man must therefore have been placed in the north, to tempt him to run after the sun, in order that the different parts of the earth might be peopled [p. 16].

When Mary returned to England at the end of the summer she was devastated to learn that Imlay had taken a mistress while she was away, and she tried to commit suicide by throwing herself into the Thames. She was rescued by some boatmen on the river. Eventually, and gradually, Mary was able to put her life back together.

She married William Godwin; they weren't married very long when she died after giving birth to her second daughter, also named Mary. That Mary became the wife of Percy Bysshe Shelley and the author of *Frankenstein*.

SOURCE: *Dictionary of Literary Biography.*

WORKS

Wollstonecraft, Mary. *Letters Written During a Short Residence in Sweden, Norway and Denmark*. Edited with an introduction by Carol H. Poston. Lincoln, Nebraska: University of Nebraska Press, 1976.

Fanny Bullock Workman,
1859–1925. American.

Fanny was born in Worcester, Massachusetts, but was schooled in New York, Dresden and Paris. She returned to Worcester; in 1881 she married William Hunter Workman, a prominent physician. In 1886 they went to Europe, where they made a lengthy tour of Germany and Scandinavia. Three years later William retired from his medical practice, and the family moved to Germany, where they remained about nine years.

Germany was the base for their travels to Algiers, Greece and Palestine. Both enjoyed mountain climbing and climbed in the Alps. They also were ardent bicyclers and toured Spain and northern Africa.

In 1897 they began their extensive bicycle tours through India, Cochin China, Java, Ceylon, and Sumatra. Their bicycle trip through the south of India resulted in *Through Town and Jungle*. While many of their books were collaborative efforts, this book was written solely by Fanny.

It was their bicycling and mountaineering that attracted the most attention. Fanny first climbed in the Himalayas in 1899. Both Fanny and William had become fascinated with the Karakorum range, a region that was little known at that time.

The Workmans defined themselves as equal working partners. They divided the obligations of each expedition in half and alternated their responsibilities from one trip to the next. They were equally adept at the scientific and logistic aspects of their travels.

Over the next thirteen years they made seven major expeditions to chart glaciers and peaks. Their last Himalayan trek was in 1912.

> We went to the East in October 1897 with the purpose of seeing something of the treasures of Buddhist, Hindu, and Mohammedan Architecture and Art, with which it is enriched. We proposed to use our bicycles as a means of travel, so far as the existence and condition of roads would permit. In the prosecution of our design, we have, during the past two and a half years, cycled over large portions of India, Ceylon, and Java, besides travelling to some extent in Sumatra, Indo-china, and Burma, and have thus been able to visit many places that would otherwise have been difficult to reach.
>
> In order to escape from the heat of the Indian plains, we have spent two summers among the higher Himalayas [*In the Ice World of the Himalayas*, Introduction].
>
> The descent to Askole is long and tiresome, like that from most of the high Asiatic passes, but the views of the mountains at the foot of the Biafo and Baltoroglacirs,

as the valley is approached, compensate for a lot of wear and tear. After eleven hours of hard marching we reached, at sunset, the rope-bridge, which spans the two hundred and seventy foot wide Braldu river before Askole.

> We regarded it with some trepidation, as it hung in a long catenary, high over the water, with its three ropes made of twisted twigs placed in the form of an isosceles triangle, the lowest rope for the feet and the upper ones to be grasped by the hands and arms; but with camp to be pitched and darkness approaching, we did not stop to consider our nerves, which is perhaps the best way to act, when obliged to cross such aerial bridges. It is not a pleasant sensation, particularly about midway, to find one's self swaying on these slender structures over such turbulent, swiftly flowing currents, as the Himalayan snows produce, and, aside from the danger of falling through the bridge, one cannot escape the thought, what if one or all of these ropes should part, as has been known to happen.
>
> Askole has been called, not inaptly, "the world's end." The name is given to seven villages scattered about this remote valley, each with its separate *lambardar*. The last and principal village, connected with the outer world only by the swaying rope-bridge and the pathless glaciers towards Hunze and Turkestan, is indeed a last gîte for human beings, the final patch of green on the ragged edge of a world of ice. As if to accentuate the stern environment, Nature inflicts upon this mountain-hemmed town an eight months' winter, during which time of cold and silence, communication even with Shigar, the next large town towards civilization is either cut off or rendered hazardous; for the lower route to Shigar is so rough and cut up by rivers, gullies, and precipitous ridges, that, even in summer, it is often more difficult and dangerous than the higher one we crossed [pp. 101–102].
>
> The surface rocks of the Skoro La group, so far as we could observe, consist mainly of shales, among which mica shale is largely represented. These are very friable and easily split up, which accounts for the extensive tali and great amount of detritus, both large and small, which covers all exposed

surfaces. The south-west or Shigar side of the Siegfriedhorn and other adjoining heights is particularly ragged and rotten. In climbing in this region one must be careful to keep to the arêtes and avoid the couloir, down which stones are constantly falling.

In these higher Himalayan regions, everything is fashioned on such a grand scale, and the atmosphere is so clear, that individual features seem dwarfed, and it is difficult to realize the enormous size of mountains, till one attempts to pass or ascend them. In like manner estimates of distance are illusory. Ordinary standards fail and what seems like one mile is likely to prove two or three.

Amid these vast solitudes some faint conception may be formed of the magnitude and energy of the forces, which are slowly, but none the less surely at work in changing the face of nature. Sun, frost, and moisture contending among the mountain tops, split off immense fragments of hardest rock from the massive bulwarks, of which they have formed a part form the foundation of the world. Gravity seizes them within its grasp. They start form their places, they slide, they roll, they bound through the air with ever-increasing velocity. With hissings, crashings, and echoing thunders, they plunge downward in wild career, the avalanche of rock, smashing opposing obstacles, scoring and pulverizing the mountain sides, sending up clouds of snow and rock dust, till they find a resting-place on the talus at the base, or imbed themselves in the glacier thousands of feet below.

These mountain fragments are borne onward by the river of ice, with its imperceptible movement of a few hundred feet at most a year, till at last it piles them, one upon another, to build a giant moraine miles from their source of origin [pp. 134–135].

Fanny made many ascents, many of them the first by a woman, and in 1906 she established a world mountaineering record for women. She calculated the altitude she'd reached at 23,300 feet. In 1908 her record was challenged by Annie Smith Peck, who claimed to have reached 24,000 feet on a guided climb in the Andes. [See entry for **Annie Smith Peck.**] Fanny hired a team of surveyors to calculate the altitude of Peck's climb; they reported it as only 21,812 feet. The altitude of Fanny's climb was later surveyed and revised to 22,815 feet; her record was not broken until 1934.

Well versed in languages, Fanny spoke before learned societies in America and Europe; she was the first woman to lecture before the Sorbonne in Paris. She was honored by ten European geographical societies with their highest awards.

The Workmans retired to France in 1912. Fanny died in Cannes in 1925. William survived until 1937.

SOURCE: *American National Biography.*

WORKS

Books are usually listed under Fanny E. Workman, but they have joint authorship: Fanny E. Workman & William H. Workman.

Workman, Fanny. *Algerian Memories: A Bicycle Tour Over the Atlas to the Sahara.* London: T. F. Unwin, 1895
_____. *The Call of the Snowy Hispar.* New York: C. Scribner's Sons 1910.
_____. *Ice-bound Heights of the Mustagh.* New York: C. Scribner's Sons, 1908.
_____. *In the Ice World of the Himalayas.* New York: Cassell & Company, Limited, 1900.
_____. *Peaks and Glaciers of the Nun Kun* New York: C. Scribner's Sons 1909.
_____. *Through Town and Jungle.* New York: C. Scribner's Sons, 1904.
_____. *Two Summers in the Icy Wilds of Eastern Karakorum.* London: T. F. Unwin, 1917.

Mrs. Marianne Postans Young see *Marianne Postans*

Part II

Additional Women Travelers of Interest

While many women who traveled were not as adventurous as those in the main part of this book, their travels still were more extensive than the norm and almost certainly had elements of adventure. In retrospect, travel at that time, by ship or overland in isolated areas, seems a risky and fragile undertaking. Few, if any, of these journeys were without adventure.

I have listed the pertinent travel books written by these women. Many of them wrote extensively — books, articles, and stories — fiction and non-fiction, on a range of subjects. When known, I have indicated that these authors wrote more than their travel books.

Jessie Ackerman, 1860–1951.

Jessie Ackerman was a world missionary for the Women's Christian Temperance Union. She spent her life working for temperance and for women's rights, and in doing so she traveled around the world six times.

WORKS

Ackerman, Jessie. *Australia from a Woman's Point of View.* New York: Cassell, 1913.
_____. *What Women Have Done with the Vote.* New York: William B. Feakins, 1913.
_____. *The World Through a Woman's Eyes.* Private, 1896.

BOOKS ABOUT OR INCLUDING JESSIE ACKERMAN

Rushing, Jenny. Master's thesis: "Jessie Ackerman, 'The Original World Citizen,' Temperance Leader, Suffrage Pioneer, Feminist, Humanitarian." East Tennessee State University, August 2003.

Harriet Georgiana Maria Aynsley (Mrs. J. C. Murray), 1827?–1898.

Harriet Aynsley lived in India from 1875 to 1896. During this time she traveled extensively, seeing much more of India than many British residents in India at that time.

WORKS

Aynsley, Harriet. *An Account of a Three Months' Tour from Simla Through Bussahir, Kunowar and Spiti to Lahoul.* Calcutta: Thacker, Spink, 1882.
_____. *Our Tour in Southern India.* London: F. V. White, 1883.
_____. *Our Visit to Hindostan, Kashmir and Ladakh.* London: W. H. Allen, 1879.

Mary Ann Serrett Barber, 1801–1864.

WORKS

Her books include:

Barber, Mary Ann. *Oshielle, or Village Life in the Yoruba Country.* London: James Nisbet & Co., 1857.

Fanny Alexandra Barkly

Fanny Alexandra Barkly accompanied her husband, who was in government service, to his various assignments. They spent five years in the Seychelles, followed by an interlude in the Falklands, then duty in Heligoland in the North Sea, where they remained for two years.

While they were in Southern Africa she lived an isolated life at a remote outpost;

there was no doctor, clergyman, or white woman around. As trouble developed between the British and the Basuto, life became more difficult. While she was seriously ill following the birth of her fourth child, her home was attacked and she had to flee by night to the Orange Free State. She struggled to find food and look after her children — but she also copied out military dispatches late at night that were smuggled out of her besieged home.

WORKS

Barkly, Fanny. *Among Boers and Basutos*. London: Remington, 1893.
_____. *From the Tropics to the North Sea*. London: Roxburghe, 1896.

Catherine Barter, sometimes listed as Charlotte Barter (A Plain Woman), d. 1895.

WORKS

Barter, Catherine. *Alone Among the Zulus*. London: Society for Promoting Christian Knowledge, 1866.
_____. *Alone Among the Zulus: The Narrative of a Journey Through the Zulu Country South Africa/ Catherine Barter*. Edited by Patricia L. Merrett. Durban: Killie Campbell Africana Library, Pietermaritzburg, University of Natal Press, 1995.
_____. *Home in South Africa*. London: Society for Promoting Christian Knowledge, 1867.

Mrs. D. B. Bates

WORKS

Bates. *Incidents on Land and Water, or Four Years on the Pacific Coast Being a Narrative of the Burning of the Ships Nonantum, Humayoon, and Fanchon, Together with Many Startling and Interesting Adventures on Sea and Land*. Boston: James French, 1857.

Nellie Sims Beckman (Mrs. William Beckman)

Her book recounts eighteen months in Europe, Asia Minor, Egypt, Syria and Palestine. She wrote several books about her life and experiences.

WORKS

Beckman, Nellie. *Backsheesh: A Woman's Wanderings*. San Francisco: The Whittaker & Ray Company, 1900.

Mary Elizabeth Blake, 1840–1907, with Margaret Frances Sullivan

WORKS

Blake, Mary, with Margaret Sullivan. *Mexico: Picturesque, Political, Progressive*. Boston: Lee & Shepard, 1888.
_____. *On the Wing: Rambling Notes on a Trip to the Pacific*. Boston: Lee & Shepard, 1883.
_____. *A Summer Holiday in Europe*. Boston: Lee & Shepard, 1890.

Eliza Jane Bridgman (Mrs. Gillett Bridgman)

WORKS

Bridgman, Eliza Jane. *Daughters of China; or Sketches of Domestic Life in the Celestial Empire*. New York: R. Carter & Brothers, 1853.
_____. *The Pioneer of American Missions in China. The Life and Labors of Elijah Coleman Bridgman*. [n.p.] 1864.

Lucy Broad

WORKS

Broad, Lucy. *A Woman's Wanderings the World Over*. London: Headley Bros., 1909.

Eliza Bush

WORKS

Bush, Eliza. *My Pilgrimage to Eastern Shrines.* London: Hurst and Blackett, 1867.

Lady Mary Rhodes Carbutt

Lady Mary's account of her tour is a recital of cities and destinations, with a little description and assessment of each place. She gives no personal information or anecdotal accounts. The itinerary included Banff, Vancouver, San Francisco, Virginia City, Colorado Springs, El Paso, Zacatecas, and Mexico City, with various excursions out of Mexico City to Patzcuaro, Guadalajara, Puebla, Veracruz and Jalapa.

WORKS

Carbutt, Lady Mary. *Five Months Fine Weather in Canada, Western Unites States and Mexico.* London: Sampson Low, Marston, Searle, & Rivington, 1889.

M. L. M. Carey

WORKS

Carey, M.L.M. *Four Months in a Dahabeeh.* London: L. Booth, 1863.

Mary Carpenter

A British educator and penologist, she also wrote books on prisons.

WORKS

Carpenter, Mary. *Six Months in India.* London: Longman, 1868.

Mrs. Julie D. Carrothers

WORKS

Carrothers, Julie D. *Japan's Year.* Illustrated by Japanese Artists. Tokyo: T. Hasegawa, 1905.

_____. *Kesa and Saijiro or Lights and Shades of Life in Japan.* New York: American Tract Society, 1888.
_____. *The Sunrise Kingdom, or Life and Scenes in Japan.* Philadelphia: Presbyterian Board of Publication, 1879.

Mrs. [Charles] Ellen Clacy

WORKS

Clacy, Ellen. *A Lady's Visit to the Gold Diggings of Australia in 1852-1853.* London: Hurst and Blackett, 1853.
_____. *A Lady's Visit to the Gold Diggings of 1852 1853, Written on the Spot.* Edited by Patricia Thompson. Melbourne: Landsdowne Press, 1963.
_____. *Light and Shadows of Australian Life.* Two volumes. London: Hurst and Blackett, 1854.

Harriet Elizabeth Abbott Clark, 1850 or 1851–1927.

WORKS

Clark, Francis E. & Mrs. Harriet Elizabeth Clark. *Our Journey Around the World: An Illustrated Record of a Year's Travel of Forty Thousand Miles Through India, China, Japan ... with Glimpses of Life in Far-off Lands as Seen Through a Woman's Eyes.* Hartford, Conn.: A. D. Worthington, 1894. The book is written with Francis Edward Clark; the last part of the book is by Harriet.

She wrote many additional books, including Bible stories and a book for young people on immigrants at Ellis Island (1912).

Mrs. Clemons

WORKS

Clemons. *The Manners and Customs of Society in India.* London: Smith, Elder & Co., 1841.

Mrs. Septima Collis, 1842–1917. [Mrs. General Charles H. T. Collis]

Collis, Septima. *A Woman's Trip to Alaska: Being an Account of a Voyage Through the Inland Seas of the Sitkan Archipelago in 1890.* New York: Cassell, 1890.

_____. *A Woman's War Record 1861–1865.* New York: G. P. Putnam's Sons, 1889.

Maria Henrietta [May] Crommelin

Maria's trip over the Andes in 1894 was by the Transandine Railway.

WORKS

Crommelin, Maria. *Over the Andes.* London: Richard Bentley and Son, 1896.

She also wrote novels.

Hanna Davies

WORKS

Davies, Hanna. *Among Hills and Valleys in Western China.* Introduction by Mrs. Isabella [Bird] Bishop. London: S. W. Partridge, 1901.

Ménie Muriel Dowie 1867–1945.

WORKS

Dowie, Ménie. *A Girl in the Karpathians.* New York: Cassell, 1891.

Dowie, Ménie. *Women Adventurers.* London: F. T. Unwin, 1893.

Jane Duncan

WORKS

Her book recounts a trip on horseback she made alone through the Himalayas.

Duncan, Jane. *A Summer Ride through Western Tibet.* London: Smith, Elder & Co., 1906.

Jane Anthony Eames, 1816–1884.

Eames, Jane. *Another Budget: Or Things Which I Saw in the East.* Boston: Ticknor & Fields, 1855.

_____. *A Budget of Letters: Or Things Which I Saw Abroad.* London: W. D. Ticknor and Company, 1847.

_____. *The Budget Closed.* London: Ticknor & Fields, 1855.

_____. *Letters from Bermuda.* Concord, New Hampshire: Republican Press Association, 1875.

Note: an old meaning of "budget" is a small bag and its contents — a collection.

Lady Elizabeth Eastlake, 1809–1893.

She sometimes is listed under **Elizabeth Eastlake Rigby**.

A critic and a writer, she started her writing career in 1836. She was well placed socially; many of her friends were writers and artists. Trips to Europe heightened her interest in art. In 1849 she married Sir Charles Eastlake, an artist, who later was director of the National Gallery. She wrote extensively on art and artists.

SOURCE: *Dictionary of National Biography.*

WORKS

Eastlake, Elizabeth. *A Residence on the Shores of the Baltic, Described in a Series of Letters.* London: Murray, 1841. Also as *Letters from the Shores of the Baltic.* London: Murray, 1842.

Emily Eden, 1797–1869.

Emily accompanied her brother to India in 1836; he was governor-general. She was well known for her travel writing as well as for her two novels.

WORKS

Eden, Emily. *Letters from India*. London: Bentley, 1872.

_____. *Portraits of the Princes and People of India*. London: J. Dickinson & Son, 1844.

_____. *Up the Country: Letters Written to Her Sister from the Upper Provinces of India*. London: Bentley, 1866.

Sarah Stock Farmer

WORKS

Farmer, Sarah. *Tonga and the Friendly Isles*. London: Hamilton, Adams & Co., 1855.

Fannie Feudge

WORKS

Feudge, Fannie. *Eastern Side, or Missionary Life in Siam*. Philadelphia: Bible & Publications Society, 1871.

_____. *India*. Boston: D. Lothrop & Co., 1880.

_____. *Many Lands and Many People*. Philadelphia: J.B. Lippincott & Co., 1875.

_____. *A Queer People*. Boston: D. Lothrop & Co., 1878.

Marianne Finch

Marianne Finch, a British woman, attended a Woman's Rights convention in Boston in 1851, then toured America.

WORKS

Finch, Marianne. *An Englishwoman's Experience in America*. London: Bentley, 1853.

_____. *An Englishwoman's Experience in America*. New York: Negro Universities Press, 1969.

Gertrude Adams Fisher

WORKS

Fisher, Gertrude. *A Woman Alone in the Heart of Japan*. London: Sisley's, 1906.

Mrs. Harriet E. Francis

WORKS

Francis, Harriet E. *Across the Meridians, and Fragmentary Letters*. New York: The DeVinne Press, 1887.

Lady Jane Franklin, 1792–1895.

Jane Franklin was the second wife of Sir John Franklin. After their marriage in 1828, Sir John held command in the Mediterranean; they traveled extensively throughout the region. He then held a post in Van Dieman's Land, Australia and New Zealand, and the couple again took advantage of their location to travel.

In 1845 Sir John left on an expedition to find the Northwest Passage through the Arctic region north of North America. There were two ships on the expedition; both were provisioned for three years. When nothing was heard of the expedition by the winter of 1846–47, doubts began to arise about its well-being.

In the spring of 1848 several relief and search expeditions, public and private, English and American, were launched. These various expeditions accomplished much in gaining information about the unknown area of the Arctic regions, but they also gleaned a grim picture of the difficulties faced by the expedition. Traces were found of the ships and of abandoned provisions which had turned putrid. Between 1850 and 1857 Lady Jane fitted out five ships for the search to determine the fate of the expedition and Sir John. The last attempt, in 1857, finally determined that Franklin and the others had died.

SOURCE: *Dictionary of National Biography*.

WORKS

Franklin, Jane. *The Journal of Lady Jane Franklin at the Cape of Good Hope, November 1836:*

Keeping up the Character. Edited, annotated, and introduced by Brian and Nancy Warner. Cape Town: Friends of the S. A. Library, 1985.
_____. *The Life, Diaries, and Correspondence of Jane Lady Franklin, 1792–1875.* Edited by Willingham Franklin Rawnsley. London: E. Macdonald, 1923.

Amy Fullerton

WORKS

Fullerton, Amy. *A Lady's Ride Through Palestine and Syria with Notices of Egypt and the Canal of Suez.* London: S. W. Partridge & Co., 1872.

Alexandra Gripenberg,
1857–1912.

Alexandra was a Finnish woman who came to the United States as a delegate to the 1888 International Woman's Conference in Washington, D.C., then traveled throughout the northern states.

WORKS

Gripenberg, Alexandra. *A Half Year in the New World; Miscellaneous Sketches of Travel in the United States.* Published in Finland in 1889. Translated and edited by Ernest J. Mayne. Newark, Delaware: University of Delaware, 1954.

Geraldine Mary Guinness later Mrs. Howard Taylor, 1865–1949.

Geraldine, a missionary to China, wrote several missionary biographies and histories of the mission.

WORKS

Her books are sometimes listed under **Mrs. Howard Taylor.**

Guinness, Geraldine. *The Call of China's Great North-west; or, Kansu and Beyond.* Edited by

her sister. London and Philadelphia: China Inland Mission, 1923.
_____. *In the Far East: Letters from Geraldine Guinness in China.* London: Morgan and Scott, 1889.

Iza Duffus Hardy

WORKS

Hardy, Iza. *Between Two Oceans: or Sketches of American Travel.* London: Hurst & Blackett, 1884.
_____. *Through Cities and Prairie Lands: Sketches of an American Tour.* London: Chapman & Hall, 1881.

Annie Jane Harvey, d. 1898.

WORKS

Her books are usually listed under Andree Hope.

Harvey, Annie. *Cositas Espanolas, or Everyday Life in Spain.* London: Hurst and Blackett, 1875.
_____. *Our Cruise in the Claymore.* London: Chapman and Hall, 1861.
_____. *Turkish Harems and Circassian Homes.* London: Hurst and Blackett, 1871.

Mary Hield

WORKS

Hield, Mary. *Glimpses of South America, or The Land of the Pampas.* New York: Cassell & Co., 1882.
_____. *The Land of Temples, or Sketches from Our Indian Empire.* New York: Cassell, 1882.

Mrs. Matilda Charlotte Houstoun, 1815?–1892.

WORKS

Houstoun, Matilda. *Hesperos; or, Travels in the West.* Two volumes. London: John W. Parker, 1850.

_____. *Texas and the Gulf of Mexico, or Yachting in the New World.* Two volumes. London: John Murray, 1844.

_____. *Twenty Years in the Wild West; or Life in Connaught.* London: John Murray, 1879.

She also wrote novels and nonfiction and an autobiography, *Records of a Stormy Life by Mrs. Houstoun.* London: S. Blackett, 1888.

Howard of Glossop, Lady Windfred.

Her name is listed variously.

WORKS

Howard of Glossop, Lady Windfred. *Journal of a Tour in the United States, Canada and Mexico.* London: Sampson Low, Marston & Company Limited, 1897.

Louisa Hutchinson

Louise was a British army wife.

WORKS

Hutchinson, Louisa. *In Tents in the Transvaal.* London: Bentley, 1879.

Fanny Chambers Gooch Iglehart, 1842–1913.

Iglehart, Fanny. *Face to Face with the Mexicans.* New York: Fords, Howard & Hulbert, 1887.

_____. *Face to Face with the Mexicans.* Edited and with an Introduction by C. Harvey Gardiner. Carbondale: Southern Illinois University Press, 1966.

Lady Julia Selina (Thesiger) Inglis, 1833–1904.

WORKS

Inglis, Lady Julia. *The Siege of Lucknow.* London: James R. Osgood, McIlvaine & Co., 1892.

Emily Innes

Emily Innes wrote her book in response to Isabella Bird's book, *The Golden Cheronese and the Way Thither* in which Bird recounts her five-week stay in Malaysia. The title refers to an ancient Roman traveler's tale of a paradise of riches that lies east of India. Innes says that in writing her book she had no intent to contradict Bird, and that her book is true. But she points out that it is written from the perspective of a celebrated traveler, who came with introductions to government officials and higher ranking members of society, and stayed only five weeks. Hers — Innes's — tale is written from the perspective of one who was a resident for over five years and the wife of a minor official.

WORKS

Innes, Emily. *The Cheronese with the Gilding Off.* London: Bentley, 1885.

_____. *The Cheronese with the Gilding Off.* Introduction by Khoo Kay Kim. New York: Oxford University Press, 1974.

Laura Fish Judd, 1804–1872.

WORK

Judd, Laura. *Honolulu, Sketches of Life, Political and Religious, in the Hawaiian Islands from 1828 to 1861.* New York : A. D. F. Randolph & Co., 1880.

_____. *Honolulu, Sketches of Life, Political and Religious, in the Hawaiian Islands from 1828 to 1861.* Edited by Dale L. Morgan. Chicago: Lakeside Press, 1966.

Emily Georgina Kemp, b. 1860.

The Face of China recounts her travels from 1893 to 1894, and from 1907 to 1908.

WORKS

Kemp, Emily. *Chinese Mettle*. London: Hodder & Stoughton, 1921.
_____. *The Face of China: Travels in East, North, Central and Western China*. London: Chatto & Windus, 1909.
_____. *The Face of Manchuria, Korea, Russian Turkestan*. London: Chatto & Windus, 1910.
_____. *Wanderings to Chinese Turkestan*. London: Wightman, 1914.

Paula Kollonitz, b. 1830. German.

Paula Kollonitz made a short visit to Mexico, sailing in April 1864 and returning December 1864. She was accompanying Austrian archduke Ferdinand Maximilian, who was to be Emperor of Mexico, and his wife Carlotta, the Empress of Mexico.

WORKS

Kollonitz, Paula. *The Court of Mexico*. Translated by J. E. Ollivant. London: Saunders, Otley, and Co., 1868.

Kate Kraft

WORKS

Kraft, Kate. *The Nilometer and Sacred Soil: A Diary of a Tour through Egypt, Palestine and Syria*. New York: G.W. Carleton, 1869.

Lilian Leland

WORKS

Leland, Lilian. *Traveling Alone, A Woman's Journey Around the World*. New York: The American News Company, 1890.

Alicia H. M. Bewicke Little, d. 1926.

Alicia Little was an early missionary in China. Her books are often listed under **Mrs. Archibald Little**.

WORKS

She wrote a variety of books including:

Little, Alice. *Intimate China: The Chinese As I Have Seen Them*. London: Hutchinson, 1899.
_____. *The Land of the Blue Gown*. London: Unwin, 1902. Also published as *In the Land of the Blue Gown*. New York: Appleton, 1909.

Harriette Lloyd

WORKS

Lloyd, Harriette, *Hindu Women, with Glimpses into Their Life and Zenanas*. London: James Nisbet & Co., 1882.

Frances Anne Emily, Marchioness of Londonderry

WORKS

Londonderry, Frances. *A Journal of a Three Months' Tour in Portugal, Spain, Africa, etc.* London: J. Mitchell, 1843.
_____. *Narrative of a Visit to the Courts of Vienna, Constantinople, Athens, Naples, etc.* London: Colburn, 1844.
_____. *Russian Journal of Lady Londonderry, 1836–7*. Edited by W. A. L. Seaman and J. R. Sewell. London: Murray, 1973. From a manuscript in the Londonderry family archives.

Fanny Loviot

WORKS

Loviot, Fanny. *A Lady's Captivity Among the Chinese Pirates in the Chinese Seas*. Translated by Amelia Edwards. London: G. Routledge & Co., 1858.

Mrs. [Colin] Helen Douglas Mackenzie

WORKS

Mackenzie, Helen. *Life in the Mission, the Camp, and the Zenana*. Three volumes. London: Richard Bentley, 1853.

Sarah Mytton Hughes Maury,
1803–1849.

WORKS

Maury, Sarah. *An Englishwoman in America.* Two volumes. London: Thomas Richardson & Son, 1848.

Elizabeth Melville

Mrs. Melville began her stay in Sierra Leone with optimism and interest in her new surroundings, but over the years she became overwhelmed. The natural beauty she'd admired so much at first became sinister; the climate that produced so much beauty was also a source of suffering. When she finally returned to England, her personality had been changed by her experiences; her optimism and cheerful disposition had darkened.
SOURCE: *Victorian Women Travel Writers in Africa.*

WORKS

Melville, Elizabeth. *A Residence at Sierra Leone, Described from a Journal Kept on the Spot, and from Letters Written to Friends at Home.* By a Lady. Edited by Mrs. Norton. London: Murray, 1849. Reprint: London: Cass, 1968.

Louisa Anne Twamley Meredith, 1812–1895.

Although Louisa Meredith was born in England, she is often regarded as Australia's first professional female writer. Her nature writing and artwork began to be published when she was young. In 1839 she married Charles Meredith. Subsequently they went to Van Deiman's land and also traveled around Australia. She then began writing about her travels. She was an advocate of conservation and animal rights.

SOURCE: *Dictionary of Literary Biography,* p. 166.

WORKS

Her books may also be listed under **Mrs. [Charles] Louisa Anne Meredith.**

Meredith, Louisa. *My Home in Tasmania.* Two volumes. London: John Murray, 1852.
_____. *Notes and Sketches of New South Wales.* London: John Murray, 1844.
_____. *Over the Straits: A Visit to Victoria.* London: Chapman and Hall, 1861.
_____. *Some of My Bush Friends in Tasmania.* London: Day and Son, 1860.
_____. *Tasmanian Friends and Foes Feathered, Furred, and Finned.* London: Marcus Ward, 1880.

Ellen Clare Pearson Miller
(sometimes listed under **Ellen Clare Pearson**)

WORKS

Miller, Ellen. *Eastern Sketches. Notes of Scenery, Schools and Tent Life in Syria and Palestine.* London: Oliphant & Co., 1871.

Ellen E. Miller

WORKS

Miller, Ellen E. *Alone Through Syria.* London: Kegan Paul, Trench, Trübner & Co., 1891.

Mrs. Louise Jordan Miln,
1864–1933.

WORKS

Miln, Louise. *Quaint Korea.* London: Osgood and McIlvaine, 1895.
_____. *When We Were Strolling Players in the East.* New York, Charles Scribner's Sons, 1894.

She wrote novels and stories set in the Far East, particularly China.

Lady Geraldine Edith Mitton

(afterward **Scott**)

WORKS

Mitton, Lady Geraldine. *Austria Hungary*. London: A. & C. Black, 1914.
_____. *A Bachelor Girl in Burma*. London: Hutchinson, 1898.
_____. *The Lost Cities of Ceylon*. London: Murray, 1916.
_____. *Round the Wonderful World*. London: T. C. & E. C. Jack, 1914.

She wrote extensively; her work includes children's books.

Montgomery, Hon. Mrs. [Alfred] Fanny Charlotte,

1828–1893.

WORKS

Montgomery, Fanny. *On the Wing: A Southern Flight*. London: Hurst and Blackett, 1875.

Georgina Adelaide Grenfell Max Müller

She usually is listed under **Max Müller** but is sometimes listed under **Müller**.

WORKS

Letters from Constantinople. London: Longman, 1897.

Amelia Matilda Murray,

1795–1884.

Murray, Amelia. *Letters from the United States, Cuba and Canada*. Two volumes. London: John W. Parker and Son, 1856. Reprint: New York: Negro Universities Press, 1969.
_____. *Recollections from 1803–1837: with a Conclusion in 1868*. London: Longmans, Green, 1868.

Mrs. Maria Hay Flyter Mitchell,

d. 1907. Occasionally she is listed under [last name] **Murray Mitchell**.

WORKS

Her books include:

Mitchel, Maria. *In India*. London: T. Nelson and Sons, 1876.
_____. *In Southern India: A Visit to Some of the Chief Mission Stations of the Madras Presidency*. London: Religious Tract Society, 1885.
_____. *Sixty Years Ago*. Edinburgh: Macniven & Wallace, 1905.

Mrs. Elizabeth Murray,

d. 1882.

Murray, Elizabeth. *Sixteen Years of An Artist's Life in Morocco, Spain and the Canary Islands*. Two volumes. London: Hurst and Blackett, 1859.
_____. *Travels and Adventures of an Officer's Wife in India, China, and New Zealand*. Two volumes. London: Hurst and Blackett, 1864.

Helen Sanford C. Nevius,

1833–1910.

Helen and her husband, both missionaries, left Boston in September, 1853, and reached the Straits of Timor in January, 1854. Her health was poor, and steadily worsened; in December, 1856, she left China without her husband to return to the United States, where she stayed a year, returning to China in June, 1864.

WORKS

Nevius, Helen. *Our Life in China*. New York: R. Carter and Brothers, 1869.

Mrs. C. P. Noyes

WORKS

Noyes, Mrs. C. P. *Recollections of India, or Reminiscences of a Six Years' Residence in Orissa*.

Providence, Rhode Island: G. H. Whitney, 1852.

Mrs. Fanny Parks

Fanny's husband was employed by the Bengal Company. They went to India in 1822 and lived there for twenty-four years. Fanny traveled widely, usually on her own with a train of servants. She was a collector of information that she recorded in her diary, from which her book is taken.

WORKS

Parks, Fanny. *Wanderings of a Pilgrim, in Search of the Picturesque.* Two volumes. London: Pelham Richardson, 1850.
Wanderings of a Pilgrim, in Search of the Picturesque. Edited with notes and an introduction by Indira Ghose and Sara Mils. Manchester, England: Manchester University Press, 2001.

Maud Parrish, 1878–1976.

When she was a teenager Maud ran away from a dull marriage. She began her travels in Klondike, Alaska, then wandered all her life. She wrote her book when she was in her 60s.

WORKS

Parrish, Maud. *Nine Pounds of Luggage.* New York: J. B. Lippincott, 1939.

Lady Charlotte Maria Pepys, 1822–1889.

WORKS

Pepys, Lady Charlotte. *A Journey on a Plank from Kiev to Eaux-Bonnes.* Two volumes. London: Hurst and Blackett, 1860.

Belle Marsh Poate, 1847–1896.

Belle Marsh was born in Truro, Nova Scotia, one of thirteen children. One or both of her parents died while she was a child, and Belle, along with some of her younger brothers and sisters, went to live with friends or relatives in the United States. She attended and graduated from Lake Erie Female Seminary (present-day Lake Erie College) and then may have taught for several years. In the fall of 1876 she enrolled as a Presbyterian missionary assistant and went to Japan, where she taught in mission schools in Yokohama.

She married Thomas Pratt Poate, an Englishman, and she joined him in his work in Baptist missionary service, moving to a more remote northern town. There they worked for twelve years; they had five children. In 1892 the family returned to the United States. Belle was then in poor health and died within four years.

WORKS

Poate, Belle. *Letters.* In Richard Poate Stebbin, *The Japan Experience: The Missionary Letters of Belle Marsh Poate and Thomas Pratt Poate, 1876–1892.* New York: Peter Lang, American University Studies, Series 9, History, Vol. 110, 1992.

Fanny Rains

WORKS

Rains, Fanny. *By Land and Ocean; of The Journal and Letters of a Young Girl Who Went to South Australia with a Lady Friend.* London: S. Low, Marston, Searle, & Rivington, 1878.

Pandita Ramabai, 1858–1922.

Pandita was born in a high caste family in India. Her father, defying tradition, taught Pandita's mother Sanskrit. Faced with strong disapproval, the couple went to southern India, where they lived in a simple home. Their children, including Pandita, were born there. Her parents taught school and farmed. Their increasing poverty resulted in a family life of pilgrimage throughout India; the children were taught Sanskrit language and literature by their parents. Eventually India suffered a terrible famine; Pandita and one brother were the only members of the family who did not die from starvation.

The two settled in Calcutta, where they met up with Hindu reformers and Christians; Pandita began to learn about Western culture. She became known as a brilliant scholar. When her brother died of cholera she married a Bengali lawyer; they had one daughter. In 1882 her husband also died of cholera. In 1883 she left India with her daughter to travel to England, to study and learn and to attain the freedom she believed came from knowledge. She began medical studies but had to give that up as she became increasingly deaf. In 1886 she was invited to the United States by the Dean of the Woman's Medical College of Pennsylvania. She traveled through the United States for two years, studying the educational system and the position of women; she frequently spoke to raise funds to build a home for Hindu widows in India. In 1888 she went back to India, where she followed through on her plan to help women.

Pandita wrote at least a dozen books, many of them focusing on Indian women and on religion. Many were written in English or have been translated.

WORKS

Of particular interest:

Ramabai, Pandita. *Pandita Ramabai Through her Own Words: Selected Works.* Edited and translated by Meera Kosambi. New Delhi: Oxford University Press, 2000.

Elizabeth Rigby *see* Lady Elizabeth Rigby Eastlake

Anne Newport Royall, 1769–1854.

Anne Newport Royall is often considered to be the first American newswoman.

In 1813 she married Captain William Royall, a gentleman farmer who had served in the Revolution. He died in 1813. Anne then began traveling across the country. She published ten accounts of her travels, which today are a valuable source of social history.

Anne also began a newspaper *Paul Pry* in Washington, which existed for several years. She then began the newspaper *The Huntress.* She crusaded against government corruption and incompetence. She was an outspoken woman; in 1829 she was tried and convicted in Washington of being a "common scold."

WORKS

Royall, Anne. *Black Book: or A Continuation of Travels in the United States.* Washington: Printed for the author, 1828–29.
_____. *Letters from Alabama on Various Subjects.* Washington: 1830.
_____. *Mrs. Royall's Pennsylvania.* Washington: The author, 1829.
_____. *Mrs. Royall's Southern Tour, or Second Series of the Black Book.* Washington: 1830–31.
_____. *Sketches of History, Life, and Manners in the United States. By a Traveller.* New Haven: Printed for the Author, 1826.

There have been various reprintings of her books including:

_____. *Letters from Alabama, 1817–1822.* With a biographical introduction and notes by Lucille Griffith. University: University of Alabama Press, 1969.
_____. *Sketches of History, Life and Manners in the United States. By a Traveller.* New York: Johnson Reprint Corp., 1970.

Mrs. Ernestine Sartorius

Mrs. Ernestine was with her husband Colonel George Conrad Sartorius and her stepdaughter in the Soudan during a period of great unrest.

WORKS

Sartorius, Ernestine. *Three Months in the Soudan.* London: Kegan Paul, Trench & Co., 1885.

Eliza Ruhamah Scidmore,

1856–1928.

WORKS

Scidmore, Eliza. *Alaska, Its Southern Coast and the Sitkan Archipelago.* Boston: D. Lothrop & Co., 1885.
_____. *As the Hague Ordains: Journal of a Russian Prisoner's Wife in Japan.* New York: Henry Holt & Co, 1907.
_____. *China, The Long-Lived Empire.* New York: The Century Co, 1900.
_____. *Java, The Garden of the East.* New York: The Century Co, 1898.
_____. *Jimrikisha Days in Japan.* New York: Harper & Brothers, 1891.
_____. *Winter India.* London: Unwin, 1903.

Mrs. Anna M. Scott

WORKS

Scott, Anna. *Glimpses of Life in Africa.* New York: American Tract Society, 1857.

Caecilie Sachs Seler, 1855–1935.

Louise (Vescelius) Sheldon

Louise, no relation to May French-Sheldon, traveled with her two sisters.

WORKS

Sheldon, Louise. *An I. D. B. in South Africa.* New York: John W. Lovell, 1888.
_____. *Yankee Girls in Zulu Land.* London: F. Warne and Co, 1888.

Henrietta Hall Shuck, 1817–1844.

Henrietta Shuck was a married missionary who was sent to China in 1835 by the Baptist Board of Foreign Missions to evangelize. She was the first woman missionary in China. During this time she focused her efforts on providing education for Chinese children, especially girls.

WORKS

Shuck, Henrietta. *Scenes in China; or Sketches of the Country, Religion and Customs of the Chinese.* Philadelphia: American Baptist Publications Society, 1852.

BOOKS ABOUT OR INCLUDING HENRIETTA HALL SHUCK

Jeter, J. B. *A Memoir of the First American Female Missionary to China.* Boston: Gould, Kendall, & Lincoln, 1850.

Ann Eliza Brainerd Smith [Mrs. J. Gregory Smith]

Her husband was the first president of the Northern Pacific Railroad Company. The town Brainerd, Minnesota, is named in her honor.

WORKS

Her books are often listed under **Mrs. J. Gregory Smith**. She wrote a variety of books including:

Smith, Ann. *Notes of Travel in Mexico and California.* St. Albans, Vermont: Printed at the Messenger & Advertiser Office, 1886.

Millicent, Marchioness of Stafford

WORKS

Stafford, Millicent. *How I Spent My Twentieth Year: Being a Short Record of a Tour Round the World 1886–87,* London: William Blackwood and Sons, 1889.

Julia A. Stone

WORKS

Stone, Julia. *Illustrated India, Its Princes and People. Upper, Central and Farther India, Up the Ganges, and Down the Indus. To Which Is Added an Authentic Account of the Visit to India of His Royal Highness the Prince of Wales.* Hartford,

Conn.: American Publishing Company, 1877. Reprint: New Delhi: Asian Educational Services, 2000.

Jane M. C. Turnbull

WORKS

Turnbull, Jane, with Marion E. Turnbull. *American Photographs: Travels.* London: T. C. Newby, 1859. This recounts a photographic trip of thousands of miles through the United States, Canada, and Cuba between 1852 and 1857.

Mary Adelaide Walker

WORKS

Walker, Mary. *Eastern Life and Scenery, with Excursions in Asia Minor, Mitylene, Crete and Roumania.* London: Chapman and Hall, 1886.
_____. *Old Tracks and New Landmarks,: Wayside Sketches in Crete, Macedonia, Mitylene etc.* London: Richard Bentley, 1897.
_____. *Through Macedonia to the Albanian Lakes.* London; Chapman and Hall, 1864.
_____. *Untrodden Paths in Roumaina.* London: Chapman and Hall Limited, 1888.

Susan Arnold Elston Wallace,

1830–1907.

Susan was the wife of Lew Wallace, who had several careers. He was a Civil War general, governor of New Mexico from 1878 to 1881, then minister to Turkey from 1881 to 1885. He was also a novelist, best known for *Ben Hur.*

Susan wrote many articles and several books in addition to her travel books.

WORKS

Wallace, Susan. *Along the Bosphorus, and Other Sketches.* London: Unwin, 1898.
_____. *The Land of the Pueblos.* New York: J. B. Alden, 1888.
_____. *The Repose in Egypt, a Medley.* New York: J. B. Alden, 1888. This includes *Along the Bosphorus.*
_____. *The Storied Sea.* Boston: Osgood, 1883.

Harriet Ward

During Harriet Ward's stay, Southeastern Africa was a place of unrest and racial tension, with armed exchanges and a war. Mrs. Ward gives a good picture of the problems and dangers of a military wife in such a setting; disease, poor food, and hardship were constant. She also praises the British soldiers and defends them from criticism; she criticizes the government for the low pay and inadequate supplies for the soldiers.

WORKS

Ward, Harriet. *The Cape and the Kaffirs, a Diary of Five Years in Kaffirland.* London: H. G. Bohn, 1851.
_____. *Five Years in Kaffirland.* London: H. Colburn, 1848.

Clara Clement Waters,

1834–1916.

WORKS

Waters, Clara. *Constantinople, The City of the Sultans.* Boston: Estes and Lauriat, 1895.
_____. *Egypt.* Boston: D. Lothrop & Co., 1880.
_____. *Naples, the City of Parthenope and its Environs.* Boston: Estes and Lauriat, 1894.
_____. *The Queen of the Adriatic or Venice, Mediaeval and Modern.* Boston: Estes and Lauriat, 1893.
_____. *A Simple Story of What One of Your Lady Friends Saw in the East.* Boston: Printed for private distribution by Rand, Avery and Fry, 1869.

Clara also wrote many books on art and artists.

Mrs. H. Dwight Williams

Mrs. Williams was returning from China on the ship *Jacob Bell* when the ship was captured by Confederate sympathizers and burnt.

WORKS

Williams, Mrs. *A Year in China; and a Narrative of Capture and Imprisonment when Homeward Bound.* New York: Hurd & Houghton, 1864.

Mrs. Rosa Carnegie Williams

WORKS

Williams, Rosa. *A Year in the Andes or A Lady's Adventures in Bogota*. London: London Literary Society, 1884.

Francis Wright, 1795–1852.

She is sometimes listed as **Francis Wright D'Arusmont**.

Frances was from a wealthy Scottish merchant family. Her parents both died when she was three, and she and her younger sister lived with their aunt, Frances Campbell, who relocated them to Devonshire. Frances inherited the family properties in India when she was eight; she was already a precocious student with a gift for languages. She was also keenly aware of social inequities in the rural life around her, laying the groundwork for her life as a social reformer. She was also very interested in the United States.

In 1825 she bought land in Tennessee to form a "colony," Nashoba, where slaves could be educated and work for their freedom. The community never became self–sufficient and was dissolved four years later, the ex–slaves being transported to Haiti.

In 1831 she married D'Arusmont, who had been a member of Owen's community in New Harmony, Indiana. The couple lived in England for a while, and then Francis returned to the United States, settling in Cincinnati.

Francis was very active lecturing and writing. She was passionately in favor of sexual freedom, racial equality, economic justice, and public education. She believed in gradual emancipation. Although she denounced the women's movement, her stand for the independence and equality of all humans made a substantial impact on the feminist movement.

WORKS

Wright, Francis. *Views of Society and Manners in America; in a Series of Letters from That Country to a Friend in England, during the Years 1818, 1819, and 1820. by an Englishwoman*. London: Longman, 1821.

Francis Wright also wrote non–travel books, including collections of lectures and addresses.

Marie Robinson Wright, 1866–1914.

WORKS

Wright, Marie. *Bolivia, the Central Highway of South America, a Land of Rich Resources and Varied Interest*. Philadelphia: George Barries & Son, 1907.

_____. *Mexico, a History of its Progress and Development in One Hundred Years*. Philadelphia: George Barries & Son, 1911.

_____. *The New Brazil. Its Resources and Attractions; Historical, Descriptive and Industrial*. Philadelphia: George Barries & Son, 1901.

_____. *The Old and the New Peru: A Story of the Ancient Inheritance and the Modern Growth and Enterprise of a Great Nation*. Philadelphia: George Barries & Son, 1908.

_____. *Picturesque Mexico*. Philadelphia: J. B. Lippincott & Co., 1897.

_____. *The Republic of Chile; the Growth, Resources, and Industrial Conditions of a Great Nation*. Philadelphia: George Barries & Son, 1904.

Bibliography

Books

Adams, William Davenport. *Celebrated Women Travellers of the Nineteenth Century*. London: Sonnenschein, 1883.

Agosín, Marjorie, and Julie H. Levison. *Magical Sites: Women Travelers in 19th Century Latin America*. Buffalo, NY: White Pine, 1999.

Allen, Alexandra. *Travelling Ladies*. London: Jupiter, 1980.

Birkett, Dea. *Spinsters Abroad: Victorian Lady Explorers*. London: Basil Blackwell, 1989.

Foster, Shirley. *Across New Worlds: Nineteenth-Century Women Explorers and Their Writings*. New York: Harvester Wheatsheaf, 1990.

_____, and Sara Mills, eds. *An Anthology of Women's Travel Writing*. Manchester, England: Manchester University Press, 2002.

Frawley, Maria H. *A Wider Range: Travel Writing by Women in Victorian England*. Rutherford, NJ: Farleigh Dickinson University Press, 1994.

Hamalian, Leo, ed. *Ladies on the Loose: Women Travellers of the 18th and 19th Centuries*. New York: Dodd, Mead, 1981.

Harding, Les. *The Journeys of Remarkable Women: Their Travels on the Canadian Frontier*. Waterloo, Ontario: Escart, 1994.

Hodgson, Barbara. *Dreaming of East: Western Women and the Exotic Allure of the Orient*. Vancouver, British Columbia: Greystone, 2005.

Middleton, Dorothy. *Victorian Lady Travellers*. London: Routledge & Kegan Paul, 1965.

Miller, Luree. *On Top of the World: Five Women Explorers in Tibet*. London: Paddington, 1976.

Morris, Mary, ed. *Maiden Voyages: Writings of Women Travelers*. New York: Random House, 1993.

Netzley, Patricia D. *The Encyclopedia of Women's Travel and Exploration*. Westport, CT: Oryx, 2001.

Newby, Eric, ed. *A Book of Travellers' Tales*. New York: Viking, 1985.

Niles, Blair. *Journeys in Time, from the Halls of Montezuma to Patagonia's Plains: A Treasury Gathered from Four Centuries of Writers*. New York: Coward-McCann, 1946.

Oliver, Caroline. *Western Women in Colonial Africa*. Westport, CT: Greenwood, 1982.

Robinson, Jane. *Wayward Women: A Guide to Women Travellers*. Oxford: Oxford University Press, 1990.

_____, compiler. 1994. *Unsuitable for Ladies: An Anthology of Women Travelers*. Oxford: Oxford University Press, 1994.

Scribner, Mary Suzanne, ed. *Telling Travels: Selected Writings by Nineteenth Century American Women Abroad*. DeKalb: Northern Illinois University Press, 1995.

Stevenson, Catherine Barnes. *Victorian Women Travel Writers in Africa*. Boston: Twayne, 1982.

Tinling, Marion. *Women into the Unknown: A Sourcebook on Women Explorers and Travelers*. New York: Greenwood, 1989.

_____. *With Women's Eyes: Visitors to the New World 1775–1918*. Norman: University of Oklahoma Press, 1993.

Van Thal, Herbert. *Victoria's Subjects Travelled*. London: A. Barker, 1951.

Encyclopedias

American National Biography. Published under the auspices of the American Council of Learned Societies. General Editors: John A. Garraty and Mark C. Carnes. New York: Oxford University Press, 1999.

Biographie Universelle Ancienne et Moderne. Graz, Austria: Akademische Druck-u. Verlagsanstalt, 1970.

Dictionary of Literary Biography.
Volume 166, British Travel Writers, 1837–1875. Edited by Barbara Brothers and Julia Gergits. Detroit: Gale Research, 1996.
Volume 174, British Travel Writers, 1876–1909. Edited by Barbara Brothers and Julia Gergits. Detroit: Gale Research, 1997.
Volume 189, American Travel Writers, 1850–1915. Edited by Donald Ross and James J. Schramer. Detroit: Gale Research, 1998.

Encyclopedia Judaica. Jerusalem: Keter, 1971.

Oxford Dictionary of National Biography. Oxford: Oxford University Press, 2004.

Index

Index